THE THEORY OF ECONOMIC

The Theory of Economic Growth

An Introduction

GRAHAM HACCHE

M

First published 1979 by
THE MACMILLAN PRESS LTD
London and Basingstoke
Associated companies in Delhi Dublin
Hong Kong Johannesburg Lagos Melbourne
New York Singapore and Tokyo

Typeset in IBM Press Roman by
Reproduction Drawings Ltd
Sutton, Surrey

Printed and bound
in Great Britain by
REDWOOD BURN LIMITED
Trowbridge & Esher

British Library Cataloguing in Publication Data

Hacche, Graham
    Theory of economic growth.
    1.   Economic development
    I.   Title
    339.5   HD82

    ISBN 0-333-23570-3
    ISBN 0-333-23571-1 Pbk

To my parents

Contents

Contents

Preface

The purpose of this book is to provide an introductory but fairly comprehensive account of the modern theory of economic growth. The exposition assumes no prior knowledge of growth theory, but it does assume that the reader is acquainted with the principles of macro- and micro-economics; it is intended mainly for undergraduates, beyond their first year, and graduate students. Elementary differential calculus is used extensively, and integral calculus occasionally; it will therefore be helpful, to say the least, if the reader is familiar with these branches of mathematics. (The usual introductory mathematics course for university economics students, for example, should have equipped him with most of the tools he will need.) But I have tried generally to supplement the mathematics with verbal explanation, and I hope that the non-mathematician will not feel shut out.

The book is concerned with the descriptive aggregative growth theory which has stemmed from the work of Harrod and Domar; for treatments of both multi-sector (or non-aggregative) and optimal growth theory (which may be traced back to the work of von Neumann and Ramsey, respectively) the reader is referred to more advanced texts – for example the second half of Burmeister and Dobell (1970). This book attempts to provide a fairly comprehensive account of the field thus defined, and it is hoped that it will be found useful as such by the reader who lacks the time to benefit from much study of the original sources. The more serious specialist will not trust or be satisfied with my exposition alone; for him, it is hoped that what follows will assist and guide the reading of the literature. (Some chapters – particularly those in which certain subjects are treated only briefly – are accompanied by supplementary lists of references suggesting possibilities for further reading.)

There are two particular respects in which the content of this book differs from that of most other texts on the subject. First, it provides a fuller account of the 'neo-Keynesian' approach to growth theory. Most textbooks allocate by far the greater part of their space to the 'neo-classical' approach, and provide at most one or two chapters – sometimes even only one or two pages – for a discussion of neo-Keynesian theory. I have attempted to provide a more balanced treatment of the differences between the two schools, and in so doing have included a fuller account than usual of the constructive (as opposed to the critical) efforts of neo-Keynesian theorists. Their critique of neo-classical theory is discussed partly in Chapter 9 but mainly in Chapter 10; together these two chapters may be regarded as forming a bridge between the neo-classical analysis of Chapters 4–8 and the neo-Keynesian theory of Chapters 11–13. Second, whereas most other textbooks have negligible empirical content, I have attempted, in Chapters 14 and 15, to provide an introduction to applied analysis by considering the empirical interpretation of the theory and some of the problems involved in confronting the theory with data. How is growth theory related to growth in real economies? What does growth theory tell us about economic history and vice versa? These questions are worthy of consideration. They are, indeed, worthy of more consideration than I have managed to give them: despite Part IV this book does no more than scratch the surface of empirical growth analysis.

As a student at Cambridge in the late 1960s, I would have found it difficult to ignore the theory of economic growth. More specifically, I owe my original interest in the subject to the lectures and teaching of Professor Kaldor and David Newbery. The book began to develop when I was a graduate student at Oxford, and it owes a considerable debt to the advice of my supervisor, Nicholas Stern; it would have foundered at a very early stage without his encouragement. David Newbery, Roger Pownall, Maurice Scott, Susan Symes and Tony Thirlwall provided valuable comments on parts or the whole of the draft at various stages. My debt to the written work of, in particular, Professors Hicks, Kaldor, Meade, Robinson and Solow will be obvious from the bibliography and also, I hope, from the text. Last, but not least, I am grateful to my employers, the Bank of England, and in particular to Leslie Dicks-Mireaux and Tony Carlisle, for their co-operation, and for their toleration of the distraction which this project has formed at various times while I have been with them. The charts were drawn, under the supervision of Amy Crosby, mainly by Gill Fitzgerald, Amanda Waldie, and Susan

Taylor; the typing of the final manuscript, organised by Jenny Bunkall, was done mainly by Hilary Abbott, Diane Coombs, Christine Hale, Glenys Harris and Lynne Ross. I am very grateful for their help.

It goes without saying that no part of the book - not even those parts which are right - necessarily reflects any Bank of England view, and that I alone am responsible for the final product.

July 1978   GRAHAM HACCHE

Part I

INTRODUCTION

1

The Emergence of Modern Growth Theory – The Harrod–Domar Models

1.1 Harrod, Domar and Keynes

The birth of modern growth theory, in the work of Harrod (1939, 1948) and Domar (1946, 1947), was one of the earliest by-products of Keynes's (1936) *General Theory*. Both writers aimed to extend Keynes's analysis into the 'long period'. Keynes had been concerned with the *short period*, in which the implications of the level of investment and saving for the stock of capital, and hence for productive potential, may be ignored: in the short run the overriding significance of investment is its influence on effective demand, and the stock of capital may be taken as given and independent of it.[1] But in the *long run* investment expenditure does augment the capital stock; and in the analysis of the long run this cannot be neglected. Domar took account of it directly, by distinguishing between the dependence of actual output on effective demand, and the dependence of potential output on the capital stock. Harrod took the relationship between capital growth and output growth the other way round, by adopting the acceleration principle, whereby producers' demand for capital goods is held to be proportional to output. But both writers were seeking to dynamise the *General Theory* by considering under what conditions, given certain assumptions, an economy could realise growth with continuous full employment; and they arrived at results which in some important respects are similar. In fact their models are commonly referred to in the singular.

We shall concentrate on Harrod's version, since it is the more comprehensive, and since most of the ensuing discussion has employed his terminology. Before proceeding to his model it is interesting to note Keynes's personal involvement in it. Harrod was one of Keynes's closest colleagues: he had been one of the four recipients, in 1935, of the proofs of the *General Theory* (the others were Hawtrey, Kahn and Joan Robinson), and he was later Keynes's official biographer. Moreover, Keynes was editor of the *Economic Journal* when Harrod submitted his 'Essay on Dynamic Theory' for publication, and there was a lengthy correspondence between them about the article (see Moggridge, 1973, pp. 321–50). In fact this was 'the final theoretical subject arising out of the *General Theory* to which Keynes turned his attention' (Moggridge, 1973, p. 320). Keynes's final verdict on Harrod's paper was ambiguous: 'In the final result, I do not find myself in agreement, but I do think that he has got hold of a very interesting point which, subject to the necessary qualifications, is of real importance' (Moggridge, 1973).

1.2 Harrod's model in outline

As is commonly the case in economic theory, Harrod's model begins with an identity. The reader will already be familiar with the *Keynesian identity* between actual (or *ex post*) investment (I) and saving (S) at any time t:

$$I(t) \equiv S(t)$$

Using this, we may decompose the proportional rate of growth, G, of output Y^2 as follows:

$$G(t) \equiv \frac{\dot{Y}(t)}{Y(t)} \equiv \frac{I(t)}{Y(t)} \div \frac{I(t)}{\dot{Y}(t)} \equiv \frac{S(t)}{Y(t)} \div \frac{\dot{K}(t)}{\dot{Y}(t)} \tag{1.1}$$

where K is the volume of capital (both fixed capital and stocks) and a dot above a variable indicates its derivative with respect to time:

$$\dot{Y} \equiv \frac{dY}{dt} \; ; \; \dot{K} \equiv \frac{dK}{dt}$$

The appearance of these derivatives is due to the fact that we are here treating time as a *continuous* variable, and thinking in terms of 'points' rather than 'periods' of time. Then $Y(t)$, for example, is a continuous function, and $\dot{Y}$ is the instantaneous rate of change of Y with respect to time; as such it is not to be confused with the proportional rate of growth of Y, which is $\dot{Y}/Y$, the rate of change in proportion to the level. In economics the term 'rate of growth' almost invariably means 'proportional rate of growth', and the word 'proportional' can safely be dropped.[3] If we were treating time as a *discrete* variable, then instead of $\dot{Y}$ we would have ΔY, which would represent the change in Y between two successive periods, say years; and similarly for $\dot{K}$. Some readers may prefer to think in these terms, and they will arrive at similar results by doing so (see section 1.4).

The first identity in (1.1) gives the definition of the (proportional) rate of growth of output, and the validity of the second identity is seen simply by cancelling the two $I(t)$s. The third identity follows from the equivalence of *ex post* investment and saving, and from the fact that, since we are abstracting from the depreciation of capital, investment is the same as the rate of change of the capital stock. The first and last steps of (1.1) form the *Harrodian identity*:

$$G(t) \equiv \frac{S(t)}{Y(t)} \div \frac{\dot{K}(t)}{\dot{Y}(t)} \tag{1.2}$$

It states that the growth rate of output can be expressed as the ratio of the proportion of income saved to the incremental capital–output ratio (I.C.O.R.). So as to make the interpretation of the identity as simple as possible, we shall assume a closed economy with no government; but it holds for any economic system, as long as the variables are defined appropriately.

Identities are of little interest in themselves. An identity is significant and useful only if the way it classifies economic phenomena is helpful to or suggestive of an understanding of them. The Harrodian identity has been a corner-stone of modern growth theory, and we now turn to examine how Harrod himself used it.

First, suppose that at some point in time the proportion of income saved, S/Y, matches the average propensity to save of the community, and that the I.C.O.R., $\dot{K}/\dot{Y}$, satisfies producers' investment demand. Then (1.2) shows that G is an equilibrium growth rate, in the sense that it leaves producers and income-earners, in the aggregate, satisfied. So far, we have made no behavioural assumptions about the determination of desired (or *ex ante*) saving or investment: at the next point in time the average propensity to save and the desired I.C.O.R. may be quite different. Now let us go that step further.

Suppose that the saving function is of the simple proportional form

$$S(t) = sY(t); \quad 0 < s < 1 \tag{1.3}$$

where s is the average (and marginal) propensity to save. We now assume it to be constant. Suppose also that the investment function is governed by the acceleration principle

$$I(t) = v\dot{Y}(t); \quad v > 0 \tag{1.4}$$

where v is the desired I.C.O.R. (or acceleration coefficient), also assumed to be constant. From (1.3) and (1.4) the Keynesian condition for equilibrium in the goods market

$$I(t) = S(t) \tag{1.5}$$

implies

$$G(t) \equiv \frac{\dot{Y}(t)}{Y(t)} = \frac{s}{v} \tag{1.6}$$

This is the 'fundamental equation' of Harrod's 'dynamic theory', 'constituting the marriage of the acceleration principle and the multiplier theory' (Harrod, 1939, p. 16). It may be compared with the Harrodian identity (1.2). Starting from some equilibrium, and given constant and positive s and v, it shows that there exists a unique growth path of output (and investment and saving, from (1.3) and (1.4)) which satisfies the Keynesian condition for macro equilibrium, and that along this path all three variables of the system grow at the same constant rate s/v.[4] But this is not necessarily a full-employment equilibrium growth path: we have not considered the labour market. In much of this book it will be convenient to restrict the term 'equilibrium' to mean 'full-employment equilibrium' (*pace* the Keynesian concept of under-employment equilibrium); and here we retain Harrod's terminology, in which (1.6) describes the *path of 'warranted' growth; s/v* is then the *'warranted' growth rate*, G_w, in this model.[5]

Turning to the labour market, let us assume that the labour force, L, is growing at a constant exogenous rate, λ, and that labour productivity (output per head), y, is growing – on account of technical progress and increasing capital per head – at a constant exogenous rate, τ. Then the necessary and sufficient conditions for the continuous maintenance of full employment are, first, full employment at the starting-point, and second, output growth at a rate equal to $\lambda + \tau$.[6] Output must grow at a rate sufficient to absorb both the new members of the labour force, net of those retiring, and those workers who would otherwise be made redundant by productivity growth. If we define the *natural growth rate*, n, of output as the growth rate which allows the continuous maintenance of full employment, then in Harrod's system n is given by $\lambda + \tau$: it is exogenous and constant. Labour-market equilibrium requires this rate of growth to be attained and maintained.

Now if we define an *equilibrium growth path* as a growth path which is both warranted (actual investment and saving = desired investment and saving) and natural (labour force fully employed), then in Harrod's model there is a unique equilibrium growth path represented by

$$G(t) = G_w = s/v = n = \lambda + \tau \tag{1.7}$$

and the starting conditions, namely saving–investment equilibrium and full employment at the starting-point.

This equilibrium path satisfies the conditions for steady-state growth, a concept which has been central to modern growth theory and which may be defined thus:

A *steady-state growth path* is a path along which each economic aggregate grows at a proportional rate which is constant over time, the growth rates of all aggregates being equal to the same value G, except that the growth rate of the labour force may differ from G.

Thus along Harrod's equilibrium path, Y, I and S all grow at the same constant rate $G = n = s/v$, while the labour force (equal to employment) grows at a different constant rate $\lambda = n - \tau = G - \tau$. Because all aggregates grow at constant rates, the ratio between any two aggregates either also grows at a constant rate or is constant. Thus output per head y increases at the rate τ, while the investment ratio I/Y, is constant.[7] Harrod avoids explicit use of the capital stock K (as opposed to $\dot{K}$ or I, which is its rate of increase) in his model (owing to measurement problems: Harrod, 1973, p. 48) but if we choose to define K at time T as the integral (sum) of all past investment, then along Harrod's equilibrium path

$$K(T) = \int_{-\infty}^{T} I(t)dt = s\int_{-\infty}^{T} Y(t)dt = sY(0)\int_{-\infty}^{T} e^{nt}dt$$

$$= \frac{sY(0)e^{nT}}{n} = vY(T) \tag{1.8}$$

so that the capital–output ratio K/Y is constant, and equal to the accelerator coefficient v. (A growth path along which the capital–output ratio is constant is sometimes referred to as a *balanced growth path*. A steady growth path is always a balanced growth path, and for most purposes the two concepts can be thought of as being the same.)

We have now described the bare bones of Harrod's dynamic theory. The next section adds some of the flesh.

1.3   The implications of Harrod's model: equilibrium growth as an unlikely and unstable coincidence

Two problems arise from the above model, concerning the existence and stability respectively of the equilibrium solution.

The Existence Problem

First, expression (1.7) shows that the existence of an equilibrium solution requires that four parameters – s, v, λ and τ – which are apparently mutually independent, be related to one another in a particular way. If the values of these parameters are such that $s/v \neq \lambda + \tau$, there is no equilibrium solution. It therefore seems that an equilibrium growth path can exist only as a coincidence, and that in all probability s/v, the growth rate warranted by saving and investment behaviour, will differ from $\lambda + \tau$, the natural growth rate which would ensure full employment. In particular, if s/v falls short of n, continuous equilibrium between investment and saving (i.e. growth at the warranted rate) will not mean full employment: an echo of Keynes! As will be seen below, the subsequent development of growth theory has to a large extent been concerned with the question of whether one or more of Harrod's parameters should be considered endogenous rather than given exogenously, so that the equality between warranted and natural growth rates which is required for equilibrium could be seen as a more probable phenomenon than he suggested.

Harrod recognised that the constancy of his s and v were simplifying assumptions. Thus the assumption of constant s was only an 'ad hoc expedient' (Harrod, 1948, p. 130) and in fact the propensity to save should be expected to vary with 'the size of income, the phase of the trade cycle, institutional changes, etc.' (Harrod, 1939, p. 16) and also with the distribution of income (Harrod, 1948, p. 131) and the rate of interest (Harrod, 1939, p. 32). And the desired I.C.O.R., v, should be regarded as a function of the rate of interest, the phase of the trade cycle, and the state of technology (Harrod, 1939, p. 17). But assuming the form of technical progress to be such that at a given interest rate, v (or the capital–output ratio) remains unchanged (i.e. assuming technical progress to be *Harrod-neutral*)[8] and also assuming the interest rate to be constant, v would remain unchanged, apart from cyclical influences.

Thus Harrod recognised that the assumed constancy of s and v was a simplification of reality.[9] But it did point to what he regarded as *the absence, in the real world, of any mechanism whereby warranted growth and natural growth would tend to coincide.*

The Stability Problem

The second problem arising from Harrod's model was what he saw as the unstable nature of warranted growth. Ignoring the existence problem for a moment, let us consider the less ambitious task of maintaining growth at the warranted rate. Suppose that the economy is disturbed from its warranted growth path so that the actual growth rate G becomes less than $G_w = s/v$. The implication, which may be seen by comparing (1.2) and (1.6), is that either income-earners are saving less than they desire $(S/Y < s)$, or producers are accumulating more capital than they require (I.C.O.R. $> v$), or both. In any event the corrective action taken by the dissatisfied income-earners and/or producers will, Harrod argued, be contractionary. Either income-earners will save more, or producers will invest less; either action will reduce G further. Similarly, an upward departure of G from G_w will feed on itself and cause the system to diverge further from the warranted growth path.

Harrod's intuitive argument is attractive. There has, however, been a lengthy discussion in the literature about whether his 'Instability Principle' can be demonstrated satisfactorily in formal terms. In this discussion it has generally been assumed that disequilibrium, when it arises, is on the side of investment alone, so that actual saving and investment are always equal to *ex ante* saving. The problem then lies in specifying *disequilibrium investment behaviour*, which Harrod does not do in a precise way.[10]

Perhaps the most satisfactory derivation of Harrod's result is that provided by Rose (1959). Producers' desired capital stock, K^*, is proportional to output:

$$K^* = vY$$

(K^* and Y are, of course, functions of time, $K^*(t)$ and $Y(t)$. But we now begin to omit '(t)' from our algebra in order to simplify it.) Then the shortage of capital, h, at any point of time is given by

$$h \equiv K^* - K = vY - K$$

so that

$$\dot{h} = v\dot{Y} - \dot{K} \tag{1.9}$$

If we assume that initially there is no shortage or surplus of capital:

$$h(0) = 0$$

then it seems reasonable to interpret Harrod as meaning that producers behave in such a way that

$$\frac{d}{dt}\left(\frac{I}{I}\right) \gtreqless 0 \text{ as } \dot{h} \gtreqless 0 \tag{1.10}$$

That is, if h remains at its initial value of zero, then producers will be happy to continue increasing investment at its current rate of growth; but if a shortage of capital is developing ($\dot{h} > 0$) then their expenditure will accelerate, while if a surplus is developing ($\dot{h} < 0$), it will decelerate. In order to obtain a model which is linear in the rate of growth, Rose takes a particular case of (1.10):

$$\frac{d}{dt}\left(\frac{I}{I}\right) = \gamma\frac{\dot{h}}{Y}; \ \gamma > 0 \tag{1.11}$$

Now since planned saving (proportional to income) is assumed to be realised, we have

$$S = sY = I = \dot{K} \tag{1.12}$$

From (1.9) and (1.12), (1.11) can be expressed as

$$\frac{d}{dt}\left(\frac{I}{I}\right) = \gamma\left(v\frac{\dot{Y}}{Y} - s\right) \tag{1.13}$$

But also from (1.12), $\dot{I}/I$ may be replaced by $\dot{Y}/Y$ in the left-hand side of this expression, which thus becomes a first-order linear differential equation in $\dot{Y}/Y$ or $G(Y)$. Its solution may be shown to be

$$G(Y) = s/v + \left\{G(Y(0)) - s/v\right\}e^{\gamma vt} \tag{1.14}$$

Thus if initially Y is growing at the warranted rate, $G(Y(0)) = s/v$, it will continue to do so. But if the initial growth rate exceeds s/v, then since $v > 0$, it will increase continuously, and conversely.

Thus Rose seemed to justify Harrod's less formal argument. But the subsequent discussion has shown how sensitive is the conclusion about stability to the assumptions adopted about disequilibrium behaviour. In fact Rose went on in the same paper to show that if, in the above system, (1.10) is replaced by

$$I = v\dot{Y} + \gamma'h ; \quad \gamma' > 0 \tag{1.15}$$

so that the level of investment, rather than its rate of growth, is stepped up if h increases, then warranted growth is stable![11] Further, an investment function similar to (1.15) would be

$$I = G_wK + \gamma''h ; \quad \gamma'' > 0$$

or, equivalently, $\qquad\qquad\qquad\qquad\qquad\qquad\qquad\qquad$ (1.16)

$$\frac{I}{K} = G_w + \gamma''\frac{h}{K}$$

and it can be shown that if investment plans of this form are realised with a simple exponential lag (see Allen, 1967, p. 88), then whether or not warranted growth is stable depends on the relationship between the parameters γ'' and G_w (Hahn and Matthews, 1964, pp. 807–8; Allen, 1967, pp. 188–90). The parameter γ'' measures what proportion of h producers plan to eliminate per unit of time; and the solution tends to imply that for stability, with credible values of G_w, this proportion would need to be implausibly small – producers would have to be implausibly sluggish in responding to disequilibrium – so that Harrod's argument is in fact supported.

More recently some writers have adopted a different approach to demonstrate Harrod's result, by assuming that investment is proportional to the *expected* rate of change of current output (Hahn and Matthews, 1968; Sen, 1970). It then remains to specify how producers' expectations are formed. Sen shows that if the rate of growth which is expected to occur in the current period[12] is directly related to actual growth in the previous period – for example, current expected growth may be related to past actual growth rates by a geometrically distributed lag[13] – then unstable warranted growth results.

These investigations into Harrod's Instability Principle have shown that its validity depends on the precise disequilibrium behaviour assumed, but that there is a variety of not implausible specific assumptions which may be used to support it. Meanwhile Harrod continued to assert it with confidence, and this so-called *knife-edge* characteristic of his warranted growth path remained a central and distinctive part of his growth theory.[14] Thus in his last work on the subject Harrod (1973, p. 45) wrote: 'I am confident that the theory that the "warranted" equilibrium growth rate of laissez-faire capitalism, without management or interference, is unstable, stands firm.'

The *significance of the Instability Principle* is clear. If G happens to fall below or to rise above G_w to any significant extent, there will be an apparently limitless tendency to depression or demand inflation, whatever the value of the natural growth rate n. Such an occurrence could be due to a change in the value of G_w as much as to a change in G. For example, if growth is proceeding at the warranted rate, a rise in the propensity to save will both depress G directly (via the Keynesian multiplier effect on output) and entail a rise in G_w. Thus G and G_w are pushed in opposite directions, and a cumulative downward movement of the actual growth rate is set off.

The problem is magnified when the first, Existence Problem of the model is recalled. In particular, if s and v are such that G_w tends persistently to exceed n, then since G cannot exceed n for long, there must be a persistent tendency for G to fall short of G_w, and thus for the system to be continually depressed. Harrod stressed the likelihood of this danger for the advanced economies in his earlier work: in fact, 'the idea which underlies' Harrod's *Towards a Dynamic Economics* 'is that sooner or later we shall be faced once more with the problem of stagnation' (Harrod, 1948, p. v) owing to an excessive warranted rate. Harrod's concern was based on evidence of a declining growth rate of population – of a declining λ – and on his expectation that s would tend to rise with increasing prosperity (Harrod, 1948, Lectures 2 and 5). More recently, with the benefit of post-war experience, he placed much less emphasis on this danger (Harrod, 1973, p. 103). The opposite problem, of chronically deficient saving and warranted growth, with its implied tendency to persistent demand inflation, is often considered to be a feature of less-developed countries.

The Instability Principle, unmodified, suggests that once an economy's actual growth rate has departed from its warranted growth rate there is nothing to prevent either ever-deepening depression (in the case of a downward departure) or ever-increasing inflationary pressure (in an upward departure). Without some initiative of economic policy, catastrophe seems inevitable! But the Instability Principle is not the end of Harrod's story, and we now need to consider the rest.

1.4 Harrod and the theory of the business cycle

The rest of Harrod's story comprises a theory of *turning-points* which, when married with the Instability Principle, provides a theory of cyclical movements about his warranted and natural growth paths. Briefly, his theory of turning-points consists of two features. The first is the ceiling of full employment. This is sufficient to provide an upper turning-point for G if G_w exceeds n, for G can exceed n only as long as there is unemployment, and so G must fall below G_w once full employment is reached. In fact Harrod (1959) expects the ceiling to become effective in reducing G towards n before full employment proper is reached, first because of factor specialisation and immobility which result in localised 'bottlenecks', and second because producers will anticipate an imminent downturn of G by reducing the growth of their output before they really have to. If G_w is below n, the full-employment ceiling will not necessarily reduce G below G_w. To obtain an upper turning-point, Harrod invokes the second element in his theory: the regular cyclical variation of s and v, and hence of G_w. In a boom, when G exceeds G_w, s will tend to rise, both because the growth of consumer spending is likely to be limited by income-earners' perception of the more normal, long-term growth of their resources, and because the distribution of income will tend to shift in favour of profits. Similarly, in a recession, when $G < G_w$, the resistance of consumption in the face of more slowly growing (or falling) incomes will tend to reduce s, and hence to reduce G_w towards G.

The Instability Principle thus occupies a place in the development of trade-cycle theory as well as in the development of growth theory. From one aspect it points towards the precariousness of steady growth with full employment; but also, for Harrod (1973, p. 45), it provides 'the fundamental explanation of the business cycle'. This book is more concerned with the former aspect; but it is worth while to digress briefly for the remainder of this section to indicate the relationship between Harrod's theory and other trade-cycle models.

At the same time as Harrod was discovering that a combination of the multiplier and the accelerator implied a constant warranted rate of growth, on the other side of the Atlantic Hansen and Samuelson were discovering that the same combination could imply something else. Their results were published in the same year as Harrod's: in Samuelson (1939). To see how the two models differ, we first need to reformulate *Harrod's model in terms of discrete time:* we replace (1.3), (1.4) and (1.5) with

$$S_t = sY_t; \quad 0 < s < 1 \tag{1.17}$$

$$I_t = v\Delta Y_t = v(Y_t - Y_{t-1}); \quad v > 0 \tag{1.18}$$

$$I_t = S_t \tag{1.19}$$

where the subscript t now refers to a 'period' of time. These three expressions imply

$$\frac{\Delta Y_t}{Y_t} = \frac{Y_t - Y_{t-1}}{Y_t} = \frac{s}{v} \tag{1.20}$$

which may be interpreted in the same way as was (1.6) – constant warranted growth – as long as $s < v$. If $s > v$, (1.20) implies that ΔY_t exceeds Y_t, which can be true only if Y_t and Y_{t-1} have opposite signs; the solution implies that in this case Y oscillates about zero. If we reject the possibility of negative output, the model thus makes economic sense only if $s < v$. There is then a constant warranted growth rate; but in period terms the growth rate would normally be defined, not as in (1.20), but as

$$G_t \equiv \frac{Y_t - Y_{t-1}}{Y_{t-1}} = \frac{s}{v-s} \tag{1.21}$$

by manipulation of (1.20). Thus in this model the warranted growth rate is not s/v.[15]

The essential difference in the *Hansen–Samuelson model* is that planned consumption and investment are assumed to depend on lagged, rather than current, values of Y and ΔY. Consumption, C, is proportional to the income of the previous period

$$C_t = (1 - s)Y_{t-1}$$

so that saving is given by

$$S_t = Y_t - (1 - s)Y_{t-1} \tag{1.22}$$

Similarly, planned investment is determined by the change in output last period:

$$I_t = v\Delta Y_{t-1} = v(Y_{t-1} - Y_{t-2}) \tag{1.23}$$

Substituting (1.21) and (1.22) into the equilibrium condition (1.19) gives

$$Y_t = [v + (1-s)]\,Y_{t-1} - vY_{t-2} \tag{1.24}$$

which is much less clear as a description of the new 'warranted' path of output than was (1.20) as a description of the old.

The important difference is the presence of the Y_{t-2} term which comes from the lagged accelerator: the one-period lag in the consumption function could in fact have been omitted and the same complication would have arisen. It may be shown that the characteristics of the path of Y implied by (1.24) depend on the values of the parameters s and v. Here we do not need to provide either the details of the solution or an account of the economic sense which lies behind them (see the reading list at the end of this chapter). What we need to note is the following. Steady growth, as in the Harrod model, is a possibility; but now it is not the only possibility. A second possibility is that Y approaches the constant value of zero. But the third possibility is potentially the most interesting: a cyclical movement of Y about zero. That is, the values of s and v may be such that the interaction of the multiplier with the lagged accelerator generates not a warranted growth path, but what may be called, using Harrod's terminology, a 'warranted cycle'.

But this cycle is centred on a constant value of Y. (The latter is zero in the model we have set out, but it is not necessarily so. In the original Hansen–Samuelson model it was positive, owing to their inclusion of an item of exogenous expenditure, spending by the government.) The fact that Harrod's cycle is centred on a growth path does seem to make it more realistic. Hicks saw this disadvantage of the Hansen–Samuelson model. But he also regarded the absence of lags in Harrod's saving and investment functions as unrealistic. In his review of Harrod (1948) he sought to avoid the disadvantages of both models (Hicks, 1949; amplified in *Hicks*, 1950). He amended the lagged accelerator by assuming that there is a component of investment which is *autonomous* and which follows the natural growth path of the economy rather than short-term changes in output. Hicks's investment function is thus

$$I_t = v\,(Y_{t-1} - Y_{t-2}) + A(1+n)^t; \quad A > 0 \tag{1.25}$$

Replacing (1.23) with (1.25) in the Hansen–Samuelson model, we obtain, in place of (1.24),

$$Y_t = [v + (1 - s)] Y_{t-1} - v Y_{t-2} + A(1 + n)^t \qquad (1.26)$$

Now the natural growth path, rather than some constant value, provides the base for the warranted movement of output.

The warranted path of Y again depends on the values of s and v. Hicks assumed that the values of these parameters are such that Y tends to diverge upwards or downwards from its base path but not necessarily such that Y oscillates in cycles about it. He preferred to propose that cycles would result from the presence of a ceiling and a floor, as in Harrod; again we need not go into details. But Hicks's equation for warranted output, (1.26) alone, is capable of generating cycles about the natural growth path, if the values of s and v lie within certain ranges.

We are now able to observe a distinctive characteristic of Harrod's trade-cycle theory. For him, the warranted path of output is a steady growth path, and the trade cycle is a consequence of departures from it – a consequence of disequilibrium between investment and saving. Once there is disequilibrium the Instability Principle, and ceiling and floors do the rest. But the warranted path of output is not necessarily a steady growth path, and if Harrod's saving and investment functions are amended in a relatively minor way – by the inclusion of lags – it can become a cycle. Thus trade-cycle models may be, and have been, constructed in which the path of the economy is for the most part dictated by the equilibrium of investment and saving, and in which disequilibrium behaviour plays a much less central role than in Harrod.

1.5   Domar's model, and a summary of Harrod–Domar

The essentials of Domar's model can now be treated briefly. Adopting the same proportional saving function as Harrod, he added, not an investment function, but a proportional relationship between the rate of increase of productive capacity or full-employment output $\overline{Y}$ and investment:

$$\dot{\overline{Y}} = \sigma I \qquad (1.27)$$

Each unit of investment or new capital increases full-employment output by σ units. His model thus comprises (1.27) together with the saving function.

$$S = sY \qquad (1.28)$$

and the equilibrium conditions

$$I = S \qquad (1.29)$$

and

$$Y = \overline{Y} \qquad (1.30)$$

From (1.27) – (1.30) we obtain the solution:

$$\frac{\dot{Y}}{Y} = \frac{\dot{I}}{I} = \sigma s \qquad (1.31)$$

which states that (1.27) and (1.28) together imply that for saving–investment equilibrium and full employment, income and investment must grow at a constant rate which is the product of the parameters σ and s. But why should investment grow at this particular rate? It seems probable that it will not, so that we shall not have equilibrium growth. Harrod's Existence Problem thus arises again, but in different guise.

Domar's equilibrium growth rate, σs, looks suspiciously like Harrod's warranted growth rate s/v, and it is tempting to infer that σ is the reciprocal of v. But it would be wrong to do so; indeed, it should be clear that the two growth rates cannot be equivalent, since one entails full employment, while the other generally does not. The point is that Domar's σ in effect embodies Harrod's natural growth rate: it embodies the influences of labour-force growth and technical progress on productive potential, as well as the idea of an optimal I.C.O.R. Thus σ measures more than the increase in full-employment output which is directly caused by investment. As Domar (1946, p. 140) emphasises, 'σ refers to an increase in capacity which accompanies, rather than one which is caused by investment' and, in particular, 'its magnitude depends to a very great extent on technological progress'.

Domar chose to represent potential growth by (1.27) because he wished to emphasise its dependence on capital accumulation. By also adopting the Keynesian multiplier to describe the determination of the level of actual output, he obtained a model in which investment plays a clear dual role, and in which the maintenance of full-employment equilibrium requires investment to grow at a particular exogenous rate. He has no theory of what determines investment; his model shows what the path of investment is required to be.

Harrod, on the other hand, preferred to adopt a theory of investment – the acceleration principle – and to show that the interaction of the accelerator with the multiplier implied a warranted growth rate which bore no necessary relation to the growth rate which would ensure full employment. He thus took the natural growth rate to be exogenous in order to emphasise the apparent lack of any automatic tendency for warranted growth to conform with it. He did not ignore the dependence of natural growth on capital accumulation: in his model the growth of output per head is in part a consequence of increasing capital per head. But the relationship is not in the foreground as in Domar; it is hidden by the assumption that technical progress is such that if the capital–output ratio is constant (which it is, given a constant interest rate and Harrod-neutrality), then the growth rate of output per head is a constant, τ. (We shall return to this conception of technical progress in Chapter 7.)

But both writers, by different routes, arrived at the same conclusion that in an unmanaged capitalist economy there would be no automatic tendency for a full-employment equilibrium growth path to exist.

And for Harrod there was a second obstacle facing the attainment of steady growth with full employment, in addition to the apparent absence of any mechanism whereby the warranted and natural growth rates would be brought into equality. Aggravating the Existence Problem, there was the instability of the warranted growth path. To him, the lesson was clear: active demand management was required, to tackle both the long-term problem of a chronic tendency towards unemployment or inflation and the short-term problem of the trade cycle.

Thus Harrod and Domar's extension of Keynes's analysis to a dynamic economy appeared to confirm his conclusions and policy prescription.

Further reading

Readers seeking mathematical help will benefit from Allen (1967), particularly chapters 1, 10 and 11 (pp. 197–207), where an alternative treatment of Harrod–Domar is provided. Differential and difference equations are treated in, for example, Chiang (1967), chapters 14–17. In the Harrod–Domar literature, highest priority should be given to the original papers, Harrod (1939) and Domar (1946), which are widely reprinted, for example in Sen (1970). Harrod (1973) provides a fuller and more recent account of his thoughts on growth; this has superseded Harrod (1948) but the latter is still of some interest in its own right. A fuller account of trade-cycle theory is provided in most macro-economic textbooks; useful surveys are provided in Matthews (1959), particularly chapter 2, and at a higher level in Evans (1969), chapters 13 and 14.

2

The Development of Modern
Growth Theory – A Preview

2.1 What is 'growth theory' about?

The implication of the Harrod–Domar models was that the automatic maintenance of equilibrium steady-state growth, with full employment, was unlikely to be one of the virtues of a free-market capitalist economy. Other economists responded by suggesting that this pessimism – at least as far as the Existence Problem was concerned – was overdone, and that it was merely due to the excessively and unrealistically rigid assumptions on which the models had been built. If the assumptions could be relaxed, so that (in Harrod's terms) one or more of the four parameters involved (s, v, λ and τ) could adjust in some way so as to tend to lead to equality of the warranted and natural growth rates, then the prospect for the real world would be less dismal. Attention was soon drawn to such possibilities.

Almost simultaneously (in the mid-1950s) two schools of thought began to develop. One maintained that the introduction of the neo-classical production function, and the variability of factor proportions which it allowed, pointed towards a mechanism whereby v could take on the value required for equilibrium growth. The other school objected to this argument but introduced the notion of a saving function which differentiates between the saving propensities attached to different kinds of income, and suggested that the distribution of income could adjust so as to enable the saving propensity of the community as a whole, s, to take on the value required. These two propositions, not always exclusively of each other, are at the heart of a large part of the growth-theory literature. (The other possibilities – endogenous λ and τ – have received much less attention.) The models of the first, 'neo-classical', school are considered in Part II. The approach of the second, 'neo-Keynesian', school is discussed in Part III.

The basic characteristics of most of the growth models which have emerged in the wake of Harrod–Domar are, then, as follows. They are concerned chiefly with the movement over time of aggregate quantities, relative prices and income distribution. Certain technical and behavioural relationships are postulated, and the movement of the economy implied by the interaction of these relationships is examined. *But almost universally, the chief concern is with the possibility of steady-state growth*, as defined above (p. 7). This is to say that most writers have been concerned primarily with establishing under their assumptions the *existence* of an equilibrium path for the economy which is a path of steady growth, the *uniqueness* of such an equilibrium path, and its *stability*.

It would therefore seem to the novice that what has been written under the name of 'growth theory' is of rather more limited scope than the name suggests. Questions concerning the determinants of actual growth, differences in growth rates over time and space, and policies for raising growth rates – questions which the student may have expected 'growth theory' to be about – seem to have been peripheral to the main task of the characterisation of steady states. This apparent lack of practical orientation is surprising; it is not as if applied economists and policy-makers in the post-war period have been uninterested in growth problems. Indeed, many writers claim that the intellectual energy that has been spent on growth theory since the war is to be accounted for by a new (or revived) practical preoccupation with the growth of productivity and productive potential in a post-Keynesian era in which the former object of concern – the problem of the gap between productive potential and realised output – has come to need less urgent attention. The work on growth theory may well have been practically motivated; yet what 'growth theory' has been about seems far removed from reality. In some respects, 'It is as if a poor man collected money for his food and blew it all on alcohol' (Sen, 1970, p. 9).

There has certainly been disillusionment with the results of the effort put into growth theory. To those who have been dissatisfied with the usefulness of modern progress in economic theory, growth theory has looked like a prime example.[1] But the reader is not about to hear a confession that the rest of this book is not worth reading – even less that growth theory is not worth studying.

The object of this chapter is not to discourage the reader. It is partly to warn the novice, at an early stage, that growth theory may well be rather different from what he expected it to be, so that he is helped to avoid the confusions which might otherwise have arisen; and it is partly to provide some idea as to why growth theory has been largely a study of steady states.

The significance of the concept of steady growth can be considered at two levels – the theoretical and the empirical.

2.2   The steady state as a device of dynamic theory

First of all, it is clear that *growth theory must be a branch of dynamic theory*.   Static theory is concerned with states of rest; dynamic theory is concerned with processes of change. And economic growth is, *par excellence*, a process of change – of change through time. This point needs some elaboration.

Static theory serves where we are considering the question of how the value of some economic variable is determined at any single point (or, in discrete analysis, in any single period) of time, and where it seems that the operation of time may be treated as inconsequential to the problem. Familiar examples are the determination of the equilibrium price of a commodity by supply and demand, and the determination of equilibrium aggregate output by investment and saving. The behavioural relationships are specified without reference to time, and the equilibrium in each case is a state of rest. The only way change can be introduced is by means of comparative statics (e.g. the implication for the equilibrium price of a higher demand curve) accompanied by some time-independent rule of disequilibrium behaviour (e.g. 'price will tend to rise or fall according as there is excess demand or excess supply'). That is the limit of static theory. Time does not enter the behavioural (or technical) relationships, either in equilibrium or in disequilibrium; the norm is a state of rest – and change is seen as a disturbance from one state of rest to another.

If it is thought that behaviour cannot adequately be described without reference to time, static theory will not suffice. For instance, suppose that in the supply–demand model of equilibrium price, it is believed that, owing to the existence of a time lag between decisions to produce and actual production, the quantity supplied in any period should be described as a function not of current price but of price some time past. Then although the equilibrium solution may be the same as before, disequilibrium behaviour is now time-dependent, and what may have appeared to be a stable equilibrium price under the time–independent rule may, in certain conditions, be unstable under this new assumption. This is the 'cobweb theorem', which should be familiar from price theory. The operation of time (in this case through a lag) is essential to it: it is dynamic theory. So is the Harrod growth model (since the rate of change of output with respect to time enters the investment function), and so is the Domar model.

Now it is conceivable that growth could be analysed by means of static theory: it could be regarded as a succession of states of rest, joined together by a succession of disturbances. And models can be constructed in which each static equilibrium implies the disturbance which leads on to the next.[2] But there are two objections to this approach. First, it seems unsatisfactory to treat what we are interested in as a succession of disturbances rather than as the norm. Second, and more fundamentally, in any growing economy behaviour will be influenced by the experience and expectation of growth and change. Thus even if one chooses to treat growth as a succession of states of rest, behaviour in each state of rest cannot be regarded as independent of time. At each point of time there is a past which is inherited – most obviously in the form of accumulated capital, knowledge, experience and skill – and a future which is expected; and the expected future differs from the inherited past. That surely is an implication of the presence of change. Behaviour and decisions will depend on the inheritance from the past, and on the expectations of the future; and the expectations of the future will depend upon the inheritance from the past. Time is of the essence, and static theory will not do.

We are now beginning to see the complexity of the influences which determine the growth path of any actual economy. At any point of time inputs of the factors of production will depend on investment decisions made over a long past. And the time patterns of past investment decisions (not merely their aggregated value) may be of vital importance if capital embodies the technical knowledge prevailing at the time of its installation, and if it has been unable to take advantage of subsequent progress; or if the capital installed was designed to be worked in fixed proportions with other factors; or if the capital has deteriorated with age. The services rendered by the capital stock will then depend on a long and detailed history. In addition, at the same point of time current decisions will be affected by expectations about the future: most obviously, decisions about the volume and form of investment expenditure (since the purpose of new capital is to produce output in the future) and about the volume and form of saving (a purpose of which is to delay consumption until the future). The present, as well as being dependent on a long past, is dependent on expectations of a long future.

To build a theoretical model attempting to specify all these influences would be a monumental task; it would also be futile. A theory of growth, like any other economic theory, is bound to simplify. And the process of growth, involving the movement of an economy through time, is more complex than most phenomena with which economic theory is concerned. The simplifying assumptions which have been adopted have thus generally been drastic. The question which the reader will need to bear in mind is to what extent the assumptions of a model make possible an enlightening analysis of the process (or of some aspect of it) and to what extent they cause essential features of the process, and the interesting questions surrounding it, to be lost from sight.

Referring back to the last paragraph but one, the reader should be alert through the following chapters for such assumptions as the following: there is no technical progress; technical progress affects all capital, old and new, uniformly; capital can be worked in any proportions with other factors even after its installation; saving is always in some constant proportion to income; investment is always 'given' by saving at full employment; there is only one capital good; and so on. These assumptions, and more (e.g. constant exogenous rates of labour-force growth and technical progress), have been adopted in various models. This should give some idea of how growth theorists have been forced to simplify; and even then, it has not all been easy.

So where does the *steady state* fit in? It should be clear that a steady state – in which, let us recall, every variable is either constant or growing at a constant rate – is the simplest conceivable form of growth path. It may therefore be regarded as the natural and indeed necessary starting-point for growth analysis. Then the analysis of steady states may 'be understood as one stage of a research strategy' since they 'provide a convenient method, and in some cases . . . the only available method, of getting a conceptual handle on the difficult problems of dynamic economics' (Dixit, 1976, p. 8). This goes a long way towards explaining how growth theory has turned out. But there is a further point. In the analysis of growth, as elsewhere in economic theory, positions of equilibrium provide the standard of reference. Equilibrium usually means a balance of forces which is maintained because the preferences of individuals are mutually consistent and thus satisfied.[3] Dynamic theory requires a concept of *inter-temporal equilibrium* in which the expectations which help to determine individuals' behaviour are mutually consistent and fulfilled. This conception may seem inapplicable to the real world, but if we are to use it as a bench-mark, it seems natural that it should take the form of a steady state: 'If all prices and quantities are either constant or changing at constant rates through time, we at least have a logically credible setting in which agents can form confident and correct forecasts' (Dixit, 1976, p. 8).

Thus *growth theory has been about steady states because they are a particularly simple and manageable form of a complex process, and because they seem logically consistent with the concept of inter-temporal equilibrium.*

But this does not say much about what the analysis of steady states can teach us about the real world. It is not the complete answer, and for some writers it is not even the main part of the answer.

2.3   The empirical relevance of steady states

We have just been emphasising how a steady state simplifies the actual growth process. In fact an equilibrium path of steady growth is only one step removed from the stationary state of static theory. In a stationary state all variables are constant; in steady growth those variables which are not constant are growing at constant rates. Thus a stationary state may be regarded as a special case of steady growth (with growth rate zero); and steady growth may be regarded as 'semi-static' (Hicks, 1965, p. 14), or 'quasi-stationary' (Hahn, 1971, p. viii), or 'semi-stationary' (Bliss, 1975).

Since in steady growth the growth rates of all aggregates (other than the labour force) are not only constant but equal, structural change is necessarily excluded. Every form of income, every form of expenditure and every form of output grows at the same rate. This may be regarded as a considerable limitation on the usefulness of steady states for the analysis of growth in developed industrialised economies; but it is clearly a greater limitation on their usefulness for the analysis of development, since structural change must be considered an essential feature of the development process. This is one reason why it is generally said that *'growth theory', as we are using the term in this book, is relevant to advanced industrialised economies if it is relevant at all*; it has little to contribute to development economics. Another reason for saying this is that in growth theory, land - the fixed factor of production - is usually neglected.

So the hope seems to be that an analysis of steady states will shed light on the actual growth process in developed economies: 'Knowledge about the necessary mutual relations between variables, exogenous or dependent, in a regular advance ought to throw light on observed relations in an irregular advance' (Harrod, 1963, pp. 402–3). And one way in which it may do so is by allowing us to compare different steady states; i.e. through *comparative dynamics*, which is analogous to the comparative statics of static theory. Thus if we wish to examine the consequences of a change in the propensity to save, we could construct two steady-state equilibria using assumptions differing only in the values of the saving propensities assumed. The comparison between the two paths will show the implications for equilibrium steady growth of the difference between the saving propensities. Then if we can provide an adequate demonstration of *stability* – a big 'if' – we can conclude that the differences between the two paths show what (on our model, and starting from equilibrium) will be the eventual result of the change in behaviour. This example illustrates the fact that despite the concentration on steady states, non-steady-state behaviour is not excluded from consideration. (This is of course analogous to the way in which, in static theory, concentration on states of rest does not exclude an analysis of change.) Indeed, unless we can show, by non-steady-state analysis, that our steady states are, in some sense, stable, the analysis of steady states loses much of its significance.

But we are still apologising for steady states. Is the concept of steady growth in fact that far removed from reality?

In constructing his models Kaldor (e.g. 1961, pp. 177–8) has consistently stated his objective to be the explanation of 'the characteristic features of the economic process as recorded by experience': he seeks to 'concentrate on broad tendencies, ignoring individual detail' and so to isolate what he calls the 'stylised facts' of macro-economic history which are to be the object for explanation. His *stylised facts* will be listed in full in Chapter 14; here we only need to note that they suggest that the history of advanced capitalist economies over the long run is characterised by: steady growth rates of output and labour productivity; equal growth rates of output and capital, and hence a constant capital–output ratio; constant proportions of aggregate income accruing to capital and labour; and a constant rate of profit on capital. They therefore suggest that economic history is in many respects like the steady state of theory, so that theories of steady growth do indeed have direct empirical relevance. More recently, Solow (1970, pp. 2, 11) has agreed with Kaldor that the theory of growth is aimed at reproducing and explaining the 'broad facts about the growth of advanced industrial economies', and has also adopted the approach that growth theory as it has developed may be seen as an attempt to 'explain' steady growth, divergences from which appear on the empirical evidence to have been 'fairly small, casual, and hardly self-accentuating'. For this reason, apart from any other, the steady state is at least 'not a bad place for the theory of growth to start' (Solow, 1970, p.7). Again, Dixit (1976, p.8) refers to Kaldor's stylised facts as a consideration which makes steady states 'an interesting subject'.

So perhaps growth theory has not been so far removed from reality after all, and perhaps a study of steady states will help us to understand (by helping to explain) the fundamental trends in economic aggregates in industrialised countries.

But on this issue, as on most other issues in growth theory, there is not unanimous agreement. Robinson does not appear to recognise any direct usefulness in 'explaining' equilibrium steady growth: growth of this kind can only sensibly be regarded as a 'golden age', a name she gives to it 'intending thereby to indicate its mythical nature' (Robinson, 1962, p. 52). She uses the concept of steady growth merely to indicate the simplest possible course of events and as a basis for examining the ways in which actual growth is liable and likely to depart from it: 'To set out the characteristics of a golden age by no means implies a prediction that it is likely to be realised in any actual period of history. The concept is useful, rather, as a means of distinguishing various types of disharmony that are liable to arise in an uncontrolled economy' (Robinson, 1962, pp. 98-9).

Hicks is on the same side as Robinson. Referring to the steady state, Hicks (1965, p. 14) writes: 'Such uniformity of growth is of course quite unrealistic . . . we do not greatly diminish the violence that we do to the facts when we fit them to a steady growth model, instead of a static model.' And again: 'the real world is not in a steady state, never has been, and (probably) never can be' (Hicks, 1977, p. xvi). Thus he is keen to emphasise the limitations of growth theory. In Section 2.1 we suggested that, at least on first glance, 'growth theory' seems something of a misnomer. After rather more than a first glance, Hicks (1965, p. 131) sees much to be said for that view: 'I would not myself claim for it that it is a theory of Economic Growth, if by that one means a theory that can hope to give at all an adequate explanation of actual

Growth phenomena; it seems to me to have a much narrower scope. It is just one of the methods of Dynamic Economics.' By that he means that it is characterised by a particular way of handling time – the adoption of the steady state as the equilibrium path which is central to the analysis. The use of this method can be instructive; but the claim of empirical significance made for it by Kaldor (and others) cannot be supported.

More than one issue seems to be involved in this controversy. First, is it justifiable to construct a theory to explain long-term trends alone? Kaldor thinks that it is; but Hicks (1965, p. 4) does not, because he considers that 'We have no right to conclude . . . that the economic forces making for trend and fluctuation are any different, so that they have to be analysed in different ways.' If we accept Hicks's view, then the significance of Kaldor's stylised facts is weakened. Second, how strictly should the concept of 'steady growth' be interpreted when we come to examine how closely the real world conforms to it? Hicks's (1965, pp. 132–4) interpretation is strictly uniform growth, whereas Kaldor's is less severe (see Chapter 14). Third, is it justifiable to treat history as if it was in equilibrium? Kaldor considers that it is, at least for this purpose. If economic history looks like a steady state, and if, consequently, we believe there may be forces tending to produce steady-state behaviour, then is it not natural to treat the real-world steady state as a 'balance of forces' when we try to explain it in theory? Robinson would disagree (see Chapter 10); and so might Hicks.

Finally, to what extent are the stylised facts stylised, and to what extent are they facts? In what sense, and with what qualifications, are they a fair description of history? The steady state is a convenient starting-point for growth theory, as we saw in the previous section; but are the stylised facts 'no more than convenient assumptions without which determinate solutions of theoretical problems could not be obtained' (Worswick, 1972, p. 78)? We take up this question in Part IV.

Further reading

This chapter has relied heavily on parts of Dixit (1976), and on Hicks (1965, part I). The latter is a masterly survey of the methodology of dynamic theory and of the place of modern growth theory in the history of dynamic economics. It is essential reading for the specialist. Though not easy, it assumes little prior knowledge of growth theory. Chapter 1 of Solow (1970) would be a useful easier read at this stage.

Part II

NEO-CLASSICAL
GROWTH THEORY

Part II

NEO-CLASSICAL GROWTH THEORY

3

Fixed versus Variable Coefficients –
The Neo-classical Approach

3.1 Harrod–Domar again

Two characteristic features of most neo-classical growth models are
some form of production function relating output to factor inputs and
the absence of an investment function so that investment is determined
passively by saving. Harrod's model – set out in Chapter 1 – possesses
neither of these features (though it could be argued that a production
function of the kind we are about to introduce is implicit in the investment behaviour he assumes). But a model with these characteristics can
be constructed having the same formal equilibrium properties as
Harrod's model proper, and it is this model which we shall explore in
this section. It may seem more akin to Domar's model, since that does
have a kind of production function (equation (1.27) above) and since it
does not possess an investment function; but the new model is not the
same as that either. It may be regarded as the 'neo-classical' version of
the Harrod-Domar models; it is what is called 'the Harrod-Domar
model' in many textbooks.

As in Chapter 1, we take a closed economy with no government, and
we continue to assume that capital does not depreciate. We also carry
over the assumption that the labour force L – measured in, say, number
of men or man-hours – is growing at a constant exogenous rate λ:

$$L(t) = L(0)e^{\lambda t} \tag{3.1}$$

But we now introduce a two-factor production function, of the specific
form:

$$Y(t) = \frac{\bar{K}(t)}{v(t)} = \frac{\bar{L}(t)}{u(t)} ; \quad u, v > 0 \tag{3.2}$$

where $\overline{K}$ is utilised capital stock, and L is employed labour force. So as to put aside measurement problems, we assume there is only one good, in units of which $\overline{K}$ and Y are measured. The production function states that at any time t output is related proportionally to the volume of capital in use and to employment of labour by the parameters v and u (which, however, as will be seen, may vary over time). Thus at every moment of time the ratios between Y, $\overline{K}$ and $\overline{L}$ are fixed: there is a *fixed-coefficients technology*. If, for example, an attempt is made to equip the employed labour force with more capital than is implied by this ratio, the additional capital will, in effect, be redundant: $\overline{K}$ cannot be pushed above $(v/u)\overline{L}$. $\overline{K}$ can be increased only if $\overline{L}$ is increased in proportion.

This technology is illustrated in an isoquant map in Figure 3.1. From (3.2), it may be seen that for unit output, $\overline{K} = v$ and $\overline{L} = u$. This defines the point P, the ray through which from the origin has slope v/u, equal to the fixed $\overline{K}/\overline{L}$. Holding L at u, any attempt to raise $\overline{K}$ - i.e., to move vertically from P towards P' - will be in vain: the additional capital will be redundant, and there will be no rise in output. Similarly, if we hold $\overline{K}$ constant at v and attempt to move horizontally towards P'', output will remain at unity and the additional labour will be redundant. Thus the unit-output isoquant is a right-angled corner at P. For higher levels of output we move along the ray through the origin and P, to higher corners. At each corner a unit increase in capital, *ceteris paribus*, has no effect on output and is redundant, while a unit reduction will reduce output by $1/v$ (and make u/v units of labour redundant). This is to say that at each corner the *marginal product* of capital is indeterminate between zero and $1/v$. Similarly, the marginal product of labour is indeterminate between zero and $1/u$.

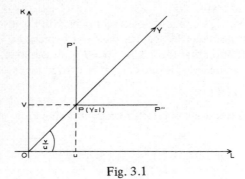

Fig. 3.1

Technical progress raises output per unit of factor input. Let us suppose, then, that v and u are both falling over time at exogenous constant rates α and β:

$$\left.\begin{array}{l} v(t) = v(0)e^{-\alpha t} \\ u(t) = u(0)e^{-\beta t} \end{array}\right\} \qquad (3.3)$$

This completes the description of the technology.

As in Chapter 1, we suppose that saving is a constant proportion s of output (income); with no independent investment function all saving is invested, and without depreciation all investment adds to the available capital stock K:

$$\dot{K} = I = sY \qquad (3.4)$$

Now for equilibrium, we require the capital stock and the labour force to be fully employed:

$$\left.\begin{array}{l} K = \bar{K} \\ L = \bar{L} \end{array}\right\} \qquad (3.5)$$

For full utilisation of K, it may be seen from (3.2)–(3.5) that we require

$$\frac{\dot{Y}}{Y} = \frac{\dot{K}}{K} - \frac{\dot{v}}{v} = \frac{sY}{K} + \alpha = \frac{s}{v} + \alpha = \frac{s}{v(0)e^{-\alpha t}} + \alpha \qquad (3.6)$$

Similarly, for full employment of L, using (3.1)–(3.3) and (3.5):

$$\frac{\dot{Y}}{Y} = \frac{\dot{L}}{L} - \frac{\dot{u}}{u} = \lambda + \beta \qquad (3.7)$$

Hence, for equilibrium, it may be seen from (3.6) and (3.7) that we need

$$\frac{\dot{Y}}{Y} = \frac{s}{v(0)e^{-\alpha t}} + \alpha = \lambda + \beta \qquad (3.8)$$

It may now be seen that the maintenance of equilibrium depends on the satisfaction of three requirements, which may be enumerated as follows:

(i) $\alpha = 0$, for otherwise (3.6) – the growth rate needed for full utilisation of the capital stock – is increasing continuously through time,

while (3.7) – the growth rate needed for full employment of labour –
is constant. With $\alpha = 0$, we have $v(t) = v(0) = v$, a constant. Then (3.8)
becomes

$$\frac{\dot{Y}}{Y} = \frac{s}{v} = \lambda + \beta \tag{3.9}$$

The second requirement is thus:

(ii) $s/v = \lambda + \beta$.

(iii) At some point of time K and L must have been fully employed,
for otherwise the satisfaction of (3.9) will merely maintain constant
rates of unemployment.

Requirements (ii) and (iii) will be familiar from Chapter 1; in particular, we again need the sum of the rates of growth of the labour force
and output per head (Harrod's natural growth rate) to equal the ratio
between the propensity to save and the capital–output ratio (Harrod's
warranted growth rate), though the last parameter, v, now has a rather
different interpretation. But what of requirement (i)? In Chapter 1 we
assumed Harrod-neutrality of technical progress and a given interest
rate; this meant that the capital–output ratio v (the accelerator coefficient in that context) was unaffected by technical progress. Requirement (i) is in effect equivalent to that assumption; at least in this
model, Harrod-neutrality as defined in Chapter 1 is equivalent to labour
being the only factor whose average productivity is increased by technical progress. This will be seen (in Chapter 7) to be generally true in the
two-factor case.

As before, then, if the above three conditions are satisfied, there
exists an equilibrium solution which is unique and which describes a
path of steady growth. But, in particular, the satisfaction of (ii) seems
to require an unlikely coincidence.

3.2   The neo-classical reaction

Tobin (1955) and Solow (1956) reacted to the Harrod–Domar model
in a similar way: it was the unrealistically rigid assumption of a fixed-
coefficients technology (or a given accelerator coefficient) which explained its pessimistic implications. In the real world production coefficients are variable, and this provides the economic system with a
flexibility which, particularly in the analysis of the 'long run', can

hardly be ignored. Factor proportions, far from being fixed, may be expected to adjust to market conditions and relative factor scarcities. This was the first step in the argument towards a 'neo-classical' analysis of growth, based on the pre-Keynesian neo-classical theory of markets which formed the core of orthodoxy before Keynes, and which is still the basis of orthodox micro-economics today. It was the first step on a return, in the words of Solow (1956, p. 162), to the 'land of the margin'.

In the neo-classical framework perfectly competitive conditions are assumed for both product and factor markets. Thus factor prices adjust freely to equilibrate (or 'clear') factor markets, and so are equal to the respective marginal products of the factors. In particular, the real wage maintains equilibrium in the labour market, and continuous full employment is assured. The Keynesian problem of the possibility of unemployment arising from a deficiency of aggregate demand is put to one side, and it is assumed that there is always sufficient investment expenditure to match saving out of full-employment income. The neo-classical analysis is therefore concerned with equilibrium growth paths which are characterised by the perfect adjustment of relative prices to supply and demand conditions; the continuous realisation of plans and expectations; and, in particular, the continuous maintenance of full employment. The question of whether disequilibrium behaviour is such that the warranted growth path is unstable – one of the questions raised by Harrod – is practically ignored; the only stability question which arises is that of whether equilibrium paths which do not exhibit steady growth converge on one that does – a question which does not arise in the Harrod–Domar model since there is only one equilibrium path, which is a steady state.

Most neo-classical writers would accept that this approach needs to be supplemented by a Keynesian theory of deviations from equilibrium; this is agreed by, for instance, Meade (1962, pp. 40-2) and Solow (1956, pp. 189-92). They would not regard themselves as anti-Keynesian.[1] But they would argue that Keynes's theory belongs to the analysis of the short period, and that for the analysis of the long period it is legitimate, first, to assume full employment, and second, having put Keynesian problems aside, to adopt the neo-classical theory of relative prices, resource allocation and income distribution. The acceptance of Keynes is sometimes made clear by the way in which the assumption of full employment is 'justified' by a further assumption that there is a government or monetary authority which ensures by its policy actions the continuous maintenance of full employment.[2] This assumption, that 'the authorities have read the *General Theory* or that they are socialists who don't need to' (Swan, 1963, p. 205), so that sufficient investment is always forthcoming to balance full-employment saving, may then be considered to be empirically validated by post-Keynesian economic history. And once the full-employment hypothesis has been justified, the neo-classicals can argue that they are taking their cue from Keynes himself, for in a well-known passage in his Concluding Notes to the *General Theory* (1936, pp. 378–9), he wrote:

> if our central controls succeed in establishing an aggregate volume of output corresponding to full employment as nearly as is practicable, the classical theory[3] comes into its own again from this point on-wards . . . there is no objection to be raised against the classical analysis of the manner in which private self-interest will determine what in particular is produced, in what proportions the factors of production will be combined to produce it, and how the value of the final product will be distributed between them.

The neo-classical theorist can therefore, it seems, enlist Keynes's support for the view that 'when Keynes solved "the great puzzle of Effective Demand", he made it possible for economists once more to study the progress of society in long-run classical terms' (Swan, 1956, p. 334).

Thus *whereas Harrod and Domar sought to extend Keynes's analysis into the long run, the neo-classicals consider that, for the analysis of the long run, the appropriate framework is provided mainly by the application and extension of pre-Keynesian theory.*

Although Keynes argued that neo-classical economics 'comes into its own' in a full-employment world, it has in fact been argued, in his name, that this is not so: that even given full employment, Keynes's analysis cannot be ignored, and that the neo-classical theory of markets (and income distribution) needs to be replaced by an alternative which is Keynesian in spirit if not in fact. This is the starting-point of the 'neo-Keynesian' theory of growth which is considered in Part III.

4

The One-good Model without Technical Progress – The Simplest Case

4.1 The model

We begin with the very simplest of models. In this section we list its assumptions and indicate the significance of some of them. They are by no means all essential to the neo-classical approach, and the following chapters will consider how they may be relaxed. They may be enumerated as follows:

(i) As before we are considering a closed economy, with no government expenditure or taxation.

(ii) There is no technological progress.

(iii) Only one good is produced, for both consumption and investment. Output (Y) and the capital stock (K) are measured unambiguously in terms of this good.

(iv) There are two factors of production, capital (K) and labour (L), each of which is homogeneous. In particular, capital does not depreciate, and all capital goods in use are the same.

(v) The labour force grows at a constant exogenous rate λ:

$$L(t) = L(0)e^{\lambda t} ; \quad \lambda > 0 \tag{4.1}$$

(vi) Capital is perfectly malleable, so that the capital–labour ratio is perfectly flexible. Both factors are fully employed, and Y (which is both gross and net output, by (iv)), is related to K and L by the production function

$$Y = F(K,L) \tag{4.2}$$

which is a non-negative function defined for all positive K and L, and which is twice continuously differentiable. Also: (a) both marginal products are always positive:

$$\frac{\partial Y}{\partial K} \equiv F_K > 0; \quad \frac{\partial Y}{\partial L} \equiv F_L > 0 \tag{4.3}$$

and (b) there are diminishing returns to each factor:

$$\frac{\partial}{\partial K} F_K \equiv F_{KK} < 0; \quad \frac{\partial}{\partial L} F_L \equiv F_{LL} < 0 \tag{4.4}$$

and (c) there are constant returns to scale, i.e. F is homogeneous of degree 1:

$$F(\mu K, \mu L) = \mu F(K,L), \text{ for any } \mu > 0^1 \tag{4.5}$$

(vii) There is perfect competition, so that factor prices are equal to the respective marginal products:

$$\begin{aligned} \text{Wage rate of labour,} \quad & w = F_L \\ \text{Rental rate of capital,} \quad & r = F_K \end{aligned} \Bigg\} \tag{4.6}$$

(viii) The saving function is of the simple proportional form

$$S = sY; \quad 0 < s < 1 \tag{4.7}$$

(ix) Since there is only one good and no financial asset, all saving is invested in the good; because there is no depreciation, all investment adds to the capital stock:

$$\dot{K} = I = S \tag{4.8}$$

In common with the Harrod–Domar model, there is a proportional saving function and a constant growth rate for the labour force. But in contrast with the Harrod–Domar model, the production function now allows the two factors to be continuously substitutable in production, so that full employment of both is always technically feasible, whatever the proportion in which they are supplied. Moreover, both factors are fully employed, with the markets for them being kept in equilibrium by the competitively determined factor prices. In contrast with Keynes, there is no money wage, for there is no money: wages are paid in the form of the single good, and so are always 'real'. Also, there is no distinction between decisions to save and decisions to invest: with only one good (and no financial asset) the two are inseparable. With the one-good assumption we are not in a Keynesian (or Harrodian) world, and Keynesian problems do not arise. The *one-good assumption* therefore does much more than remove aggregation difficulties. And it simplifies the analysis in other ways besides. With only one good the competitive factor prices can simply be read off the single production function, once K and L are known; with more than one good (and hence more than one production function) we would need simultaneously to determine the allocation of the factors among the different goods, and the relative prices of the goods. It is only in the one-good case that factor prices (marginal-value products) can be determined independently of demand conditions, by the technology alone. Furthermore, consider the rental rate of capital. This is to be interpreted, analogously to the wage rate, as the price of the use (or services) of a capital good per unit of time, or as the income to be derived, per unit of time, from the hiring-out of a capital good. Now if we had more than one good, we would measure this income in terms of some *numéraire* (which might be money) and in order to calculate the rate of return or profit we would add the appreciation (or deduct the depreciation) of the value of the good (also in terms of the *numéraire*), and express the sum as a proportion or percentage of the good's initial value. In competitive equilibrium with perfect foresight all such rates of return, for all capital goods, would be equal to one another, and to the rate of interest; the rate of profit would be 'normal'. But in our model there is no possibility of appreciation or depreciation, and the single good is the *numéraire*: its value is always unity. Hence the rental rate r is the rate of return, or rate of profit; and under the conditions we are assuming it is the rate of normal profit, and it may be regarded as the interest rate.

Next consider the *constant returns to scale assumption*. This means that if both factors are increased by some equal proportion, output will expand in the same proportion: there are no 'economies' or 'diseconomies' of scale. In other words, the average productivity of each factor is invariant to scale and is a function only of the ratio between the factors. Formally, if we substitute

$$\mu = \frac{1}{L}$$

in (4.5), we obtain

$$Y = F(K,L) = L \times F\left(\frac{K}{L}, 1\right) = L \times f\left(\frac{K}{L}\right) \tag{4.9}$$

or

$$y = f(k) \qquad (4.10)$$

where the lower-case letters denote *per capita* variables. Thus the average productivity of labour is simply a function of the capital–labour ratio. We shall call (4.10) the *labour-productivity function*. By the properties assumed for F, f is twice continuously differentiable; and from (4.9) it may be seen that the marginal product of capital, F_K, is simply the first derivative of it:

$$F_K \equiv \frac{\partial Y}{\partial K} = f'(k)$$

Also,

$$\left. \right\} \qquad (4.11)$$

$$F_{KK} \quad = f''(k)$$

Similarly, from (4.9), the marginal product of labour is

$$F_L \equiv \frac{\partial Y}{\partial L} = f(k) - kf'(k) \qquad (4.12)$$

Hence, the marginal, as well as the average, products of the two factors are functions of the capital–labour ratio only. Further, since the factors are being paid their marginal products, the sum of all factor payments is

$$Kf'(k) + L[f(k) - kf'(k)] = Lf(k) = Y \qquad (4.13)$$

We have thus shown that under constant returns, output, Y, is exactly exhausted by total factor payments when the factors are paid their marginal products; we have proved what is known in more general mathematical terms as *Euler's theorem*. The result shows how naturally the constant-returns assumption fits into the neo-classical scheme.

A labour-productivity function derived from a production function satisfying the above conditions is shown in Figure 4.1. The general shape of f is defined by assumption (vi) and (4.11); we also assume here that it goes to the origin. To examine some properties of the diagram, suppose that the capital–labour ratio is Ok^*. Then output per head is Oy^*, and the output–capital ratio Oy^*/Ok^* is the slope of the ray OX. In the Harrod–Domar model this was fixed at a given value, but it is now variable along f. The rental rate or rate of profit, $f'(k^*)$, is shown by the slope of the straight line RX, which touches $f(k)$ at X, i.e. by

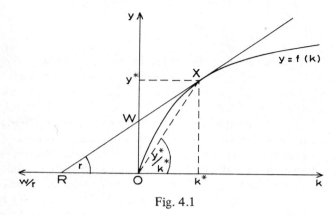

Fig. 4.1

OW/OR or Xk^*/Rk^*. The slope of RX is also shown by Wy^*/y^*X, and since y^*X is the same as Ok^*, Wy^* measures the product of the profit rate and capital per head, which is profits per head (of the labour force). The difference between output per head and profits per head is the wage rate (wages per head), which is thus shown by OW (see (4.12)). The ratio of Wy^* to OW is therefore the ratio of profits per head to wages per head, which is the same as the ratio of total profits to total wages in the economy; the share of wages in total income is shown by OW/Oy^*, and the share of profits by Wy^*/Oy^*. This last ratio can be expressed in another way: dividing both numerator and denominator by the capital-labour ratio, we see that it is the same as the product of the profit rate, Wy^*/y^*X, and the capital–output ratio, Ok^*/Oy^*. Thus the share of profits, Wy^*/Oy^*, is the elasticity of $f(k)$ at X. Finally, the ratio of the wage rate to the rental rate – the *wage-rental ratio* – is the ratio of OW to OW/OR, so that it is shown by OR.

4.2   The existence and uniqueness of steady-state equilibrium

We now bring our assumptions together to examine the implications of equilibrium.

From (4.1), (4.7), (4.8), and the definitions of k and y, we have that in equilibrium

$$\frac{\dot{k}}{k} \equiv \frac{\dot{K}}{K} - \frac{\dot{L}}{L} = \frac{sY}{K} - \lambda \equiv \frac{sy}{k} - \lambda = \frac{sf(k)}{k} - \lambda \quad (4.14)$$

so that

$$\dot{k} = sf(k) - \lambda k$$

which is a first-order linear differential equation in k. In order to obtain the equilibrium path of k, we would need to assume a particular form for f. But, as Solow (1956) showed, we can make considerable progress in general terms.

We can *ask first whether there exists a steady-state equilibrium*. From our definition of steady growth, we know that a necessary feature of a steady state is that Y and K grow at the same constant rate. But our production function (4.2) has constant returns; and it follows that if any two of the variables Y, K and L grow at the same constant rate, the third must as well. Hence a requirement for steady growth in this constant-returns, no-technical–progress case is that K and L grow at the same constant rate, or that k is constant. Therefore, for steady growth, (4.14) is zero, and

$$\frac{s}{k/f(k)} = \lambda, \text{ or } \frac{f(k)}{k} = \frac{\lambda}{s} \qquad (4.15)$$

The similarity between the first version of (4.15) and condition (ii) for equilibrium in the Harrod–Domar model of the previous chapter is clear. (The term β in (3.9) disappears with no technical progress.) But there are two important differences. First, (4.15) is not a necessary condition for equilibrium in this model; it is only a condition for steady-state equilibrium. With fixed coefficients and no technical progress, equilibrium implies constancy of k and steady growth; but with variable co-efficients, non-steady-state equilibrium ($\dot{k} \neq 0$) is not precluded. Second, the capital–output ratio v is now a variable: in (4.15) it is shown as $k/f(k)$, a function of k. (In Figure 4.1 it is the reciprocal of the slope of OX.) The second version of (4.15) shows, in terms of the parameters λ and s, the value which $1/v$ must take for steady-state equilibrium; and if $f(k)$ is such that there exists an output–capital ratio equal to λ/s, for given values of those parameters, then there exists a steady-state equilibrium.

Further, if $f(k)$ is such that $1/v$ can take any positive value, there must exist a steady-state solution whatever are the (positive) values of λ and s. Now assume that $f(k)$ is *well-behaved*, a property defined by (4.3), (4.4), (4.11) and the additional condition:

$$\lim_{k \to 0} f'(k) = \infty; \quad \lim_{k \to \infty} f'(k) = 0 \qquad (4.16)$$

We already know from (4.3), (4.4) and (4.11) that $f'(k)$ is a positive and decreasing function of k; the additional restriction (4.16) now ensures that $f'(k)$ can take any positive value. But it can be shown that (4.16) implies that

$$\lim_{k \to 0} \frac{f(k)}{k} = \infty; \quad \lim_{k \to \infty} \frac{f(k)}{k} = 0$$

so that the assumption of well-behavedness is sufficient to ensure that $f(k)/k \equiv 1/v$ can take any positive value, and hence that it can always take the value λ/s. In other words, *if $f(k)$ is well-behaved, the warranted growth rate, s/v, can always take the value of the natural rate λ: Harrod's Existence Problem no longer exists!*

Furthermore, with f well-behaved, it is clear that for each value of λ/s, there is only one value of k which will satisfy (4.15): *for each value of λ/s, there is a unique steady-state solution.*

The *characteristics of this solution* are filled out easily. First, we know that the output–capital ratio is constant at λ/s, and that k takes the constant value which makes this so: we may thus suppose that the slope of OX in Figure 4.1 is λ/s, so that k^* is the steady-state value of k. The steady-state values of

$$y = y^* = f(k^*) = \frac{\lambda}{s} k^*$$

$$r = f'(k^*)$$

$$w = f(k^*) - k^* f'(k^*)$$

are then all determined in terms of k^* and the productivity function. We see immediately that the share of profits, P, in income

$$\frac{P}{Y} = \frac{rK}{Y} = \frac{k^* f'(k^*)}{f(k^*)} \tag{4.17}$$

is constant, as is its complement, the share of wages W. The steady-state paths of K and Y are then obtained, in terms of k^* and the parameters of the model:

$$K(t) = k^* L(t) = k^* L(0) e^{\lambda t} = K(0) e^{\lambda t} \tag{4.18}$$

where

$$K(0) = k^* L(0), \quad \text{and}$$

$$Y(t) = y^* L(t) = f(k^*) L(0) e^{\lambda t} = \frac{\lambda}{s} k^* L(0) e^{\lambda t}$$

$$= Y(0) e^{\lambda t} \tag{4.19}$$

where

$$Y(0) = \frac{\lambda}{s} k^* L(0)$$

Thus K and Y (and also $I = S$, W and P) grow at the rate λ of the labour force, which is the natural growth rate in this model.

4.3 Comparing steady states

We can now compare steady-state paths with differing parameter values. It is to be stressed again that these exercises in *comparative dynamics* will not describe the *effects of changes in parameter values*, at least until we have established the stability of steady-growth paths, i.e. at least until we have established that, following a disturbance from one steady state, the economy described in the model will converge on another; and even then they will only describe the long-run effects, after convergence. We shall be concerned with stability in the next section; meanwhile these exercises can be interpreted as showing only *the implications for equilibrium steady growth* of differences in parameter values.

First, consider two steady states with *different saving propensities*. We can simply compare the steady-state solution of the previous section – call it G – with what that solution would be if, *ceteris paribus*, the propensity to save took a value, s', greater than s. In this 'alternative' steady state – which we may call G' – the satisfaction of (4.15) requires a lower output–capital ratio than in G, and this will be obtained (given diminishing returns to capital) with a k higher than k^*. That is, in Figure 4.1 we shall have a lower y/k, a higher k, a higher y, a lower r, and a higher w; and since there is no difference in $L(t)$, it follows that at each point of time K, Y and W must all be higher in G' than in G. Investment $I(= S)$ must also be higher, both because Y is higher and because $s' > s$. But we do not know whether aggregate consumption C (and consumption per head c) is higher or lower: on the one hand, the proportion of income consumed is lower in G', while on the other hand $Y(t)$ (and y) are higher. We shall return to this question later in the section. Again, we cannot tell how profits, P, differ between the two paths, since r is lower in G', while $K(t)$ is higher. We therefore have insufficient information to say whether the ratio of profits to wages, P/W, is higher or lower. This question of relative factor shares will also be examined below. So far, we have not considered growth rates. It may be seen from (4.18) and (4.19) that although $K(t)$ and $Y(t)$ are always higher in G' than in G, their rate of growth is no different: it is still λ. And the same is true of all aggregates in the model; i.e. *in equilibrium steady growth the growth rate is independent of the propensity to save, since it is given by the natural growth rate which (we are assuming) is independent of saving behaviour.*[2]

Now consider two steady states with the same propensity to save, but *different natural growth rates*. We can compare G with a different 'alternative', G'', with a λ'' lower than λ. First, from (4.15) we see that G'', like G', is characterised by a lower output–capital ratio than G. We thus again have a higher k, a higher y, a lower r, and a higher w; and since y is higher while s is the same, consumption per head, c, is also higher. But now for all $t > 0$, $L(t)$ is lower in G'', so we cannot say that the aggregates K, Y, W and C are always higher than in G. From (4.18) we see that although K and Y are initially higher in G'', their growth is at the lower rate λ'', so that eventually, beyond some point in time, they must both be lower. Indeed, *initially* every aggregate in the model must be higher in G'' than in G, except L (whose initial value is the same) and P (whose initial value may be higher or lower, depending on whether the higher $K(0)$ outweighs the lower r); and *eventually* every aggregate, without exception, must be lower. Thus for each aggregate except L and possibly P there is some time $t(> 0)$ at which its G path crosses its G'' path. This is illustrated, for K and Y, in part (b) of Figure 4.2.

In both parts of the diagram the steady-state paths of K and Y are drawn in terms of natural logarithms; they are therefore shown as straight lines, with the slope of each measuring the constant exponential growth rate. Part (a) compares G with G'. With a higher propensity to save, each G' path is higher than, but parallel to, its corresponding G path. Part (b) compares the G and G'' paths. With a lower natural growth rate, each of the two G'' paths is initially higher than its corresponding G path, because G'' (like G') has more capital per head and output per head than G. But the G'' paths are less steep than the G paths, reflecting the lower growth rate. Consequently, the two Y paths cross at some time t_1, and the two K paths cross at t_2. For $t < t_1$, Y is higher in G'', and so, therefore, are S, I and C; but for $t > t_1$, the order is reversed. For $t < t_2$, K is higher in G'', while we cannot say whether

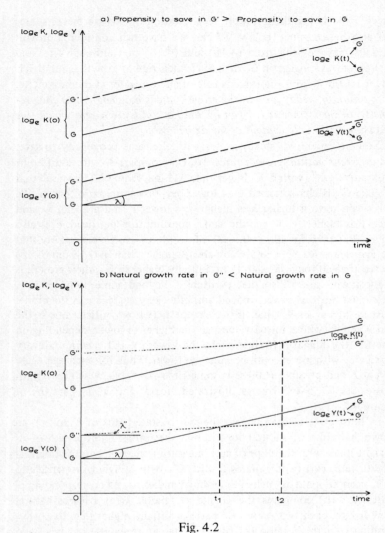

Fig. 4.2

P is higher or lower; but for $t > t_2$, both K and P are lower in G''. (If we were to draw the paths for P, they would cross at some time $t_3 < t_2$.)[3]

Thus *differences in s and differences in* λ *have contrasting implications for equilibrium steady growth.* In steady growth (at least in our present model, which excludes technical progress) we must have

$$\frac{\dot{Y}}{Y} = \frac{\dot{K}}{K} = \frac{\dot{L}}{L} = \lambda$$

so that it is only differences in λ which can mean different rates of steady growth. But in both cases the output–capital ratio differs. In the case of a difference in s, Y/K must differ to the same extent in the *opposite* direction in order that the equilibrium

$$\frac{\dot{K}}{K} = \frac{sY}{K}$$

be maintained at the given λ. In the case of a difference in λ, Y/K must differ in the *same* direction for the equilibrium $\dot{K}/K$ to conform with the natural growth rate.

There are two questions left to be considered, one concerning the composition of income between wages and profits, the other concerning the level of consumption in the comparison between G and G'.

We first consider how the *distribution of income between wages and profits* will differ among steady states. We already know from our definition of steady growth that distributive shares are constant in a steady state. We also know that in our present model the steady-state share of profits (and its complement, the share of wages) is determined by the steady-state value of k, and by the competitive factor prices which are implied by that k and the productivity function (see expression (4.17)). To see how factor shares will differ among states, it is therefore sufficient to see how competitive factor shares change when k changes, for given $f(k)$.[4]

Consider the ratio of profits to wages:

$$\frac{P}{W} = \frac{rK}{wL} \equiv \frac{k}{w/r} \qquad (4.20)$$

It is the same as the capital-labour ratio divided by the wage–rental ratio. Now suppose k rises; of itself, this increase in capital intensity will favour capital's share. But as k rises, the rental rate r will fall while the wage rate w will rise, because of diminishing returns; there will be a change in relative factor prices in favour of labour. (In Figure 4.1 we would have, as k increases, the wage–rental ratio OR increasing as the point X moves to the right along f.) From (4.20), P/W, and hence

$$\frac{P}{Y} \equiv \frac{P/W}{1 + P/W}$$

will fall, remain constant, or rise, depending on whether k rises by a proportion less than, equal to, or greater than the proportionate rise in w/r, i.e. the direction in which P/Y changes following a change in k depends on the elasticity of k with respect to w/r. This is defined as the *elasticity of substitution*, σ, between K and L, since it measures how readily one factor is substituted for the other when their relative prices change:[5]

$$\sigma \equiv \frac{d \log K/L}{d \log w/r} \equiv \frac{w/r}{K/L} \times \frac{d(K/L)}{d(w/r)} \tag{4.21}$$

Whether P/Y falls, remains constant, or rises as k rises (and thus whether P/Y is lower, the same, or higher in a steady state with a higher k - e.g. in G' or G'' as compared with G) depends on whether σ is less than, equal to, or greater than unity: it depends on the 'shape' of the production (or productivity) function.

With constant returns σ may be expressed in terms of k, f and the derivatives of f as follows:[6]

$$\sigma = - \frac{f'(k)[f(k)-kf'(k)]}{kf(k)f''(k)} = - \frac{f'(f-kf')}{kff''} \tag{4.22}$$

which, it may be seen, is always positive: k always changes in the same direction as w/r, which we knew already.

Generally, the elasticity of substitution in a production function will vary with the inputs of the factors: for σ to be constant, the production function must have a particular form. The form required for σ to take any constant value is known as the *constant elasticity of substitution (or C.E.S.) production function*. We do not need to use this,[7] but we shall need to use the form required for σ to take the particular constant value of unity. It is derived easily. Retaining our assumption of constant returns, we know that if $\sigma = 1$ for all K and L, the competitive share of profits is invariant with respect to k.[8] We can therefore write

$$\frac{P}{Y} = \frac{kf'(k)}{y} = \frac{k}{y}\frac{dy}{dk} = \alpha \text{ (a constant)} \tag{4.23}$$

Thus

$$\int \frac{dy}{y} = \alpha \int \frac{dk}{k}$$

Therefore

$$\log y = \alpha \log k + \log A$$

where A is an arbitrary constant. Therefore

$$y = Ak^{\alpha} \tag{4.24}$$

This gives the productivity function $f(k)$. Multiplying through by L:

$$Y = AK^{\alpha}L^{1-\alpha} \tag{4.25}$$

This is the *constant-returns Cobb–Douglas production function*. Now when factors receive their marginal (social) products, the share of each factor in total income is the same as the elasticity of output with respect to the input of the factor.[9] For total output to be exactly exhausted by marginal-product factor payments, the production function must therefore be such that those elasticities always sum to unity; this is the same as saying that there must be constant returns. In (4.25) the elasticities (factor shares) are the exponents α and $1 - \alpha$ of the respective factor inputs; and not only do they sum to unity (constant returns) but they are also constant (elasticity of substitution equal to unity). Now if the right-hand side of (4.25) is raised to a power $\beta(\neq 1)$, the exponents of K and L will no longer sum to unity, though they will still be constant:

$$Y = [AK^{\alpha}L^{1-\alpha}]^{\beta} = BK^{\alpha\beta}L^{(1-\alpha)\beta}; \quad \beta \neq 1 \tag{4.26}$$

where

$$B = A^{\beta}$$

The exponents sum to β; if $\beta < 1$ there are decreasing returns to scale, while if $\beta > 1$ there are increasing returns to scale. But in either case we still have $\sigma = 1$; (4.26) is the *Cobb–Douglas production function with non-constant returns*.

Finally, we consider how *aggregate consumption and consumption per head* differ among steady states. We have already answered this question for steady states with different natural growth rates: we saw that in G'' (which has the lower growth rate) consumption per head is higher than in G, while aggregate consumption is initially higher but eventually lower. But in our comparison of G' with G, we could not say whether the lower propensity to consume outweighs, or is outweighed by, the higher y and $Y(t)$. We now return to that comparison.

In all steady states which have the same $L(t) = L(0)e^{\lambda t}$, $\dot{K}/K = \lambda$, so that investment per head $\dot{K}/L = \lambda k$. Thus consumption per head, c, may be written as follows in terms of λ and the steady-state values of k and $f(k)$:

$$c = y - \frac{\dot{K}}{L} = f(k) - \lambda k \qquad (4.27)$$

In Figure 4.3 a well-behaved productivity function is drawn, together with the steady-state investment per head function λk; the distance between these at any k shows the value of c in the steady state represented by that capital–labour ratio. As we move to the right along Ok

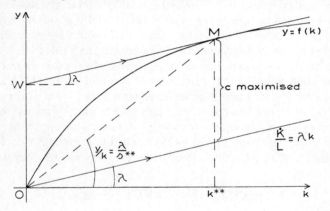

Fig. 4.3

from the origin, from one steady state to another, each increment of k raises output per head by $f'(k)$, and investment per head by λ. The well-behavedness assumption ensures that initially the marginal product of capital is sufficiently large to exceed λ, so that c increases. But the same assumption also ensures that $f'(k)$ declines continuously, so eventually we must reach a steady state where $f'(k) = \lambda$; there c stops rising, and if we move further to the right, $f'(k) < \lambda$, so that c must fall. Thus the steady growth path with the highest c is such that $f'(k) = \lambda$.[10] This is the so-called *golden rule of accumulation*, established by Phelps (1961) and others. Given the rate of growth of the labour force, for steady growth with maximum consumption per head, we should want the saving propensity s to take that value s^{**} in Figure 4.3, which gives equality between the rate of growth λ and the rate of profit.

It is now easy to compare G and G'. In G, c is given by

$$c^* = f(k^*) - \lambda k^*$$

while in G', we have

$$c^{*'} = f(k^{*'}) - \lambda k^{*'}$$

Consequently:

$$c^{*'} \gtreqless c^*, \text{ according as } \frac{f(k^{*'}) - f(k^*)}{k^{*'} - k^*} \gtreqless \lambda$$

That is, the steady state with the higher propensity to save, G', has the higher consumption per head (and the higher aggregate consumption) if the ratio of the difference in y to the difference in k – the discrete analogue of the marginal product of capital – exceeds the natural growth rate. This depends on the value of λ and the shape of the productivity function.

4.4   The stability of the steady state: equilibrium dynamics

In Section 4.2 we established that for any given values of the parameters λ and s, and a well-behaved productivity function $f(k)$, there exists a unique steady-state equilibrium solution to the model. We have since been describing and comparing the steady-growth paths associated with different values of the parameters. But we started with the equilibrium condition (4.14), which does not require steady growth; and we now need to examine *non-steady-state equilibrium behaviour*.

In *non-steady-state equilibrium*, (4.14) is satisfied, but not (4.15):

$$\dot{k} = sf(k) - \lambda k \neq 0 \tag{4.28}$$

so that

$$\frac{f(k)}{k} \neq \frac{\lambda}{s} \tag{4.29}$$

Now suppose $f(k)/k > \lambda/s$: the output–capital ratio is too high for steady growth, which means, by the properties of f, that k is too low.

But then $sf(k) > \lambda k$, so that, as (4.28) shows, in equilibrium k will be rising: the growth rate of the capital stock, $\dot{K}/K = sY/K = sf(k)/k$, will be greater than the growth rate of the labour force, λ. With k rising, $f(k)/k$ must be falling. Similarly, if $f(k)/k < \lambda/s$, the equation in k shows that equilibrium implies that k will be falling; and hence the output–capital ratio will be rising. In sum, if the output–capital ratio differs from the value λ/s required for steady-growth equilibrium, the continuous maintenance of equilibrium implies that the divergence must diminish continuously. By this argument – the simplicity of which may seem surprising – Solow (1956) demonstrated that in the simple one-good neo-classical model, steady-growth equilibrium is stable, in the sense that every equilibrium path approaches a steady state asymptotically. (Whether equilibrium growth is stable – i.e., whether disequilibrium paths converge on equilibrium paths – is, of course, another question, which for the most part neo-classical theory does not attempt to answer.)

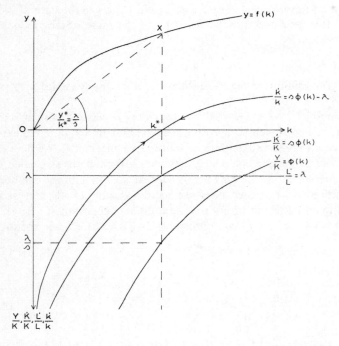

Fig. 4.4

The argument is illustrated in Figure 4.4. The upper quadrant reproduces, more or less, Figure 4.1 : $f(k)$ is a well-behaved productivity function, and the point X represents the unique steady-state solution, determined by $y*/k* = \lambda/s$, λ and s being given. Now well-behavedness ensures that the output–capital ratio is a decreasing function of k which can take any positive value: $Y/K \equiv y/k = \phi(k)$ is drawn in the lower quadrant (where the vertical axis has a different scale). In equilibrium $\dot{K}/K = sY/K = s\phi(k)$ is also a decreasing function of k, and it also is drawn in the lower quadrant. Labour-force growth is represented simply by a horizontal straight line at λ. We know that when $k = k*$, $\dot{K}/K = s\phi(k*) = \dot{L}/L = \lambda$: thus $s\phi(k)$ and λ meet at this unique steady-state value of k. As we move to the left from $k*$, $Y/K = \phi(k)$ rises above λ/s, and $\dot{K}/K = s\phi(k)$ rises above λ; at any value of k, $\dot{k}/k$ is shown by the difference between $s\phi(k)$ and λ. Conversely as we move to the right from $k*$, $\dot{K}/K$ falls below λ, and $\dot{k}/k$ becomes negative. Thus either side of $k*$ any value of k represents an unstable equilibrium since it implies movement towards $k*$. The stability of $k*$ is indicated by the arrows on the $\dot{k}/k$ curve.

The examination in Section 4.3 of the differences among steady growth paths with differing parameter values now has the added significance of showing the long-run equilibrium effects of parameter changes from a starting-point of steady growth. Thus suppose that s rises. Our comparative-dynamics analysis showed that there will exist a new steady state (G') with a lower output–capital ratio and a higher k than in the old (G); and our stability analysis has shown that the system will approach the new steady state asymptotically by way of a (non-steady-state) path on which the capital intensity of production increases. Whether, on this transitional path, the distribution of income changes in capital's favour, or in labour's favour, or not at all, will depend on the elasticity of substitution between the two factors. And so on.

4.5 Summary

The model defined by the assumptions listed in Section 4.1, and by the additional assumption that the productivity function implied by the production function is well-behaved, is such that there always exists a unique equilibrium steady state, and that the system will converge on this steady state if it remains in equilibrium. It is in this sense that the model 'explains' steady growth. It is, as Solow (1970, p. 23) remarks, only a 'partial explanation', because it does not consider disequilibrium behaviour; but in contrast with the Harrod–Domar model, at least steady growth does not seem to depend on a fluke.

Further reading

'The neo-classical one-sector growth model has become a standard piece of equipment in the economic theorist's tool kit' (Johnson, 1967, p. 143), and there are many alternative expositions of variants of that model which are essentially similar to what we have called the 'simplest case'. The most celebrated are the original papers by Solow (1956) and Swan (1956), and chapters 1–7 of Meade (1962). (The earlier paper by Tobin (1955) is more relevant to the next chapter; he introduced money as well as the neo-classical production function, and was less concerned with steady growth than with the behaviour of the money supply and prices which various forms of growth would require.) Solow's paper is more comprehensive than Swan's; it is also more general in that Swan restricted his attention to the Cobb–Douglas production function. Most of Solow's paper ignores technical progress, while both Swan and Meade are a few chapters ahead of us in that respect. Both Swan and Meade take account of land as a third (fixed) factor. Solow (1970, ch. 2) has since revisited the model. Chapter 3 of Allen (1967) provides a helpful introduction to the algebra of production functions.

5

The One-good Model
without Technical Progress –
Altering some Assumptions

5.1 Introduction

While retaining the neo-classical framework, we shall in the remainder of Part II be examining the sensitivity of the conclusions reached in Chapter 4 to the assumptions on which they were based, paying particular attention to the question of how well the conclusions about the existence, uniqueness and stability of a steady-state solution withstand alterations to the model. In this chapter we continue to assume that there is only one good and no technical progress; and we consider the consequences of adopting different assumptions about saving, labour-force growth, the technology, of introducing a monetary asset, and depreciation.

5.2 The saving function

Hitherto, we have been assuming that saving is related proportionally to aggregate income:

$$S = sY; \quad 0 < s < 1 \tag{5.1}$$

An alternative hypothesis is that the average propensity to save out of wages, s_w, is less than the average propensity to save out of profits, s_p:

$$S = s_w W + s_p P; \quad 0 \leqslant s_w < s_p \leqslant \tag{5.2}$$

This plays a large role in neo-Keynesian growth theory, and is frequently called the *neo-Keynesian saving function*. When $s_w = 0$, (5.2) reduces to

$$S = s_p P; \quad 0 < s_p \leqslant 1 \tag{5.3}$$

This assumption, that all wages are consumed so that all saving is out of profits, arises most naturally in models where wages fail to rise above 'subsistence' levels; it is associated with the classical economists of the early nineteenth century, and (5.3) is called the *classical saving function*. All three of these functions are embodied in

$$S = s_w W + s_p P; \quad 0 \leqslant s_w \leqslant s_p \leqslant 1 \tag{5.4}$$

It collapses to the proportional function if $s_w = s_p = s$; it gives the neo-Keynesian function when $s_w < s_p$; and it gives the classical function when $0 = s_w < s_p$. Since most growth models employ one of these three hypotheses, (5.4), which embraces all of them, may be called the *general saving function*.

It is, however, obviously far from 'general' in any wider sense. The average propensities to save, s_w and s_p, are constrained to be constant and thus equal to the marginal propensities; and they are not related to any variables which may have an influence on saving separate from that of income. In fact each of the saving functions contained in (5.4) is little more than a simple rule which neglects any consideration of how rational individuals will allocate their income between consumption and saving, or plan that allocation through time. To some economists, simple rules of this kind are often acceptable; but since the assumption of rational, maximising behaviour is one of the traits of neo-classical theory (as we shall see in Chapter 10) it is not surprising to find neo-classical economists dissatisfied with all the above hypotheses. Thus Johnson (1967, p. 148) argues that the proportional function is 'completely arbitrary and theoretically indefensible, an analytical relic of naive Keynesianism deriving no logical support from utility maximisation theory', and that 'little of theoretical advantage can be gained by complicating the model' with a neo-Keynesian function.

It is, nevertheless, instructive to 'complicate' the model in that way. The reasoning behind the *neo-Keynesian function* will be considered in Part III; here we merely substitute it for the proportional function in the model of the previous chapter. From (5.2) and the identity

$$Y \equiv W + P$$

we have

$$S = s_w Y + (s_p - s_w)P$$

so that the over-all propensity to save, s, depends on the distribution of income and can be expressed as a function of the share of profits:

$$s \equiv \frac{S}{Y} = s_w + (s_p - s_w)\frac{P}{Y} = s_w + (s_p - s_w)\frac{kf'(k)}{f(k)} \quad (5.5)$$

Substituting (5.5) into (4.14), we obtain a new differential equation in k:

$$\dot{k} = s_w f'(k) + (s_p - s_w)kf'(k) - \lambda k \quad (5.6)$$

Putting this equal to zero, we see that steady growth now implies

$$s_w \frac{f(k)}{k} + (s_p - s_w)f'(k) = \lambda \quad (5.7a)$$

or

$$\frac{f(k)}{k} = \frac{\lambda}{s_w + (s_p - s_w)\dfrac{kf'(k)}{f(k)}} \quad (5.7b)$$

which may be compared with (4.15).

Consider (5.7a). If $f(k)$ is well-behaved, both $f(k)/k$ and $f'(k)$ are monotonically decreasing functions of k, taking all positive values, and since $s_w < s_p$, the same is true of the whole left-hand side of the expression. Hence, for any set of values of λ, s_w and s_p there is a unique k which allows the equality to be satisfied: there exists a unique steady-state solution. It is also stable, for the left-hand side of the equation is nothing but the warranted $\dot{K}/K = sY/K$; since this is a decreasing function of k, the system approaches the steady state if it remains in equilibrium, in the way illustrated in the lower quadrant of Figure 4.4.

But the system is not quite the same as that illustrated in Figure 4.4. With proportional saving, the over-all saving propensity, s, is independent of both k and the characteristics of $f(k)$. In consequence the steady-state output–capital ratio, λ/s, is independent of k and $f(k)$; in the upper quadrant of Figure 4.4 it can be drawn without any knowledge of the production function. But with neo-Keynesian saving, as

(5.5) shows, s will generally depend on both k and the form of $f(k)$. There is one special case in which it is independent of k: this is when the elasticity of substitution, σ, is unity everywhere, i.e. when the production function is of the Cobb–Douglas form. Then factor shares, and hence s, are invariant with respect to k, so that in the lower quadrant of Figure 4.4 we would again have the $\dot{K}/K$ curve differing from the Y/K curve by a fixed proportion of Y/K, and in the upper quadrant we would again find the steady-state solution by putting $y/k = \lambda/s$. But even in this case, though s is the same for all k, its value depends on the production function; specifically, it depends on the parameter α which specifies the invariant share of profits (see (4.23–4.25)). Thus even when $\sigma = 1$, the steady-state output–capital ratio is dependent on the form of $f(k)$. For $\sigma \neq 1$ Figure 4.4 would, strictly speaking, need to be redrawn: if $\sigma < 1$, s, as well as Y/K, is a decreasing function of k, so that as k increases the difference beteeen Y/K and $\dot{K}/K$ is an increasing, rather than a constant, proportion of Y/K; and conversely, if $\sigma > 1$ the vertical gap between the two curves narrows in proportionate as well as absolute terms as k rises.[1] In both cases, with $\sigma \neq 1$, the over-all propensity to save in the steady state is determined simultaneously with the output–capital ratio and the rate of profit (which together define the share of profits) in the way shown by (5.7).

But now take the *classical function*. Putting $s_w = 0$ in (5.7) we see that the requirement for steady growth simplifies to

$$\left. \begin{array}{l} s_p f'(k) = \lambda \\[2ex] \text{or} \\[2ex] f'(k) = \dfrac{\lambda}{s_p} \end{array} \right\} \tag{5.8}$$

In this case, although the over-all propensity to save, $s_p P/Y$, is still generally dependent on k and the form of $f(k)$, $\dot{K}/K = sY/K = s_p P/K$ is simply a constant proportion of the profit rate $f'(k)$. Thus Figure 4.4 would need to be redrawn: in the lower quadrant we would replace the Y/K curve with an $f'(k)$ curve, and the $s\phi(k)$ curve with a curve showing $\dot{K}/K = s_p f'(k)$. Well-behavedness of course ensures the existence, uniqueness and stability of steady growth as before. But now, as (5.8) – which may be compared with (4.15) – shows, it is the steady-state rate of profit – not the output–capital ratio – which is determined independently of the production function by the natural growth rate and saving parameters. The steady-state k would be such that in the lower quadrant of the new Figure 4.4 $\dot{K}/K = s_p f'(k) = \lambda$, while in the upper quadrant $f'(k) = \lambda/s$. The steady-state output–capital ratio will then clearly depend on the form of f.

In sum, *the neo-Keynesian saving function (including its special classical case) leaves intact the conclusions reached with the proportional function about the existence, uniqueness and stability of a steady state. But the three particular cases of the general function lead to different conclusions about the dependence of* Y/K *and* r *on the form of the production function in steady growth.* In the proportional case Y/K is independent of f but r is not; in the classical case r is independent of f but Y/K is not; otherwise – in the non-classical neo-Keynesian case – neither Y/K nor r is independent of f.

Before moving on we should note that with classical saving if $s_p = 1$, the steady-state profit rate equals the growth rate; $f'(k) = \lambda$, from (5.8). Recalling the 'golden rule of accumulation' we thus see that when all wages are spent and all profits saved, the steady-state solution is the steady state in which consumption per head is at a maximum.

It should be clear from the above, and from the bench-mark provided by Figure 4.4, that any function which makes the over-all saving propensity s a decreasing function of k will leave secure the existence, uniqueness and stability of steady growth. The neo-Keynesian function with $\sigma < 1$ is one example; but there are two other possibilities which have more of a neo-classical flavour. First, we could on familiar grounds make s *an increasing function of the rate of return on capital*, r, which is the same as the rate of interest in this model.[2] Second, we could make s *a decreasing function of the capital–output ratio*: the greater is wealth in relation to income, the less prepared are people to sacrifice consumption to accumulate more.[3]

What kind of saving function would lead to different conclusions about steady growth? The possibilities may be indicated in terms of three cases. First, it may be that beyond some value of k at which steady growth is possible (i.e. at which $\dot{K}/K = s\phi(k) = \lambda$), s is such a strongly increasing function of k that $s(k)\phi(k)$ increases to intersect λ again at a higher k. This case is illustrated in Figure 5.1. Initially, at low levels of k, $\dot{K}/K$ is a decreasing function of k, and there is a steady-state solution similar to that of Figure 4.4 at $k_1{}^*$. But beyond $k_1{}^*$, s rises as k rises: perhaps because s *is an increasing function of income per head (or the wage rate)* when the standard of living has attained levels in this range. Then, despite the continued decline of

Y/K, $\dot{K}/K = s(k)\phi(k)$ reaches a minimum at M, thereafter rising to equal λ again at k_2*. This gives a second steady state solution. But $\dot{K}/K$ cannot go on rising, since Y/K is monotonically decreasing and s cannot exceed unity: even if s is rising towards 1 as k increases, $\dot{K}/K$ can only be tending towards Y/K. Thus $\dot{K}/K$ eventually reaches a second turning-point at M', and declines again, crossing λ a third time at k_3*. There are thus three steady-state solutions; and it should be clear, by inspection of $\dot{k}/k = s(k)\phi(k) - \lambda$, that those represented by k_1* and k_3* are stable, like that shown in Figure 4.4, while that represented by k_2* is unstable. This case therefore shows the possibility of *multiple equilibrium steady states, not all of which are stable*. If $k < k_2$* the economy will be moving towards the low-level steady state k_1*; if $k > k_2$* it will be moving towards k_3*. The steady state represented by k_1* is an example of what is known in development theory as *a low-level equilibrium trap* (see Nelson, 1956). It illustrates the possibility that an economy may be stuck in a position of relatively low income unless or until there is some critical change which allows it to realise its greater potential. In this example the changes which could most obviously release the economy from its 'trap' would be an exogenous increase in k to beyond k_2* (by, for example, an injection of foreign capital), or an increase in thriftiness which would raise the $\dot{K}/K$ curve above λ for all $k < k_3$*: M would then be raised above λ and k_3* would become the unique and stable steady state.

Second, it may be that s, and therefore $\dot{K}/K$, are zero at low levels of k and y. This case could be represented in Figure 5.1 with the $\dot{K}/K$ curve amended so that it falls from M', not to the turning-point M, but to the k-axis at some point k_0. The steady states at k_2* and k_3* remain; and, as before, the former is unstable while the latter is stable. The difference is that now, if $k < k_2$*, there is nothing to stop k falling. To the left of k_0, with $\dot{K}/K$ zero, k will decline at the same rate as L is increasing, and in the limit the economy will disappear at the origin! - a 'low-level equilibrium trap' with a vengeance which has no economic sense, but which serves to draw attention to the unsatisfactory nature of the assumption that the growth rate of the labour force is entirely independent of income per head (see section 5.3).

In the third case, s is again zero at low levels of k and y, but even when it is positive it is so low that $\dot{K}/K$ is always less than λ. There is then *no steady-state solution*: k will fall continuously, and in the limit the economy will reach the origin.

These three illustrative cases point towards some more general conclusions. It should be clear, first, that if s is always positive, there must exist at least one stable steady-state solution; second, that there may more than one steady-state solution if s is ever an increasing function of k; third, that if there is more than one steady state, at least one of them will be unstable; and fourth, that if s is zero at low levels of income, there will either be more than one steady state, or no steady state at all.

It should also be clear that every case of non-existence, non-uniqueness and instability is dependent not on the saving function alone but on its relationship to the natural growth rate and the production function. Thus in our first case, illustrated in Figure 5.1, a higher λ or a

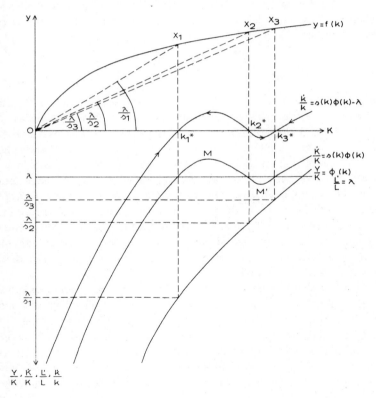

Fig. 5.1

lower $f(k)$ could produce a unique and stable low-level steady state, while a lower λ or a higher $f(k)$ could produce a unique and stable high-level steady state. Again, in our third case (non-existence) steady-state solutions could be brought into existence by a lower λ or a higher $f(k)$.

5.3   The labour force

We now return to the model with proportional saving, and consider the consequences of altering the assumption that the growth rate of the labour force is exogenous.

Referring again to Figure 4.4 it may be seen that the existence, uniqueness and stability of steady growth are secure with any hypothesis which makes λ a monotonically increasing function of k. One such hypothesis would be a *'neo-Malthusian' population growth* function, where λ rises with the real wage (or income per head).[4] In steady growth, as before,

$$\frac{\dot{Y}}{Y} = \frac{\dot{K}}{K} = \frac{\dot{L}}{L} = \lambda$$

but now, since λ takes different values at different values of k, the growth rate will vary from one steady state to another. This means, in particular, that *the steady-state growth rate is no longer independent of the propensity to save*. If, for example, we start in one steady state and s rises, then at the initial k, $\dot{K}/K$ rises above $\dot{L}/L$, so that – as before – k will rise and Y/K will fall towards their new steady-state values, but now the accompanying increase in the real wage will induce λ to rise towards a higher value in the new steady state, and this will reduce the required adjustment of k and Y/K. In terms of the Harrod–Domar equilibrium condition both the output–capital ratio and the natural growth rate are endogenous; and the endogeneity of λ provides the neo-classical model with added flexibility.

The neo-Malthusian hypothesis may justifiably be regarded as more realistic than the assumption that λ is the same for all values of k and y.[5] It is, however, open to two particular objections. First, although it is not unreasonable to assume that λ is an increasing function of income per head when the latter is close to subsistence levels, it is not clear that the same assumption is appropriate at higher incomes. Population growth may then be determined less closely by the biologically feasible (which may indeed be an increasing function of income per head) than by the availability of birth-control methods (which may make λ a decreasing function of income per head). Moreover, as is well known, the 'income effect' of rising wages on the choice between work and leisure may offset the 'substitution effect' and actually reduce the supply of labour. There is thus the possibility that at 'affluent' incomes, λ *may be a decreasing function of the wage or income per head*; and this may entail non-uniqueness and instability. An example is shown in Figure 5.2. There is a well-behaved productivity function and a proportional saving function; but λ is now endogenous, being related to k (via the real wage) in the way shown by the $\lambda(k)$ curve. When $k = k_o$ the real wage (shown by OW_o) is just sufficient to maintain a constant labour force: when $k < k_o$, λ is negative. As k rises above k_o, λ rises above zero but reaches a maximum at M; it then declines towards the constant value λ. It may be seen that there are three steady-state equilibria, represented by k_1*, k_2* and k_3*, and that only the first and third of these are stable. That represented by k_1* is another *low-level equilibrium trap*; to be released from it the economy would need either a downward shift in $\lambda(k)$ or an upward shift in $\dot{K}/K$, or an exogenous jump in k to beyond k_2*.

The second objection to the neo-Malthusian function is that it appears to ignore the fact that there is bound to be a *positive 'floor' to the real wage* below which workers would fail to subsist. In terms of Figure 5.2 the consequence of reducing the wage below OW_o may be such a drastic fall in the labour force that the $\dot{L}/L$ function is best represented in that region by the vertical line $k_o X_o$, with a discontinuity in the function at k_o. OW_o would then, in effect, be the minimum wage. The introduction of this refinement into Figure 5.2 does not interfere with the steady-state characteristics of the model. But it is easy to see that if the minimum real wage acceptable to the labour force is higher than that which just maintains a constant labour force, it may be incompatible with the marginal product of labour in a steady state. This is one example of how *factor-price rigidities* may hinder the equilibration of factor markets and so make the neo-classical mechanisms inoperative. Another such rigidity will arise in section 5.5.

5.4   The production function

With *non-well-behaved productivity functions* either non-existence, or non-uniqueness with instability is possible. An example of non-existence would be provided by a productivity function whose output–capital ratio is always higher than λ/s, however large is k. It would be tedious to describe other cases, though the reader may like to give the matter a few minutes' thought.

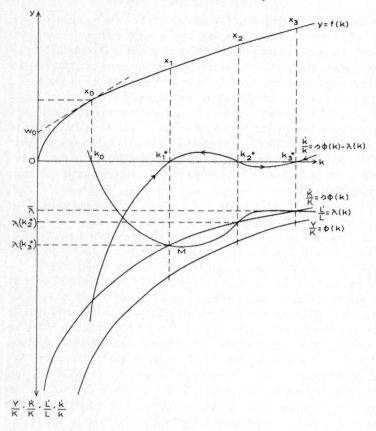

Fig. 5.2

It is more interesting to consider the implications and significance of *non-constant returns to scale*. Without constant returns *Euler's theorem* does not hold; with decreasing returns the sum of marginal-product factor payments would fall short of total output and income, while with increasing returns the reverse would be true. Thus the factors cannot be being paid their marginal social products: either the economy is imperfectly competitive and some factors are not receiving their (private) marginal-value products, or private and social marginal products diverge – i.e. there are externalities in production. In any event a production function with non-constant returns does not fit happily into the simple neo-classical scheme.

Since increasing returns may, as much as technical progress, be a source of growth in 'output per unit of input', is this not a serious indictment of that scheme as a basis for the analysis of growth and for the explanation of steady growth in the real world? A neo-classical economist might reply by making two points.

First, *an increasing-returns production function is not necessarily inconsistent with steady growth.* Take the general two-factor production function

$$Y = F(K,L) \tag{5.9}$$

and relax the assumption that F is linearly homogeneous. The total differential of F is

$$dY = F_k dK + F_L dL \equiv \frac{\partial Y}{\partial K} dK + \frac{\partial Y}{\partial L} dL$$

so that

$$\frac{1}{Y} \frac{dY}{dt} \equiv \frac{\dot{Y}}{Y} = \left(\frac{K}{Y} \frac{\partial Y}{\partial K} \right) \frac{\dot{K}}{K} + \left(\frac{L}{Y} \frac{\partial Y}{\partial L} \right) \frac{\dot{L}}{L} \equiv$$

$$\equiv E_K \frac{\dot{K}}{K} + E_L \frac{\dot{L}}{L} \tag{5.10}$$

Thus the growth rate of output is a weighted sum of the growth rates of the factors, the weights being the respective factor elasticities of output, which we are calling E_K and E_L. Now assume that $\dot{L}/L (= \lambda)$ is positive and constant. Steady growth requires that $\dot{Y}/Y$ and $\dot{K}/K$ are positive, constant and equal to each other; putting $\dot{Y}/Y = \dot{K}/K$ in (5.10)

$$\frac{\dot{Y}}{Y} = \frac{\dot{K}}{K} = \frac{E_L}{1 - E_K} \times \lambda \tag{5.11}$$

which is positive and constant only if

$$\frac{E_L}{1 - E_K} \equiv \eta \tag{5.12}$$

is positive and constant. With constant returns E_K and E_L – the factor shares under perfect competition – sum to unity: then $\eta = 1$ and from (5.11) $\dot{Y}/Y = \dot{K}/K = \lambda$. That is the kind of steady growth we have been considering in this and the previous chapter. If there are increasing returns, the sum of the elasticities will exceed unity. There are then two particular cases in which η will be constant and positive, so that steady growth will be possible.

The first is when F takes the Cobb-Douglas form (4.26), with $\beta > 1$ because returns to scale are increasing:

$$Y = BK^{\alpha\beta}L^{(1-\alpha)\beta} ; \quad \beta > 1, 0 < \alpha < 1 \tag{5.13}$$

Here E_K, the elasticity of Y with respect to K, is $\alpha\beta$, and E_L is $(1-\alpha)\beta$; both are constant, and therefore η is constant:

$$\eta = \frac{E_L}{1 - E_K} = \frac{(1-\alpha)\beta}{1 - \alpha\beta} \tag{5.14}$$

But this is positive if and only if

$$E_K = \alpha\beta < 1 \tag{5.15}$$

If this condition is satisfied, steady growth is possible with

$$\frac{\dot{Y}}{Y} = \frac{\dot{K}}{K} = \eta\lambda = \left(\frac{(1-\alpha)\beta}{1 - \alpha\beta} \right)\lambda > 0 \tag{5.16}$$

But if $\alpha\beta > 1$, then $\eta < 0$, and Y and K could have a common positive growth rate only if λ were negative. (This is because β, the degree of homogeneity in the production function, would then be so large in relation to α - the tendency to increasing returns would be so strong – that there would be increasing returns to capital by itself, and these would have to be offset by a declining labour force for Y to grow at a rate no higher than K.) Steady growth is thus compatible with the Cobb-Douglas production function (5.13) only if (5.15) is satisfied. With the growth of Y and K given by (5.16), the growth rate of output per head is

$$\frac{\dot{y}}{y} \equiv \frac{\dot{Y}}{Y} - \lambda = \left(\frac{\beta - 1}{1 - \alpha\beta} \right)\lambda \tag{5.17}$$

which is positive, given (5.15). This shows that with increasing returns steady growth of labour productivity may be possible even without technical progress, as long as $\lambda > 0$; and the greater is λ, the faster can productivity grow.

In the Cobb-Douglas case η is constant by virtue of the fact that both E_K and E_L are constant. But η may also be constant if the variations in the two elasticities are always mutually offsetting. It may be shown that this will occur when F can be written alternatively as a linearly homogeneous function G in K and L^η, with $\eta > 1$:

$$Y = F(K,L) = G(K,L^{\eta}), \eta > 1 \qquad (5.18)$$

The increasing returns are then, in effect, transmitted through labour alone; and steady growth is possible with Y and K growing at a constant rate higher than λ. Formally, since G is linearly homogeneous, we know that

$$\frac{K}{Y} \frac{\partial Y}{\partial K} + \frac{L^{\eta}}{Y} \frac{\partial Y}{\partial L^{\eta}} = 1$$

and from this it can easily be shown that

$$\frac{E_L}{1 - E_K} = \eta > 1$$

Thus an increasing-returns production function is compatible with steady growth only if it takes one of two particular forms; and since there is no theory to explain why it should, we seem far away from a satisfactory explanation of steady growth in labour productivity. Moreover, since factor prices cannot be adequately accounted for by marginal products, we are lacking a theory of distribution and an explanation of why distributive shares and the rate of profit should be constant. It still seems, therefore, that the simple neo-classical explanation of steady growth cannot readily be extended to an increasing-returns technology.

But the force of this criticism depends on the importance of increasing returns in the real world; and the second argument that might be put forward by a neo-classical economist is that *increasing returns are in fact a relatively unimportant source of productivity growth* – in relation, that is, to technical progress. This argument might be supported in the following way. Take as an example the U.K. economy between 1948 and 1962, and suppose that the steadily rising income per head over that period is to be explained by increasing returns without technical progress. Then if the technology can be described by a production function of the general form (5.9), it may be seen from (5.11) and (5.12) that the value of η may be inferred from empirical values of $\dot{Y}/Y$ and λ. Now over that period, real G.D.P. grew by 2.5 per cent per annum on average, and employment by 0.6 per cent per annum (Matthews, 1964, table 1); the implied value of η is thus 0.025/0.006, which exceeds 4. But if there were steady growth, F must have been either of the Cobb-Douglas form (5.13) or of the form (5.18). If the true form was (5.13), (5.16) applies, and we can derive the value of β if we know α. Assume that income was distributed between capital and labour approximately in the ratio it would have been if there had been perfect competition and constant returns, i.e. $\alpha/(1 - \alpha)$. Then the value of α can be approximated by the share of profits, which was about 20 per cent (Feinstein, 1972, table 18). Thus from (5.16)

$$\beta = \frac{\eta}{\alpha\eta + (1 - \alpha)} \doteq \frac{4}{0.8 + 0.8} = 2.5$$

which may be claimed to be an implausibly high estimate of the degree of homogeneity of the production function. It implies that if K and L are both raised by 1 per cent, say, Y will rise by 2.5 per cent: no one would claim that increasing returns are as powerful as that! And if the true form of the production function was (5.18), with $\eta > 4$, a similar inference may be drawn without any need for assumptions about the income distribution.

Results similar to this are generally obtained from calculations of this kind. The implication is taken to be that empirical growth rates of labour productivity are too high to be explicable by increasing returns alone, and further that for more plausible values of η the role of technical progress must be greater than that of increasing returns. Dixit (1976, pp. 80–1) uses this argument, as does Solow (1970, p. 34), who claims that 'It is difficult to believe that the United States is enabled to increase output per man at something over 2 per cent a year mainly by virtue of unexploited economies of scale. This is not to deny the existence of economies of scale . . . but only to suggest that their effect is probably overshadowed by those of technological progress.' If that is the case it seems justifiable, at least as a first approximation, to ignore increasing returns and to attribute productivity growth to technical progress alone; and that is what most neo-classical theory has done. With technical progress, as with increasing returns, the production function must take a particular form to be compatible with steady growth (as will be shown in Chapter 7); but, as is not the case with increasing returns, there are theories to explain why it should do so (as will be seen in Chapter 8).

Neo-classical economists, therefore, are not particularly worried by the difficulty of fitting increasing returns into their theoretical framework. But, as will be seen in Chapter 9 and Part III, there are others who think they ought to be.

5.5 A monetary asset

A one-good economy in which there is money may seem an even stranger conception than a one-good economy without money: if there is only one good there is little need for a medium of exchange, which is money's primary function. Nevertheless, the introduction of money into the one-good model allows some interesting questions to be considered. For example, is money 'neutral', or do steady states which have different growth rates of the money stock differ in real respects, for example in the technique of production? Second, how is the theory of the interest rate – so far treated as the same as the rate of return on capital – affected by the presence of a monetary asset? These are some of the questions which will arise in this section. The analysis originates with Tobin (1955; 1965). We introduce into the model of Chapter 4 a monetary asset which, like real capital, is a store of value: it is an alternative to real capital as a form in which wealth may be held. It is also a unit of account, and we introduce a new variable p to measure the price of the good in terms of it; thus since Y is real output, measured in terms of the good, pY is nominal output, measured in terms of money. We now need to specify how the money is supplied and demanded.

Suppose there is a government which buys goods and services for public consumption and levies taxes. If government expenditure in real terms is G, we have a new identity

$$Y \equiv C + I + G \tag{5.19}$$

which shows that there are now three forms of expenditure in the model. The real government deficit, D, is given by

$$D \equiv G - T \tag{5.20}$$

where T is taxation in real terms. We now assume that *money is supplied solely by the government as a consequence of its deficit spending*; $\dot{N}$, the rate of increase of the nominal money stock N, is equal to the nominal government deficit:

$$\dot{N} = pD \equiv p(G - T) \tag{5.21}$$

Since money is supplied solely by the government, the whole of the money stock is a private-sector asset without any corresponding private-sector liability. It is thus regarded by the community as part of its net wealth: it is what is sometimes known as *outside money* (Gurley and

Shaw, 1960), like currency in the real world but unlike bank deposits. The community's total wealth in real terms, W, is thus the sum of the capital stock and the real money stock M:

$$W \equiv K + M \equiv K + \frac{N}{p} \qquad (5.22)$$

Similarly, the rate of increase of real wealth is the sum of the rates of increase of the real capital stock and the real money stock. From (5.22)

$$\dot{W} \equiv \dot{K} + \dot{M} \equiv \dot{K} + \frac{\dot{N}}{p} + M\left(-\frac{\dot{p}}{p}\right) \qquad (5.23)$$

From this it may be seen that the increase in the real money stock, $\dot{M}$, is composed of the real value of the increase in the nominal money stock, $\dot{N}/p$, and the increase in the real value of the money stock resulting from any decline in the prive level, $-\dot{M}p/p$;[6] this second component will be negative if $\dot{p}/p$ is positive, i.e. if there is a positive rate of inflation.

Identity (5.23) may be interpreted in another way if it is rewritten as follows, using (5.21):

$$\dot{K} \equiv \dot{W} - M\left(-\frac{\dot{p}}{p}\right) - D \qquad (5.24)$$

The first two terms on the right-hand side of this identity give what would be defined by the normal conventions of national-income accounting as private-sector saving: the increase in private-sector wealth *minus* capital gains. The identity would then say that investment is the same as private-sector saving *minus* the government's dissaving (i.e. its deficit), which is nothing but a reinterpretation of the Keynesian saving–investment identity for a closed economy with a government. (The same identity could be obtained from (5.19) and (5.20), since private-sector saving is defined as what remains after consumption has been deducted from disposable income, with the latter defined as factor incomes *minus* taxation.) For present purposes, however, it is more convenient to treat capital gains like income, and thus to include them, first, in private-sector saving S, so that (5.24) may be rewritten as

$$\dot{K} \equiv S - M\left(-\frac{\dot{p}}{p}\right) - D \qquad (5.25)$$

or as

$$\dot{K} \equiv S - \dot{M} \qquad (5.26)$$

and second, in disposable income Y_d, now defined as

$$Y_d \equiv Y + M(-\frac{\dot{p}}{p}) - T \qquad (5.27)$$

This will enable us to take capital gains into account in our saving function in a straightforward way. (5.25) shows that S is now defined in such a way that it is absorbed partly by investment, partly by government dissaving, and partly also by capital gains; but the sum of government dissaving and capital gains is the same as the increase in the real money stock, so (5.26) shows, equivalently, that S is absorbed partly by investment and partly by $\dot{M}$. (Note that (5.25) can still be derived from (5.19) and (5.20), using the new definition of disposable income.)

We can now go straight to the saving function. The obvious analogue to the proportional function $S = sY$ is now

$$S = sY_d \equiv s\left\{ Y + M\left(-\frac{\dot{p}}{p}\right) - T \right\}; \quad 0 < s < 1 \qquad (5.28)$$

The remainder of Y_d is consumed:

$$C = (1 - s)\left\{ Y + M\left(-\frac{\dot{p}}{p}\right) - T \right\} \qquad (5.29)$$

Assume also that the government spends a constant proportion of 'national' income Y:

$$G = gY; \quad 0 < g < 1 \qquad (5.30)$$

We may then obtain the following equation in investment, $\dot{K}$, as a condition for goods-market equilibrium, either from (5.26) and (5.28), or from (5.19) and (5.29), using (5.20), (5.21) and (5.30):

$$\dot{K} = s(1 - g)Y - (1 - s)\dot{M} = s(1 - g)Y - (1 - s)M\left(\frac{\dot{N}}{N} - \frac{\dot{p}}{p}\right) \qquad (5.31)$$

On dividing through by K, we obtain an equation in the growth rate of the capital stock. And for equilibrium steady growth this must, as in Chapter 4, equal λ:

$$\lambda = \frac{\dot{K}}{K} = s(1 - g)\frac{Y}{K} - (1 - s)m\frac{Y}{K}\left(\frac{\dot{N}}{N} - \frac{\dot{p}}{p}\right) \qquad (5.32)$$

where m is defined as the ratio of the money stock to income, i.e. as the reciprocal of the income velocity of money. This steady-state-equilibrium condition may be rewritten in terms of the productivity function $f(k)$:

$$\lambda = \frac{s(1-g)}{k/f(k)} - \frac{(1-s)m}{k/f(k)}\left(\frac{\dot{N}}{N} - \frac{\dot{p}}{p}\right) \qquad (5.33)$$

which is more easily comparable with the first version of (4.15).

With no government ($g = 0$) and no money ($m = 0$), (5.33) would reduce to (4.15). With a government which had always balanced its budget ($m = 0$), (5.33) would reduce to

$$\lambda = \frac{s(1-g)}{k/f(k)} \qquad (5.34)$$

which differs from (4.15) simply because $s(1 - g)$, not s, would in this case be the ratio of saving to output. Since (5.34) is the same as the first term in (5.33), the second term clearly arises on account of unbalanced budgets and the presence of money. Its interpretation is more straightforward if we step back to (5.31), which may be re-written as follows:

$$\dot{K} = s(1-g)Y + s\dot{M} - \dot{M}$$

$$= s(1-g)Y + s\left\{D + M\left(-\frac{\dot{p}}{p}\right)\right\} - \left\{D + M\left(-\frac{\dot{p}}{p}\right)\right\} \qquad (5.35)$$

Thus $\dot{K}$ differs from 'balanced-budget saving' (the first term in (5.35), corresponding to the first term in (5.33)) because saving is augmented by the proportion s of the addition to disposable income of the current deficit and capital gains (i.e. by the second term in (5.35)), but also because the whole of that addition – which constitutes $\dot{M}$, the increase in the real money stock – absorbs saving, thereby displacing investment (as is shown by the third term). Since $s < 1$, $\dot{K}$ will be less than 'balanced-budget saving' if the real money stock is increasing; and the faster it is increasing, the greater will be the difference.

We cannot proceed much further without considering how m, $\dot{N}/N$, and $\dot{p}/p$ are determined. In particular, it is clear that (5.32) (or (5.33)) cannot be considered to provide a complete specification of steady-state equilibrium because we have said nothing to ensure that the money stock embodied in m is willingly held. We now turn to consider the determinants of the demand for money and the requirements for *portfolio balance*; i.e. the requirements for the composition of wealth between money and real capital to be such as to satisfy the preferences of the community.

One possibility would be to assume that there is a *fixed desired money-to-income ratio*, $\bar{m}$. For portfolio balance we would then substitute $m = \bar{m}$ in (5.32); and since m must be constant at this value, the growth rate of the real money stock, $\dot{M}/M$, must be the same as the growth rate of output. The steady-state Y/K is then determined in terms of $\bar{m}$ and the other parameters:

$$\frac{Y}{K} \equiv \frac{f(k)}{k} = \frac{\lambda}{s(1-g) - (1-s)\bar{m}\,\lambda} \qquad (5.36)$$

This is clearly higher than the steady-state Y/K in the non-monetary case; and it is higher the larger is $\bar{m}$, i.e. the greater is the demand for money or the lower is the velocity of circulation $1/\bar{m}$. But it is independent of $\dot{N}/N$, the growth rate of the nominal money stock determined by government policy. The higher is $\dot{N}/N$, the higher must be $\dot{p}/p$, so that $\dot{M}/M$ is held at λ and portfolio balance is maintained. In this case, therefore, the fiscal–monetary policy of the government helps to determine the rate of inflation in equilibrium steady growth, but it has no 'real' significance; in that sense, *money is 'neutral'*.

This conclusion is analogous to the 'classical dichotomy' of pre-Keynesian monetary orthodoxy based on the quantity theory of money; and the correspondence is not surprising given our assumptions of full-employment output and fixed velocity. But the assumption of fixed velocity now seems primitive; it takes no account of the influence on the demand for money of its relative rate of return (or its opportunity cost), nor does it take account of the influence of the volume of wealth which is to be allocated between money and real capital. We therefore leave that case, and go on to a more general function which is more in accord with modern portfolio-choice theory.

We still assume that the demand for money is an increasing function of real income Y, because our monetary asset is assumed to be the medium of exchange and because Y may be regarded as a measure of the volume of transactions. But we assume that it is also an increasing function of the capital stock K and a decreasing function of the opportunity cost of holding money. Suppose (for the sake of generality) that our monetary asset bears an interest rate i, paid and fixed by the government.[7] The opportunity cost of holding money is then the rental rate of real capital (r, its marginal product) *plus* the rate at which capital is appreciating in relation to money ($\dot{p}/p$, the rate of inflation) *minus* the interest rate i.[8] For our purposes it is convenient to take the particular form of this function which expresses the *money-to-income ratio as an increasing function of the capital–output ratio and a decreasing function of $r - i + \dot{p}/p$*:

$$m = m(K/Y, r - i + \dot{p}/p) \tag{5.37}$$

Now consider the possibility of steady-state equilibrium. In steady growth K/Y and r must of course be constant; and it seems natural to add the requirement that $\dot{p}/p$ should be constant. Also, i and $\dot{N}/N$ are to be regarded as given by government policy. It may then be seen from (5.37) that m must be constant: not because it is a behavioural or institutional datum as we were assuming earlier, but as an implication of portfolio balance in steady growth. But how is the steady-state m determined? If m is constant, the real money stock must be growing at the natural rate, so $\dot{p}/p$ must be equal to the difference between $\dot{N}/N$ and λ. In (5.37), therefore, the steady-state value of $\dot{p}/p$, as well as the value of i, is given by government policy, and since r is a decreasing function of K/Y (from the properties of the production function) m may be expressed simply as an increasing function of K/Y, or, as will be more convenient, as a decreasing function of Y/K, i.e. (5.37) may be rewritten as

$$m = m(Y/K); \quad m' < 0 \tag{5.38}$$

This is represented by the downward-sloping curve in the third quadrant of Figure 5.3. The first and second quadrants need no introduction; in the third quadrant m is measured on the horizontal axis. Any point on $m(Y/K)$ gives a pair of values of m and Y/K which provide portfolio balance at the given i and $\dot{p}/p$.

But points on $m(Y/K)$ do not necessarily provide goods-market equilibrium or full employment; for these we have to return to (5.32), which may be rearranged to give a second relationship between m and Y/K:

$$m = \frac{s(1 - g)}{(1 - s)\lambda} - \frac{1}{(1 - s)Y/K} \tag{5.39}$$

Here m is an increasing function of Y/K since the greater is m, the more saving will have been absorbed, and the more investment will have been displaced, by government debt. This relationship is shown by the upward-sloping curve in the third quadrant of the diagram. It will be seen that if $m = 0$, the Y/K implied by (5.39) is $\lambda/s(1-g)$; this is the steady-state Y/K in a non-monetary (balanced-budget) economy, as we could have inferred from (5.34).

The intersection of the two curves gives the steady-state equilibrium m^* and $(Y/K)^*$. (There must exist a unique intersection, like that shown in the diagram, as long as the m required for portfolio balance becomes sufficiently small as Y/K becomes large; and it does not seem unreasonable to assume that the $m(Y/K)$ function satisfies this condition.) The steady-state solutions for all other variables may then be unravelled in the usual way; the first and second quadrants of the diagram give a start.

We may see, first, that as in the case of fixed velocity – which could be represented in Figure 5.3 by replacing the $m(Y/K)$ curve by a vertical line at the fixed $\overline{m}$ – the steady state in the monetary economy has a higher Y/K (and thus a lower k, a lower y, etc.) than does the steady state in the same economy without money. The comparison is represented in the diagram by the difference between the monetary steady state shown by $(Y/K)^*$, k^* and y^*, and the non-monetary steady-state shown by $\lambda/s(1-g)$, k_n and y_n. And again we have that the greater is the demand for money – the further from the origin is the $m(Y/K)$ curve – the greater is the difference. Now compare monetary steady states with different policy parameters. First suppose that the government raises $\dot{N}/N$ and that the economy reaches a new steady state; m must again be constant, so $\dot{p}/p$ must be correspondingly higher. The upward-sloping curve in the third quadrant is unaffected; but the $m(Y/K)$ curve must now be nearer the origin because, with i the same, the opportunity cost of holding money at any r and Y/K must be higher in the new steady state than in the old. With the $m(Y/K)$ curve nearer the origin, the steady-state m^* and $(Y/K)^*$ must both be lower. It may thus be seen that the faster is the rate at which the government expands the nominal money supply, the lower is the steady-state Y/K, the higher is the steady-state k, and so on. Thus $\dot{N}/N$ now influences the 'real' characteristics of steady growth as well as the steady-state rate of inflation; and it does so via its influence on the rate of inflation, which helps to determine the demand for money. We have a growth model in which *money is not 'neutral'*.

Variations in the rate of interest, i, will have implications for steady growth similar to those of variations in $\dot{N}/N$: an increase in i will shift the $m(Y/K)$ curve outwards from the origin, and vice versa. A reduction in the steady-state rate of inflation without any 'real' side-effects could

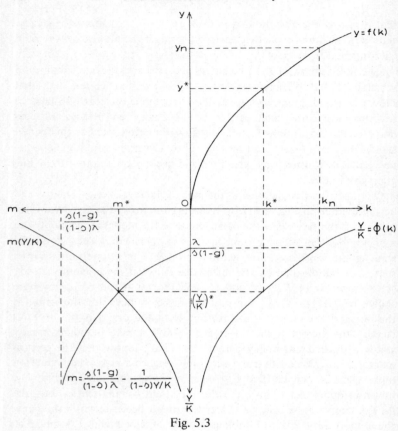

Fig. 5.3

therefore be engineered through a reduction in $\dot{N}/N$ accompanied by a reduction in i just sufficient to prevent any shift in $m(Y/K)$; without that reduction in i, the steady-state values of y would of course fall. We may also note that *the steady-state rental rate of capital, $r = f'(k)$, is now dependent on – varying directly with – the government-determined rate of interest on money.*

This last point is worthy of some further consideration. The rental rate, r, is the own rate of return on capital: it is the yield to be derived from the hiring-out of a capital good, measured in terms of that good. We saw in section 4.1 that with only one good and no financial asset, r could be regarded as the rate of interest. We have now introduced a financial asset, and we have naturally been calling the own rate of return on that asset the rate of interest, i. Thus *r is no longer the rate of interest; and furthermore, there is no necessary tendency for r and i to be equal.* The two are comparable only when the price of the good in terms of money is introduced: thus in terms of money, the rate of return on capital is the sum of the rental rate, r, and the rate of appreciation of capital, $\dot{p}/p$, and it is this sum which is comparable with i. Now we could assume that behaviour is such that the two rates of return must be equal for portfolio balance with positive supplies of both assets:

$$r + \dot{p}/p = i \qquad (5.40)$$

This could replace (5.38) as the condition for portfolio balance: it might be argued that if the rates of return were unequal – if (5.40) were not satisfied – the demand for the asset with the lower return would be zero, while if they are equal investors will be willing to hold both assets in any proportion. We would then have a different model from that constructed above.[9] But even then the rental rate would be equal to the interest rate in equilibrium only if the price level was stable; and following Tobin we have preferred to pay most attention to a condition for portfolio balance which does not require the rates of return to be equal.[10] In that case, all we can say is that, *ceteris paribus*, the steady-state r will vary directly with i.

So far, we have been concerned with the characterisation of equilibrium steady growth in the monetary economy. The analysis of *non-steady-state behaviour* is more complex than in the variants of the one-good model considered hitherto, and there is space only to give some idea of the problems which may hinder the attainment and maintenance of steady growth.

First, the steady-state $\dot{p}/p$ implied by $\dot{N}/N$ and λ may be unattainable because of *price (or wage) rigidities*. For example, $\dot{N}/N$ and λ may require a negative $\dot{p}/p$ and hence falling money wages, which may be unacceptable; deficient demand and Keynesian unemployment may then result.[11] A particularly vivid example of how steady growth with full employment may be unattainable arises when (5.40) is the condition for portfolio balance. Suppose that $\dot{p}/p$ takes its steady-state value; given i, the r required for portfolio balance is then determined, as is Y/K. The equilibrium m is then given by (5.39). But if m falls short of this value, (5.32) implies that $\dot{K}/K$ will exceed λ; goods-market equilibrium with full employment thus implies a rising k and a falling Y/K. But that is inconsistent with portfolio balance; if portfolio balance is being maintained, investment must be less than the saving available for investment, and there must be a deficiency of demand. The inconsistency may be removed if r (and hence Y/K) are reduced, either through a reduction in i, or through a reduction in $\dot{N}/N$. The problem may be regarded as an example of how the attainment of a steady state through adjustments in factor proportions and factor prices may be hampered by a monetarily determined interest rate. It thus provides a view of one of the objections to neo-classical theory put forward by Harrod and others (see section 1.3 and Chapter 10, and Hahn and Matthews, 1964, pp. 12–13).

Second, away from steady growth, portfolio imbalance may produce unstable spirals of price inflation or deflation. If there is excess demand for money, say, prices will tend to fall as wealth-holders exchange capital for money. The real value of money will thus rise, helping to correct the imbalance; but, on the other hand, the falling prices will provide a further upward twist to the demand for money, because they reduce the opportunity cost of holding it. The seriousness of this problem cannot be assessed adequately without consideration of the nature of expectations. It may be noted that a similar problem arises in non-monetary models with *different kinds of capital goods*; it arises essentially because of the dependence of relative rates of return on expectations of capital gains and losses.

5.6 Depreciation

The simplest form of depreciation of capital entails the disappearance or 'evaporation' of some fixed proportion of each unit of the stock – irrespective of age – at each point in time. If our production function F gives gross output, then net output, Y_N, is given by

$$Y_N = F(K,L) - \delta K \qquad (5.41)$$

where δ is the rate of *radioactive decay*. The net productivity function is then easily derived. The nature of the steady-state solution will depend on the saving hypothesis. If net saving is proportional to gross income, then $\dot{K} = sF$, and the steady-state ratio of gross output to capital is λ/s, as before. If net saving is proportional to net income, it may be shown that the same ratio is $\lambda/s + \delta$, dependent on the rate of depreciation, as well as the natural growth rate and propensity to save. The rate of depreciation also enters into the steady-state output–capital ratio with the other two possible variants of proportional saving.[12] But it is easy to show in all cases that the existence, uniqueness and stability of steady growth withstand any positive constant rate of 'radioactive decay'.

With radioactive decay, no 'machine' ever dies – they just become progressively less efficient. An obvious alternative assumption to adopt is that machines never become less efficient but just die, i.e. capital equipment works with unchanging efficiency for a fixed period – say *T* years – and then evaporates completely. Under this assumption of *sudden death*, the ratio of depreciation to capital stock, δ, depends on the age distribution of the stock, and hence on the history of accumulation.[13] In steady growth, however, the age distribution is constant; a constant proportion of the capital stock is *T* years old, and therefore we have what is equivalent to radioactive decay. Although this is not so away from steady growth, it is still possible to demonstrate the stability of the steady state.

Further reading

Some of the topics discussed in this chapter are treated by Solow (1956) and Johnson (1967). The life-cycle *saving* hypothesis, based on the idea of inter-temporal utility maximisation by households, has, very naturally, found a place in neo-classical growth theory. The main reference are Diamond (1965), Meade (1966), Cass and Yaari (1967), (which is summarised by Wan (1971, pp. 185-94)), Tobin (1967), and Meade (1968, ch. 12, 13). Dixit (1976, pp. 116-22) provides a brief textbook treatment. There has been a lot more work on *money* in growth models since Tobin's (1965) paper. For example, Johnson (1967) and Levhari and Patinkin (1968) criticised Tobin for his neglect of the convenience derived from the use of money in transactions. Readers interested in these and other developments are referred to the fuller textbook treatments of Burmeister and Dobell (1970, ch. 6) and Foley and Sidrauski (1971). The problems of instability which arise with a *heterogeneous capital stock* were first pointed out by Hahn (1966), and have been further explored by Shell and Stiglitz (1967) and others. Textbook expositions are provided by Wan (1971, pp. 129-36) and Dixit (1976, pp. 142-6). *Depreciation* is treated more fully by Hahn and Matthews (1964, pp. 43-6), and Dixit (1976, pp. 66-72).

6

The Two-sector Model without Technical Progress

6.1 Introduction: relaxing the one-good assumption

The one-good assumption of the last three chapters may be interpreted in two ways. First, it may be regarded as an assumption that there is a single all-purpose commodity which, in particular, is both consumed and accumulated as capital. For an advanced industrial economy this may seem an enormous simplification. It may, however, suggest itself more naturally in the analysis of a pre-industrial economy based on agriculture: agricultural products are both consumed (as food and clothing) and invested in future production (i.e. reproduced), and other forms of capital which are not consumed (machinery, buildings, etc.) may be sufficiently unimportant to be neglected. Thus some writers have illustrated their single-good models with a 'parable' of 'corn' being produced by labour and 'corn' (in the form of seed), for consumption (as food) and investment (as seed). Meade's (1962, p. 6) model is embroidered with a similar story: 'The economy produces cows which may be eaten as meat or used as instruments of production to produce more cows.' But modern growth theory is not meant to be about pre-industrial economies or agricultural production.

The second interpretation is that there is more than one good but that they are produced under a uniform technology. There may be a capital good and a consumption good which are physically distinct but which are 'perfectly substitutable in production' (Meade, 1962, p. 71): the production functions for the two goods are the same, so that with perfect competition and factor mobility, their prices in equilibrium are always equal. They can then, in effect, be aggregated without reference to relative prices, and can be regarded as one good.

This indicates the way the one-good assumption will be relaxed in

this chapter. We shall assume that *the capital good and the consumption good are produced in separate 'sectors' characterised by different
technologies or production functions.* There are thus two (but only
two) goods, which can be aggregated only by reference to their relative
prices. We retain the assumption that there are only two factors, K
(produced in the capital-good sector) and L (again increasing at an exogenous rate); and both factors are still homogeneous.
This amounts to the simplest possible relaxation of the one-good
assumption. It will be noted, in particular, that the distinction drawn
between the two sectors, based on an assumption of differing technologies, coincides with the distinction between capital goods and consumption goods which is based on their different end-uses and sources
of demand. If the former distinction were drawn between one sector
producing a capital good and another sector producing the consumption good and a second capital good, the analysis would be radically
complicated, even though there would still be only two sectors –
the reason being that capital would no longer be homogeneous. The
coincidence may be justified if capital goods do indeed tend to be
produced under different conditions from consumption goods; and the
obvious illustrating 'parable' is of an economy where food is produced
in an agricultural sector and machinery is produced in a manufacturing
sector. But there is then the problem of conceiving a homogeneous
'machine' which could be used in both sectors; thus Hicks (1965,
p. 138) has to apologise for stretching his reader's imagination by posit-
ing a capital-good sector in which 'tractors' (used in his consumption-
good sector with labour to produce 'corn') are produced by labour and
'tractors'! In fact it is probably at least as difficult to visualise a two-
sector economy of the kind we shall now be modelling as it is to visualise a one-good economy: there is a strong case for considering that
these two-sector models 'do not represent any great advance in realism
over one-sector models' (Hahn and Matthews, 1964, p. 39). Nevertheless they do introduce complications which are absent from a one-good
world, and which are instructive, particularly if they are seen as observations on a first step to *multi-sector growth theory* (see the further
reading at the end of this chapter).
    One obvious complication – which certainly does provide an advance
in realism – is that the introduction of two distinct technologies adds
the possibility of changes in the inter-sectoral allocation of output as a
new dimension to the potential flexibility of factor proportions in the
economy as a whole. This is seen most clearly if the two-sector assumption is used as a relaxation of the *Harrod–Domar model* of Chapter 3.

There will then be two sectors, each with fixed coefficients; but the coefficients will differ between the two, so that the proportion in which the factors are employed over-all will depend on the product mix. A model of this kind is constructed by Hicks (1965, part II).[1] Clearly, the greater is the difference in coefficients between the two sectors, the wider will be the range of values of s and λ for which the Harrod–Domar condition $s/v = \lambda$ can be satisfied.

Here, however, we shall be assuming that both sectors have continuous production functions of the kind we have been using in the last two chapters. We shall be following, in particular, Meade (1962, appendix II), Uzawa (1961; 1963), and Inada (1963).

6.2 The model

The capital good is produced in Sector 1, and the consumption good in Sector 2. As in the one-good model, capital and labour, the only two factors of production, are homogeneous, and capital is perfectly malleable; but now in addition we assume that the factors are perfectly mobile between the two sectors, as well as among techniques with differing factor proportions within each sector. There is no technical progress or depreciation. The two production functions have the properties of F in section 4.1; they may be written

$$\text{for Sector 1:} \quad Q_1 = F_1\,(K_1, L_1) \tag{6.1}$$

$$\text{for Sector 2:} \quad Q_2 = F_2\,(K_2, L_2) \tag{6.2}$$

Q_1, the physical output of Sector 1, is measured in units of the capital good, as are K_1 and K_2. Q_2, the physical output of Sector 2, is measured in units of the consumption good. Let p represent the price of the capital good in terms of the consumption good;[2] we then measure total output, Y, in units of the consumption good:

$$Y \equiv pQ_1 + Q_2 \equiv W + P \tag{6.3}$$

Since we have constant returns, labour-productivity functions can be derived from (6.1) and (6.2), and these have the usual properties:

$$q_1 = f_1(k_1),\ f'_1 > 0, f''_1 < 0, \text{ for all } k_1 > 0 \tag{6.4}$$

$$q_2 = f_2(k_2),\ f'_2 > 0, f''_2 < 0, \text{ for all } k_2 > 0 \tag{6.5}$$

As to saving behaviour, we adopt, not the proportional saving function of Chapter 4, but the general saving function

$$S = s_w W + s_p P,\ 0 \leqslant s_w \leqslant s_p \leqslant 1 \tag{6.6}$$

where S, W and P are all in units of the consumption good. As was seen in section 5.1, this can be reduced to either the proportional, or the neo-Keynesian, or the classical form by the adoption of specific assumptions about s_w and s_p. Our reason for adopting the general form is that the working of the two-good model is sensitive to which specific assumption is made.

The labour force, L, is again assumed to be growing at a constant exogenous rate λ; and finally, we again assume full (competitive) equilibrium with both factors fully employed. Thus

$$\left. \begin{array}{l} L_1 + L_2 = L \\ K_1 + K_2 = K \end{array} \right\} \qquad (6.7)$$

Full employment of K also means that investment, I (which is $\dot{K}$, the rate of increase of the capital stock), must be equal to the output of the capital-good sector, as well as to saving (now measured in terms of the capital good):

$$\dot{K} = I = Q_1 = \frac{S}{p} \qquad (6.8)$$

6.3 Momentary equilibrium

There are three prices in the model: p; the wage rate w (which is measured in units of the consumption good); and the rental rate r (the own rate of return on capital, which must be measured in units of the capital good). We first examine how these prices are related to one another in competitive equilibrium.

The wage rate must be equal to the marginal product of labour in Sector 2 and to the marginal product of labour in Sector 1 multiplied by the price of the capital good:

$$w = \frac{\partial Q_2}{\partial L_2} = f_2(k_2) - k_2 f'_2(k_2) \qquad (6.9a)$$

$$= p \frac{\partial Q_1}{\partial L_1} = p[f_1(k_1) - k_1 f'_1(k_1)] \qquad (6.9b)$$

Similarly, the rental rate r is equal to the marginal product of capital in Sector 1 and to the marginal product of capital in Sector 2 divided by the price of the capital good:

$$r = \frac{\partial Q_1}{\partial K_1} = f'_1(k_1) \qquad (6.10a)$$

$$= \frac{1}{p} \frac{\partial Q_2}{\partial K_2} = \frac{f'_2(k_2)}{p} \qquad (6.10b)$$

From (6.9) and (6.10) we see that the ratio of the marginal product of labour to the marginal product of capital in Sector 1 is

$$\frac{\partial Q_1/\partial L_1}{\partial Q_1/\partial K_1} = \frac{w/p}{r} = \frac{f_1(k_1) - k_1 f'_1(k_1)}{f'_1(k_1)}$$

$$= \frac{f_1(k_1)}{f'_1(k_1)} - k_1 \tag{6.11}$$

while the ratio of marginal products in Sector 2 is

$$\frac{\partial Q_2/\partial L_2}{\partial Q_2/\partial K_2} = \frac{w}{pr} = \frac{f_2(k_2) - k_2 f'_2(k_2)}{f'_2(k_2)}$$

$$= \frac{f_2(k_2)}{f'_2(k_2)} - k_2 \tag{6.12}$$

Hence

$$\frac{w}{pr} = \frac{f_1(k_1)}{f'_1(k_1)} - k_1 = \frac{f_2(k_2)}{f'_2(k_2)} - k_2 = z \tag{6.13}$$

is the ratio of marginal products, the same in the two sectors under perfect competition. The ratio z is the *wage-rental ratio* in the two-good model. It is depicted in Figure 6.1, where the productivity functions of the two sectors are drawn. As in the one-sector model, the ratio of the marginal product of labour to the marginal product of capital in Sector 1 at any point on f_1 is shown by the intersection with the horizontal axis of the tangent to f_1 at that point; this may be seen from (6.11); and similarly for Sector 2, from (6.12). We thus see that competitive equilibrium requires that k_1 and k_2 be in such a relation to each other that the tangents to $f_1(k_1)$ and $f_2(k_2)$ intersect the horizontal axis at the same point: this is exactly what (6.13) says. In Figure 6.1 $k_1{}^*$ and $k_2{}^*$ fulfil this requirement; and the corresponding wage-rental ratio is measured by OR.

Now (6.13) gives the equilibrium z in terms of k_1 and k_2; and from it, we see that

$$\frac{dz}{dk_1} = -\frac{f_1 f''_1}{(f'_1)^2} > 0; \quad \frac{dz}{dk_2} = -\frac{f_2 f''_2}{(f'_2)^2} > 0 \tag{6.14}$$

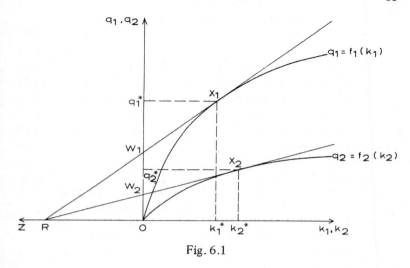

Fig. 6.1

Hence in equilibrium z, k_1 and k_2 are directly related to one another. And if f_1 and f_2 are well-behaved, it may be seen from (6.13) that $z \to 0$ as k_1 (or k_2) $\to 0$; and that $z \to \infty$ as k_1 (or k_2) $\to \infty$. Thus *with well-behaved productivity functions, z can take any positive value; any such value of z will be associated with a unique k_1 and a unique k_2; and the higher is z, the higher will be k_1 and k_2.* All this should be clear from the diagram, and may seem an unremarkable extension of the relationship between the wage–rental ratio and the capital–labour ratio in the one-good model. But we have not yet introduced the *over-all* capital–labour ratio in the two-good model; and we shall see shortly that the relationship between that and the wage-rental ratio is not quite so straightforward.

Meanwhile, we note two other features of competitive equilibrium. First, *if we know any one of the three prices of the system, we can find the other two.* If, for example, we know r, then we know $f'_1(k_1)$, and hence, given the properties of f_1, we can find w/p from (6.9b) (shown by OW_1 in the diagram) and this, together with r, gives us z. Knowing z and the form of f_2, we can then find w (shown by OW_2 in the diagram), using (6.12) and (6.9a); and the value of p then follows. Similarly, if we began with w, we could find r and p; and if we began with p, we could find r and w. In particular, therefore, p is determined if either r or w is given. In fact from (6.9) and (6.10)

$$p = \frac{\partial Q_2/\partial L_2}{\partial Q_1/\partial L_1} = \frac{\partial Q_2/\partial K_2}{\partial Q_1/\partial K_1} \qquad (6.15)$$

and since each marginal product is determined by the capital–labour ratios alone, we have that, owing to the fact that the two goods are produced in separate sectors under constant returns to scale, *the relative prices of the two goods are determined independently of the composition of output between the two sectors, and hence independently of the composition of demand between the two goods.* From (6.15), p is shown in Figure 6.1 by the ratio OW_2/OW_1.

Further, it should be clear from the diagram that *if the wage–rental ratio z is known, all three prices which make up z can be found from the productivity functions*; in particular, any z implies a value of p. What is not so self-evident is how p will differ among equilibria characterised by different values of z. This is the second feature we need to note; in what follows it will turn out to be important. It may be seen that the diagram has been drawn in such a way that $k_2^* > k_1^*$. If the same holds at every wage–rental ratio – so that the equilibrium capital-labour ratio is always higher in the consumption-good sector – Sector 2 may be said to be more capital-intensive than Sector 1. Then as z rises – as the cost of hiring labour rises in relation to the cost of hiring capital – the cost of producing a unit of the capital good must rise in relation to the unit cost of the consumption good. Thus, with competitive equilibrium being maintained, p must rise. Conversely, if the capital-good sector is the more capital-intensive, p will fall as z rises. Thus *whether p rises or falls as z rises depends on whether the capital-good sector is the less or the more capital-intensive.*

We can now turn to the *over-all capital–labour ratio k*, which may be written:

$$k = \frac{K}{L} = \frac{K_1 + K_2}{L} = k_1 \frac{L_1}{L} + k_2 \left(1 - \frac{L_1}{L}\right)$$

$$= (k_1 - k_2)\frac{L_1}{L} + k_2 \qquad (6.16)$$

It is dependent on the allocation of labour (and capital, and output) between the two sectors; and to get any further we need to bring in demand and the saving function. From (6.8), (6.6), and (6.1)

$$\dot{K} = \frac{S}{p} = s_w \frac{w}{p} L + s_p r K \qquad (6.17)$$

$$= Q_1 = F_1(K_1, L_1) = rK_1 + \frac{w}{p} L_1 \qquad (6.18)$$

From (6.17) and (6.18)

$$\frac{L_1}{L} = \frac{s_w z + s_p k}{z + k_1}$$

which may be substituted into (6.16) to give

$$k = \frac{(k_1 - k_2)(s_w z + s_p k)}{(k_1 + z)} + k_2 \qquad (6.19)$$

and solving for k

$$k = \frac{k_2(k_1 + z) - s_w z(k_2 - k_1)}{z + (1 - s_p)k_1 + s_p k_2} \qquad (6.20)$$

which expresses k in terms of z, k_1, k_2 and the saving propensities. But we know that k_1 and k_2 are continuous increasing functions of z, defined for all $z > 0$ if f_1 and f_2 are well-behaved. Hence (6.20) shows the function $k(z)$, and *for any positive z there exists a unique over-all capital-labour ratio in equilibrium.*

Further, by the properties of k_1 and k_2, $k(z)$ can take any positive value, so that given any positive k - i.e. given any positive endowments of K and L - there must exist an equilibrium wage–rental ratio satisfying (6.20). But for each k, is there only one equilibrium z? There will be a unique equilibrium wage-rental ratio associated with each value of k only if $k(z)$ is monotonically increasing; we thus have to examine the sign of the first derivative of (6.20). It may be shown that

$$\frac{dk}{dz} = \frac{\frac{dk_1}{dz}[(s_p k_2 + s_w z)(k_2 + z)] + \frac{dk_2}{dz}[(1 - s_p)k_1 + (1 - s_w)z][k_1 + z]}{[z + (1 - s_p)k_1 + s_p k_2]^2}$$

$$+ \frac{[k_2 - k_1][s_p(1 - s_w)k_2 - s_w(1 - s_p)k_1]}{[z + (1 - s_p)k_1 + s_p k_2]^2} \qquad (6.21)$$

With $z > 0$, k_1, k_2, dk_1/dz and dk_2/dz are all positive. Thus with the most general condition on the saving propensities ($0 \leqslant s_w \leqslant s_p \leqslant 1$), at least one of the first two terms in the numerator is positive, the other being at least non-negative. The denominator is also positive. Thus dk/dz is positive as long as the third term in the numerator is non-negative. Now if $s_p > s_w$, the third term is non-negative if $k_2 \geqslant k_1$; while if $s_p = s_w = s > 0$, the third term reduces to $s(1 - s)(k_2 - k_1)^2$, which is positive, irrespective of the relationship between k_2 and k_1. In summary, therefore, *the over-all capital–labour ratio k is a monotonically increasing function of z, for all z > 0 if*:

> either   (i)   *the saving function is of the proportional*
>   *form, $S = sY$, $0 < s < 1$*
>
> or   (ii)   *the saving function is of the neo-Keynesian*
>   *form, $S = s_w W + s_p P$, $0 \leqslant s_w < s_p \leqslant 1$; and*
>   *$k_2 \geqslant k_1$ for all $z > 0$*

$$(6.22)$$

This may seem a strange result. What is its meaning, and why, in particular, is the condition that Sector 2 be at least as capital-intensive as Sector 1 – what we shall call the *capital-intensity condition (C.I.C.)* – needed to ensure the monotonicity of z when $s_w \neq s_p$? We know that k_1 and k_2 are monotonically increasing functions of z; hence k can fail to be a monotonically increasing function of z only if a rise in z can mean a shift of labour towards the less capital-intensive sector (see expression (6.16)). We must ask, therefore, under what conditions a rise in z can lead to such a shift.

First, in the proportional saving case, from (6.8) and (6.3):

$$S = pQ_1 = sY = s(pQ_1 + Q_2)$$

and

$$s = \frac{pQ_1}{pQ_1 + Q_2} = \frac{1}{1 + \frac{1}{p}\left(\frac{Q_2}{Q_1}\right)}$$

$$(6.23)$$

The value of the output of the capital good, in terms of the consumption good, is a constant proportion s of total output Y measured in terms of the consumption good; and Q_2/Q_1 must vary directly with p for the saving–income ratio to remain constant. But we already know that if z rises, p will rise if the capital-good sector is the less capital-intensive, and fall if it is the more capital-intensive: thus in the former case Q_2/Q_1 will rise, while in the latter case Q_2/Q_1 will fall. Therefore, when z rises, the physical output of the more capital-intensive sector, be it Sector 1 or Sector 2, must always rise in relation to that of the other sector, so as to maintain the constancy of the saving ratio. Thus there must always be a shift of labour to the more capital-intensive sector when z rises, and so $k(z)$ must be monotonically increasing.

Turning to the neo-Keynesian function, we see that since

$$\frac{z}{k} \equiv \frac{wL}{prK} \equiv \frac{W}{P}$$

the share of wages must rise if an increase in z is not accompanied by a rise in k. The over-all saving ratio must then fall, and from (6.23) Q_2 must rise in relation to pQ_1. Now if Sector 2 is at least as capital-intensive as Sector 1 – if the C.I.C. is satisfied – p cannot fall as a result of the rise in z, so that Q_2/Q_1 must rise. But this conclusion is incompatible with the initial hypothesis that k does not rise. Hence that hypothesis is untenable: if the C.I.C. is satisfied, the monotonicity of $k(z)$ is safe. If, however, Sector 2 is less capital-intensive than Sector 1, then p will fall as z rises; then the required rise in Q_2/pQ_1 may be obtained with falling, constant or rising Q_2/Q_1. In particular, Q_2/Q_1 may rise, so that there may be a shift of resources to the less capital-intensive sector; then k may fall as z rises.

It should be clear from this argument that the C.I.C. is a sufficient not a necessary condition for $k(z)$ to be monotonically increasing. Nevertheless we now have a significant contrast with the one-good model. In the latter, given arbitrary endowments of K and L at any point in time, competitive factor-pricing and a technology satisfying no unusual restrictions are sufficient to ensure the uniqueness of the wage-rental ratio in momentary equilibrium, whether saving is proportional or neo-Keynesian. *But in the two-sector model, an arbitrary initial capital-labour ratio may be consistent with more than one momentary equilibrium – even if the technology of each sector is well-behaved – if saving is neo-Keynesian, unless the capital-intensity condition is satisfied.* The full significance of this result will become clearer when we examine the stability of steady-state equilibrium.

6.4 The existence and uniqueness of steady-state equilibrium

As with the one-good model, we are concerned first to examine whether there exists an equilibrium solution with $\dot{K}/K = \lambda$, for any $\lambda > 0$. From (6.8), (6.6) and the definition of z:

$$\frac{\dot{K}}{K} = \frac{s_w W + s_p P}{pK} = \frac{s_w w}{pk} + s_p r = \frac{s_w z f'_1(k_1)}{k} + s_p f'_1(k_1) \quad (6.24)$$

Now if f_1 is well-behaved, k_1 is a continuous function of z, defined for all $z > 0$; and, therefore, so is $f'_1(k_1)$. Also, if f_1 and f_2 are well-behaved, k is a continuous function of z, for all $z > 0$. Thus with f_1 and f_2 well-behaved (6.24) shows that $\dot{K}/K$ is a continuous function of z, $g(z)$, defined for all positive z. Further, it may be seen that $g(z) \to \infty$ as $z \to 0$, and that $g(z) \to 0$ as $z \to \infty$. Hence $g(z)$ takes all positive values, so there exists at least one z for which $g(z) = \lambda$, for any positive λ. And for each such value of z by (6.20) there exists a steady-state over-all capital–labour ratio k^*. Thus the *well-behavedness of f_1 and f_2 is sufficient to ensure the existence of a steady-state equilibrium*: a result similar to that obtained for the one-good model.[3]

The *uniqueness* of the steady-state solution is ensured if $g(z)$ is monotonically decreasing, for then there exists only one z, and hence only one k, for which $\dot{K}/K = \lambda$. From (6.24), using (6.13) and (6.14), we obtain:

$$\frac{dg}{dz} = -\frac{f'_1(k_1)(s_p k - s_w k_1)}{k(z + k_1)} - \left\{ s_w z \frac{f'_1(k_1)}{k^2} \right\} \frac{dk}{dz} \quad (6.25)$$

As was the case when we were examining the monotonicity of $k(z)$, we need to distinguish between the results obtained under two different saving assumptions. But now the distinction is not between the proportional and neo-Keynesian hypotheses but between the classical and the non-classical hypotheses. With the classical saving function, (6.25) becomes

$$\frac{dg}{dz} = -\frac{s_p f'_1(k_1)}{z + k_1} \quad (6.26)$$

which is unambiguously negative for all $z > 0$, so that uniqueness is established.[4] But with $s_w > 0$, the capital-intensity condition reappears. The second term in (6.25) is negative provided dk/dz is positive, which we have shown to be the case either when $s_w = s_p$, or when $s_w < s_p$ and the C.I.C. is satisfied. And the first term is non-positive provided $k \geqslant k_1$, which will be the case if and only if $k_2 \geqslant k_1$. Thus, whether or not $s_w = s_p$, we need the C.I.C. to ensure the monotonicity of $g(z)$ and the uniqueness of the steady-state solution. In summary, therefore, *the equilibrium growth rate of the capital-stock, $\dot{K}/K = g(z)$, is monotonically decreasing for all $z > 0$ if*:

either (i)   the saving function is of the classical
form, $S = s_p P, \ 0 < s_p \leqslant 1$

or   (ii)   the saving function is of the non-   (6.27)
classical form, $S = s_w W + s_p P$,
$0 < s_w \leqslant s_p \leqslant 1;$ and $k_2 \geqslant k_1$
for all $z > 0$

As with (6.22), we need to consider the meaning and significance of
the C.I.C. in (6.27). Let us return to expression (6.24). When $s_w = 0$ the
establishment of uniqueness is straightforward; as we have seen (in the
last two notes), the model is then very similar to the one-good model.
The unique steady-state solution can easily be worked through, for
example using Figure 6.1. (Note that in the steady state the own rate of
return on capital, r, is again given by λ/s_p.)

The problem which arises when $s_w > 0$ can best be seen by using

$$z \equiv \frac{w}{pr} \ ; \quad r = f'_1(k_1) = \frac{P}{pK}; \quad Y \equiv pQ_1 + Q_2 \equiv W + P$$

to obtain from (6.24)

$$\frac{\dot{K}}{K} \ = \ g(z) = s_w \ \frac{Y}{pK} \ + \ (s_p - s_w)f'_1(k_1) \qquad (6.28)$$

This is easily comparable with the left-hand side of (5.7a), which
was $\dot{K}/K$ in the one-good model with $s_w \neq s_p$: Y/pK has replaced
$f(k)/k$ and $f'_1(k_1)$ has replaced $f'(k)$. And when $s_w = s_p = s$, (6.28)
collapses to an expression in Y/pK which is similar to the expression in $f(k)/k$ obtained for the one-good model with proportional
saving (see expression (4.15)). Clearly, then, it is with Y/pK that the
trouble arises; and the question is why this 'value output–capital ratio'
in the two-good model[5] is, unlike the physical output–capital ratio in
the one-good model, not necessarily a monotonically decreasing function of z (and of k), given the usual properties of the production functions. Now Y/pK may be written:

$$\frac{Y}{pK} \ \equiv \ \frac{pQ_1 + Q_2}{pK} \ \equiv \left[\frac{q_1}{k_1}\right]\frac{K_1}{K} \ + \left[\frac{q_2/p}{k_2}\right]\frac{K_2}{K} \qquad (6.29)$$

Now consider how Y/pK will change as z changes.

Suppose z rises. Then by the properties of f_1 and f_2 the physical
output–capital ratios, q_1/k_1 and q_2/k_2, must both fall. Now assume

first that the C.I.C. is satisfied. With Sector 2 at least as capital-intensive as Sector 1, the rise in z cannot mean a fall in p; thus the two bracketed terms in (6.29) must both fall. Hence Y/pK can fail to fall only if either (i) $q_1/k_1 > (q_2/p) \div k_2$, and there is a shift of resources to Sector 1, or (ii) $q_1/k_1 < (q_2/p) \div k_2$, and there is a shift to Sector 2. But the C.I.C. implies that $q_1/k_1 \geqslant (q_2/p) \div k_2$ for all z.[6] This means that Y/pK can fail to fall only if there is a shift of resources to Sector 1. But we already know that if the C.I.C. is satisfied, such a shift cannot accompany a rise in z. Thus Y/pK must be a monotonically decreasing function of z.

But now suppose that the C.I.C. is not satisfied. With Sector 1 more capital-intensive than Sector 2, p will fall as z rises, so that the second bracketed term in (6.29) may rise despite the fall in q_2/k_2. We need go no further: in this case Y/pK may rise as z rises, and $g(z)$ may not be monotonically decreasing. There may thus be more than one value of z, and hence of k, compatible with $\dot{K}/K = \lambda$, i.e. there may be more than one steady-state solution.

6.5   The stability of steady-state equilibrium

Suppose z^* and k^* characterise a steady-state equilibrium. Then for stability, as in the one-good model, we require that for any $k > k^*$, k should be falling, i.e. $\dot{K}/K < \lambda$; and that for any $k < k^*$, k should be rising, i.e. $\dot{K}/K > \lambda$. Now if we have both that $k(z)$ is monotonically

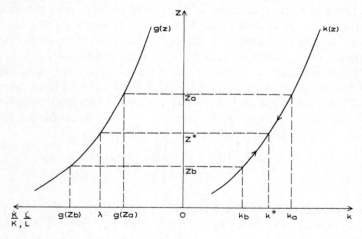

Fig. 6.2

increasing and that $g(z)$ is monotonically decreasing, this requirement is fulfilled, as may be seen from Figure 6.2. The steady-state $\dot{K}/K = \lambda$ is shown in the left-hand quadrant; z^* is then given by $g(z^*) = \lambda$, and k^* by $k(z^*)$. Then if, for example, the over-all capital–labour ratio is k_a, which exceeds k^*, the equilibrium wage–rental ratio z_a exceeds z^*, and $\dot{K}/K = g(z_a)$ is less than λ; thus k and z must be falling, and $\dot{K}/K$ must be rising, towards their steady-state values.

It follows that *stability is assured for any form of the general saving function if the C.I.C. is satisfied*. If the C.I.C. is not satisfied, we cannot be sure of the monotonicity of *both* $g(z)$ and $k(z)$ under any of the saving hypotheses. But can we do without the monotonicity of either and still be sure of stability?

First suppose that $g(z)$ is monotonically decreasing but that $k(z)$ is not monotonically increasing; this situation, represented in Figure 6.3, may arise only if saving is not proportional and the C.I.C. is not satisfied. Now suppose that $k > k^*$: can we be sure that k is falling?

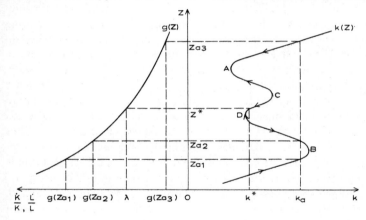

Fig. 6.3

Assume that k is as shown by k_a in the diagram. We see immediately that there is more than one z compatible with k_a: momentary equilibrium is not unique. Moreover, each equilibrium z obviously implies a different equilibrium $\dot{K}/K = g(z)$, so that we cannot know how k will move from the starting-point k_a without knowing which equilibrium the system is in; the path to be followed by k from k_a is indeterminate. We thus see that *when k(z) is not monotonically increasing, so that for some values of k there are multiple momentary equilibria, the specification of an initial value for k may be insufficient for the subsequent equilibrium motion of the system to be predictable.* The system is said then to be *causally indeterminate*, or *non-causal*. This problem never arose in the one-good model. In every variant considered in Chapters 4 and 5 momentary equilibrium was unique, and the system was causal: given initial factor endowments the equilibrium motion of the system was always determinate, and then stability depended on whether the motion was in the direction of the steady state. Instability was found to be associated with the existence of multiple steady-state solutions. We shall now see that in the two-sector model instability is associated additionally with non-uniqueness of momentary equilibrium and causal indeterminacy.

Let us return to the example of k_a in Figure 6.3 to indicate the kind of problem which may arise. In fact none of the equilibria associated with k_a will lead the system to the steady state. If the actual equilibrium z is z_{a1} or z_{a2}, the left-hand quadrant shows that k must be rising further away from k^*. It is true that if $z = z_{a3}$, k must initially be falling towards k^*; but even in this case the system will not simply move continuously along the $k(z)$ curve until it reaches the steady state. When it reaches the turning-point A, k must still be falling, so that z will have to drop to the low upward-sloping stretch of $k(z)$ for equilibrium to be maintained; k will then begin rising towards B, at which point z will jump to the high upward-sloping stretch of the curve. Thus equilibrium can be maintained indefinitely without the system ever entering the section of $k(z)$ which lies between A and B. In fact it may be seen that the system can attain the steady state smoothly along $k(z)$ only from points lying on the stretch of the curve between C and D, and that if the system is outside that stretch it cannot enter it apart from by discontinuous changes in z. In this example, therefore, the steady state is only locally stable, in the sense that the system will tend towards the steady state from equilibria in the neighbourhood of (k^*,z^*), i.e. on the *C–D* stretch, But, globally, the steady state is not stable; and it should be clear that if the example were reconstructed with $k(z)$ falling in the neighbourhood of (k^*, z^*) even local stability would be lost. We may thus conclude simply that *if k(z) is not monotonically increasing, steady growth will generally not be stable.*

Second, suppose that $k(z)$ is monotonically increasing but that $g(z)$ is not monotonically decreasing; this situation, illustrated in

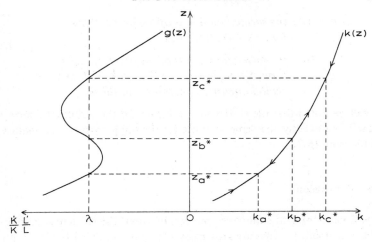

Fig. 6.4

Figure 6.4, may arise only if saving is not classical and the C.I.C. is not satisfied. We see first that there is now the possibility of more than one steady-state solution; in the diagram there are three, at $(k_a{}^*, z_a{}^*)$, $(k_b{}^*, z_b{}^*)$, and $(k_c{}^*, z_c{}^*)$. Now suppose the system is in non-steady-state equilibrium. Inspection of the diagram shows that if $k < k_a{}^*$, k will be rising; that if $k_a{}^* < k < k_b{}^*$, k will be falling; that if $k_b{}^* < k < k_c{}^*$, k will be rising; and finally, that if $k > k_c{}^*$, k will be falling. Thus k will be converging on $k_a{}^*$ or $k_c{}^*$ depending on whether k is initially less than or greater than $k_b{}^*$: if the system is not in a steady state it must be converging on one. Although $k_b{}^*$ is an unstable steady state (because in its neighbourhood $g(z)$ is increasing), we can be sure that there is a stable solution either side of it by virtue of the properties of $g(z)$. (We saw in section 6.4 that if f_1 and f_2 are well-behaved, $g(z) \to \infty$ as $z \to 0$, and $g(z) \to 0$ as $z \to \infty$, so that for sufficiently high and low z, $g(z)$ must be decreasing.) We therefore see that *if $g(z)$ is not monotonically decreasing there will be multiple steady-state solutions for some values of λ, at least one of which will be unstable, but that the system will converge on some stable solution from any non-steady-state starting point as long as $k(z)$ is monotonically increasing.* The implication is that we can dispense with the C.I.C. if saving is proportional and still be sure that the system will tend towards a steady state.

In summary, therefore, *from any starting point, all equilibrium paths approach a steady-state path asymptotically if*:

> *either* (i) *the saving function is of the proportional*
> *form, $S = sY$, $0 < s < 1$*
>
> (6.30)
>
> *or* (ii) *the saving function is of the neo-Keynesian*
> *form, $S = S_w W + s_p P$, $0 \leqslant s_w < s_p \leqslant 1$; and the*
> *capital-intensity condition is fulfilled*

It will be noted that the sufficient conditions for the stability of steady growth are exactly the same as those for the uniqueness of momentary equilibrium (6.22).

6.6 Conclusion

It will be helpful to summarise our results about the existence, uniqueness and stability of steady growth by taking the three particular forms of the general saving function in turn.

Classical saving: $0 = s_w < s_p \leqslant 1$[7]

(i) There exists a unique steady-state solution for any $\lambda > 0$ if f_1 is well-behaved.

(ii) Every equilibrium path approaches the unique steady state asymptotically if the capital-intensity condition is satisfied.

Proportional saving: $0 < s_w = s_p = s < 1$[8]

(i) There exists at least one steady-state solution for any $\lambda > 0$ if f_1 and f_2 are well-behaved.

(ii) Every equilibrium path approaches some steady state asymptotically.

(iii) For any $\lambda > 0$ the steady-state solution is unique if the capital-intensity condition is satisfied.

Non-classical, neo-Keynesian saving: $0 < s_w < s_p \leqslant 1$[9]

(i) There exists at least one steady-state solution for any $\lambda > 0$ if f_1 and f_2 are well-behaved.

(ii) If the capital-intensity condition is satisfied, the steady-state solution for any $\lambda > 0$ is unique, and every equilibrium path approaches it asymptotically.

Thus whichever particular version of the general saving function is taken, the sufficient conditions for either uniqueness or stability (or both) include the C.I.C., which seems a rather 'casual property of the technology' (Solow 1961, p. 275) in that whether or not it is empirically valid would appear to be almost fortuitous. But it must be emphasised that we have been dealing in sufficient not necessary conditions, and that alternative sufficient conditions are available and may be preferred. Thus Takayama (1963) showed that with classical saving the stability of steady growth is assured if the elasticity of substitution in the capital-good sector is not less than unity, even if the C.I.C. is not satisfied; and a complete set of sufficient conditions, for all the saving hypotheses, can be derived in terms of elasticities of substitution instead of the C.I.C.[10] We need explore these alternative requirements no further. What we need to note is that when the one-good assumption is relaxed in what may be considered the simplest possible way, more restrictive assumptions of some form are needed if the neo-classical 'explanation' of steady growth is to remain intact. This is not especially surprising; it is hardly remarkable that the relaxation of one assumption calls for the imposition of others for the properties of the model to be maintained. But the empirical significance of any particular set of new restrictions required by the two-sector model is far from clear, since the gain in realism provided by the assumption of two goods rather than one is so small. In fact whether the loss of the one-good model's simplicity and versatility is, at the end of the day, worth the candle may be considered debatable.

It is unnecessary to spell out in full the characteristics of steady growth in the two-sector model, or the implications of parameter changes; this would involve a great deal of repetition from Chapter 4. It is, however, worth observing that *steady growth in the two-sector model implies no 'structural change'*: the relative prices of the two goods are constant, and the two sectors remain in the same relation to each other as regards output and factors employed. This has a very clear empirical interpretation, which we shall refer to in Part IV.

Further reading

One of the most interesting aspects of the two-sector model is that it may be regarded as a small general-equilibrium system. This was first pointed out by Solow (1961), and was explored further in Hahn (1965). The latter is particularly recommended as supplementary reading to this chapter, as is Dixit (1976, ch. 6), which is an unconventional and illuminating textbook exposition. *Multi-sector growth theory* is beyond the scope of this book; the interested reader is referred to Hahn and Matthews (1964, part III) and to Burmeister and Dobell (1970, ch. 7) for introductions and references.

7
Technical Progress, Productivity Growth and Steady States

7.1 Technical progress and modern economic growth

In nearly all the steady states described in the last three chapters output grows at the same rate as the labour force, so that the productivity of labour is constant. The only exception arose in Section 5.4, where we showed that steady growth with rising output per head is a possibility when there are increasing returns to scale; but there are problems with that conception, as we saw. Otherwise – with constant returns – in the absence of technological change steady growth necessarily entails constant output per head; and rising output per head is a non-steady-state phenomenon, associated with rising capital–output and capital–labour ratios, i.e. capital-deepening. To explain steady growth with rising income per head – which is what Kaldor's stylised facts refer to – our neoclassical models need technical progress.

But even if the theoretical concept of steady growth has little empirical relevance, it is obvious from casual observation that no analysis of modern economic growth – by which we mean the kind of growth experienced by the 'developed' or industrialised countries over periods dating back to the late eighteenth century – can approach completeness without taking account of advances in technology. In fact it may be claimed that what, above all else, distinguishes modern economic growth from pre-industrial development is technological change at an unprecedented rate. Thus Kuznets (1966, p. 9), the most famous student of the characteristics of modern economic growth, judges that its distinctive driving-force – what he calls the 'epochal innovation' which has generated the 'modern economic epoch' – is 'the extended application of science to problems of economic production', or 'the emergence of modern science as the basis of an advancing technology'

(Kuznets, 1973, p. 249). Indeed, Kuznets (1966, p. 10) goes further, to claim that 'certainly since the second half of the nineteenth century, the major source of economic growth in the developed countries has been science-based technology'. Although, as we shall see below, there can be argument over the meaning and validity of this last statement, and over the precise quantitative contribution of technical progress to economic growth, there can be no doubt that technological change is an essential part of the story, and that it cannot be excluded from models which purport to tell the story in simplified form.

7.2 Disembodied technical progress at an exogenous rate

'Over the years technical progress has been given a wide range of meanings and interpretations' (Kennedy and Thirlwall, 1972). Nevertheless, we can offer a simple provisional definition: *technical progress means the advancement of knowledge about methods of production*. It implies that the potential output obtainable from any inputs of 'physical' factors is increased, or (which is the same thing) that the inputs required to produce any quantity of output are reduced.[1] Correspondingly it may be visualised either as an upward shift of a production function whose arguments are physical inputs, or as an inward shift of isoquants towards the origin.

More conveniently, the 'shift factor' representing technical progress may be incorporated in the production function. The simplest form of technical progress may then be represented by amending the continuous one-good production function to include time, t, as an independent variable alongside K and L:

$$Y = F(K, L, t); \quad F_t > 0 \tag{7.1}$$

Here, owing to technical progress, Y increases with the passage of time even if K and L are constant: time, representing the stock of knowledge, may be thought of almost as a third factor of production, which 'increases' of its own accord in much the same way as we have for the most part been assuming L to be increasing of its own accord. Technical progress is thus represented simply as an automatic, *exogenous* process, occurring independently of any economic variables; in particular, it is being treated as costless, falling on the economy like 'manna from heaven'. Further, it is represented as occurring irrespective of whether new units of K and L are being introduced. New units are no more efficient than old units - 'machines' and 'men' are still homogeneous - and technical progress has the same effect on the efficiency of every unit in use, however old, of each factor; the 'manna' falls indiscriminately, and technical progress is said to be *disembodied*. (An alternative hypothesis would be that technical progress, though still occurring at an exogenous rate, only affects the efficiency of new units of the factors as they come into use: each unit 'embodies' the 'state of the arts' at the time of its introduction and cannot benefit from later advances. We consider this *embodiment* hypothesis in section 7.6. Then in Chapters 8 and 9 we shall examine models in which, first, the direction or factor-saving characteristics, and then the rate, of progress are *endogenous* to the economic system.)

For many purposes it is convenient to assume that F in (7.1) is such that it may be re-expressed as follows:

$$Y = G\left[a(t)K, b(t)L\right]; \quad \dot{a}, \dot{b} \geqslant 0 \qquad (7.2a)$$

or

$$Y = G(\bar{K}, \bar{L}) \qquad (7.2b)$$

where

$$\bar{K} = a(t)K, \quad \bar{L} = b(t)L$$

Here, technical progress is *factor-augmenting*: it raises the efficiency of K at the rate $\dot{a}/a$, and the efficiency of L at the rate $\dot{b}/b$, in that its effect on output is just as if K and L were rising at those respective rates. Then if $\dot{a} = 0$ and $\dot{b} > 0$, technical progress is purely *labour-augmenting*; while if $\dot{b} = 0$ and $\dot{a} > 0$, it is purely *capital-augmenting*. $\bar{K}$ and $\bar{L}$ measure the capital stock and labour force in *efficiency units* rather than natural units, and with technical progress $\bar{K}$ and $\bar{L}$ or both will be rising even if K and L are constant.

7.3 Requirements for steady growth

Chapter 3 showed that in the Harrod–Domar model a necessary condition for equilibrium growth (which there meant steady growth) was that technical progress should be such that the average productivity of labour rises at a constant rate while the average productivity of capital is constant. We also noted that this requirement that technical progress be purely labour-augmenting[2] was equivalent to requiring Harrod-neutrality (as defined in Chapter 1) with a constant interest rate. We now ask how these results transfer to a variable-coefficients technology.

Suppose that technical progress is of the most general exogenous and disembodied form, as represented by (7.1), and that there are constant returns so that F is linearly homogeneous in K and L. The labour force is growing at the constant rate λ. What form of progress is compatible with steady growth? Differentiating (7.1) logarithmically with respect to t

$$\frac{\dot{Y}}{Y} = \left(\frac{KF_K}{F}\right)\frac{\dot{K}}{K} + \left(\frac{LF_L}{F}\right)\frac{\dot{L}}{L} + \frac{F_t}{F} \tag{7.3}$$

which may be compared with (5.10), the corresponding expression for an unchanging technology. With constant returns KF_K/F and LF_L/F are the competitive factor shares, summing to unity. Hence

$$\frac{\dot{Y}}{Y} = \left(\frac{KF_K}{F}\right)\frac{\dot{K}}{K} + \left(1 - \frac{KF_K}{F}\right)\lambda + \frac{F_t}{F} \tag{7.4}$$

or, in *per capita* terms

$$\frac{\dot{y}}{y} = \frac{KF_K}{F}\frac{\dot{k}}{k} + \frac{F_t}{F} \tag{7.5}$$

Now if K and L are constant, we see from (7.4) that output grows at the rate F_t/F, as does output per head, while if K and L are both growing at the same rate λ, the growth rate of output is $\lambda + F_t/F$ and the growth rate of output per head is F_t/F. F_t/F thus provides a natural measure of the rate of technical progress; for reasons which will become clear we call it the *Hicks rate of technical progress*. It is *the growth rate of output per head when capital per head is constant*.

Now in steady growth K and Y must grow at the same constant rate. Thus from (7.5)

$$\frac{\dot{k}}{k} = \frac{\dot{y}}{y} = \left(\frac{1}{1 - \dfrac{KF_K}{F}}\right)\frac{F_t}{F} \tag{7.6}$$

must be constant. This is the *growth rate of output per head at a constant capital-output ratio*; we call it the *Harrod rate of technical pro-*

gress, for reasons which may already be clear. Now if F_t/F, the Hicks rate, is constant, then constancy of the Harrod rate (and steady growth) requires F_K, the marginal product of capital (the rate of profit or interest), to be constant. Thus technical progress must be *Harrod-neutral*, in the sense that it must leave the marginal product of capital undisturbed at a constant capital–output ratio.[3] If the Hicks rate is not constant, the constancy of the Harrod rate would require compensating movements in F_K, and hence in factor shares. Thus although output and capital can conceivably grow at the same constant rate without Harrod-neutrality, the features of such a growth path would violate the idea of steady growth as expressed in our definition in section 1.2.

In sum, then, *with constant returns to scale and a constant rate λ of labour-force growth, steady growth is maintainable if and only if the production function F(K, L, t) is of such a form that technical progress is Harrod-neutral and the Hicks rate of technical progress is constant.* The growth rate of output per head at a constant capital–output ratio – the Harrod rate of technical progress – is then a constant, τ. In steady growth capital per head and output per head will be growing at this rate, so that capital and output will be growing at the rate $\lambda + \tau$, which may clearly be thought of as the new natural growth rate. (It is of course the same as the old natural rate of Chapters 1 and 3.)

But what form of the production function $F(K, L, t)$ will satisfy these conditions? It may be shown that *with constant returns to scale and the other usual neo-classical restrictions on F (positive and diminishing marginal products), technical progress is Harrod-neutral if, and only if, F may be re-expressed in purely labour-augmenting form,*[4] i.e. if and only if there is a function G such that

$$F(K, L, t) = G(K, b(t)L) = G(K, \bar{L}) \qquad (7.7)$$

This result was first derived by Robinson (1938); an algebraic proof was provided by Uzawa (1961a). Sufficiency is easily shown, thus. Since there are constant returns, (7.7) may be written

$$Y = G(K, b(t)L) = b(t)LG\left(\frac{K}{b(t)L}, 1\right) = b(t)Lg(\bar{k}) \qquad (7.8)$$

or

$$\bar{y} = g(\bar{k}) \qquad (7.9)$$

where

$$\bar{y} \equiv \frac{Y}{b(t)L}; \quad \bar{k} \equiv \frac{K}{b(t)L}$$

Thus just as without technical progress, constant returns allows output per head (i.e. output per natural unit of labour) to be expressed simply as a function f of capital per head, so now with purely labour-augmenting progress, constant returns allows output per efficiency unit of labour $\bar{y}$ to be expressed simply as a function g of capital per efficiency unit of labour $\bar{k}$. Now, from (7.8) the marginal product of capital is

$$\frac{\partial Y}{\partial K} = g'(\bar{k})$$

so that positive and diminishing marginal productivity ensures that g, like f, is an increasing concave function. The output–capital ratio is

$$\frac{Y}{K} = \frac{\bar{y}}{\bar{k}} = \frac{g(\bar{k})}{\bar{k}}$$

Thus if the output–capital ratio is constant, $\bar{k}$, and hence $g'(\bar{k})$, must be constant. We therefore have Harrod-neutrality. To show necessity, Uzawa (1961a) obtained from (7.1) a function relating output per head to the capital–output ratio and time; he then derived an expression for the marginal product of capital in terms of this function and showed that it was independent of t (and hence dependent only on the capital–output ratio) only if (7.7) holds.

Thus for steady growth to be possible technical progress must be purely labour-augmenting, so that the production function may be written in the particular form shown by (7.7). But this is not sufficient; in addition $b(t)$ must be increasing at a constant rate. In fact if K and Y are growing at the same constant rate $\lambda + \tau$, then constant returns means that $\bar{L} = b(t)L$ must also be growing at this rate. But L is growing at the rate λ, so $b(t)$ must be growing at the rate τ, the constant Harrod rate of technical progress. We thus reach the conclusion that *with constant returns to scale and constant labour-force growth, steady growth is feasible with exogenous and disembodied technical progress if, and only if, the production function may be written*

$$F(K, L, t) = G(K, b(t)L) \tag{7.10}$$

where $b(t) = b(o)e^{\tau t}$ and τ is constant. Neo-classical growth models which take into account technical progress (at least of the kind now being considered) need to assume that it takes this particular form if steady growth is to be explained.[5]

This may be considered 'a further limitation on the value of steady-state growth models as representations of reality. In order to defend their usefulness in this role, one must either maintain that technical progress just happens to have been neutral or else suggest reasons why a tendency to Harrod-neutrality should exist' (Hahn and Matthews, 1964, p. 53). Such reasons have been put forward, as we shall see in Chapter 8, and in our examination of Kaldor's growth model in Chapter 9 and Part III. Whether these attempts provide a satisfactory theory of *endogenous Harrod-neutrality* is a matter for debate. But there are other reasons why it may be argued that technical progress is, by its very nature, incompatible with steady growth. First, since advances in knowledge and their consequences are inherently unpredictable, 'technical progress forces us to recognise that imperfect foresight is what characterises the actual progress of an economy through time' (Bliss, 1975, p. 11). As we saw in Chapter 2, steady growth may be viewed partly as a state of affairs which allows the problems arising from imperfect foresight to be neglected; and one may argue that if the occurrence of technical progress – hardly represented satisfactorily as an exogenous, regular process, as in (7.1) – is incompatible with perfect foresight, it is also incompatible with steady growth. Second, in reality technical progress results in structural change as well as productivity growth; and structural change does not occur in a steady state. These two points indicate the limitations of what can be learned about technical progress, and about growth with technical progress, from steady-state models. But it would be rash for us to conclude at this stage, as Bliss (1975) does, that 'any interesting technical progress' is incompatible with steady growth.

We are now in a position to examine how well the results of the last three chapters survive the introduction of technical progress of the required form.

7.4   Steady growth with technical progress

We first take the *one-good model* of Chapter 4, replacing the old production function with the new, represented by (7.10). We have already derived the productivity function for effective labour, $g(\overline{k})$, and shown that its first derivative measures the marginal product of capital or rate of profit. Similarly, it may be shown that the real wage, w, is now given by

$$w = \frac{\partial Y}{\partial L} = g(\bar{k}) - \bar{k}g'(\bar{k})$$

which again is similar to the corresponding expression obtained for $f(k)$. Now in equilibrium growth

$$\frac{\dot{\bar{k}}}{\bar{k}} \equiv \frac{\dot{K}}{K} - \frac{\dot{L}}{L} = \frac{sY}{K} - (\lambda + \tau) = \frac{sg(\bar{k})}{\bar{k}} - (\lambda + \tau)$$

so that

$$\dot{\bar{k}} = sg(\bar{k}) - (\lambda + \tau)\bar{k} \qquad (7.11)$$

which has the same form as (4.14); but k has been replaced by $\bar{k}$, $f(k)$ by $g(\bar{k})$, and λ by $\lambda + \tau$. It has already been shown that in steady growth K, Y and L all grow at the same rate, $\lambda + \tau$; thus $\bar{k}$ is constant, and for steady growth we put (7.11) equal to zero, so that

$$\frac{s}{\bar{k}/g(\bar{k})} = \lambda + \tau, \quad \text{or} \quad \frac{g(\bar{k})}{\bar{k}} = \frac{\lambda + \tau}{s} \qquad (7.12)$$

which is the same as (4.15), but with the same amendments. There is clearly little need to retrace our steps much further: the alterations which have to be made to the analysis of Chapters 4 and 5 should now be apparent. Essentially, we replace the old natural growth rate, λ, with the new, $\lambda + \tau$; and the old productivity function, $f(k)$, with $g(\bar{k})$. Thus, with proportional saving, the steady-state solution is characterised by an output–capital ratio of $(\lambda + \tau)/s$; existence, uniqueness and stability are now assured for all positive λ and τ if $g(\bar{k})$ is well-behaved; in steady growth Y and K grow at the rate $\lambda + \tau$, and y, w and k grow at the Harrod rate of technical progress, τ. Again, in steady growth the output-capital ratio, the rate of profit and distributive shares are constant, as are k, y and the wage per efficiency unti of labour. And so on, through Chapters 4 and 5.

The introduction of technical progress into the *two-sector model* of Chapter 6 does, however, bring some complications, which may be noted briefly. Such complications could be banished by assuming equal rates of technical progress and Harrod-neutrality in both sectors individually. But for constant distributive shares we now require the overall capital–output ratio in value terms to be constant at a constant profit rate: Harrod-neutrality naturally takes this meaning in the two-good model, and it may be satisfied even if the volume capital–output ratio in neither sector remains constant at a constant profit rate, as long as the relative prices of the goods and the relative weights of the two sectors behave appropriately. (This may be seen from (6.29).) Thus one may imagine a steady state in which technical progress is, say, faster in the capital-good sector so that p is falling, while there are offsetting biases in volume terms in the two sectors.

7.5 Alternative notions of neutrality and bias

'The purpose of a definition of neutral technical progress is to indicate characteristics of technical progress which will in some sense leave unchanged the balance between labour and capital' (Hahn and Matthews, 1964, p. 47). *Harrod's definition of neutrality* was introduced in Chapter 1, and by now its significance has become apparent. Corresponding to it are definitions of *factor-saving (or factor-using) bias.* Thus technical progress is said to be Harrod labour-saving (capital-using) if, at a constant capital-output ratio, the return on capital (or rate of interest, or marginal product of capital) rises: at a constant capital–output ratio technical progress will then cause distributive shares to change at the expense of labour, and in favour of capital. In the opposite case technical progress is Harrod capital-saving (labour-using).

An alternative definition of neutrality, proposed by Hicks (1963, pp. 121-2) takes as its bench-mark the constancy, not of the capital-output ratio, but of the capital–labour ratio. Thus technical progress is *Hicks-neutral* if the ratio of the marginal product of labour to the marginal product of capital (the wage–rental ratio under competition) is undisturbed by technical progress at a constant capital–labour ratio. The ratio of total wages to total profits will then remain unchanged if the capital–labour ratio is held constant; this contrasts with Harrod-neutrality, under which distributive shares remain unchanged at a constant capital–output ratio. There are again associated definitions of bias. Technical progress is Hicks labour-saving (capital-using) if it causes the wage–rental ratio to fall when the capital–labour ratio is held constant, and Hicks capital-saving (labour-using) in the opposite case. In the former case factor shares shift in capital's favour if relative factor supplies do not change; in the latter case they shift in labour's favour.

With constant returns the two definitions of neutrality may be compared in the productivity-function diagram of the usual kind. From (7.1), if F is linearly homogeneous in K and L, we can write

$$y \equiv \frac{Y}{L} = F\left(\frac{K}{L}, 1, t\right) = f(k, t) \qquad (7.13)$$

Output per head is now a function of capital per head and time; and technical progress may be represented as an upward movement in our old productivity function $f(k)$, as in Figure 7.1.[6] Here $f(k, i)$ and $f(k, j)$ represent productivity function at two points of time, i and j. Now if Harrod-neutrality is satisfied, then along any ray through the origin the slope of f remains unchanged; for example, along the ray OV the slope of $f(k, i)$ at X_1 must be the same as the slope of $f(k, j)$ at X_3. For Hicks-neutrality, on the other hand, at any capital-labour ratio, the wage-rental ratio OR must remain the same as f shifts; this condition is satisfied for the capital-labour ratio k_1 by the points X_1 and X_2. The Hicks rate of technical progress will now be recognised as the rate at which y grows if we follow the movement of f vertically, holding k constant; while the Harrod rate is the rate at which y grows if we follow the movement of f outwards along any ray like OV, holding the capital-output ratio constant. It is clear that since the Harrod rate includes a capital-deepening element, whereas the Hicks rate does not, the former will always exceed the latter. Indeed this is apparent from (7.6), which shows that the differences will be the larger the higher (the nearer to 1)

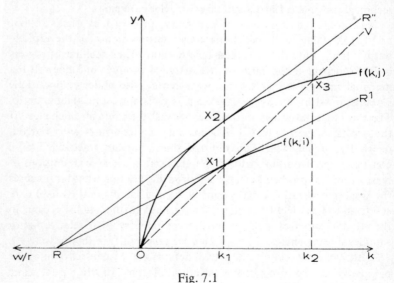

Fig. 7.1

is the elasticity of output with respect to capital (i.e. the higher the profit share).

We can now see what form the production function must take for technical progress to be both Hicks- and Harrod-neutral. Hicks-neutrality implies that factor shares remain constant when the capital–labour ratio is constant; for instance, factor shares are the same at X_1 and X_2 in Figure 7.1. Harrod-neutrality, however, implies that factor shares remain constant when the capital–output ratio is constant; they are thus the same at X_1 and X_3. Therefore, the diagram, which has been drawn to illustrate both forms of neutrality, has the property that distributive shares are the same at X_3 as at X_2; the rise in the capital–labour ratio from k_1 to k_2 along $f(k, j)$ brings with it no change in factor shares. Hence the elasticity of substitution described by k_1 and k_2 on $f(k, j)$ must be unity. The generalisation of this result is that *technical progress is both Hicks- and Harrod-neutral if, and only if, the production function has an elasticity of substitution between capital and labour of unity – the production function must be of the Cobb–Douglas form.* [7]

The sufficiency part of this theorem can be demonstrated in another way. It may be shown that with constant returns Hicks-neutrality means that technical progress augments both factors equally, so that the production function may be written: [8]

$$Y = F(K, L, t) = G[a(t)K, a(t)L] = a(t) G(K, L) \qquad (7.14)$$

Now if the capital–labour ratio is held constant, by virtue of constant returns, G must grow at the same rate as L (and K), so that output per head must grow at the same rate as $a(t)$; $\dot{a}/a$ is therefore the Hicks rate of progress. But if the production function is Cobb–Douglas, (7.14) must have the particular form

$$Y = a(t)K^\alpha L^{1-\alpha}$$

which may be rearranged to give

$$Y = K^\alpha [b(t)L]^{1-\alpha}$$

where

$$b(t) \equiv a(t)^{\frac{1}{1-\alpha}},$$

which shows that technical progress may also be considered to be purely labour-augmenting or Harrod-neutral. The Harrod rate of progress may be seen to be

$$\frac{\dot{b}}{b} = \left(\frac{1}{1 - \alpha} \right) \frac{\dot{a}}{a}$$

This expression corresponds with the more general (7.6).

We thus see that if the Hicks notion of neutrality is preferred to the Harrod notion, an elasticity of substitution of unity has to be assumed for steady growth to be possible.[9] This course was adopted by Swan (1956) and Meade (1962, esp. chs 4, 6); and Solow (1956, pp. 182–3) also took a Cobb–Douglas function with Hicks-neutrality. The more general model of steady growth, however, is provided by (7.10).

7.6   Embodied technical progress at an exogenous rate: vintage models

Technical progress of the kind we have been considering consists of advances in knowledge which are infused into the productive system independently of the introduction of new units of the factors. Although this may be a fair representation of how technological change proceeds in some cases, such as through improvement in the organisation of work (resulting perhaps from time-and-motion study), it is obvious that innovation is commonly – probably more commonly – effected through new kinds of factors, particularly new kinds of capital equipment, which are more productive than the old. The implication is that technical progress cannot be assumed to raise the productivity of capital equipment already in use in the same way as it raises the productivity of equipment installed in one period in relation to that of equipment installed earlier. In fact it may not be too unrealistic to assume that once equipment is installed, advances in knowledge have only a minor 'disembodied' effect on its productivity, or even no effect at all, so that technological change is wholly 'embodied' in new capital. The introduction of new capital – gross investment – is then identified as the necessary vehicle of technical progress; and each piece of equipment unalterably embodies the stock of knowledge of its date of construction or 'vintage'.[10]

Three main kinds of 'vintage-capital' models have been considered, differing in the assumptions adopted about factor substitutability. All we shall do here is describe these alternative assumptions, and provide a brief account of some of the results obtained. The cursoriness of this treatment does not reflect a judgement about the relative importance of the idea of embodiment,[11] and advanced students will need to explore it further. They may be encouraged to do so by Hicks's (1974, p. 25) suggested amendment of what Kuznets identifies as the 'epochal innovation' of modern economic growth (see section 7.1): ' "Science-based technology" certainly, but not just that; technology which needs for its application embodiment in physical equipment.'

In the first type of model, labelled *'putty-putty'* (after Phelps, 1963), there is assumed to be smooth substitutability between capital and labour both before capital has been installed (*ex ante*, in the terminology of Johansen (1959)) and afterwards (*ex post*). Capital is malleable - like putty - both before and after its construction. The output from machines of vintage v surviving at time t, $Q_v(t)$, may then be described by a continuous production function.

$$Q_v(t) = F[K_v(t), L_v(t), v] \; ; \quad t > v \qquad (7.15)$$

where $K_v(t)$ represents the number of units of capital[12] of vintage v extant at time t, and $L_v(t)$ is the labour employed on them. The term v represents technical progress; it shows that it is the date of manufacture of the equipment, rather than the current time t, that determines productivity. If we take (7.15) to be a Cobb–Douglas function, and the rate of labour augmentation to be a constant, τ, then we have

$$Q_v(t) = K_v(t)^\alpha [e^{\tau v} L_v(t)]^{1-\alpha} \qquad (7.16)$$

The significance of the Cobb–Douglas assumption is that it enables technical progress to be both labour-augmenting, so that steady growth is possible, and at the same time capital-augmenting or *Solow-neutral*.[13] Solow-neutrality means that it is possible to derive a scalar measure of aggregate capital, in efficiency units, by adding up the number of units of capital of different vintage, weighted according to their vintage (and hence their efficiency); an aggregate production function may then be written in terms of labour and this capital aggregate. This was shown by Solow (1959). As time passes beyond v and more productive equipment is introduced, the real wage - equal to the marginal product of labour working on machines of each vintage under competitive conditions - increases, and the labour employed on vintage v machines declines continuously, the labour released being redeployed on the new equipment. Except for declining physical efficiency, however, the machines of vintage v are never discarded, owing to their malleability.

In the second kind of model, labelled *'putty-clay'*, substitutability is allowed only *ex ante*: capital is like putty prior to installation, but afterwards it is like clay. *Ex ante*, therefore, there is a smooth production function

$$Q_v(v) = K_v(v)^\alpha [e^{\tau v} L_v(v)]^{1-\alpha} \tag{7.17}$$

(if we take the Cobb–Douglas form with a constant rate τ of labour augmentation); but *ex post*, for $t \geqslant v$, excluding physical depreciation, K_v, L_v and Q_v are fixed until the equipment of the vintage is discarded on account of *obsolescence*. With the passage of time beyond v the real wage will be bid up by the owners of the newer and more efficient capital, and so will eventually, at some time $t = v + T$, rise to equality with ·the average productivity of labour on the machines of vintage v. At that point the quasi-rents of machines of this vintage fall to zero, so that they are on the margin of being scrapped. That is, we have then that

$$\frac{Q_v}{L_v} = w(v + T) \tag{7.18}$$

where w is the real wage. To examine the determination of T, we can assume steady growth equilibrium, so that w grows at the constant rate τ of labour augmentation:

$$w(v + T) = w(v)e^{\tau T} \tag{7.19}$$

From (7.18) and (7.19) we see that:

$$T = \frac{1}{\tau} \log \left(\frac{Q_v}{w(v)L_v} \right) \tag{7.20}$$

so that the length of life T of capital equipment depends inversely both on the rate of growth τ of the real wage and on the share of wage costs in the output of the machines when new. Under competitive conditions, then, the wage is always equal to the average productivity of labour working on the equipment which is on the margin of being scrapped – the *'extensive'* margin, to be distinguished from the 'intensive' margin of factor substitution (Hahn and Matthews, 1964, p. 62). The more recent vintages will have lower labour costs per unit of output, and so will be earning positive quasi-rents. In turn these will be eaten away with the passage of time and the introduction of newer machines. The quasi-rents of each vintage are thus a temporary phenomenon. because of the reproducibility of capital; in other respects they are similar to the Ricardian rents earned by (non-reproducible) intra-marginal land.

Third, in *'clay–clay'* models, it is assumed that there are fixed co-efficients *ex ante* as well as *ex post*, so that capital is like clay both before and after installation. Again taking a constant rate τ of labour augmentation, the production function for equipment of vintage v has the form:

$$Q_v(t) = \frac{K_v(t)}{a} = \frac{L_v(t)}{b_o e^{-\tau v}} \ ; \quad t \geqslant v \qquad (7.21)$$

As with 'putty–clay', the introduction of equipment embodying new advances means that the wage will rise and eventually completely eat away the quasi-rents of older machines; and again competition implies that the wage will always equal the average productivity of labour at the extensive margin.

Under these three kinds of assumption the main concern has been with the usual properties of *steady-state solutions*, which may now need to be defined without reference to an aggregate capital stock or capital–output ratio as solutions which have a constant growth rate of output and a constant propensity to save. It will not be surprising that if suitable assumptions are adopted about labour-force growth, the constancy and neutrality of technical progress, saving and expectations (the last becoming important with non-malleability), it is not difficult to characterise steady growth. (Allen (1967, ch. 15), for example, does so for all three kinds of model.) Output again grows at the sum of the rates of labour-force growth and labour augmentation; and this natural growth rate is again independent of saving. With 'putty–putty', it is quite easy, with a Cobb–Douglas production function, to establish results (including stability) similar to those of disembodied-progress models; but there has been little joy from functions of other forms. For 'clay–clay', Solow *et al.* (1966) have shown how the variable life T of capital adds a new flexibility to the Harrod–Domar model, so that unless the labour force in efficiency units is growing so fast and the saving rate is so small that everyone cannot be employed even if T becomes infinite, there exists a steady state with T taking a constant value dependent on the model's parameters. They also established stability (in the sense, of course, of equilibrium dynamics) on the assumption of correct expectations. Thus following a rise in the propensity to save, their system is restored to steady-growth equilibrium by way of a decline in T. It is the 'putty-clay' case which has proved the most intracttable; Bliss (1968) departed from the assumption of an *ex ante* Cobb–Douglas production function and derived comparative-dynamics results, but non-steady-state behaviour has yet to be cracked.

7.7   The importance of technical progress: accounting for growth

In 7.1 we quoted Kuznets's claim that technical progress has been 'the major source' of modern economic growth, the implication being that it has been a more important source than the growth of factor inputs. It seems that prior to the 1950s and certainly before the Second World War, this view was far from widely held. Thus Fabricant (1974) relates how Cobb and Douglas (1928), in their pioneering work on the production function which bears their name, found that almost the whole of the growth of output in U.S. manufacturing between 1899 and 1922 could be explained by the growth of capital and labour inputs. It is surprising, to say the least, that practically the first empirical estimate of technical progress 'could say that it was negligible in a country and industry and period when technological and other change was widely recognised as advancing rapidly and greatly transforming the economy'. Nevertheless, the results were 'widely accepted' so that they 'found their way into textbooks'. (Fabricant, 1974, p. 240). Thus Hicks (1974, p. 21) writes that 'One has only to go back to the 1930s to find a time when the importance of technical progress did not seem at all obvious. Few economists would then have given it the priority which now seems so natural.'

Although the results obtained by Cobb and Douglas had already been challenged and contradicted in the 1940s and early 1950s, it was probably the work of Solow (1957) which caused the tide to turn. To see how he obtained his results we return to (7.3) and (7.5), which we derived from (7.1), the constant-returns production function with exogenous and disembodied technical progress. With π representing the capital-elasticity of output (the competitive share of profits), they may be rewritten:

$$\frac{\dot{Y}}{Y} = \pi \frac{\dot{K}}{K} + (1 - \pi) \frac{\dot{L}}{L} + \frac{F_t}{F} \qquad (7.22)$$

$$\frac{\dot{y}}{y} = \pi \frac{\dot{k}}{k} + \frac{F_t}{F} \tag{7.23}$$

The latter expression shows that (7.1), with constant returns, implies that the instantaneous growth rate of labour productivity comprises two mutually distinct and independent components: one being the Hicks rate of progress, and the other being due to capital-deepening. And the expressions suggest a remarkably simple way of separating the two components empirically, on discrete (e.g. annual) data. Data are available for the growth of real output and capital per head, and if we believe that factors are paid their marginal products, π is capital's share in income, for which we also have data. The only unknown is the rate of technical progress, which can thus be calculated; hence the relative contributions of technical progress and capital-deepening to productivity growth can be estimated, apparently without the need for any assumptions about the specific form of F.

In fact, however, some assumption is needed. The reason is that the actual year-to-year movements in π reflect (on the neo-classical theory of distribution) the operation of both capital-deepening, via the elasticity of substitution, and the Hicks bias or neutrality of technical progress. To provide an estimate of the contribution of capital-deepening to productivity growth – of productivity growth as it would have been without technological change – the π to be used in the application of (7.23) should reflect deepening only, and be independent of bias. Estimates of π which satisfy this criterion can be derived from the data only by means of some assumption about either the elasticity of substitution or the factor-saving characteristics of technical progress. Two simple alternatives suggest themselves. One is to calculate the rate of technical progress in each year using that year's actual π; this amounts to assuming that technical progress was Hicks-neutral so that all the variation in π was due to capital-deepening (with an elasticity of substitution different from unity). The other is to use the same π, from some base year, throughout; this amounts to assuming an elasticity of substitution of unity, so that the observed variation of π may be put down to Hicks bias, and ignored. (By this latter alternative the estimated rate of technical progress will obviously be sensitive to the choice of base year.)

Solow assumed Hicks-neutrality (on the basis of some evidence), and calculated the Hicks rate of progress – now the rate of factor augmentation, i.e. $\dot{a}/a$ in (7.14) – for the U.S. private non-farm sector for every year between 1909 and 1949. He found an average rate of progress of 1.5 per cent per annum. But the most remarkable aspect of his results was reported as follows: 'Gross output per man-year doubled over the interval (1909–49), with 87½% of the increase attributable to technical change and the remaining 12½% to increased use of capital' (Solow, 1957, p. 418).

Essentially the same calculation has since been performed for other periods and countries, with similar results – implying the overriding importance of progress – in nearly all cases. In fact Abramovitz (1956) had already published estimates, based on a similar method (but using a base year π) suggesting that between 60 and 85 per cent (depending on the base year taken) of the growth of U.S. national income per head of population between 1869–78 and 1944–53 was to be accounted for other than by the growth of labour and capital inputs per head. Kuznets (1966, p. 81) has replicated Abramovitz's calculation for a number of countries over various long periods, reaching the conclusion that 'while the results would clearly vary among individual countries, the inescapable conclusion is that the direct contribution of man-hours and capital-accumulation would hardly account for more than a tenth of the rate of growth in per capita product – and probably less'. It is this finding which underlies his claim for the relative importance of advancing technology to modern economic growth. Exceptions to the general rule that the greater part of the growth of output per head cannot, on the above method, be accounted for by the growth of physical inputs per head seem few and far between.[14]

The superficial explanation for the general applicability of Solow's result lies simply in the fact that in most of the countries and in most of the periods examined the growth rate of output is at least as large as the growth rate of the capital stock (so that the proportionate contribution of capital-deepening to productivity growth is no larger than π), while π, the share of income accruing to capital, is generally less than 30 per cent.[15] But how are the results to be interpreted, and what is their significance? We need briefly to consider two aspects of the analysis, and the subsequent research associated with them which has aimed, in effect, to clarify the answers to these questions.

First, from the point of view of policy, the most interesting implication of the analysis lies not so much in its interpretation of history, as in its prediction that the impact of increased saving and investment on the growth rate, even in the short run, will be relatively small. This may be seen by applying plausible parameter values to (7.22). Suppose the propensity to save is doubled from, say, 0.1 (i.e. 10 per cent) to 0.2, and assume an output-capital ratio of 0.3 (on annual data): the growth rate of K will then rise from 0.03 (i.e. 3 per cent per annum) to 0.06. If π is 0.25, the contribution of capital growth to output growth will thus rise from 0.0075 to 0.0150, so that the growth rate of Y will rise by 0.0075, or by less than one percentage point per annum. And that is in response to a doubling of the saving (or investment) ratio, and before taking any account of the subsequent effect of diminishing returns through the output-capital ratio on the growth rate of K.[16] The analysis of Solow and others thus 'produced a wave of investment pessimism' (Phelps, 1963, p. 550), a lack of confidence in the potential effectiveness of encouragement to investment as a policy for raising growth rates.

But of course the whole of this analysis rested on the assumption of disembodied technical progress, and the first response to the results which the analysis threw up was the *embodiment hypothesis* described in the previous section. In fact Solow (1959) was taking his cue from his previous 1957 paper, for in the latter he qualified the results described above by recognising that 'much, perhaps nearly all, innovation must be embodied in new plant and equipment to be realised at all' (Solow, 1957, pp. 411-12), so that the 'rate of technical progress' estimated by his method was bound to be dependent on the actual rate of capital accumulation. Furthermore, embodiment implies that an increase in the rate of investment will have a greater impact on the growth rate in the short run through its effect of reducing the average age of the capital stock. The embodiment hypothesis thus entails a 'new view of investment' as a variable on which policy may act to raise growth rates.[17]

The second aspect of the analysis concerns the composition of the estimated rate of technical progress. Once it is recognised that the real world does not match the constant-returns, one-good, homogeneous-factors conception of theory, it is apparent that the productivity growth which is not accounted for by the growth of physical capital per head must reflect a host of diverse influences, and that the question of its composition is worthy of investigation. Thus the large relative importance of technical progress as measured by Solow *et al.* could 'be taken to be some sort of *measure of our ignorance* about the causes of economic growth' (Abramovitz, 1956, p. 328); and it 'ought to be analysed further into such components as improvements in the skill and quality of the labour force, returns to investment in research and education, improvements in technique within industries, and changes in the industrial composition of input and output, etc.' (Solow, 1959, p. 90). The response was a vast research effort aimed at cutting back to the core the *residual* element of the growth of output which could not be accounted for by the measurable growth of inputs, now widely defined to embrace quality as well as quantity, changes in inter-sectoral distribution, economies of scale, etc. These exercises in *growth accounting* are based (at least implicitly) on much more complex production functions than the constant-returns, two-homogeneous-factors function underlying Solow's work; they also rely substantially on guess-work based on varying amounts of information. But the methodology is essentially the same, being based on a belief that relative factor prices provide a fair indication of relative marginal products, so that a share-weighted sum of growth rates of inputs – often called a *Divisia index*[18] – will provide an estimate of the contribution of inputs to output growth, with the individual components in the sum showing the individual contributions of the respective inputs.

Denison (1962) made the first report of thorough-going growth accountancy. Denison found that after taking account of such contributors as the improvement in the quality of the labour force (due mainly to more education, shorter working hours and changes in composition by age and sex), economies of scale and improvements in allocative efficiency, only 20 per cent of the growth of U.S. national income between 1929 and 1957 remained 'unexplained', as a 'residual' to be put down to 'advances in knowledge' not accounted for among the measured inputs. Similar methods were used by Denison (1967) to explain the sources of differences in growth rates among eight European countries and the United States between 1950 and 1962. A third study, Denison (1974) takes an even more detailed look at the United States between 1929 and 1969.

Although the growth accountants have succeeded in reducing the residual far below Solow's $87\frac{1}{2}$ per cent,[19] their results are clearly *not* to be interpreted as showing that technical progress is not so great a contributor to economic growth, since much of what they have taken out of the residual may be considered to comprise aspects of, or to be dependent on, the advancement of knowledge. In fact Denison (1962a, p. 374) considers that 'the main object' of his work 'has been to divide up the contribution to growth of what has been vaguely termed technological progress'.

The value and validity of growth accountancy as a method of explaining empirical growth, or of measuring the relative importance of technical progress, or of obtaining prescriptions for growth policy, are matters of dispute. Quite apart from the details of the way in which the method should be correctly applied, the usefulness of the whole approach may be questioned, even from a neo-classical viewpoint (see, for example, Mirrlees, 1973, pp. xix–xx; Nelson, 1973). Perhaps the most fundamental doubt is whether it is meaningful or valid, or positively misleading, to ignore the complementarities and interactions among the sources of growth, and so to consider the growth rate as a simple sum of implicitly independent sources. To neo-Keynesian economists, who, at a minimum, reject the neo-classical theory of distribution, growth accountancy is anathema. Kaldor has been its most strident critic, and we shall consider his objections to the neo-classical account of technical progress in Chapter 9.

Further reading

Nadiri (1970) and Kennedy and Thirlwall (1972, part I) are comprehensive surveys of the literature on the measurement of technical progress. They both discuss the problems which arise in the econometric estimation of the parameters of production functions – problems which we have not touched on. Fabricant (1974) is a shorter and more informal survey of a similar area. Allen (1967, ch. 15) is an excellent introduction to *vintage models*, and Wan (1971, ch. 5) provides a fairly comprehensive textbook treatment with references. For a lucid account of the 'clay–clay' model, with very little mathematics, see Solow (1970, ch. 3). Salter (1966) is one of the earliest studies of embodiment, and one of the most worth-while readings in the whole area of technical progress. On *growth accounting* accessible summaries of Denison's method and results are provided in Denison (1962a; 1968); readers wishing to delve below the surface will need to refer to the debate between Jorgenson and Griliches, and Denison, which is brought together in Jorgenson *et al.* (1972).

8
Technical Progress – Theories of Bias and Neutrality

8.1 Introduction

In this chapter we consider how the hypothesis that technical progress is Harrod-neutral or purely labour-augmenting may be justified, so that it may become an endogenous rather than an exogenous feature of the neo-classical explanation of steady growth. Three approaches to a theory of Harrod-neutrality will be examined.[1] All are based on the view that producers can influence the factor-saving characteristics of technical progress, and that they will do so by allocating their research and development (R & D) effort among alternative projects in a cost-minimising way. In all these models, therefore, the kinds of advances attained in applied science and productive techniques (and perhaps even the kinds of advances occurring in pure science as a result or by-product of inventive or productive activity) are subject to economic influences.

8.2 The Hicks–Ahmad theory of induced Hicks-bias

The first theory is based on an analysis associated with Hicks (1963, pp. 121-7). As a preliminary we examine the occurrence of technical progress from the point of view of a firm operating under perfect competition, by means of the usual isoquant diagram.

On the assumption that the firm's production function allows continuous substitution between K and L, and possesses the other usual properties – including, in particular, constant returns – it may be represented, at any time t, by the unit-product isoquant $I(t)$ in Figure 8.1. The firm minimises costs by choosing the capital–labour ratio

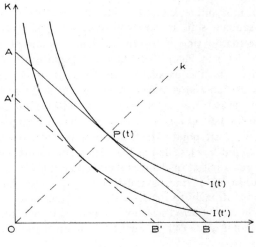

Fig. 8.1

shown by the slope of the ray *Ok* which passes through the point *P(t)*, where *I(t)* is tangent to the isocost line *AB*, whose slope is numerically equal to the wage-rental ratio determined in the competitive factor markets. Now, with the passage of time the firm's choice of technique will be subject to two influences: inward shifts of the isoquant with technical progress; and rotations of the isocost line if relative factor prices change.

The shift of the isoquant can be described by three of its characteristics (Salter, 1966, ch. 3). The first is the rate at which it shifts inwards with time. This may be measured by the rate of reduction of unit costs at an unchanged factor-price ratio, which may be regarded as the analogue for the firm of the Hicks rate of technical progress, defined in section 7.3 for the economy as a whole. Second, as the isoquant shifts inwards its curvature may alter, i.e. the responsiveness of the cost-minimising capital-labour ratio to changes in relative factor prices – the elasticity of substitution, σ – may change. If, for example, technical progress is persistently specific to one technique – say the technique originally adopted – or to a small range of techniques, with only minor spillover effects to other techniques, then σ will progressively decline, and the production function will approach a fixed-coefficients form. The empirical importance of such 'localised' progress has been stressed by Atkinson and Stiglitz (1969). The final characteristic, and the one in which we are most interested in this chapter, concerns the question of whether the isoquant shift is biased towards saving one factor or the other. Suppose that by time $t' > t$, the isoquant has shifted to the position shown by $I(t')$ in Figure 8.1. At the original wage–rental ratio, shown by $A'B'$, which is parallel to AB, the cost-minimising capital–labour ratio is the same as at time t. Assuming this to be generally true – so that at any given wage–rental ratio the optimal capital–labour ratio is the same on $I(t')$ as on $I(t)$ – we may say that the isoquant shift is Hicks-neutral. To correspond with this notion of neutrality, a technical improvement would be classified as biased towards capital-saving if the capital–labour ratio fell at unchanged relative factor prices, or as biased towards labour-saving if the capital–labour ratio rose; the isoquant would shift more strongly to the L-axis in the former case, and to the K-axis in the latter.[2] Harrod's notion of neutrality and bias may be adapted in a similar way. Thus in Figure 8.2 the shift from $I(t)$ to $I(t')$

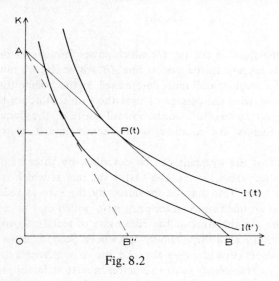

Fig. 8.2

is such that if the rental rate remains constant, so that the isocost line pivots about A, capital per unit of output, v, remains constant: the isoquant shift is Harrod-neutral. If $I(t')$ were tangent to an isocost line through A at a K lower than v, there would be capital-saving bias in Harrod's sense, while if the new tangency were above v, there would be Harrod labour-saving bias.

We now need to consider when, given the factor-saving characteristics of technical progress according to the Hicks classification, there will be Harrod-neutrality. As we have already shown in section 7.5, the link between the two classifications is provided by the elasticity of substitution; and it is easy to show, in terms of the isoquant diagram, how the link works. The argument is essentially the same as that applied previously to the productivity-function diagram. Thus in Figure 8.3 the shift from $I(t)$ to $I(t')$ is both Hicks-neutral (as is shown by the points $P(t)$ and X_1) and Harrod- neutral (as is shown by $P(t)$ and X_2); this diagram is in effect an amalgamation of the previous two. Now since the capital–labour ratio and wage–rental ratio are both the same at X_1 as at $P(t)$, the ratio of capital costs to labour costs – and the share of capital costs in total costs – must be the same at these two points. But, on account of Harrod-neutrality, the share of capital costs in total costs must be the same at X_2 as at $P(t)$; it is therefore the same at X_2 as at X_1, which means that σ must be unity. Similarly, it may easily be shown that there can be Harrod-neutrality: (i) with Hicks capital-saving bias only if $\sigma > 1$; and (ii) with Hicks labour-saving bias only if $\sigma < 1$. And in both these cases σ must differ from unity to an extent exactly sufficient to offset Hicks-bias.

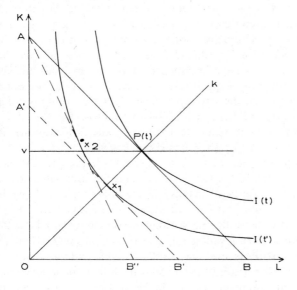

Fig. 8.3

The second kind of change which may occur with the passage of time is a movement in relative factor prices. This will lead the firm to substitute one factor for the other – to move along its isoquant – to an extent dependent on the elasticity of substitution. In particular, if for the economy as a whole the course of capital accumulation, labour-force growth and technical progress is such that the wage–rental ratio is rising through time – which is what is to be observed in practice – the firm will substitute capital for labour.

Thus with the passage of time the path traced out by the firm in its isoquant map may be considered to be determined by the combined influences of the nature of technical progress and movements in relative factor prices.

Now if we are to have a theory of endogenous bias or neutrality, we must clearly allow the firm to choose among different isoquants representing different innovations and exhibiting different factor-saving characteristics. *The essence of the Hicksian theory is then that the isoquant chosen by the firm, and hence the characteristics of technical progress in the economy as a whole, will be determined by the way relative factor prices are changing – more specifically, that there will be a bias towards labour-saving or capital-saving (in the Hicksian sense) according as the wage–rental ratio is rising or falling.* For this result to be established assumptions are needed about the range of innovation possibilities – the alternative isoquants – available to the firm. The task has been completed by Ahmad (1966). He assumes simply that the innovations among which the firm can choose at time t for introduction at time t' (for given expenditure on research) may be described by a series of isoquants, the envelope of which is a continuous *innovation possibility curve* (I.P.C.) which is convex to the origin. The I.P.C. shifts inwards over time at a rate determined by the firm's (given) research expenditure; and it moves inwards Hicks-neutrally.

Thus suppose that I.P.C.(t) in Figure 8.4 represents the range of innovation possibilities which were open to the firm for time t. At the time the choice was faced, relative factor prices were as shown by AB; in consequence the firm selected the position $P(t)$ on I.P.C.(t), which meant the selection of the innovation represented by $I(t)$. Now the firm faces its choice of innovation for time t', the possibilities being shown by I.P.C.(t'). If the isocost line is still AB (which implies that there will have been no factor substitution about $I(t)$), then the innovation represented by the isoquant $I(t'_1)$ will be cost-minimising; and, by the assumption that successive I.P.C.s are Hicks-neutral, the shift from $I(t)$

to $I(t'_1)$ must be Hicks-neutral. But if the wage–rental ratio has risen so that AD is the operative isocost line (which implies that the firm will meanwhile have substituted capital for labour by moving along $I(t)$), then it is the innovation represented by $I(t'_2)$ which will be chosen; and the movement from $I(t)$ to $I(t'_2)$ is labour-saving. In fact *the convexity of the I.P.C. and the Hicks-neutrality of its movement ensure that technical progress will be Hicks labour-saving, neutral, or capital-saving, according as the wage–rental ratio rises, remains constant, or falls.*

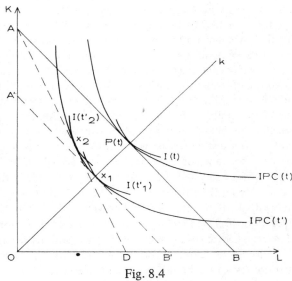

Fig. 8.4

Thus Hicks's theory is established: 'A change in the relative prices of the factors of production is itself a spur to invention, and to invention of a particular kind – directed to economising the use of a factor which has become relatively expensive' (Hicks, 1963, p. 124). In particular, with a secularly rising wage–rental ratio – the case which has most empirical relevance and in which Hicks was particularly interested – technical progress will tend to be biased towards labour-saving.

The Hicks–Ahmad analysis has a number of fairly obvious weaknesses, to which we shall turn shortly. But first, we need to consider an objection raised by Salter (1966, p. 43): he argued (in an oft-quoted passage) that the analysis was fundamentally invalid, because 'The entrepreneur is interested in reducing costs in total, not particular costs such as labour costs or capital costs. When labour costs rise any advance that reduces total costs is welcome, and whether this is achieved by saving labour or capital is irrelevant.' (The same view was expressed in similar terms by Fellner (1961).) The first sentence of this passage does not conflict with the Hicksian theory – that theory is based on the supposition that the firm 'is interested in reducing costs in total'. But whereas the Hicksian theory predicts that the behaviour of the cost-minimising firm will be such that a rise (fall) in the wage–rental ratio will induce a labour-saving (capital-saving) bias, Salter seems to argue not so much that the bias of technical progress is 'given' to the firm, but that the firm will be indifferent, whatever the factor-price ratio, among innovations with differing biases. The validity of Salter's argument is not self-evident, at least from the above passage; the Hicksian theory is based on the same assumptions about behaviour as the theory of factor substitution, which Salter certainly does not reject. But perhaps it is here, in the similarity between factor substitution and Hicksian induced bias, that his objection is founded. A distinction between the two must rest upon a distinction between movements along a production function (or isoquant) of a particular date, and shifts in it over time. Now in his own analysis Salter had chosen to include in the production function facing the firm at any one time all techniques allowed by the current stock of basic scientific knowledge, including all such techniques yet to be designed and developed. Thus technical progress is treated as comprising advances in pure science only; and the reverse side of the same coin is that Salter (1966, p. 16) regards 'the process of factor substitution as a very broad one, a part of a generalised decision spread over many persons that begins as soon as alternative lines of development are compared on the basis of cost'. Thus the shift over time of Salter's (1966, p. 15) production function 'is purely technically determined and is free from the prior influence of factor prices'. This seems to be the crux of the matter; it seems that the induced bias of Hicks and Ahmad is subsumed in the factor substitution of Salter, and that Ahmad's I.P.C.s are Salter's isoquants. Salter's rejection of Hicksian (or any other) endogenous bias then seems to correspond with Ahmad's assumption that his I.P.C.s move Hicks-neutrally. Apart from semantics, then, induced bias is not excluded from Salter's theory. What is excluded are Ahmad's isoquants, showing post-invention substitution possibilities; but then Salter was erecting a 'putty–clay' vintage model. If this interpretation is correct, Salter's objection may be put to one side, except that it does have the value of reminding us that the distinction between bias and substitution cannot be clear cut.[3] (Fellner (1966; 1967) later clarified his acceptance of the Hicksian position; see Ahmad (1967).)

But while the Hicks–Ahmad analysis does not seem invalid in the fundamental sense suggested by Salter, some of its assumptions are certainly questionable. First, although it is not unreasonable that a theory of endogenous bias should require an hypothesis that at some fundamental level the advance of knowledge is purely technically determined, immune from economic influences, and therefore neutral in some sense in its factor-saving characteristics, Ahmad's assumption that his I.P.C.s shift Hicks-neutrally is based on weak foundations. In particular, it requires that successive I.P.C.s are independent of the innovations previously selected: that the I.P.C. for any period t' is independent of the innovation chosen from the I.P.C. of period t. If, as seems more likely, current innovation possibilities are dependent on innovations adopted previously, no general statement can be made about the relationship among successive I.P.C.s without knowledge of the course of factor prices. We shall return to this question below. Second, it may be considered implausible that producers select innovations purely on the basis of current factor prices without regard to expectations, particularly in the context of a secular upward trend in the wage–rental ratio. This criticism has been made by Atkinson and Stiglitz (1969) – and Fellner (1961) suggested that firms might extrapolate the past trend of factor prices when selecting innovations; but this does not of course invalidate the long-run implications of the Hicksian theory. Third, the theory (like the others to be considered in this chapter) ignores uncertainty, in the sense that it assumes that firms know in which direction to push inventive activity in order to obtain any desired bias.

But the greatest drawback of the Hicksian approach from our point of view is that *it does not directly provide a theory of Harrod-neutrality*, which is what we are seeking. Hicks was not concerned to provide such a theory; he was concerned, rather, to explain his observation that technical progress was predominantly labour-saving. His theory provides such an explanation, given a secularly rising wage–rental ratio; but it provides a theory of Harrod-neutrality only if there are grounds for presuming not only that the elasticity of substitution, σ (described by the individual isoquants), is below unity but also that it falls short of unity to an extent just sufficient to offset the degree of bias (dependent on the curvature of the I.P.C.s).[4] There can, of course, be no such presumption, though there are various theoretical and empirical considerations which may lead one to expect σ to lie within some more or less narrow range.[5].

The Hicksian theory does, however, provide a background to the more recent search for a direct explanation of Harrod-neutrality.

8.3 The Kennedy theory of Harrod-neutrality

The approach introduced by Kennedy (1964) is distinguished by the fact that a production function does not form an explicit part of it. The possibilities opened up by technical progress are described not by a shifting production function or shifting isoquant but by a relationship showing a trade-off between increases in average labour productivity on the one hand, and increases in average capital productivity on the

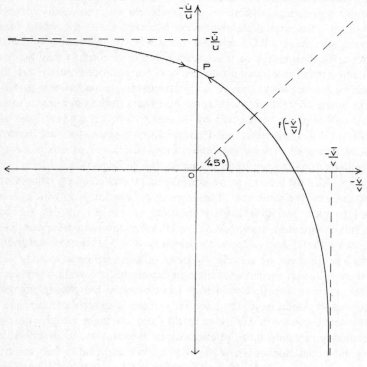

Fig. 8.5

other. This if u and v are labour and capital requirements respectively per unit of output, the options open to the firm are represented by an *innovation possibility function* (I.P.F.) of the form:

$$- \frac{\dot{u}}{u} = f(- \frac{\dot{v}}{v}) \qquad (8.1)$$

where f', $f'' < 0$; $f(0) > 0$; $- \dot{v}/v < \bar{\dot{v}}/v$, $- \dot{u}/u < - \bar{\dot{u}}/u$. Such a relationship is shown in Figure 8.5. Its first derivative is negative because it is a trade-off: more labour-saving can be attained only at the expense of less capital-saving. The second derivative is negative (i.e. the curve is concave to the origin) on the assumption that to obtain equal successive increments of saving in one factor, ever-increasing amounts of saving in the other factor have to be sacrificed. The third restriction ensures that the function exists in the first quadrant; but it is not confined to the first quadrant – negative rates of saving are allowed for each factor individually. The fourth restriction specifies upper bounds (each less than unity) to $- \dot{u}/u$ and $- \dot{v}/v$.

Kennedy's (1966, p. 442) hope was that his I.P.F. 'might be able, so to speak, to swallow up the traditional production function and replace it altogether', so that, in particular, what we have seen to be the nebulous distinction between substitution and induced bias might be avoided. However, since the model assumes that prices are formed under perfect competition and that the factor requirements per unit of output are invariant to scale, the assumption of constant returns, at least, must implicitly be present, as Kennedy (1964, p. 542) in fact appreciated. It therefore seems valid and worth while to enquire how the description of possibilities provided by Kennedy's I.P.F. differs from that provided by Ahmad's shifting I.P.C.

First, it will be noted that Kennedy's I.P.F. entails the assumption that the 'frontier' of proportionate rates of factor-saving is independent of the firm's initial position; otherwise the relationship between $- \dot{u}/u$ and $- \dot{v}/v$ would depend on u and v, and then the analysis might lead to conclusions significantly different from Kennedy's (Ahmad, 1966, pp. 351–3). The assumption is analogous to Ahmad's assumption that each I.P.C. is independent of the starting-point on the previous I.P.C. But it is not the same; and in fact it may be shown that the movement of Ahmad's I.P.C.s can be described by Kennedy's I.P.F. only if each I.P.C. has an elasticity of substitution of unity. That is, the I.P.C.s must be like the isoquants of a Cobb–Douglas production function; this is a necessary consequence of imposing the properties of Kennedy's I.P.F. on Ahmad's I.P.C.s (Ahmad, 1966, pp. 353-7). No variation in the ratio of labour costs to capital costs is then possible; this result is in clear conflict with Kennedy's theory, since the variability of this ratio (i.e. of distributive shares) is, as we shall see, essential to it.

But *second*, Kennedy rejects Ahmad's assumption that each I.P.C. is independent of the innovation selected previously. Kennedy (1967, p. 960) considers 'that the innovation possibilities open to one are relative to one's starting position; and that the innovation possibilities of tomorrow will be influenced by the innovations of today'. This view is obviously inconsistent with Ahmad's assumption. (It may also be argued to be inconsistent with Kennedy's own assumption that his I.P.F. is independent of u and v; but Kennedy does not regard it so.) Kennedy thus considers that technical progress is such that, in Ahmad's terms, there is a set of I.P.C.s for 'tomorrow', one corresponding to each point on the I.P.C. of 'today'. This means that Ahmad's Cobb–Douglas result does not hold, so that Kennedy's function seems safe.

But *third*, allowing for this, it may be shown that if factor substitution is allowed between innovations so that the firm's starting position may be at a point on an isoquant off its I.P.C., the innovation possibilities represented by the next I.P.C. cannot be described by Kennedy's I.P.F. (Ahmad, 1967a). It follows that factor substitution and Kennedy's I.P.F. cannot survive together; the only allowable starting positions for the firm are those lying on an I.P.C., and the I.P.F. can only describe the possibilities thrown up by technical progress.

It therefore seems that Kennedy's function does not live up to the hopes he initially had for it as a substitute for the production function. But although it now seems a less general and powerful tool than was originally thought, his analysis remains of interest because of the remarkably simple explanation of Harrod-neutrality which it provides.

Assume for simplicity that there is only one good. Then for any firm the unit cost of production in terms of the good is[6]

$$c = wu + rv \tag{8.2}$$

where w is the wage, and r is the rental rate of capital or the rate of interest; we assume the latter to be constant. Thus the proportional rate of reduction of unit costs is

$$-\hat{c} = \frac{wu}{c}(-\hat{u}) + \frac{wu}{c}(-\hat{w}) + \frac{rv}{c}(-\hat{v}) \tag{8.3}$$

where $- \hat{c} \equiv - \dot{c}/c$, etc. Now assume that the firm selects the combination of $- \hat{u}$ and $- \hat{v}$ allowed by its I.P.F. which maximises $- \hat{c}$. Substituting (8.1) into (8.3), we obtain

$$- \hat{c} = \left(\frac{wu}{c} \right) f(- \hat{v}) + \frac{wu}{c} (- \hat{w}) + \frac{rv}{c} (- \hat{v}) \qquad (8.4)$$

Therefore

$$\frac{d(- \hat{c})}{d(- \hat{v})} = \frac{wu}{c} f'(- \hat{v}) + \frac{rv}{c} = 0 \text{ when } f'(- \hat{v}) = - \frac{rv}{wu} \qquad (8.5)$$

The concavity of f ensures that (8.5) identifies the unique point on the I.P.F. where $-\hat{c}$ is maximised; at this point the slope of the I.P.F. is numerically equal to the ratio of capital costs to labour costs. Thus *in the short run, given the firm's capital–labour ratio v/u and the market-determined wage–rental ratio w/r, the cost-minimising innovation is determined by the ratio of capital costs to labour costs.* The greater is the relative importance of capital costs, the greater is the optimal slope of the I.P.F.; and therefore, given the curve's concavity, the more capital-saving will be the innovation chosen.

But for the long run this is not the end of the story, since the innovation chosen will itself affect the cost ratio, and thus feed back on the next choice of innovation. Thus if the initial innovation entails a change in v/u which increases the cost ratio, the next innovation will be more capital-saving: the firm will move to the south-east along its I.P.F. Conversely, if the initial innovation leads to a fall in the cost ratio, the firm will move along the curve to the north-west. Clearly, then, a point on the I.P.F. can represent a long-run equilibrium only if the factor-saving characteristics which it describes leave the cost-ratio unchanged. Now it may seem from (8.5) that the precise location of the long-run equilibrium must depend on the rate of growth of w; since r is assumed constant, the constancy of the cost ratio requires v/u to be rising at the same rate as w. If all we know is that w is rising, then all this tells us is that the long-run equilibrium must lie above the 45° line in Figure 8.5. But in fact we can go further. In competitive equilibrium, c must be unity, so that the ratio of capital costs to labour costs is $rv/(1 - rv)$, and since r is constant the cost ratio is constant if, and only if, v is constant. There is thus a unique long-run equilibrium at the point P in Figure 8.5 where $- \dot{v}/v$ is zero, i.e. where the capital–output ratio is constant and technical progress is Harrod-neutral. At points on the

I.P.F. to the south-east of P, innovations are such that v and the cost ratio are falling; at points to the north-west, v and the cost ratio are rising. Thus, apart from the possibility of explosive cobweb-like oscillations about P, the long-run equilibrium is stable.

In the long-run equilibrium the ratio of capital costs to labour costs is equal to the slope of the I.P.F. at P. Thus *whereas in the short run in Kennedy's theory the characteristics of innovation are determined by the cost ratio, in the long run the causality is reversed, in the sense that the cost ratio for the firm, and hence the distribution of income between wages and profits for the economy as a whole, is then determined by the shape of the I.P.F.* We therefore see that Kennedy's model provides not only a theory of Harrod-neutrality but also – for the long run – 'a theory of distribution in its own right' (Kennedy, 1964, p. 547).

The ease with which Kennedy's model predicts Harrod-neutrality as the long-run equilibrium seems remarkable.[7] The contrast with the Hicks–Ahmad theory in this respect is striking: the need for any restriction corresponding to the requirement that the elasticity of substitution takes a specific value is, at least apparently, absent. And the assumptions behind Kennedy's result are simple, and they do not seem unusually implausible. If (bearing in mind Ahmad's critique) the I.P.F. is accepted as a description of the possibilities opened up by technical progress, and if it is accepted as plausible that firms will seek to maximise the rate of reduction of unit costs, then the relative proportions in which the respective factors are saved will depend not (only) on relative factor prices but rather on the shares of the factors in total cost. The higher is the share of a factor, the keener will producers be to save it; but also, the more of a factor is saved, the more will its share be reduced. There is thus a two-way relationship between the choice of innovation and factor shares which, at least on casual inspection, is stabilising. Thus if the I.P.F. is stable, the system will approach an equilibrium in which factor shares are constant; given a constant interest rate, factor shares are then dependent solely on the shape of the I.P.F., and technical progress is then Harrod-neutral.

But the model is incomplete. First, Kennedy's proof of stability is casual and inconclusive. More important, changes in the capital–labour ratio and factor shares will in fact depend not only on the characteristics of innovation, but also on the rate at which capital is accumulating and the rate at which the labour force is growing, neither of which has an explicit role in the model. The production function has a curious semi-presence, and it needs to be brought more clearly into the picture.

When these defects are remedied in a manner now to be considered, the elasticity of substitution predictably reasserts its influence.

8.4 The neo-classical one-sector model with endogenous Harrod-neutrality

This third approach consists of an integration of Kennedy's I.P.F. into a standard one-good neo-classical model. The result to be described was obtained by Drandakis and Phelps (1966) and Samuelson (1966), though an earlier paper, Samuelson (1965), had also considered the question of combining the I.P.F. with the production function, but in a rather different way.

We assume that technical progress is of the factor-augmenting form defined in section 7.2. Thus with one good and two homogeneous factors the production function may be written:

$$Y = F[a(t)K, b(t)L] \tag{8.6}$$

The I.P.F. now describes the trade-off between capital augmentation and labour augmentation for every firm, and has the same form as the Kennedy function drawn in Figure 8.5. Using $\hat{b}$ to represent $\dot{b}/b$, etc.

$$\hat{b} = \phi(\hat{a}) \tag{8.7}$$

where ϕ', $\phi'' < 0$; $\phi(0) = 0$; $\hat{a} \leqslant \bar{a}$, $\hat{b} \leqslant \bar{b}$. There are constant returns and perfect competition, proportional saving, and constant labour-force growth. The following expressions need no more explanation:

$$w = \frac{\partial Y}{\partial L} = b(t)F_2 \, ; \quad r = \frac{\partial Y}{\partial K} = a(t)F_1 \tag{8.8}$$

$$\dot{K} = S = sY \, ; \quad 0 < s < 1 \tag{8.9}$$

$$L(t) = L(0)e^{\lambda t} \, ; \quad L(0) > 0, \lambda \geqslant 0 \tag{8.10}$$

Now the Hicks rate of technical progress, R, is the growth rate of Y when K and L are constant; it may thus, from (8.6) and (8.8) be written:

$$R \equiv \frac{1}{Y} \frac{\partial Y}{\partial t} = \frac{rK}{Y} \hat{a} + \frac{wL}{Y} \hat{b} = \pi\hat{a} + (1 - \pi)\hat{b} \tag{8.11}$$

where π is the share of profits. Thus R is a share-weighted average of the respective rates of factor augmentation. It is assumed that firms choose the combination of $\hat{a}$ and $\hat{b}$ allowed by the I.P.F. which maximises R; this is exactly analogous to Kennedy's behavioural hypothesis. Substituting (8.7) into (8.11) and differentiating R with respect to $\hat{a}$:

$$\frac{dR}{d\hat{a}} = \pi + (1 - \pi)\phi'(\hat{a}) = 0 \text{ when } \phi'(\hat{a}) = -\frac{\pi}{1 - \pi} \qquad (8.12)$$

This result corresponds to Kennedy's (8.5). Again, the concavity of ϕ ensures that (8.12) identifies the maximum value of R, and again firms choose the innovation represented by the point on the I.P.F. where the slope of the curve is numerically equal to the ratio of profits to wages. The higher is this ratio (i.e. the higher is π), the higher will be the chosen $\hat{a}$, and the lower will be the chosen $\hat{b}$. In fact it may be seen from (8.12) and (8.7) (or from Figure 8.5) that the optimal rates of capital and labour augmentation are continuous functions of π, with the following properties:

$$\left.\begin{array}{l} \dfrac{d\hat{a}}{d\pi} > 0; \ \lim_{\pi \to 0} \hat{a} = -\infty; \ \lim_{\pi \to \infty} \hat{a} = \overline{\overline{a}} \\[3mm] \dfrac{d\hat{b}}{d\pi} < 0; \ \lim_{\pi \to 0} \hat{b} = \overline{\overline{b}}; \ \lim_{\pi \to \infty} \hat{b} = -\infty \end{array}\right\} \qquad (8.13)$$

We now need to reintroduce two familiar concepts – the bias of technical progress and the elasticity of substitution. For bias, we adopt the Hicksian classification; and we measure the degree of labour-saving bias B by the proportional rate of decline of the wage–rental ratio at a constant capital–labour ratio:

$$B \equiv -\frac{\partial}{\partial t} \log \frac{\partial Y/\partial L}{\partial Y/\partial K} \equiv \frac{\partial}{\partial t} \log \frac{\partial Y}{\partial K} - \frac{\partial}{\partial t} \log \frac{\partial Y}{\partial L} \qquad (8.14)$$

Technical progress is biased towards labour-saving, is neutral, or is biased towards capital-saving according as B is positive, zero, or negative.

The elasticity of substitution, σ is defined in the usual way. Drandakis and Phelps (1966) show that B can be expressed in terms of σ and the rates of factor augmentation:

$$B = \frac{(1 - \sigma)}{\sigma} [\hat{b} - \hat{a}] \qquad (8.15)$$

This shows that technical progress which is predominantly labour-augmenting (in the sense that $\hat{b} > \hat{a}$) will be Hicks labour-saving or Hicks capital-saving according as σ is less than or greater than unity. Similarly, technical progress which is predominantly capital-augmenting will be Hicks capital-saving or Hicks labour-saving according as σ is less than or greater than unity. Finally, for Hicks-neutrality, either both factors must be being augmented at the same rate, or σ must be unity.[8]

We now derive an equation showing explicitly *the dependence of changes in distributive shares on the bias of technical progress, the accumulation of capital in relation to labour, and the elasticity of substitution.* From

$$\pi = \frac{K}{Y} \frac{\partial Y}{\partial K}$$

by logarithmic differentiation with respect to time

$$\hat{\pi} \equiv \frac{\dot{\pi}}{\pi} = \frac{\dot{K}}{K} + \frac{d}{dt} \log \frac{\partial Y}{\partial K} - \frac{\dot{Y}}{Y} \qquad (8.16)$$

Now a result, derived by Diamond (1965a), is that

$$\frac{d}{dt} \log \frac{\partial Y}{\partial K} = \frac{\partial}{\partial t} \log \frac{\partial Y}{\partial K} - \frac{(1-\pi)}{\sigma} \left(\frac{\dot{K}}{K} - \frac{\dot{L}}{L} \right) \qquad (8.17)$$

Also, total differentiation of the production function (8.6) with respect to time gives

$$\hat{Y} = \pi\hat{K} + (1-\pi)\hat{L} + \pi\hat{a} + (1-\pi)\hat{b} \qquad (8.18)$$

This differs from (7.3) or (7.22) only in that we now have factor-augmenting progress. It may be seen from either of those previous expressions, or from (8.11), that the last two terms in (8.18) give the Hicks rate of technical progress, R. We may obtain a different expression for R by partial differentiation of the equation

$$Y = K \frac{\partial Y}{\partial K} + L \frac{\partial Y}{\partial L}$$

with respect to time, holding K and L constant:

$$R \equiv \frac{1}{Y} \frac{\partial Y}{\partial t} = \pi \frac{\partial}{\partial t} \log \frac{\partial Y}{\partial K} + (1-\pi) \frac{\partial}{\partial t} \log \frac{\partial Y}{\partial L} \qquad (8.19)$$

This may be substituted into (8.18) to give

$$\hat{Y} = \pi\hat{K} + (1 - \pi)\hat{L} + \pi\frac{\partial}{\partial t}\log\frac{\partial Y}{\partial K} + (1 - \pi)\frac{\partial}{\partial t}\log\frac{\partial Y}{\partial L} \quad (8.20)$$

Then, by substituting (8.17) and (8.20) into (8.16), using the definition of bias (8.14), we obtain

$$\hat{\pi} = (1 - \pi)\left[B - \frac{(1 - \sigma)}{\sigma}\left(\frac{\dot{K}}{K} - \frac{\dot{L}}{L}\right)\right] \quad (8.21)$$

Finally, using (8.15) for B, and the labour-force equation (8.10), we obtain the required differential equation:[9]

$$\hat{\pi} = (1 - \pi)\frac{(1 - \sigma)}{\sigma}[(\hat{b} - \hat{a}) - (\hat{K} - \lambda)] \quad (8.22)$$

Interpreting $\hat{b}$ and $\hat{a}$ as optimal, we know that they are functions of π only, as shown by (8.13). Thus (8.22) is a differential equation in π, except for the presence of $\hat{K}$.

The rate of capital accumulation, $\hat{K}$, is clearly a second endogenous variable, for which we need another differential equation. From the saving function (8.9) we have

$$\log \hat{K} = \log s + \log Y - \log K$$

so that

$$\frac{d}{dt} \log \hat{K} = \hat{Y} - \hat{K} \quad (8.23)$$

Substituting (8.18) into (8.23):

$$\frac{d}{dt} \log \hat{K} = (1 - \pi)\left[\hat{b} + \frac{\pi}{1 - \pi}\hat{a} - (\hat{K} - \lambda)\right] \quad (8.24)$$

This forms the second of the two differential equations in π and K which describe the operation of the model.

We now examine the model for the *existence, uniqueness and stability of a steady-state solution.*

In steady growth $\hat{K}$ and π must take constant values, which we may call K^* and π^*. We therefore set (8.22) and (8.24) to zero. Excluding from now on the case of $\sigma = 1$, we thereby derive two expressions for $\hat{K}^*$ in terms of λ and the rates of factor augmentation. From (8.22):

$$\hat{K}^* = \hat{b} - \hat{a} + \lambda \tag{8.25}$$

And from (8.24):

$$\hat{K}^* = \hat{b} + \left(\frac{\pi^*}{1 - \pi^*} \right) \hat{a} + \lambda \tag{8.26}$$

These two expressions together imply that $\hat{a}$ must be zero, i.e. that the constancy of π and $\hat{K}$ requires technical progress to be purely labour-augmenting (or Harrod-neutral). It follows from (8.12) that π^* must be such that

$$- \frac{\pi^*}{1 - \pi^*} = \phi'(0) \tag{8.27}$$

By the properties of ϕ, we know that there exists such a π^* lying between 0 and 1, and that it is unique. The steady-state rate of labour augmentation is then

$$\hat{b}^* = \phi(0) > 0 \tag{8.28}$$

Also, from (8.25) and (8.28)

$$\hat{K}^* = \phi(0) + \lambda > 0 \tag{8.29}$$

so that $\hat{\pi}^*$ implies a unique and positive $\hat{K}^*$. Further, it may be seen from (8.18) that $\hat{\pi}^*$ and $\hat{K}^*$ imply a growth rate of output, $\hat{Y}^*$, equal to $\hat{K}^*$. Thus the capital–output ratio is constant, equal to the ratio of the natural growth rate, $\phi(0) + \lambda$, to the average propensity to save, s, in the usual way. In sum, there exists a unique steady-state solution.

As regards *stability*, it may be shown using (8.25) and (8.26) that *the unique steady-state equilibrium represented by π^* and $\hat{K}^*$ is globally stable (in the sense of equilibrium dynamics) if $\sigma < 1$, but both locally and globally unstable if $\sigma > 1$*. The formal proof is provided by Drandakis and Phelps (1966); its sense may be conveyed as follows. Suppose $\pi > \pi^*$, so that there must be a shift of income away from profits towards wages if the steady state is to be attained. Now from the I.P.F. we know that if $\pi > \pi^*$, then in equilibrium $\hat{a} > 0$ and $\hat{b} < \hat{b}^*$. Thus in comparison with the steady-state path, the rate of capital augmentation is higher and that of labour augmentation lower. This means by (8.15) that if $\sigma > 1$ technical progress is less capital-saving (in the Hicksian sense) than in the steady state, where π is constant; hence π must be rising further away from π^*. If, on the other hand,

$\sigma <$, technical progress must be less labour-saving than in the steady state, so that π must be falling back towards its steady-state value, π^*, A similar argument can be used for a starting-point with $\pi < \pi^*$, to show instability with $\sigma > 1$ and stability with $\sigma < 1$.

The elasticity of substitution thus plays a critical role in the determination of the model's behaviour. On the assumption that $\sigma < 1$, steady growth is stable; and in the stable steady state, technical progress is Harrod-neutral and (since $\sigma < 1$) Hicks labour- saving. Although factor prices are equal to marginal products, factor shares are determined solely by the shape of the I.P.F. (more specifically, by $\phi'(0)$) and independently of, in particular, the propensity to save, the elasticity of substitution and the growth rate of the labour force.

In contrast with what we labelled the *Hicks–Ahmad theory* of Harrod-neutrality, there is no need to assume that the elasticity of substitution takes that particular value below unity which is required by an exogenously given Hicks labour-saving bias; in the Drandakis–Phelps model the Hicks bias of technical progress becomes adapted to σ by way of movements in distributive shares along the I.P.F. In contrast with the *Kennedy theory* of Harrod-neutrality, the production function is explicitly present and factor substitution is allowed; indeed, it is on this account that bias has become dependent on the elasticity of substitution.

8.5   Summary and conclusions

The achievement of Drandakis and Phelps, then, was to show that in the standard one-good neo-classical model with disembodied technical progress and proportional saving, the assumption that technical progress is Harrod-neutral or purely labour-augmenting can be dispensed with, leaving the neo-classical 'explanation' of steady growth intact. This may seem a remarkable accomplishment. But one should not lose sight of the fact that the old restrictive assumption, that technical progress takes the form required for steady growth, needs to be replaced not only by the less restrictive assumption that technical progress is factor-augmenting but also by three altogether new assumptions: that there exists a stable Kennedy-type I.P.F.; that firms select innovations in such a way as to maximise the current rate of technical progress; and that the elasticity of substitution in the production function is less than unity. Whether these four assumptions combined are more or less restrictive than the old single assumption is debatable.[10] And since the position of the I.P.F. is exogenous to the model, the rate (as opposed to the factor-saving characteristics) of technical progress is still essentially unexplained: it is still little more than costless 'manna from heaven'.

9
Technical Progress at an Endogenous Rate

9.1 The stages and sources of technical progress

Technical progress, defined in Chapter 7 simply as the advancement of knowledge about methods of production, is often thought of as proceeding in a number of distinct stages. The first is *invention* or *discovery*, which may be defined as the occurrence of new ideas or as 'the devising of new ways of attaining given ends' (Kennedy and Thirlwall, 1972, p. 51). Generally, a new idea will not be suitable for application in production without some effort and expenditure on its refinement and *development*. When the idea has become applicable, the next stage is its *adoption*; and it is this which constitutes *innovation*, defined as 'the commercial application of inventions for the first time' (Kennedy and Thirlwall, 1972, p. 56). (The innovation may or may not need to be embodied in some new kind of productive factor.) All this can occur within one firm; we should usually expect there to follow *diffusion* of the new knowledge through the economy as a whole, and *imitation* of the original innovation.

A purist may consider that it is only the first stage in this sequence which improves production possibilities and constitutes technical progress, and that the other stages refer to the way the system attains the new production function implied by the original new idea. But the sequence is a stylised description of the process; in practice the stages merge into one another and 'it is not possible to operate with such purity' (Kennedy and Thirlwall, 1972, p. 12). Even in theory there are senses in which both development and diffusion add to society's stock of knowledge and improve production possibilities, so that they may quite legitimately be regarded as aspects or stages of the process of technological advance.[1]

Having broken down the process in this way we can see more clearly how it may be subject to economic influences.

First, the speed of the process may be expected to be dependent upon the volume of resources deliberately and specifically committed to each of its stages. Thus the rate of invention and discovery will depend on the resources committed to research, and what is achieved at the subsequent stages will be related to expenditure on development, reorganisation, new capital equipment, education and training, etc. In part, therefore, technical progress may be regarded as the direct outcome of deliberate and costly effort on the part of individual producers and society as a whole; and its rate, like its factor-saving characteristics, may be expected to depend upon directly related economic choices.

But not all technical progress is the result of a conscious and deliberate search for new methods. Although the schoolboy's history of invention and discovery – Newton's apple, Watt's steaming kettle, etc. – may be more myth than reality, technical progress obviously does depend to some extent on accident, on individual insight and inspiration, and on forces – historical, cultural and sociological – which are not amenable to economic analysis; and this is not only true of the invention stage. But, on the other hand, even advances which do not stem from economic decisions about the allocation of resources to technical progress may be economically determined, because they may be a by-product of other kinds of economic activity such as production and investment. This is the second way in which the rate of technical progress may be considered endogenous to the economy.

In the following two sections we consider the best-known descriptions in the growth-theory literature of how the rate of technical progress may be related to other economic variables. In section 9.2 we examine Arrow's model of 'learning by doing'. In section 9.3 we list Kaldor's criticisms of the neo-classical account of technological change, and introduce his 'technical progress function', which forms part of his growth model (to be described in Chapter 13). The section on Kaldor would be more at home in Part III; but its inclusion here helps us provide a unified treatment of technical progress, and perhaps it will also be an appetiser for the neo-Keynesian theory which follows. The models of Arrow and Kaldor are both based on the idea that technical progress is a by-product of capital accumulation. Other approaches, which have so far occupied a less prominent place in the corpus of growth theory, are discussed in section 9.4.

9.2 Learning by doing

The acquisition of knowledge by an individual would usually be called 'learning'. Analogously, the process of technological change, whereby production possibilities alter over time in man's favour, may be regarded as 'a vast and prolonged process of learning about the environment' in which he operates (Arrow, 1962, p. 131). In this light Arrow borrowed from the theory of learning (by individuals) in psychology the empirical generalisation that learning is primarily the product of experience, which is not simply a function of time, but is dependent on practice or on 'doing'; and this is the basic hypothesis of his model. The current level of knowledge or technical expertise in an economy is seen as the result of past experience; and improvements in productive techniques are a consequence of growing experience of the problems involved in production.

Arrow assumed that technical progress is wholly embodied in new capital equipment – in effect that it takes place only in the sector producing capital goods, the design of which is being continuously improved as experience in their production increases. With the design improvements assumed to be of a purely labour-augmenting kind, technical progress thus proceeds by way of a direct relationship between the experience of the capital-good sector and the efficiency of labour operating new machines. The natural index of experience in this framework is the cumulative past gross output of the capital-good sector, which is the same as cumulative past gross investment for the economy as a whole. Arrow's learning function thus comprises a direct relationship between cumulative investment and the efficiency of manpower working on new machines.

It is sufficient for our purpose to examine a simplified, non-vintage version of Arrow's model, which we obtain simply by amending the familiar one-good model to take account of 'learning by doing'.[2] We start with the constant-returns Cobb–Douglas production function:

$$Y = AK^{\alpha}[b(t)L]^{1-\alpha} \tag{9.1}$$

The rate at which $b(t)$ is increasing - the rate of labour augmentation - is now not exogenously given, but is determined by the *Arrow learning function, B*:

$$b(t) = B\left[\int_{-\infty}^{t} I(\tau)d\tau\right]; \quad B' > 0 \tag{9.2}$$

where I is gross investment. Thus b, the efficiency index of labour, is an increasing function B of cumulative gross investment.[3] Now, on the assumption that capital does not depreciate, cumulative gross investment is the same as the current capital stock, so that (9.2) becomes

$$b(t) = B[K(t)]; \quad B' > 0 \tag{9.3}$$

We again assume constant labour-force growth:

$$L(t) = L(0)e^{\lambda t}; \quad \lambda > 0 \tag{9.4}$$

We now ask what form the learning function B must take for steady growth to be possible. From (9.1), (9.3) and (9.4) we have that

$$\frac{\dot{Y}}{Y} = \alpha\frac{\dot{K}}{K} + (1 - \alpha)\lambda + (1 - \alpha)\frac{\dot{b}}{b}$$

$$= \alpha\frac{\dot{K}}{K} + (1 - \alpha)\lambda + (1 - \alpha)\frac{KB'(K)}{B(K)}\frac{\dot{K}}{K}$$

In steady growth $\dot{Y}/Y = \dot{K}/K = G$, a constant, so that

$$\frac{KB'(K)}{B(K)} = \frac{(1 - \alpha)G - (1 - \alpha)\lambda}{(1 - \alpha)G} = \frac{G - \lambda}{G} \equiv m \tag{9.5}$$

This is to say that the elasticity of $B(K)$ must be a constant, m, which we also know must be positive; in addition, with λ positive, m must be less than unity. The sense of this result is clear: in steady growth Y and K grow at the same constant rate; with constant returns bL must also be growing at this rate; but L is growing at a positive constant rate, so b must be growing at a positive constant rate smaller than that of Y and K; and with b a function B of K, this is possible only if the elasticity of $B(K)$ is constant, positive and less than unity.[4]

By integration of (9.5), the required form of the learning function is seen to be

$$b(t) = CK^m; C \text{ some constant}; 0 < m < 1 \tag{9.6}$$

In steady growth Y and K will be growing at the rate G, obtained from (9.5) in terms of λ and m,

$$G = \frac{\lambda}{1 - m} \qquad (9.7)$$

which is the natural growth rate in this model; and y, k and b will be growing at the rate g:

$$g = G - \lambda = \left(\frac{m}{1 - m}\right) \lambda \qquad (9.8)$$

But why should the learning function take the particular form (9.6) which permits steady growth? Arrow assumed this form for his model not merely in order that there would be a steady state solution but on the basis of empirical evidence obtained at the micro level. In particular, aeronautical engineers had found a 'remarkably precise' (Arrow, 1962, p. 132). Similar relationships had been found for other capital goods, labour efficiency appeared to be described accurately by a function of form (9.6), with K the number of airframes produced previously and m equal to about 0.3. In fact this specific relationship had 'become basic in the production and cost-planning of the US Air Force' (Arrow, 1962, p. 132). Similar relationships had been found for other capital goods, though the rate of learning (value of m) appeared to vary from case to case. This evidence both gave support to Arrow's basic hypothesis that the principle of 'learning by doing' was applicable in the economic analysis of technical progress, and led to his adoption of the particular form of the learning function which allows steady growth.

It may be seen from (9.7) and (9.8) that with learning, the steady-state growth rates of output and productivity are proportional to λ, the growth rate of the labour force. This is just as was found to be the case in section 5.4 with increasing returns and no technical progress (cf. the Cobb–Douglas expressions (5.16) and (5.17).[5] And the similarity between learning by doing and increasing returns does not end there; in fact if (9.6) is substituted into (9.1), we obtain

$$Y = A C^{1-\alpha} K^{\alpha+(1-\alpha)m} L^{1-\alpha} \qquad (9.9)$$

This is exactly like a Cobb–Douglas function with increasing returns and no technical progress: the degree of homogeneity, obtained from the sum of the exponents of K and L, is $1 + (1 - \alpha)m$. *Thus when*

*Arrow's learning function is combined with a constant-returns produc-
tion function, the implicit result is an increasing-returns production
function.* Its degree of homogeneity exceeds unity by the product of
m (the elasticity of b with respect to K) and $(1-\alpha)$ (the elasticity of Y
with respect to b); this measures what may be called the 'indirect'
elasticity of Y with respect to K, which is due to the effect of learning
on the efficiency of labour.

It follows that the two factors cannot be paid their marginal products. If labour is paid its marginal product, it may be seen from (9.9)
that the real wage will be

$$w = \frac{\partial Y}{\partial L} = (1 - \alpha)\, \frac{Y}{L} \qquad (9.10)$$

so that labour will receive the proportion $(1 - \alpha)$ of the total product.
But if capital receives its marginal product, the rate of return will be

$$r = \frac{\partial Y}{\partial K} = [\alpha + (1 - \alpha)m]\, \frac{Y}{K} \qquad (9.11)$$

so that total profits will exceed the income available after labour has
been paid its marginal product by the proportion $(1 - \alpha)m$ of total
income. The marginal product of capital (9.11) comprises two elements, the first $\alpha Y/K$, representing the direct effect on Y of an increase
in K, and the second, $[(1 - \alpha)m]\, Y/K$, representing the indirect effect
which occurs by way of endogenous technical progress. Following
Arrow, we may treat the latter as an external economy which goes
unrewarded in the market; the rate of return will then be given not by
the marginal social product of capital (9.11), but by the marginal
private product:

$$r' = \alpha \frac{Y}{K} \qquad (9.12)$$

This solves the 'adding-up' problem. But an implication of the solution
is that the allocation of resources between the production of capital
goods and the production of consumption goods is likely to be ineffi-
ciently weighted in favour of the latter, since investors are not being
paid for the benefit which accrues to society from their activities
through the presence of learning. This provides a case for state intervention to raise investment.

Thus although the implicit, 'reduced-form' production function (9.9) is formally equivalent to an increasing-returns function without technical progress, the learning model which underlies it gives its parameters a particular meaning and leads to a distinctive interpretation of marginal products and factor pricing. Furthermore, the formal equivalence depends on our assumption of no depreciation. If this assumption is removed, (9.9) no longer holds, because (9.3) no longer follows from (9.2). With depreciation, the capital stock may contract; this will occur if depreciation exceeds gross investment so that net investment is negative. But gross investment can never be negative, so that cumulative gross investment can never contract. Thus suppose that gross investment is zero, so that b is constant (by expression (9.2)), and that K and L both fall in some proportion; then by (9.1) Y will fall in the same proportion. With increasing returns, of course, this would not be the case; *whereas any increase in efficiency brought about purely by an increase in scale will be lost if the scale is reduced, 'learning' gained by 'doing' cannot be lost since experience cannot be undone.*

Nevertheless, learning by doing and increasing returns are obviously related. With learning, efficiency is in effect an increasing function of the 'scale' of all current and previous activity; and, equally, one source of increasing returns proper may be the 'learning' derived from current operations.

Arrow thus showed how a plausible description of the determination of the rate of technical progress provided a relationship which could be fitted into neo-classical models of steady growth without too much disturbance. The shortcomings of his approach may be considered to be threefold.

First, as was indicated at the beginning, Arrow's own model ignored any increase which may be taking place in the proficiency with which new machines are operated after their installation; he assumed that it is only the builders of machines who learn, and not their users. He acknowledged this omission, and recognised that the learning hypothesis is equally applicable to disembodied progress (Arrow, 1962, p. 148).

Second, the empirical evidence supporting Arrow's assumption that the learning function takes the form compatible with steady growth seems narrowly based for a macro model. On the other hand, it is something, and it is interesting; and the hypothesis that learning proceeds in such a way that the elasticity of knowledge or efficiency with respect to experience is a positive constant less than unity is, in a sense, a natural one to adopt *a priori*. (It implies diminishing returns to experience; with $m < 1$ the second derivative of the learning function is negative.)

Third, there must obviously be doubts of a more general nature about the adequacy of the learning hypothesis – or at least of Arrow's learning function – as a description of how technical progress occurs. In fact it is clearly not true that technical knowledge keeps step with experience in the regular manner suggested by this model. The history of technical progress appears to consist, to quite a large extent, of 'bursts' of innovative activity associated with critical breakthroughs in technology – from the smelting of iron with coal in the mid-eighteenth century, through the steam-engine, etc., to the micro-electronics of the 1970s. This suggests, in Arrow's terms, that there are important discontinuities in the learning function. This may be considered not a very telling criticism as far as the analysis of the long term is concerned; and if the explanation of such discontinuities is judged to be a task for growth theory, it is unlikely to be provided by any model within the confines of steady-state analysis. Our third point is therefore as much a comment on steady-growth theory generally as on Arrow's model *per se*.

9.3 Kaldor's technical progress function

It will be recalled from Chapter 7 that a production function of the form

$$Y = F(K, L, t) \tag{9.13}$$

implies, if constant returns prevail, that the growth rate of output per head may be expressed as the sum of two independent components, the Hicks rate of progress and the growth rate of capital per head *times* capital's competitive share in income:

$$\frac{\dot{y}}{y} = \frac{F_t}{F} + \left(\frac{KF_K}{F}\right) \frac{\dot{k}}{k} \tag{9.14}$$

In section 7.7 we saw how this has provided the basis for empirical estimates of the relative importance of technical progress to productivity growth and for more detailed exercises in growth accounting, whereby output growth is attributed to the independent contributions of identifiable inputs and a 'residual' representing unidentified technical advances. Now (9.14) may be regarded as a linear relationship between $\dot{k}/k$ and $\dot{y}/y$; and it will be a stable relationship through time if the Hicks rate of progress and factor shares are constant. Stability requires, in particular, that factor shares should be constant when $\dot{k}/k = 0$, which demands Hicks-neutrality, and when $\dot{k}/k = \dot{y}/y$, which demands Harrod-neutrality. Thus the elasticity of substitution must be unity, and (9.13) must be a Cobb–Douglas function with factor-augmenting progress; and since F_t/F must be constant, the rate of augmentation must be constant. More formally, if (9.14) is a stable linear relationship, it may be written as

$$\frac{\dot{y}}{y} = h + \alpha\frac{\dot{k}}{k} \qquad (9.15)$$

where h and α are constants. On integration we obtain

$$y = \left[\frac{y(0)}{k(0)}\alpha\right] e^{ht}k^{\alpha} \qquad (9.16)$$

where $y(0)$ and $k(0)$ denote initial values. This is a Cobb–Douglas function, with a Hicks rate of progress of h or a Harrod rate of $h/(1-\alpha)$.

At an early stage in the development of modern growth theory Kaldor emphatically rejected this kind of analysis. He denied that production possibilities or technical progress could be represented adequately by a relationship like (9.13), and, *a fortiori*, that a relationship such as (9.14) could be used validly to interpret empirical growth. As will be seen, Kaldor's objections may be regarded partly as being directed against the particular conception of (disembodied and exogenous) technical progress represented by (9.13), and as having been met by more recent developments within the neo-classical framework, i.e. through embodiment, endogenous Harrod-neutrality, learning, etc. Indeed, he could justly claim to have played a part in stimulating these developments. But his strictures go deeper than this, and they are to be regarded more as *an aspect of the neo-Keynesian critique of neo-classical theory*; and although we are here associating them particularly with Kaldor, they may be found, at least implicitly, in the writings of other neo-Keynesians. His objections are as follows.

First, he considers that even if there is no technical progress, the concept of the aggregate production function is inapplicable, apart from as a means of comparing the combinations of output and inputs which would obtain in different steady-state equilibria (Kaldor, 1961, pp. 204-5). The production function is the efficient boundary of the production set: it shows the maximum output obtainable from each combination of inputs. The boundary will be attained by an economy employing a particular technique of production (represented by a capital-labour or capital-output ratio) only if its capital stock is efficiently adapted to that technique. Since in reality capital is neither homogeneous nor perfectly malleable, this will be the case only if the technique has been employed 'for a long enough period for the actual assortment of capital goods to have become optimally adapted to it' (Kaldor, 1961). Otherwise, if techniques are changing, the capital stock will always contain items of equipment appropriate to techniques other than that currently employed, and output will be less than is implied by the boundary or production function. Thus, generally, outside steady-state equilibrium, the production function is irrelevant; indeed, there will be no unique relationship between Y on the one hand and K and L on the other. (Kaldor draws from this the inference that the partial derivatives of the production function must be irrelevant to factor-pricing and the distribution of income.)

Second, Kaldor holds that it is illegitimate to include the 'state of knowledge' among the arguments of a production function (see, for example, Kaldor, 1961, p. 205). Rather ironically, he accepts Samuelson's (1947, p. 84) rule that only 'measurable quantitative economic goods and services' may properly be used as independent variables in a production function, and argues that since the 'state of knowledge' is by its nature immeasurable – and 'time' cannot be a satisfactory proxy – it should be treated not as a productive input but as a 'background element' influencing the form of the relationship between output and inputs correctly defined. This means that even when technology is changing Kaldor would reject (9.13) as invalid, and would replace it with a relationship like

$$Y = N(K, L) \qquad (9.17)$$

This is not a production function of the neo-classical kind. It cannot describe how output will respond to changes in inputs in a 'given' state of knowledge; nor can it describe how output will respond to technical progress with 'given' inputs. And it certainly cannot be used to separate the contribution of technical progress to growth from the contributions of factor inputs, or to estimate its relative importance. Since technical progress is immeasurable, such questions are seen as artificial, meaning-less and unanswerable.[6] What is described by (9.17) – the only kind of aggregate 'production function' Kaldor regards as admissible – is, in effect, the observable time-series correlation between output and measurable inputs. It includes the influence of technological change, which Kaldor, in contrast to Solow and the growth accountants, be-lieves cannot be isolated. For this reason alone, and even if we do not believe in economies of scale in the usual sense, 'In terms of the true variables, capital and labour, the production function will not be linear-homogenous' (Kaldor, 1961, p. 206), so that if the factors were paid their 'marginal products', as described by (9.17), total output would be more than exhausted.

But in any case Kaldor (e.g. 1972) does believe in the existence of economies of scale, internal to the firm, in industry, if only as a neces-sary consequence of the three-dimensional nature of space; and this forms his *third* objection to the neo-classical theory of production. He would, of course, reject the kind of argument referred to in section 5.4 that scale economies must be relatively unimportant to productivity growth; and he appeals to evidence obtained at the micro level (see for example, Pratten, 1971) to support his contention that in reality in-creasing returns play a 'dominating role' (Kaldor, 1972, p. 1242). He thus argues that neo-classical perfect-competition models which are forced to assume constant returns neglect the fact that 'on an empirical level, nobody doubts that . . . in industry increasing returns dominate the picture for the very reasons given by Adam Smith. . . reasons that are fundamental to the nature of technological processes and not to any particular technology' (Kaldor, 1972).

Fourth, Kaldor (1961, p. 204) criticises neo-classical theory for hav-ing to assume Harrod-neutrality in order to explain steady growth. (He would presumably reject the Drandakis–Phelps model of section 8.4 for other reasons, which will now be obvious.)

Fifth, Kaldor argues that technical progress and capital accumulation are necessarily interdependent features of the growth process, and that this is another reason why they cannot be separated from each other empirically or in a theoretical production function. On the one hand, it is difficult to conceive of capital-deepening without technical progress, not only because accumulation takes time, but also because changes in technique inevitably 'require "inventiveness" of some kind' (Kaldor, 1957, p. 264).[7] And, on the other hand, technical progress usually en-tails and requires capital-deepening: 'most . . . technical innovations which are capable of raising the productivity of labour require the use of more capital per man – more elaborate equipment and/or mechanical power' (Kaldor, 1957). And even if technical progress does not require *more* capital per man, it will usually need to be embodied in *new kinds* of equipment, which will require gross investment: 'improved knowledge is, largely, if not entirely, infused into the economy through the introduction of new equipment' (Kaldor, 1961, p. 207). These considerations suggest that the rate of technical progress, and hence the rate of growth of labour productivity, are likely to depend directly on the rate of capital-deepening or capital accumulation; and this inference is strengthened if there are thought to be learning effects[8] and economies of scale of a dynamic kind[9] associated with the production of capital goods.

These arguments lead directly, first, to Kaldor's rejection of any kind of production function for his growth model, and second, to his alternative technological relationship. Feasible output at any point in time will depend not only on the volume of capital and labour employed, but also on the age structure of the capital stock (because of embodiment) and, which is almost the same thing, on the history of accumulation (because of learning and dynamic economies of scale). Hence the form of N in (9.17) cannot be known independently of the growth path, so it can be of little use for a growth model. Thus Kaldor abandons the only kind of production function he finds acceptable.

He replaces it with a relationship which follows naturally from his view that the rate of technical progress is an increasing function of the rate of capital-deepening, and that the direct effect of capital-deepening on productivity is inseparable from the indirect effect through technical progress. In the *non-vintage versions* of his model he makes the growth rate of output per head an increasing function of the growth rate of capital per head. The relationship is assumed to be subject to diminishing returns: the higher is $\dot{k}/k$, the greater is the extent to which new ideas are already being exploited, so the lower will be the return in terms of faster productivity growth to any further increase in $\dot{k}/k$. Also, it is assumed that $\dot{y}/y$ is positive when $\dot{k}/k$ is zero, because, even if k is constant, new equipment will be introduced both to equip additions to the labour force and to replace worn-out capital, and also because there will be some disembodied improvements. Thus Kaldor's *technical progress function* (T.P.F.) has the form:

$$\frac{\dot{y}}{y} = T\left(\frac{\dot{k}}{k}\right); \quad T(0) > 0, T' > 0, T'' < 0 \qquad (9.18)$$

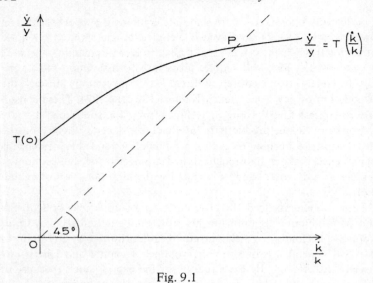

Fig. 9.1

It is illustrated in Figure 9.1. The height of the curve – the rate of productivity growth at any rate of deepening – depends, in Kaldor's phrase, on the 'technical dynamism' of the economy and, in particular, of its entrepreneurs. He recognises that in reality the function will be caused to shift by, for instance, important scientific discoveries; but for the purpose of his model he assumes that the T.P.F. is stable – in other words, that the degree of technical dynamism is stable.

In the *vintage-capital version* of the model he assumes the same kind of relationship, but one between the growth of output per head on new equipment and the growth of investment per head. He thus makes quite explicit the fact that he does not consider the T.P.F. as reliant solely on the embodiment hypothesis: 'the annual gain of productivity due to "embodied technical progress" will tend to be all the greater the larger the number of plants constructed per year' (Kaldor, 1972, p. 1243). This draws attention to the close relationship between Kaldor's T.P.F. and Arrow's learning function; they are not, however, equivalent (see Kaldor, 1962).

Kaldor's T.P.F. represents an attempt to break clearly away from the neo-classical production function; but it turns out in fact that the break is not all that clear cut. The way the function is specified in (9.18) rules out linearity; and a function of this form is generally not integrable into a production function (Black, 1962). But if the T.P.F. is linear, then – lo and behold! – we are back with (9.15), which, as we saw, implies that there is a production function, and one of a very specific kind: with constant returns, an elasticity of substitution of unity, and neutral technical progress. From the point of view of Kaldor's analysis the significance of this is twofold. First, the non-linearity of his T.P.F. does not play any significant role in the working of his growth model. His model is concerned essentially with explaining how investment behaviour will be such that the system will converge on the point P in Figure 9.1 where there is steady growth. His attempts to demonstrate the stability of this position nowhere relies on the non-linearity of the T.P.F.; all that matters is that P should exist (i.e. that the T.P.F. should intersect the 45° line); that to the left of P the T.P.F. should lie above the 45° line (implying a falling capital–output ratio); and that to the right of P the T.P.F. should lie below the 45° line (implying a rising capital–output ratio). These conditions will be satisfied by any linear T.P.F. with a slope between zero and unity, as well as by any T.P.F. like (9.18). Second, Kaldor sometimes in fact assumes linearity (though only to simplify the solution) and thereby implicitly assumes a Cobb–Douglas function.

He can of course avoid this difficulty by insisting that the T.P.F. should have the form of (9.18); then there is no implicit production function, and no implicit assumption of Harrod-neutrality. But it seems unsatisfactory that his quite fundamental critique of the neo-classical analysis of productivity change appears, in the end, to boil down to an argument about curvature which is anyway unimportant to his model.

9.4   The frontiers of steady-state equilibrium analysis and beyond

Although both Arrow and Kaldor see the rate of technical progress as being dependent on the rate of capital accumulation, the steady-state growth rate in each of their models is independent of the propensity to save – a not unfamiliar feature. For Arrow, the steady-state growth rate is determined by the growth rate of the labour force and the elasticity of the learning function (see expression (9.7)); for Kaldor, it is determined by the growth rate of the labour force and the height of the T.P.F. at its intersection with the 45° line (see Figure 9.1).

Eltis (1973, esp. ch. 6) argues that this indicates that both models fail to do justice to the ideas underlying them about the strong linkages between investment and productivity growth. He thus suggests, and for other reasons as well, that Kaldor's T.P.F. should be discarded in favour of a *relationship between the growth rate of labour productivity and the proportion of income saved and invested.* In contrast with the T.P.F. there is no confusion between this and a production function; and it enables Eltis to construct a model in which the natural growth rate – the equilibrium growth rate in the long run – does depend on saving and investment behaviour.

The same is true of the steady-state growth rate in a model constructed by Conlisk (1969). There are two sectors, one producing a consumption good, and the other producing capital equipment and technical progress. Production possibilities in the latter 'productivity' sector may be represented, for given inputs of capital and labour, by a frontier similar to the Kennedy I.P.F. of sections 8.3 and 8.4, except that the horizontal axis now shows, not the rate of capital augmentation, but the rate of growth of capital in efficiency units; no distinction is drawn between capital accumulation (in natural units) and capital augmentation. The economy thus faces two choices. The first – the saving decision – determines how much resources are to be used for productivity growth as opposed to consumption; this *fixes endogenously the position of the frontier of possibilities in the productivity sector.* The second is the selection of a point on the frontier; this determines, for a given exogenous growth rate of the labour force in natural units, the relationship between the growth rates, in efficiency units, of capital and labour. It is the presence of the first choice which leads to Conlisk's result that the rate of labour augmentation is not only endogenous to the economy (which it is, in different ways, in the Arrow model and even in the Drandakis–Phelps model) but also dependent, even among steady states, on economic decisions.

Conlisk's model is the closest we have come to a theory which treats the rate of technical progress explicitly as the direct outcome of a deliberate and costly search for new methods and productivity growth. Even in Arrow, Kaldor and Eltis technical progress is still costless manna, even though it may be falling from machines rather than heaven.[10] Other models have been constructed in which technical progress is an increasing function of the resources devoted to research, and *normative 'rules' for optimum research expenditure* have been derived which are analogous to the 'golden rule of accumulation' of section 4.3 (see, for example, Nordhaus, 1969). The formulation of a positive theory of the determinants of investment in technical progress – investment in learning *per se*, 'learning before doing', if you will – is a similar problem to the formulation of a theory of investment in capital, and the answer can be no more straightforward, not least because of the risk and uncertainty which are inherent in research activity, even more than in the 'hostage to fortune' that is capital investment.

Some interesting conclusions can be reached more easily if we broaden our view and bring into focus the possibility of *disequilibrium*. We can then, in particular, allow factors to be in excess demand or supply, and firms to be earning super-normal (or sub-normal) profits as a reward (or penalty) for innovating (or not innovating).

Then the pressure on, or incentive to, producers to innovate, and hence the rate of technical progress, may be the greater *the shorter is the supply of the factors* – more precisely, the non-reproducible factors, labour and land – in relation to demand or capital. The incentive may be transmitted through pressure on profitability from rising factor prices,[11] or through physical bottlenecks which reflect profitable opportunities being missed. Since most formal growth theory – including that of Kaldor – has assumed equilibrium in the labour market and given little consideration to land, this possible form of endogenous technical progress has received little attention (Hahn and Matthews, 1964, p. 73). Robinson's writing, which is deliberately less restrictive in this respect, forms an exception, for example (1956, p. 96). 'When entrepreneurs find themselves in a situation where potential markets are expanding but labour hard to find, they have every motive to increase productivity', and moreover 'the experience of wage rates rising with output overcomes the reluctance of the workers to assist them to do so.' In fact, she argues, 'the capitalist rules of the game produce the most flourishing results when. . . a rise in real wages (due to scarcity of labour) is constantly threatening a fall in the rate of profit, which technical progress is constantly fending off'.[12] An implication of these ideas is that *endogenous technical progress may help to resolve Harrod's Existence Problem*. If the rate of technical progress increases when there is scarcity of labour arising from the warranted growth rate pushing up against the natural rate, then the latter may rise sufficiently for equilibrium growth to be attained – and conversely.

On this view technical progress is a means by which competing firms struggle to overcome factor scarcities. A more general view is that it is *a means whereby competing firms struggle for profits, survival and growth*, a view associated with Marx and Schumpeter. It has been revived in a most ingenious way by Nelson and Winter (1974; 1975) in a model based on the modern 'behavioural' theories of the firm, which reject assumptions of maximisation as being implausible and even meaningless in an environment dominated by change and uncertainty. Instead, firms are assumed to adopt set 'decision rules', and the decision rules are allowed to differ among the firms. Some firms adopt successful or profitable rules; their profits enable them to invest and thus to grow. Other firms adopt unsuccessful rules; their lack of profits induces them to search for new rules. The 'rules' in the Nelson–Winter model are essentially coefficients of production; and what the unsuccessful firms search for are new techniques. (The distinction between technical progress and factor substitution, in the conventional sense, hardly requires to be made, but a change of rule provides 'a natural definition of innovation' (Nelson and Winter, 1974, p. 894).) The outcome of a firm's search is a stochastic process, specified in such a way that what is turned up by it is likely to be close to the technique already used by the firm, or to the most common techniques in use elsewhere. The latter consideration allows for diffusion and imitation. The search may be successful, or it may not; persistent failure means no profit, no growth, and ultimately collapse. Thus for the economy as a whole growth is the outcome of the expansion of successful firms, a search process by unsuccessful firms and a 'selection environment' which distinguishes the fit, who survive and flourish, from the weak, who stagnate and perish.

Nelson and Winter constructed a specific model of this kind, and used it in an attempt to simulate the aggregate behaviour of the U.S. economy between 1909 and 1949, using the data of Solow (1957). The results were 'quite successful': successful enough in relation to Solow's results, at any rate, to suggest that 'neo-classical models are unlikely to be decisively superior in this area' (Nelson and Winter, 1974, pp. 898–9).

As will be seen more clearly in the following chapter, the approach adopted by Nelson and Winter has much in common with neo-Keynesian theory: there is no aggregate production function; there is no sharp 'growth-accounting' distinction between substitution and technical progress; the economy is not 'efficient', either in the simple sense that aggregate output is maximised, or in a Pareto allocative sense; firms are not straightforward profit-maximisers; and neither individual firms, nor the economy as a whole, are in equilibrium in any meaningful sense. This is not to say there are no differences; most obviously, there is no Keynesian treatment of saving and investment. Also, there is little of Kaldor's emphasis on economies of scale. But despite these differences one would expect neo-Keynesians to be sympathetic to their model as an analysis of technological change.

The *appeal* of the Nelson–Winter approach is the attractiveness and plausibility of the Schumpeterian view of growth and technical progress as the outcome of a competitive struggle among firms with different advantages and capabilities. In this view diversity and structural change are essential to the whole process, and steady-state equilibrium analysis misses the point: 'the diversity and change that are suppressed by aggregation, maximisation, and equilibrium are not the epiphenomena of technical advance. They are the central phenomena' (Nelson and Winter, 1974, p. 903). The *achievement* of Nelson and Winter is to have constructed a formal, operational model embodying these ideas, a formal model of growth which is not a model of steady growth. The specification of their model is more complex than that of more orthodox models; but it is conceptually simple and appealing. The approach is at an early stage of development; but it at least seems promising, and it may be a pointer to the future of the subject.

All this takes us back to Bliss's remark that 'any interesting technical progress' is incompatible with steady growth (see page 105). While this is surely an exaggeration – learning by doing and Kaldor's analysis are surely of some interest – there seems a strong case for saying that a lot of interesting technical progress is incompatible not only with steady growth but with equilibrium more generally.

Further reading

There is a large literature on what may be called the empirical microeconomics – or micro-economic history – of technical progress. It is particularly concerned with such questions as the relationship between firm size and market structure on the one hand and innovative effort and achievement on the other. Kennedy and Thirlwall (1972, part II) and Kamien and Schwartz (1975) are surveys; Mansfield (1968) is a textbook. Rosenberg (1971) is an excellent collection of readings on the theory and economic history of technical progress.

Part III

NEO-KEYNESIAN
GROWTH THEORY

10

Neo-Keynesian Criticisms of Neo-classical Theory

10.1   The neo-Keynesian heritage: Keynes and the classics

Chapter 3 showed how, in the mid-1950s, neo-classical growth theory emerged from the view that for long-run analysis it was appropriate to relax the Harrod–Domar assumption of fixed coefficients, legitimate to ignore Keynesian problems, and natural to assume that prices and distribution are determined by the equilibration of competitive product and factor markets.

At that time at Cambridge University – the university of Keynes – analysis of growth and distribution had already begun to develop along different lines. Before the appearance of the papers by Tobin, Solow and Swan, Joan Robinson (1954) had argued that with heterogeneous capital the aggregate production function of neo-classical theory simply could not provide an explanation of income distribution. (At the time the best-known example of the production function explicitly being put to this use was probably Hicks (1963).) Kaldor (1956) also rejected neo-classical distribution theory, and offered an alternative 'Keynesian' theory of distribution for the long run in a growing economy. Robinson's book, *The Accumulation of Capital*, followed in the same year. Her approach to growth theory was similar to Harrod's, in that she considered the problem to be 'the generalisation of the *General Theory*, that is, an extension of Keynes's short-period analysis to long-run development' (Robinson, 1956, p. vi). For Robinson and Kaldor, therefore, the *General Theory* was not to be cast aside; it had to be an essential ingredient, if not the starting-point. Not that there was nothing to be learned from pre-Keynesian neo-classical economics; but the

work of the neo-classicals had been dominated by the problems of resource allocation and relative prices in a stationary economy. Just as
Keynes had found that it was not equipped to cope with the problem
of effective demand, so now it seemed ill-equipped for the analysis of
growth.

The *classical* economists, however, *had* been concerned with dynamics. Adam Smith's *Inquiry into the Nature and Causes of the Wealth
of Nations* of 1776 might have been entitled, in modern language, *An
Inquiry into the Nature and Causes of Economic Growth*. And for
Ricardo (1817, Preface) the main subject-matter of economics was the
explanation of distributive shares in a growing economy:

> The produce of the earth . . . is divided among three classes of the
> community; namely, the proprietor of the land, the owner of the
> stock or capital necessary for its cultivation, and the labourers by
> whose industry it is cultivated. But in different stages of society, the
> proportions of . . . rent, profit, and wages, will be essentially different;
> depending mainly on the actual fertility of the soil, on the accumu-
> lation of capital and population, and on the skill, ingenuity, and in-
> struments employed in agriculture. To determine the laws which re-
> gulate this distribution is the principal problem in Political Economy.

To Robinson and Kaldor, it seemed that in the wake of Keynes the
time was ripe for the restoration to their rightful prominence of the
classical questions, from which neo-classical economics had been a distraction. Robinson (1956) began: 'Economic analysis, serving for two
centuries to win an understanding of the Nature and Causes of the
Wealth of Nations has been fobbed off with another bride - a Theory
of Value.' In particular, the neo-classical production function, 'in which
the relative prices of the factors of production are exhibited as a function of the ratio in which they are employed in a given state of technical knowledge. . .has distracted attention from the more difficult but
more rewarding questions of the influences governing the supplies of
the factors and of the causes and consequences of changes in technical
knowledge' (this was the first sentence of Robinson, 1954). It was true
that the classical answers were largely inapplicable to a modern industrial economy - the 'Malthusian' view of population growth and subsistence wages, the emphasis on diminishing returns from land, Ricardo's
underestimation of the importance of technical progress, and, of course,
the inadequate treatment of effective demand - but the classical

approach provided clues which were not to be found in neo-classical theory. And the lessons of classical economics were meanwhile being clarified by the work of Sraffa, also at Cambridge. The first volume of his edition of the works of Ricardo had been published in 1951 (Ricardo, 1817); and his treatise on production and value from a classical, non-marginalist viewpoint, conceived in the 1920s, was nearing the end of its extraordinarily long gestation period (Sraffa, 1960).

Even as the first neo-classical growth models were appearing, the foundation had thus been laid for an alternative approach to growth and distribution theory. The battle-lines had thereby been drawn for a controversy which was to be unique in modern economics for its combination of rancour, a virtual absence of compromise, over more than twenty years, on either side, the high distinction of the principal combatants on both sides, and the fact that despite these features and despite the voluminous literature, probably the majority of students, teachers and practitioners of economics have been left either untouched or mystified.

The alternative approach is still associated mainly with economists at Cambridge University: Robinson and Kaldor, who have remained its most prominent exponents, Champernowne, Kahn, Pasinetti and Sraffa. These are the recognised leaders of a school of thought which considers its main progenitors to be the classical economists (particularly Ricardo and Marx), Keynes, Kalecki, and Harrod. Although the work of some pre-Keynesian neo-classicals - particularly Wicksell and Cambridge's own Marshall - is sometimes acknowledged, not infrequently by Robinson, the flavour is that in the light of Keynes, Kalecki and Harrod, 'The post-Keynesian theories of economic growth and income distribution can be directly grafted on to the Ricardian theoretical framework, as if nothing happened in between' (Pasinetti, 1974, p. 92).

Because of what the school claims to be its inheritance from Keynes, and also because of the personal association several of its main proponents had with Keynes himself, it has been labelled 'Keynesian', or neo-Keynesian' (the label adopted here), or 'post-Keynesian'. It is also sometimes referred to as the 'Cambridge school', and elsewhere as the 'neo-Ricardian school'. None of these labels can be regarded as descriptively adequate. As noted in section 3.2, most neo-classiclas (or neo-neo-classicals as they are sometimes called, to distinguish them from the genuine pre-Keynesian article) would regard themselves as Keynesians. And by no means all economists at Cambridge are neo-Keynesians; in particular,

Meade, a neo-classical growth theorist, has been at Cambridge almost from the start of the controversy, and was, moreover, personally associated with Keynes in the 1930s. To confuse matters further, the recognised centre of the neo-classical school is M.I.T., which happens to be located in Cambridge, Massachusetts; and the opposing sides are frequently referred to as 'the two Cambridges'.[1] It has even been suggested by Hicks (1973a, p. 13), whose recent writing has been sympathetic towards the neo-Keynesians,[2] that 'It is the post-Keynesians who would better be called neo-classics; for it is they who, to their honour, have wrought a Classical Revival', whereas the so-called neo-classical school ought really to be called anti-classical. These confusions serve at least to remind us that names written on labels have to be interpreted with care.

Another danger with labels attached to schools of thought is that they may obscure divergences of view which there will usually be within them. There are differences of view within the neo-Keynesian school concerning both the question of which aspects of neo-classical theory are most objectionable (or most vulnerable) and the question of which alternative direction growth theory should take. On the latter question there is, as we shall see, a clear divergence between Kaldor, on the one hand, whose aim has been to provide an alternative formal model of equilibrium steady growth, and Robinson, on the other, who has eschewed formal model-building and been primarily concerned (like Harrod) to emphasise obstacles which are liable to prevent the attainment of a 'Golden Age' by an unplanned capitalist economy. The latter approach reflects a less sanguine view of the workings of capitalism than the former. With respect to the first question the differences are mainly on points of emphasis.

The neo-Keynesian attack on neo-classical theory may be regarded as being prosecuted on two fronts. First, it is alleged to be empirically irrelevent because it is based on artificial and unrealistic assumptions. Second, it is alleged to be logically inadequate even on its own assumptions, once the crucial hypothesis of homogeneous capital is removed. Most of the literature has been concerned with the latter – the so-called 'capital controversy'. But we shall pay more attention, in sections 10.2–10.5, to the former, partly because our ultimate object in Part III is to describe Kaldor's theory of steady growth, and he has placed more emphasis on this allegation, partly because the capital controversy has been extensively surveyed elsewhere, and partly because it seems to provide the more rewarding line of investigation in the limited space, not least because it seems – not only to the present writer – to form the more important challenge.

10.2 Keynes

The first 'neo-Keynesian' objection to the neo-classical approach is as implied in the name: neo-classical growth theory is alleged to be anti-Keynesian. It is accused of illegitimately ignoring Keynes's analysis of the working of the capitalist economy, and the problem of effective demand which it tackled. To appreciate the meaning of this charge, we need to return briefly to Keynes.

Pre-Keynesian neo-classical theory relied on two mechanisms to establish that the maintenance of full employment was ensured in the absence of market frictions. First, although it was recognised that an act of saving did not automatically entail an act of investment, it was argued that the rate of interest would perform the task of bringing saving and investment into equilibrium. Hence once the economy was at full employment, a fall in investment, for example, would quickly, through its effect on the interest rate, be accompanied by an equal contraction of saving, and therefore an equal expansion of consumer spending, so that aggregate spending (and income) would remain unchanged; only its composition would alter. With the interest rate playing this role, it seemed that 'Say's Law'[3] – 'supply creates its own demand' – could be retained, and that there would be no problem of deficient aggregate demand. This theory of the interest rate was also used as a basis for arguments that when there was unemployment, a policy of raising investment (more particularly, of increasing government expenditure) could offer no solution to the problem, since by raising the cost of finance it would merely divert expenditure from elsewhere. This was, in effect, the standpoint of the White Paper issued by the British Government in 1929.[4]

It was the second mechanism which implied how the problem could be solved. The real wage was seen as the price whose function was to clear the labour market. With unemployment the real wage would tend to fall under the pressure of excess supply, and this would induce the required expansion of the demand for labour through an adjustment of factor proportions. If unemployment was persistent, the inference was that there were frictions preventing this mechanism from operating, and that wages should be reduced as a matter of policy. As the Professor of Political Economy at Cambridge put it three years before the publication of the *General Theory*, when unemployment in the United Kingdom was 20 per cent (it had exceeded 10 per cent in the previous twelve years):

> With perfectly free competition among work-people and labour perfectly mobile . . . there will always be a strong tendency for wage-rates to be so related to demand (for labour) that everybody is employed. Hence in stable conditions every one will actually be employed. The implication is that such unemployment as exists at any time is due wholly to the fact that changes in demand conditions are continually taking place and that frictional resistances prevent the appropriate wage adjustments from being made instantaneously' (Pigou, 1933, p. 252).

Keynes overthrew this analysis[5] in a way which should be familiar. With regard to the first mechanism, he did not deny that both investment and saving are in some degree dependent on the rate of interest, but he did deny that the interest rate performs the function of equilibrating them. He emphasised, first, that investment is liable to fluctuate in response to changes in expectations about profitability (i.e. shifts in the marginal efficiency of capital schedule); and second, that saving is much more closely dependent on current income than on the interest rate. Thus when investment falls, for instance, the large fall in interest rates which would be needed to induce an equal contraction of saving and an equal expansion of consumption is simply not forthcoming; in consequence, effective demand is reduced, so that income and employment will decline, via the multiplier (introduced by Kahn, 1931), until there has been a fall in saving equal to the initial drop in investment. It is therefore primarily income, rather than the interest rate, which responds to changes in investment (and also to changes in the propensity to save); and, contrary to Say's Law, there is no necessary tendency for effective demand to be consistent with full employment. Keynes completed the picture by arguing that interest is determined not by the forces of 'productivity and thrift' which lay behind the neo-classical investment and saving schedules but by purely monetary influences. With the demand for money (or 'liquidity preference') related directly to real income and the price level, and inversely to the interest rate (for given, probably inelastic, interest-rate expectations), the rate would tend to the level at which demand is satisfied by the supply fixed by the authorities.

With regard to the second mechanism, Keynes emphasised the distinction between real and money wages. Specialisation in production and the institution of wage labour, which are essential features of capitalist economies, require, given the costliness and inconvenience of barter, the existence of money. In fact 'a society which had not succeeded in inventing money could not develop a capitalist economy' (Robinson, 1956, p. 27). It is in terms of money, not goods, that wages are agreed and paid; and it is money wages not real wages, Keynes (1936, p. 13) observed, which respond to conditions in the labour market: 'In assuming that the wage bargain determines the real wage the classical school have slipt in an illicit assumption. . . . There may exist no expedient by which labour as a whole can reduce its *real* wage to a given figure by making revised *money* bargains with the entrepreneurs.' If there is unemployment, money wages may fall; but real wages will fall to an equal extent only if prices do not respond to the resulting decline in money costs of production. This is clearly unlikely: prices will tend to fall, and if they fall in equal proportion, real wages will be the same as before. And in fact Hicks (1974a, pp. 59–60) attributes to Keynes the *wage theorem*: that usually, provided that monetary policy is accommodating, a change in money wages will be followed by an equi-proportional change in prices, so that real wages will not be materially affected.[6] But suppose that prices fall by less than money wages, so that real wages are reduced to some extent; even then, Keynes argued, an increase in employment cannot confidently be expected, since falling real wages will tend to be accompanied by falling consumption and effective demand. The second neo-classical mechanism therefore seemed fallacious: not only is there no natural tendency for the real wage to clear the labour market and prevent unemployment, because real wages depend on prices as well as money wages, but also government action to reduce real wages, even if successful, may fail to reduce unemployment, because the demand schedule for labour depends on the effective demand for goods.

There was, however, Keynes admitted, one way – and only one way in a closed economy – in which the second mechanism might work: falling wages and prices, by reducing the transactions demand for money, would tend to reduce the interest rate, and this might encourage investment if producers' expectations and confidence were not adversely affected by the increasing real burden of debt. 'It is', Keynes (1936, p. 266) wrote, 'on the effect of a falling wage and price-level on the demand for money that those who believe in the self-adjusting quality of the economic system must rest the weight of their argument.' They had not, of course, done so. But anyway, the same effect could be achieved more directly by increasing the nominal supply of money; and more directly again (and more surely if, as Keynes believed, reducing the interest rate sufficiently might be a difficult task, or if investment expenditure was interest-inelastic) by raising government expenditure.

This, very roughly, was Keynes's analysis; and *the first neo-Keynesian contention is basically that it is no less relevant or valid for the economics of the long period than it is for that of the short.* What are the implications of this view for neo-classical growth theory?

In all the models of Part II investment was assumed to be given by saving at full employment; Keynes's problem of effective demand was thus, in Solow's (1956, p. 189) phrase, 'shunted aside'. One consequence of this assumption of continuous full-employment equilibrium which conflicts starkly with a Keynesian analysis is that when a rise occurs in the propensity to save, the theory entails an instantaneous equal increase in the ratio of investment to output, and hence an increase in the rate of capital accumulation – this, indeed, is how the capital-deepening approach to a new steady state is set off. The depressive effect of increased thriftiness on effective demand, fully acknowledged in Harrod's Keynesian model, is suppressed. As shown in section 3.2, it is not that the neo-classical writers believe that the above mechanisms actually do operate in the real world, but rather that long-run analysis can proceed as if they did, or as if government policy compensated for their absence.

Robinson (1962, pp. 14, 25) disagrees fundamentally: 'The argument of the *General Theory*, which shows that there is no . . . mechanism (to keep accumulation going at the right rate for full-employment equilibrium) in a private-enterprise economy, cannot be true at each moment of time and yet untrue "in the long run" [and] A model applicable to actual history has to be capable of getting out of equilibrium'; in her view it is quite illegitimate, even in growth theory, to assume away disequilibrium and ignore Keynes.

What form, then, should growth theory take? Harrod's model – as described in Chapter 1, not the neo-classical version of it described in

Chapter 3 – in at least one respect shows the way. To Robinson (1971, p. 109), 'The great strength of Harrod's model is that it is not an equilibrium scheme. It is a projection into the long period of the concepts of the General Theory.' It is not an equilibrium scheme, not because *s* and *v* are 'rigidly fixed', but because the rate of accumulation is not, as in neo-classical theory, always given by the ratio between them, and also because even growth at the warranted rate does not normally entail full employment. There is no assumption, or implicit neo-classical mechanism involving the rate of interest or the real wage, whereby investment is kept in balance with full-employment saving, or the demand for labour kept in balance with supply. If, starting in equilibrium steady growth, *s* rises, the growth rate does not as in neo-classical analysis, immediately follow the warranted rate upwards: it departs from the warranted rate, downwards, because investment does not respond in the neo-classical manner. What is to be learned from Harrod, then, is the need for an independent, Keynesian treatment of investment which acknowledges that it is not governed by, or somehow implicitly kept in balance with, full-employment saving. Thus in Robinson's (1964, p. 99) view, neo-classical theory 'leaves out of account the most important element in the whole affair – the decision governing the rate of accumulation of capital'. Sen (1965, p. 230) agrees that 'If growth theory is to have any relevance to policy, it cannot do without an investment function.'

It is then necessary to consider what kind of *investment function* is appropriate. Kaldor's attempts at formalising the determinants of investment are described in Chapter 13. Robinson (1961, p. 16) regards Harrod's accelerator function as 'peculiar'. She prefers to start with Keynes's emphasis on 'prospective profits' (see, for example, Robinson, 1962, pp. 36–7) but rejects the formalism of his marginal efficiency of capital schedule: Keynes himself 'did not take [this] seriously' (Robinson, 1962), as is shown by the importance he attached to the 'animal spirits' of entrepreneurs, meaning their 'spontaneous urge to action rather than inaction' (Keynes, 1936, p. 161). In Robinson's (1964, p. 101) view, 'To understand the motives for investment, we have to understand human nature and the manner in which it reacts to various kinds of social and economic system in which it has to operate. We have not got far enough yet to put it into algebra.' She considers that the rate of accumulation emerges out of the competitive urge of firms to grow, and that 'to account for what makes the propensity to accumulate high or low we must look into historical, political, and psychological characteristics of an economy' (Robinson, 1962, p. 37). But if pressed for a formal economic relationship, she would assume the desired rate of accumulation to be an increasing function of the rate of profit (Robinson, 1962, pp. 36–51).

In neo-Keynesian theory, therefore, investment decisions are explicitly treated as being independent of saving decisions; and disequilibria between investment and saving are allowed to have real (i.e., Keynesian) rather than 'merely' financial (i.e., neo-classical) repercussions.

Yet some neo-Keynesian theory, like neo-classical theory, assumes *full employment*, and not always merely for fun. Kaldor (1960, pp. 12–13), whose model describes equilibrium growth with full employment, writes:

> it now seems to me essential that a theory of growth should be based on the hypothesis of full employment. Fruitful as it has proved in the analysis of short-period fluctuations, the Keynesian under-employment hypothesis. . . is obviously inappropriate to the analysis of conditions in a prolonged boom. Such a boom may be taken as a first approximation to the conditions one is isolating in studying growth.

This could have been written by a neo-classical theorist! But Kaldor, like other neo-Keynesians when they assume full employment, would claim that he does not throw out the baby of Keynesian analysis with the bath-water of unemployment. He claims to retain the Keynesian insight that goods markets rather than financial markets equilibrate saving and investment (and respond to disequilibria between them), and to provide two mechanisms, consistent with this insight, which justify his full-employment assumption. The first, to be considered in section 11.3, forms part of his growth model, and is meant to provide a theory of income distribution while ensuring the *local* stability of full employment. The second, to be described in section 12.1, is external to his models, and is intended to demonstrate the *global* stability of full employment in a growing economy. Here Kaldor is clearly departing from Keynes, though in a way which he would regard as Keynesian.

Unlike Kaldor, Robinson attaches no empirical significance or validity to the assumption of full employment; for her, the determinants of the level of employment cannot be left out of account in growth analysis. This, and her reluctance to formalise economic relationships in 'closed' determinate models are two characteristics features of her writing; and she attributes them to the influence of Keynes's analysis. They are associated with what Coddington (1976) calls her 'fundamentalist' interpretation of Keynes's message. This involves an emphasis on *uncertainty* and *disequilibrium* as essential features of real life – essential features of the operation of time and change[7] – which are central to Keynes's analysis,[8] but which are missing from neo-classical equilibrium models which assume that expectations are always realised and mistakes never made: 'On the plane of theory, the main point of the General Theory was to break out of the cocoon of equilibrium and consider the nature of life lived in time – the difference between yesterday and tomorrow. Here and now, the past is irrevocable and the future is unknown' (Robinson, 1972, p. 95). Thus the main lesson for economic theory from Keynes's breakthrough is considered to be the limitations of equilibrium analysis, and the importance for economic behaviour of disappointed expectations of the present and uncertain expectations of the future. The major problem with neo-classical growth theory is considered to be that it has not learned the lesson. Furthermore, according to Robinson and other neo-Keynesians, Keynes himself failed to appreciate fully the far-reaching implications of his own lesson. They have therefore been seeking to extend his analysis, and his critique of neo-classical theory, into other fields.

10.3 Competition, markets and prices

The second neo-Keynesian objection to neo-classical theory is that *the assumption of competitive markets on which it relies is unrealistic, and therefore invalid, even given full employment.* This seems a clear departure from Keynes, for, as we saw in section 3.2, he proclaimed in the *General Theory* that the neo-classical analysis 'comes into its own again' in a full-employment world. Robinson (1964, pp. 81, 76) regards this as representing merely one of Keynes's 'moments of nostalgia for the old doctrines . . . Keynes himself was not interested in the theory of relative prices[9]. . . . On those topics he was content to leave orthodoxy alone. . . . The Keynesian revolution is only now slowly fighting its way into this terrain.'

In fact the fight may be considered to have begun before the *General Theory* was written. In 1926 Sraffa questioned the applicability of the perfect competition model to most markets for manufactured goods.

Casual empirical evidence showed that even in the industries commonly regarded as competitive – so that perfect competition rather than monopoly was supposed to be the appropriate model – most firms were producing under conditions of diminishing costs, with output limited not by diminishing returns but by a downward-sloping demand curve which reflected 'the absence of indifference on the part of the buyers of the goods as between the different producers' (Sraffa, 1926, p. 190) and which could be shifted to the right by expenditure on marketing. The conclusion was that monopoly theory was more generally applicable than had been supposed. Robinson's *Economics of Imperfect Competition* followed in 1933 (see Robinson, 1969). She showed how, if firms' demand curves are not perfectly elastic, profit maximisation implies that price will exceed marginal cost even if profits are no more than 'normal'. The real wage will then equal labour's marginal-revenue product, and fall short of its marginal-value product. This breaking of the link between wage and marginal product was to her 'the main point' of her analysis (Robinson, 1969, p. xii).

But this still shared with neo-classical theory the assumption that firms maximise profits under demand conditions which are known. The 'Keynesian' breakthrough was still to come; but already, without the restraint of perfect competition, the assumption of profit maximisation was vulnerable.

It was Kalecki who provided the key. Writing in the 1940s, he argued that an essential distinction needed to be drawn between primary products and manufactured goods. In the case of the former, supply was inherently price-inelastic in the short term, and prices were consequently sensitive to changes in demand; in fact, prices could be regarded as being predominantly 'demand-determined'. But for the latter, prices were mainly 'cost-determined': 'The production of finished goods is elastic as a result of existing reserves of productive capacity. When demand increases it is met mainly by an increase in the volume of production while prices tend to remain stable. The price changes which do occur result mainly from changes in costs of production' (Kalecki, 1954, p. 43). He proceeded to consider the formation of 'cost-determined'[10] prices at the level of the firm, prefacing his analysis with the characteristically bald remark that 'In view of the *uncertainties* faced in the process of price fixing it will not be assumed that the firm attempts to maximise its profits in any precise sort of manner' (Kalecki, 1954, p. 44, my emphasis). This may be regarded as the birth of 'The Keynesian theory of prices, that money-wage rates are the main determinant of prime costs and that the general level of prices moves more or less proportionately to the level of wage rates' (Robinson, 1969, p. viii). Its role in the neo-Keynesian theory of income distribution will be examined in the following chapter.

The neo-Keynesians thus reject not only the 'parable' of perfect competition but neo-classical assumptions of optimising behaviour generally. Robinson (1977, pp. 1318, 1325) now considers *Imperfect Competition* to have been a 'blind alley': 'The doctrine that firms "maximise profits" collapses as soon as it is taken out of the equilibrium world and set in historical time. . . . Certainly, it is true that firms pursue profit, for without profits they would perish, but to "maximise" profits over the long run is a meaningless phrase.' Neo-Keynesians prefer simple *rules of thumb* as descriptions of behaviour in an imperfectly competitive, uncertain world. The neo-Keynesian saving function may be regarded as an example (see sections 10.4 and 12.2); another instance is Kaldor's adoption of the 'pay-off-period criterion' for his investment function (13.5).

It is appropriate at this point to refer back to Chapter 9, to recall, first, Kaldor's emphasis on the empirical importance of *economies of scale* and their inconsistency with perfect competition, and second, Nelson and Winter's rejection of profit maximisation in favour of a *behavioural* theory of the firm.

10.4 Saving: Kalecki and the classics

As we saw in Part II, most neo-classical growth models assume either proportional, or classical, or neo-Keynesian saving – i.e., one of the particular cases embodied in what we referred to in section 5.2 as the general saving function:

$$S = s_w W + s_p P ; \quad 0 \leqslant s_w \leqslant s_p \leqslant 1 \tag{10.1}$$

But this function, and each of its particular cases, are all simple rules ('of thumb') having no foundation in a theory of optimising behaviour. In this sense even the proportional function, with $s_w = s_p$, is more in keeping with the neo-Keynesian approach than with the neo-classical. It may have been sensible for neo-classical theory initially to retain

Harrod's saving assumption, to focus on the more crucial differences between his model and the neo-classical approach, but there is nothing 'neo-classical' about proportional saving. Some neo-classical writers have therefore been keen to dissociate themselves from each variant of (10.1) – from any assumption of fixed saving propensities – and to follow their natural inclination by seeking a more adequate treatment in theories of inter-temporal utility maximisation. We quoted Johnson in section 5.2;[11] the same view is held by Dixit (1976, esp. pp. 65–6) and Bliss (1975, p. 126): 'The habit of assuming "propensities to save", here meaning given fractions of income or profit, has badly infected the theory of economic growth, so that the assumption that ratios of saving to other quantities are given constants is quite usual . . . to assume such a ratio constant in advance is to take as given something that ought to be the subject of economic analysis.'

But to the neo-Keynesians by far the most important 'fact' about saving, staring in the face of anyone whose vision and 'economic analysis' are not restricted by neo-classical conceptions, is that most saving comes from profits; and this 'fact' is satisfactorily embodied in the assumption that s_p exceeds s_w. The validity of the assumption, and the neo-classical objections to its use, will be discussed in section 12.2. Here we need to say something about the history of the hypothesis and its role in neo-Keynesian theory.

It was the assumption that most saving emanated from profits that lay behind the importance which Ricardo attached to the question of distributive shares. With workers too poor and landlords too profligate to save, the bulk of saving was seen as being done by capitalists out of their profits. With profits determining saving, and saving determining the rate of capital accumulation, the importance of distributive shares was clear: they determined the rate of growth. Furthermore, as capital accumulated, the operation of diminishing returns would result in a declining rate and share of profits until accumulation and growth would cease. In this ultimate stationary state distributive shares would be such as to be compatible with a zero rate of growth; in this sense distribution would in the long run be determined by the rate of growth rather than vice versa.

Although the classical or neo-Keynesian hypothesis is implicit in some of Keynes's writing,[12] it was through Kalecki that it returned to prominence. Whereas Ricardo had considered investment to be governed by saving, Kalecki showed that if investment behaviour is independent of saving, the hypothesis that all wages are consumed implies that profits are determined by investment rather than vice-versa, even in the short run. For our purposes his model may be written simply as

$$S = s_p P; \quad 0 < s_p \leqslant 1$$

$$I = \bar{I}$$

$$S = I$$

Therefore

$$P = \frac{\bar{I}}{s_p} \tag{10.2}$$

This was set out in Kalecki (1933), a paper written in Polish which anticipated the central analysis of Keynes's work published three years later.[13] For Kalecki the importance of the dependence of saving on income distribution was that it provided a theory of profits, and hence, given his theory of distribution based on his analysis of pricing behaviour (see section 11.2 below), a theory of output. The neo-Keynesians adopted this work (see section 11.5); and they have adapted it to provide their theory of distribution at full employment (section 11.3 below) and their theory of the rate of profit (section 12.3), which are meant to fill the gap left by their rejection of marginal-productivity theory.

That Kalecki played a vital role in the development of neo-Keynesian analysis will now be clear from this and the preceding section. Robinson (1977a, p. 14) puts it this way: 'Kalecki was able to weave the analysis of imperfect competition and of effective demand together, and it was this that opened up the way for what goes under the name of post-Keynesian theory.' He understood the far-reaching implications of the Keynesian breakthrough better than Keynes himself, because he 'was free from the remnants of old-fashioned theory which Keynes had failed to throw off. Kalecki gets Keynes back on to the rails where his "classical" education led him astray' (Robinson, 1977a, p. 15).

10.5 Capital: malleability

The final set of objections to the neo-classical approach is concerned with its treatment of capital as a homogeneous and malleable factor of production.

First, with regard to malleability, the neo-Keynesians generally insist on retaining the Marshallian distinction between the short run and the long run. In the short run, though there may be a 'utilisation function' relating output to the labour employed on given equipment (for example, Kaldor, 1961, p. 202), substitution possibilities are viewed as limited and costly, because capital goods are designed for specific uses, to be worked in combination with fairly specific inputs of labour, material and land. And even for the long-run, *ex ante* choice of techniques, Robinson would prefer to assume a finite range of possibilities (a 'book of blue-prints') rather than smooth substitutability, while in Kaldor the technology develops through the interaction of an investment function with his technical progress function (cf. section 9.3 and Chapter 13).

The neo-Keynesians regard malleable capital and the smooth production function which it allows as part of the neo-classical mythology which is required for the equilibrium story to be told. But in fact neo-classical equilibrium stories can be told without malleable capital and variable technical coefficients in production. First, as was indicated in Chapter 6, factor substitution for the economy as a whole may take place through changes in the composition of output among goods produced with different (fixed) factor proportions, as well as through changes in the techniques used to produce individual goods. Second, in the 'clay–clay' vintage model of section 7.6 there are fixed coefficients both *ex post* and *ex ante*, and yet there exists a steady-state solution in which factor prices have a neo-classical interpretation, and to which the economy converges owing to the flexibility of the life span of capital equipment, which plays the accommodating role performed by the capital–output ratio in variable-coefficients models. In both these cases Harrod's Existence Problem is resolved, and there is a neo-classical theory of steady growth, even though capital is not malleable.

There is a third example which is worth describing. We return to the Harrod–Domar model of section 3.1, and simply replace the proportional saving function entailed in (3.4) with the neo-Keynesian function

$$S = s_w Y + (s_p - s_w)P \qquad (10.3)$$

We immediately see that the condition for equilibrium (steady-state) growth, $s/v = \lambda + \beta$, is now less daunting, since from (10.3) the over-all saving propensity s is now a variable, dependent on the distribution of income:

$$s = s_w + (s_p - s_w)P/Y \qquad (10.4)$$

If the share of profits (and the share of wages) can take any value between zero and unity, then s can take any value between s_w and s_p. Hence, provided that the parameters are such that

$$s_w/v < (\lambda + \beta) < s_p/v$$

then if the income distribution is appropriate, in fact if

$$\frac{P}{Y} = \frac{v(\lambda + \beta) - s_w}{s_p - s_w} \tag{10.5}$$

then by (10.4), $s/v = \lambda + \beta$, so that the equilibrium condition is satisfied, and equilibrium steady growth is, at least on this account, feasible. Thus *as long as s_w and s_p are sufficiently different, and P/Y sufficiently versatile, the neo-Keynesian saving function can resolve the Existence Problem of the fixed-coefficients model, without malleable capital.*

But we have said nothing about stability: why should P/Y take the required value (10.5)? A theory of distribution is needed. We adopt the approach of, for example, Meade (1962, ch. 7) and Solow (1970, pp. 14–16), which is neo-classical in two respects. First, although with fixed coefficients a marginal-productivity theory is precluded (cf. section 3.1), it is still assumed that relative factor prices react to supply and demand conditions in the appropriate way. Second, it is assumed that all saving is invested: that we are always on the warranted growth path. But unemployment is (necessarily) not excluded.

Suppose, then, that the distribution of income is not appropriate to equilibrium growth: that, say, $s/v < \lambda + \beta$. The capital stock must then be growing at a lower rate than the labour supply (in efficiency units) so that capital must be becoming increasingly scarce in relation to the other factor. Factor markets respond by raising the return on capital in relation to the real wage; and with fixed coefficients, this must entail a rise in the profit share. Thus the over-all propensity to save and the growth rate of capital increase; and the process continues until the rate of accumulation has risen sufficiently to match the natural rate of growth. Conversely, if $s/v < \lambda + \beta$ initially, there will be a redistribution of income in favour of labour – now the factor whose scarcity is increasing – until equilibrium growth is attained. Thus as long as all saving is invested and factor prices respond appropriately to factor-market conditions, equilibrium steady growth is stable.

This model is helpful in a number of ways. It is, as previously stated, a third example of a neo-classical theory of steady growth without malleable capital and flexible coefficients. It also shows – what we knew already – that neo-classical models can accommodate neo-Keynesian saving. Although fixed coefficients and neo-Keynesian saving are essentially non-neo-classical hypotheses, the model is still neo-classical because of its treatment of investment and its assumptions about factor-pricing and distribution. (The neo-Keynesian version of the model will be described in sections 11.3 and 11.4.) It thus seems to suggest that *rejection of capital malleability and insistence on neo-Keynesian saving are not, in isolation, to be regarded as of central significance to the neo-Keynesian critique.*

10.6   Capital: homogeneity

The neo-Keynesians argue that when the assumption of homogeneous capital is relaxed, critical problems of two kinds confront neo-classical theory.

First, as we indicated in section 4.1, the assumption entails the absence of Keynesian problems. In his survey of the history of dynamic theory Hicks (1965, pp. 35, 41) argues that 'It is the big thing that was wrong with [pre-Keynesian] theory. If there is just one homogeneous "capital", there is nothing to do with our savings but to invest them in this "capital". . . . The "frugal man" must put his savings into "corn"; for, in the model, there is nowhere else to put them.' *Once heterogeneous capital is admitted, the Keynesian problem of effective demand, and the importance of expectations, are less easily ignored;* then, as Hicks (1963, p. 182) appreciated in his neo-classical period, 'an entrepreneur by investing in fixed capital gives hostages to fortune' .

Even with attention restricted to equilibrium dynamics, the question of the stability of steady growth in neo-classical models has to be reconsidered. (We mentioned this in section 5.5.) Following Hahn (1966) it has been established that owing to the possibility of destabilising speculation, convergence to the steady state can be relied upon generally only if expectations are initially such as to allow the economy to follow a path where expectations are always fulfilled – a path difficult to conceive of in the real world owing to the rareness of futures markets. This conclusion is obviously markedly more pessimistic than that of Solow (1956).

The neo-Keynesians have, however, been more concerned with a different kind of question.

They consider that heterogeneity of capital means that the marginal-productivity theory of the rate of profit and income distribution is invalid, even for a competitive system, so that even on its own assumptions the neo-classical approach does not have a complete theory to offer. This objection was first raised when Robinson (1954) asked about the meaning of the variable 'K' in the neo-classical production function. If the capital stock consists of different kinds of capital goods, any scalar measurement of it requires knowledge of the relative values of the individual goods; and this requires knowledge of the price vector of the economy and of the rate of profit. Thus, Robinson argued, the aggregate capital stock, the production function and the marginal products of the factors are defined meaningfully only when the rate of profit is already known, so that they cannot be used for a theory of the rate of profit and distribution. Thus in Robinson's view even neo-classical theory has to fall back on Kalecki and Keynes for a theory of the rate of profit once the homogeneity postulate is relaxed. From (10.2), an extremely simple relationship is derived between the rate of profit and the rate of capital accumulation:

$$\frac{P}{K} = \left(\frac{1}{s_p}\right) \frac{I}{K} \tag{10.6}$$

This shows that the level of prices 'has to be such that the rate of profit is such that the distribution of income is such that the ratio of saving to the stock of capital is equal to the rate of accumulation' (Robinson, 1962, p. 12). With the rate of accumulation given by the natural rate of growth n, the equilibrium value of the profit rate is determined by n and s_p, quite independently of the technology (cf. sections 5.2 and 12.3). The only role then left for the production function and marginal products is to describe how the choice of techniques is made by firms in a competitive system.

The neo-classical response to this attack may be said to have taken two forms. Some writers, while continuing to employ an aggregate production function, have emphasised that the homogeneity postulate provides no more than a 'parable' but have argued that it is an illuminating and empirically useful one. Thus Swan (1956, p. 344) confessed to the assumption that 'Capital is made up of a large number of identical Meccano sets', while Meade (1962, p. 5) took 'the unreal but simple assumption that all machines are alike (they are simply a ton of steel)'. But Robinson has not taken seriously this search for a homogeneous (and malleable) physical substance in units of which capital might be aggregated independently of the rate of profit; referring to Meade's 'steel' she suggests, 'let us write it "leets"', so as to be continuously reminded that we do not know what it means' (Robinson, 1961, p. 23);[14] and elsewhere she has suggested that 'jelly' (Robinson, 1967), 'butter' (Robinson, 1971a) or 'ectoplasm' (Robinson 1965) might fulfil the requirements – the implication being that the substance being sought is mythical or metaphysical rather than physical. Most recently, she just calls it 'stuff' (Robinson, 1975). What she will not call it is 'capital'. So how misleading is the 'parable'? One problem with it, which Robinson (1956) had noted[15] and which Sraffa (1960) had clarified, was acknowledged by the neo-classicals during the *reswitching* debate of the mid-1960s, which Harcourt (1976) refers to as the climax of the Cambridge capital controversy. It was shown that, with a heterogeneous capital stock, it is possible that in comparing different steady states the relationship between the profit rate and the capital–labour ratio may not be monotonically decreasing unless the different capital goods stand in the same relation to one another, as regards the capital-intensity with which they were produced, at every stage of their production. Thus neo-classical parables based on the assumption of such a relationship in terms of homogeneous capital are not generally valid. Although the neo-classicals now accept this, they question its importance, because they judge that the conditions under which reswitching can be ruled out are acceptably weak. Thus Stiglitz (1974) and Solow (1975) both consider the reswitching phenomenon to be no more significant than the Giffen paradox of demand theory: just as we carry on drawing downward-sloping demand curves despite the (usually irrelevant) Giffen paradox, we can carry on drawing well-behaved production functions in spite of the (usually irrelevant) reswitching phenomenon.

The second response has been to emphasise that neo-classical theory can withstand the abandonment of capital aggregation and parables entailing homogeneous capital. Every individual capital good can be considered separately, and the rates of return on capital goods become a question of inter-temporal equilibrium (see, in particular, Bliss, 1975; Dixit, 1977). The neo-Keynesians complain that this system does not generally deliver a uniform equilibrium profit rate. But first, 'as all the world knows, there is no such thing as "the rate of profit". . . . The crudest empirical observation will convince one that there is no unique rate of profit to be observed in the economy. . . . Why is the "rate of profit" an interesting unknown? Ask the neo-Ricardians. If we know all relative prices from here to doomsday, could we ask for more?' (Hahn, 1975, pp. 360–1). And second, the system does deliver a uniform equilibrium rate of profit on special assumptions – assumptions which neoclassicals would regard as no more special than the assumption about saving embedded in (10.6). So could we ask for more? Some would ask for more empirical *applicability*; for example, 'The general neo-classical theory is too complex to allow straightforward statements to be made about factor shares' (Atkinson, 1975, p. 173). Thus although 'with our armchair omniscience we can take account of each machine separately. . . [it is]. . . of little comfort to the empirically inclined' (Hahn and Matthews, 1964, p. 110). If the only alternative is general-equilibrium theory, the 'empirically inclined' would prefer parables. And Robinson (1961, p. 26) would ask for more empirical *validity*: 'Postulate full employment in continuous competitive equilibrium and the assumptions we choose to make about technical and thriftiness conditions will see us through, right on till Kingdom Come, without any need to resort to ectoplasm' – Hahn is right. But the problem is that 'What they cannot do is to tell us anything about the history of the world we live in.' But this is of course a separate issue.

10.7 Summary

What is the most important issue in this controversy? What is the main point of the neo-Keynesian critique? First, Kaldor (1966a, p. 301n) 'the whole dispute between Keynesian and non-Keynesian theories is whether investment determines saving, or vice versa'. Second, Robinson (1973, p. xii): referring to the 'Cambridge debates in capital theory' she writes, 'The argument was not really anything to do with the problem of valuing capital. It was concerned with reconstructing a pre-Keynesian equilibrium in which . . . accumulation . . . is governed by the desire of society as a whole to save, and where full employment is guaranteed by real wages finding the level at which the existing stock of jelly will be spread out or squeezed up to employ the available labour.' To the neo-Keynesians the main thing wrong with neo-classical growth theory is that it ignores Keynes and adopts the framework of competitive equilibrium which he discredited. The force of this charge may be regarded partly as an issue of methodology, and partly as an issue not so much of ideology but of the ideological interpretation of neo-classical theory.

Neo-classicals are committed to competitive equilibrium analysis as the appropriate framework for growth theory, or at least as the framework with which to start and on which to build; and they do not consider that this commitment is inconsistent with Keynes. Many (e.g. Solow) would emphasise the view that for the long run it provides a reasonably realistic descriptive framework: that for the long run Keynesian problems can legitimately be ignored, and that at least in the long run capitalist economies really are ruled by the fundamental forces of *supply and demand, competition* and *optimising or 'rational' behaviour.* Others would emphasise the view that competitive equilibrium is, almost by definition, the correct framework for growth theory *qua* steady-state analysis. Bliss (1975) stresses how the steady state may be seen as a device which makes sense of inter-temporal equilibrium with perfect foresight (cf. section 2.2); and steady-state analysis is for him largely a theoretical exercise for which competitive equilibrium is naturally and necessarily the appropriate framework. Keynes, uncertainty, corporate saving, etc., are simply irrelevant: 'the conditions of semi-stationary growth are wildly unrealistic and, if we were to treat of them as a theoretical exercise, it would be better if they were not sweetened by grafting on to them "realistic" embellishments that are in fact quite foreign to stationary conditions' (Bliss, p. 135).

Kaldor (like Solow) sees more direct empirical relevance in steady-state analysis than does Robinson (or Bliss); this is a dispute which divides each of the two schools (cf. section 2.3). For Robinson, steady-state analysis is little more than a theoretical exercise but one which cannot be completed within the confines of the neo-classical framework, while for Kaldor steady-state analysis is about the real world. But for both – and this seems to be the main point of the neo-Keynesian critique – the real world, even in the long run, is ruled by *market failure, uncertainty, imperfect competition, economies of scale* and *behaviouristic rules* 'of thumb', and so cannot be described in terms of the 'unrealistic' abstractions of competitive equilibrium. The neo-classical framework is a tired and discredited structure of irrelevant assumptions: 'Very drastic assumptions are useful to hack out a new path, but it hardly seems worthwhile making them in order to stroll up a well-trodden blind alley' (Robinson, 1967, p. 132).

This seems so obvious to the neo-Keynesians that the loyalty to neo-classical economics of the greater part of the economics profession in capitalist countries has to be understood in terms of ideology:

The criteria by which [hypotheses] are chosen to survive and enter into the corpus of economic teaching are of two kinds. One is that a hypothesis seems life-like and offers some explanation that appears sufficiently promising to be worth exploring, and the other is that it fits into and supports received doctrine. Clearly the model of competitive equilibrium has a low score on the first criterion and owes its support to the second (Robinson, 1977, p. 1323).

In particular, the marginal-productivity theory of distribution, by confusing capital as 'machines' which co-operate with labour, with capital as wealth which is owned by capitalists, succeeds in appearing to demonstrate that 'The labourer is worthy of his wage and the capitalist is worthy of his profit' (Robinson, 1971b, p. 17). This was certainly how J. B. Clark (1891, p. 313), to whom the aggregate production function is often attributed, saw marginal-productivity theory: 'What a social class gets is, under natural law, what it contributes to the general output of industry.' Present-day neo-classicals dissociate themselves from such naïve normative inferences; but to Robinson (1967, p. 129) this merely means that the role of ideology is nowadays more subtle: 'Nowadays, of course, no one would put it so crudely [as did Clark]. Nowadays the hidden persuaders are concealed behind scientific objectivity, carefully avoiding value judgements; they are persuading all the better so.' For Robinson, neo-classical theory is best understood as an attempt to defend and justify *laissez-faire* capitalism.

It is the neo-Keynesians, like Keynes and the classical economists before them, who are trying to understand capitalism, as opposed to justifying it. At least that is how the neo-Keynesians see it.

Further reading

The basic neo-Keynesian readings are Kaldor (1956) (summarised in the article on 'Distribution, Theory of' by 'N. K.' in *Chambers's Encyclopaedia*), Robinson (1962) and Kahn (1959). The easiest and most systematic account of Robinsonian economics is the textbook by Robinson and Eatwell (1973). Pasinetti (1974, essays II and IV) are also helpful general accounts of the neo-Keynesian approach.

The relevant papers by Kalecki are in his collection of 1971. Feiwel

(1975) is a comprehensive study of Kalecki's work. See also the February 1977 issue of the *Oxford Bulletin of Economics and Statistics*.

For a comprehensive guide to the literature on the capital controversy, the reader is referred to Harcourt (1972). Harcourt and Laing (1971) is a useful collection of readings. Harcourt (1976) is a survey of more recent developments. Harcourt is a neo-Keynesian; for a survey critical of the neo-Keynesian approach see Blaug (1974). Dixit (1977) is a guide to Bliss (1975), which is the definitive account of general-equilibrium capital theory. For a very clear contrast of methodologies, compare Bliss (1975, ch. 6) with Pasinetti (1974, essay II). Pasinetti prefers 'causal models' with one-way causal relations to general-equilibrium analysis, where 'everything depends on everything else', and argues that this preference is inherited from Keynes and Ricardo. (He presents the Keynesian model as a causal system by ignoring the dependence of the demand for money on income. Then 'investment determines saving' unambiguously, since the influence of the propensity to save on income has no financial feedback on investment. In terms of the *IS-LM* paradigm, the *LM* curve is horizontal. Whether this is an accurate representation of Keynes is debatable.)

11

Income Distribution and Effective Demand

11.1 Introduction

In neo-Keynesian theory the distribution of income between labour and capital is explained in terms of two distinct though interrelated sets of forces. The first, usually attributed to Kalecki, is the 'degree of monopoly' of producers, or the relationship between the power of producers to control prices in the goods market and the power of labour to control wages in the labour market. The second – aggregate demand – is associated mainly with Kaldor's theory that in the region of full employment distributive shares are determined, for given propensities to save out of wages and profits, by the level of investment. Kalecki had no particular interest in the hypothesis of full employment, and although aggregate demand does have a role in his analysis, he never adopted the Kaldorian theory. Kaldor, having as his main concern the analysis of full-employment growth, rejected Kalecki's theory for this purpose and proposed his own as a substitute. Nevertheless the two may be regarded as complementary constituents of neo-Keynesian theory, and Robinson uses them both.

We examine Kalecki's analysis in section 11.2. In sections 11.3 and 11.4 we proceed to the Kaldorian theory, which will form a component of the growth model of Chapter 13. In section 11.5 we show how the relaxation of the full-employment assumption in Kaldor's theory allows the reintroduction of Kalecki's degree of monopoly to provide a neo-Keynesian theory of effective demand and output.

11.2 Distribution determined by the degree of monopoly (Kalecki)

In both Kalecki and Kaldor the share of profits in aggregate income is related to the profit margin of a 'representative firm'[1] operating in an imperfectly competitive environment, and in both cases the macro theory of distribution is based on an analysis of cost conditions and pricing behaviour at the micro level.

Much of economic theory is constructed in terms of variables whose precise empirical meaning is ambiguous; the problem of matching the variables of theory to the empirical variables measured by statisticians is then left as a problem for the applied economist (see Chapter 15). The object of Kalecki's analysis, however, was to explain the behaviour of specific, empirical, statistical variables. His main concern was with the determination of the share in private-sector G.D.P. of the income of manual labour. He distinguished between the income of manual labour – *wages* – and the income of non-manual labour – *salaries* – because he considered that the former constituted prime (or variable or direct) costs, while the latter constituted supplementary (or fixed or overhead) costs to the firm. This distinction between wages and salaries is based 'upon the degree of contact with the manual operations and thus the degree to which the worker's employment is dependent on the current volume of production' (Kuznets, 1966, pp. 191-2).

Kalecki's theory hinges on an analysis of costs, prices and distribution in manufacturing. Consider a firm producing an output x of a manufactured good, with given equipment. The price of the good, p, may be regarded as the sum of three elements: average prime cost, a (the sum of unit wage cost a_w and unit raw materials cost a_r); an allowance f for overhead or fixed costs (comprising salaries, interest and depreciation charges, normal profit, and rent of land and buildings); and additional profit or entrepreneurial income per unit of output, e:

$$p \equiv a + f + e \equiv a_w + a_r + f + e \qquad (11.1)$$

Deducting marginal cost m from both sides:

$$p - m \equiv (a - m) + f + e \qquad (11.2)$$

Now Kalecki assumes that over the relevant range of output a and m are equal. Underlying this assumption is the proposition that cost conditions in manufacturing industry are such that average variable

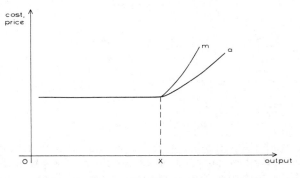

Fig. 11.1

cost does not change significantly with output until the 'practical capacity' of plant is reached, while the attainment of capacity output is a rare occurrence, even in cyclical booms. The cost conditions of the representative firm are therefore as shown in Figure 11.1. The a and m curves have a 'reverse-L' shape; and since output will normally be below OX, where marginal cost begins to rise owing to pressure on 'practical capacity', they may for most purposes be regarded as flat and coincident with each other. Thus substituting $a = m$ in (11.2):

$$p - m = f + e \tag{11.3}$$

We now introduce the 'degree of monopoly', μ, as defined by Lerner (1934):

$$\mu \equiv \frac{p - m}{p} \tag{11.4}$$

This is the excess of price over marginal cost (and over marginal revenue if we were assuming profit maximisation) expressed as a proportion of the price; under perfect competition its value would be zero. Substituting (11.4) into (11.3):

$$\mu p = f + e \tag{11.5}$$

Now let v denote the firm's value added per unit of output:

$$v \equiv p - a_r = a_w + f + e \tag{11.6}$$

Thus (11.5) may be rewritten in terms of v and a_w:

$$\mu p = v - a_w \tag{11.7}$$

Hence

$$\frac{v - a_w}{a_w} \equiv \left(\frac{v - a_w}{p}\right) \frac{p}{a_w} = \mu \frac{p}{a_w} \qquad (11.8)$$

and

$$\frac{a_w}{v} \equiv \frac{1}{1 + (v - a_w)/a_w} = \frac{1}{1 + \mu p/a_w} \qquad (11.9)$$

Thus the ratio of the firm's wage costs per unit of output to its value added per unit of output, and hence the share of wages in the value added of the firm, may be expressed in terms of Lerner's degree of monopoly and the ratio of price to unit wage cost.

We now obtain the corresponding expression for the share of wages in the total value added of manufacturing industry. We take (11.7), multiply through by the firm's output x, and sum over all firms:

$$\Sigma x \mu p = \Sigma x v - \Sigma x a_w$$

Thus

$$\frac{\Sigma x v - \Sigma x a_w}{\Sigma x a_w} = \frac{\Sigma x \mu p}{\Sigma x a_w} \equiv \frac{\Sigma x \mu p}{\Sigma x p} \times \frac{\Sigma x p}{\Sigma x a_w} \equiv \bar{\mu} \frac{\Sigma x p}{\Sigma x a_w} \qquad (11.10)$$

where $\bar{\mu}$ is a weighted average of the firms' degrees of monopoly, the weight for each firm being the ratio of its total revenue to the total revenue of the industry. We thus obtain an expression for the wage share:

$$\frac{\Sigma x a_w}{\Sigma x v} = \frac{1}{1 + \bar{\mu} \Sigma x p / \Sigma x a_w} \qquad (11.11)$$

The share of wages in the value added of manufacturing industry varies inversely with both the average degree of monopoly of the industry and with the ratio of the value of sales (or total revenue) to total wage costs.

This was how Kalecki's (1939) analysis was originally formulated. It is obviously messy; in particular, the two variables which are found to determine the wage share – the ratio of the value of sales to wage costs, and the degree of monopoly – must be interrelated. In a later version Kalecki (1954; 1954a) adopted an approach which isolates more clearly the influence of raw-material costs by defining the degree of monopoly differently, as the ratio of price to average prime cost:

$$k \equiv \frac{p}{a} \qquad (11.12)$$

We then obtain for the individual firm, from (11.1)

$$f + e \equiv (k-1)a \equiv (k-1)\,(a_w + a_r)$$

so that

$$\frac{a_w}{v} \equiv \frac{a_w}{a_w + f + e} \equiv \frac{1}{1 + (k-1)\,(j+1)} \qquad (11.13)$$

where j denotes a_r/a_w. Now the degree of monopoly of the firm enters only through k: the ratio j will be determined by 'demand-determined' primary-product prices, and by wage costs and degrees of monopoly at lower stages of production. A corresponding expression may then again be obtained for the wage share in manufacturing industry as a whole, by aggregation over all firms in the sector:

$$\frac{\Sigma x a_w}{\Sigma x v} \equiv \frac{1}{1 + (\bar{k} - 1)\,(\bar{j} + 1)} \qquad (11.14)$$

where $\bar{k}$ is the ratio of total sales to total prime costs for the sector – another measure of the average degree of monopoly – and $\bar{j}$ is the ratio of total material costs to total wage costs.

From what we have seen so far it is not surprising that Kalecki's analysis has been criticised on the ground that it is merely a tautology rather than a theory proper. The share of wages is shown to be dependent on the 'degree of monopoly'; but the latter is defined as the relationship between prices and prime costs, which is not far removed from the reciprocal of the share of wages! For example, (11.13) is based merely on the definitions of v, k and j, and the definitional decomposition of p. This expression – and indeed each expression included in the above statement of Kalecki's later formulation – is valid in any situation, and under any assumptions: they are all identities, with no theoretical content. It thus seems that Kalecki's analysis provides a theoretical contribution only in so far as it proceeds to put forward a refutable theory for the determination of k (or $\bar{k}$).

Kalecki proposed, in fact, that k is determined by the relationship between the monopoly powers of producers and labour; and this is one aspect of the theoretical content of his analysis. But is it a testable theory? If it is to have predictive power, we should be able to measure the relationship of monopoly powers independently of the variable k which it is alleged to determine; otherwise, to 'explain' a change in relative shares due to a change in k (which we happen to call the degree of monopoly) by a change in the monopoly relation is still merely tautological. This does not mean that we require a precise measure or index of monopoly power – rather, that we can be sufficiently specific in postulating the way the monopoly relation is determined to be able to recognise changes in it without reference to profit margins or distributive shares. Now Kalecki enumerates quite clearly the influences which he regards as the main determinants of monopoly power: the degree of industrial concentration; the prevalence of formal or tacit cartel agreements (which, he suggests, will be particularly strong when producers need to protect their margins over prime costs from relatively burdensome overheads, e.g. during a slump); trade-union strength, etc. Nevertheless doubts arise with regard to, first, whether we can tell when each of these determinants has changed; second, whether we can tell by how much it has changed; and third, whether we can know the nature of the functional relationship between monopoly power and its several determinants. Consider, for example, the prediction that a rise in trade-union strength, *ceteris paribus*, will raise the wage share. To test this proposition we need to be able to recognise an increase in trade-union power; to recognise whether *cetera* (e.g. the degree of employer or government resistance) remains *pares*; and also to be able to say, when other things are not equal, which forces are the dominant ones. The first problem is difficult; the second and third, perhaps even more so. Since it is therefore difficult to conceive of a satisfactory method of measuring monopolistic strengths,[2] the 'theory' seems to have little predictive value; it may not be tautologous, but it is not easily testable in any rigorous way, and it therefore seems that it cannot be very helpful. This is a common criticism of Kalecki's analysis (see, for example, Kaldor, 1956; and Reder, 1959).

This is not, however, sufficient reason to reject Kalecki's analysis. First, a theory which (in our current state of knowledge) is not easily testable in a rigorous fashion, and which is not, therefore, a 'good theory' by the criteria of positive science, is not necessarily empty or invalid. As Kaldor (1956, p. 366) himself recognised, 'the proposition that the distribution of income between wages and profits depends on market structures, on the strength or weakness of the forces of competition, is not a tautological one; it asserts *something* about reality (which may in principle be proved false) even if that "something" cannot be given a logically precise formulation'. This much is clear from the observation that it does *not* assert that distribution is determined, for example, by relative factor supplies and the nature of the technology.[3] In fact Kalecki's analysis has provided the framework for several investigations of the causes of observed movements in distributive shares conducted by himself and others, as will be seen in Part IV. Essentially these consist of searches for historical events or processes which, on Kalecki-type theories, might explain the behaviour of factor shares. The absence of rigorous statistical verification of the 'explanations' put forward does not necessarily invalidate them or detract from their plausibility.

But second, Kalecki's propositions about the determination of *k* do not comprise the total theoretical content of his analysis. We also have to note the reasons for his rejection of the neo-classical analysis, which are more apparent in his earlier formulation. First, he inferred from observation of manufacturing industry that in the short period output expands and contracts without any substantial effect on marginal cost (or, almost by implication, on the marginal productivity of the variable factor). This implies that there cannot be perfect competition, for if there were, price would be equal to marginal cost and hence to average prime cost, and firms would be making losses. Competition must be imperfect. Moreover, as we saw in the previous chapter, Kalecki rejected the hypothesis of profit maximisation 'in view of the uncertainties faced in the process of price-fixing'.[4] These arguments add further theorectical content to the basic tautological structure of identities. The validity of Kalecki's cost-curve assumption has been questioned by Reder (1959), Hahn (1972), and others. In particular, the point has been made that the observations on which it was based were made during the 1930s, and that the excess-capacity conditions which it represents may be inapplicable more generally and inappropriate to the levels of activity of the post-war period. But Kalecki stood by his hypothesis to the end: in a paper written shortly before his death in 1970 Kalecki (1971a, p. 164) wrote that 'even contemporary capitalism, where deep depressions are avoided as a result of Government intervention, is in general still fairly remote from . . . a state of full utilisation of resources. This is best shown by the fact that prices of finished goods *are* fixed on a cost basis rather than determined by demand.'

All this has been concerned with the manufacturing sector, in which Kalecki included industries not normally classified as manufacturing but which could be expected to have a similar cost structure and pattern of price formation – e.g. construction, transportation and some other services. He divided the remainder of the economy (excluding the government sector) into trade, finance and related service activities on the one hand, and agriculture and mining on the other. In the former the wage share could be assumed to be practically zero, owing to the negligible employment of manual labour; in the latter the wage share could be considered to be given by the relationship between demand-determined primary-product prices and unit wage costs. *Thus even when the primary and tertiary sectors are brought into account, the determinants of the private-sector wage share remain essentially the same: the degrees of monopoly of manufacturing firms; the relationship between primary-product prices and wage costs; and the industrial and sectoral composition of output and activity.* (With regard to this third determinant, Kalecki referred to a tendency for the composition of demand and private-sector value added to shift away from the low-wage-share service sector towards the high-wage-share manufacturing sector during a slump). Although the theory is based on short-term analysis, ignoring capital accumulation and technical progress, Kalecki considered that even such long-term influences could affect distribution only by way of these three determinants.

In conclusion we list some characteristics of Kalecki's analysis, and this will assist our examination of Kaldor's amendments to and extensions of it:

(i) Kalecki excludes from consideration the public sector.

(ii) Within the private sector he restricts to manufacturing industry the assumption that marginal cost is constant within the normal range of output.

(iii) In his analysis of distribution in manufacturing industry he restricts his attention to this normal range of output.

(iv) The analysis is concerned primarily with the determination of the share of the income of manual labour ('wages') rather than labour as a whole. Salaries are regarded as overheads, and are in a sense included in the share of profits. When, as an addendum to his analysis, Kalecki (1954a, pp. 74–7) considers the share of the sum of wages and salaries, he indicates that he expects there to be a secular upward trend in the share of salaries in fixed costs, as well as an inverse correlation between the share of salaries in income and output over the cycle (owing, of course, to the overhead nature of salary costs).

(v) There are *four ways in which, on Kalecki's theory, distributive shares may be affected by aggregate demand*: through the prevalence of cartel agreements (which will tend to raise the degree of monopoly and *reduce* the wage share in a slump); through inter-sectoral shifts of demand and income (which will also tend to *reduce* the wage share in a slump); through the relationship between wage costs and primary-product prices (which will tend to *raise* the wage share in a slump); and through the stable employment of salaried labour (which will tend to *raise* the share of salaries in a slump). Kalecki argued that the observed cyclical stability of the wage share was to be explained by the first three influences offsetting one another, and that the observed inverse correlation between the share of labour income as a whole and the cycle of output was therefore to be attributed primarily to the over-head nature of salary costs.[6]

11.3 Distribution determined by investment and saving (Kaldor)

Kaldor's amendments to Kalecki's analysis form the basis of a distinctively different distribution theory. They may be enumerated as follows:

(i) Kaldor's (1961, p. 197) 'representative firm' is 'assumed to behave like a small-scale replica of the economy as a whole': no sector is explicitly excluded from consideration along these lines.

(ii) The firm is fully integrated vertically, so that it does not purchase raw materials from other firms (or from overseas). Hence prime costs comprise labour costs only, and (11.1) becomes

$$p = a_w + f + e \qquad (11.15)$$

The omission of raw-material costs also means that the firm's value added is simply the value of its output and that value added per unit of output is measured by the price, p.

(iii) Kaldor does not distinguish salaries from wages: 'wages' now refers to all labour incomes, and all labour costs are treated as prime costs. Thus a_w represents labour costs per unit of output, and a_w/p measures the share of labour income in value added. Correspondingly, $(f + e)/p$, the ratio of fixed costs plus (super-normal) profit per unit to price, now measures the share of capital costs or profit in value added. There are thus only two forms of income – wages and profits – and the distinction between them matches the distinction between prime costs on the one hand and fixed costs and super-normal profit on the other.[7]

Since $(f + e)/p$ is the same as $(p - a_w)/p$, the proportional margin of price over average prime cost – which is Lerner's degree of monopoly under the Kaleckian cost assumption – now provides a direct measure of the share of profits.

(iv) Kaldor accepts Kalecki's hypothesis about the relationship between costs and output (and his inference about the absence of perfect competition). But he considers that Kalecki has ignored something crucial. This is that although it may be reasonable to assume that output is below the levels at which *physical capacity* is sufficiently stretched for marginal costs to be increasing, it is not reasonable to neglect the constraint of *labour* shortage. Full employment of labour, ignored by Kalecki, is regarded by Kaldor as a restriction on output which must be brought into account, in a way now to be described.

(v) Kaldor, like Kalecki, uses the concept of 'degree of monopoly', but it plays a peripheral role in his model. For Kaldor, it describes an exogenously determined minimum proportional margin of price over average prime cost:

$$\mu' = \min \left[\frac{p - a_w}{p} \right] \tag{11.16}$$

It provides a floor to the share of profits, and the position of the floor is dependent, in Kaleckian fashion, on competitive conditions. In Figure 11.2, where the a and m curves are similar to those of Figure 11.1, the SS curve embodies a given μ' and in effect represents a Kaleckian supply curve for the firm. Kaldor is prepared to agree that

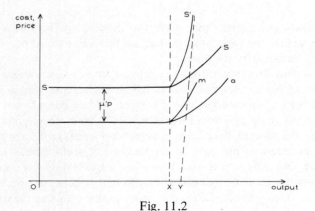

Fig. 11.2

below full employment this is the operative supply curve, and that the profit margin and profit share may then be regarded as being given by μ'. But before the *SS* curve turns up significantly to the right of *OX* – on account of rising costs – the full-employment barrier at *OY* restricts output much more severely: the Kaldorian supply curve is thus shown by *SS'*, and in the full-employment range the constraint represented by the degree of monopoly, (11.16), will generally not be binding. *The profit margin and profit share will be higher than μ' to an extent directly dependent on demand.*

Thus in Kaldor's theory the share of profits is determined with – indeed is equal to – the margin of profit over average prime cost of the 'representative firm'; this both indicates the way Kaldor amended Kalecki's analysis below full employment, and provides the basis for the mechanism whereby the distribution of income at full employment is determined in Kaldor's theory. The nature of the 'demand curve' in this analysis will be considered in section 12.1; meanwhile we proceed to a closer examination of full-employment distribution – the Kaldorian strand of neo-Keynesian distribution theory – at the *macro* level.

As in the neo-classical models of Part II, there are two forms of income, wages (*W*) and profits (*P*):

$$Y \equiv W + P$$

Real income or output, *Y*, is fixed at the full-employment level, $\overline{Y}$:

$$Y = \overline{Y} \tag{11.17}$$

(We are thus in effect assuming that the representative firm's supply curve is strictly vertical.) The saving function needs no introduction:

$$S = s_w W + s_p P \equiv s_w Y + (s_p - s_w)P; \, 0 \leqslant s_w < s_p \leqslant 1$$

But now, in contrast to the neo-classical models, *ex ante* investment is independent of saving. As a first approximation we assume it to be exogenous:

$$I = \overline{I}$$

From the Keynesian condition for goods-market equilibrium

$$I = S \tag{11.18}$$

we then obtain

$$\overline{I} = s_w \overline{Y} + (s_p - s_w)P \tag{11.19}$$

in which there is only one unknown: equilibrium profits. Rearranging this expression, we obtain the equilibrium profit share:

$$\frac{P}{\bar{Y}} = \frac{(\bar{I}/\bar{Y}) - s_w}{s_p - s_w} \tag{11.20}$$

This solution makes economic sense only if it lies between zero and unity, which will be the case, given $s_p > s_w$, as long as

$$s_w < \bar{I}/\bar{Y} < s_p \tag{11.21}$$

and this we assume. *Thus, at full employment, the Keynesian condition for goods-market equilibrium, (11.18), implies a solution for distributive shares which, given full-employment output, is dependent solely on investment and the saving propensities.*

If s_p were equal to s_w, the equilibrium income distribution in this model would be indeterminate, and we would have to look elsewhere for a distribution theory. But *the significance of the neo-Keynesian saving hypothesis* to the Kaldorian model goes deeper than this, for it ensures that if at full employment the 'representative firm' behaves in such a way that its profit margin (and hence the profit share) rises or falls according as there is excess demand or excess supply in the goods market, the equilibrium distribution shown by (11.20) will be stable. This may be seen as follows. Suppose we start from a full-employment position, with distribution shown by (11.20); and suppose there is a rise in investment $\bar{I}$. In terms of comparative statics the direction in which $P/\bar{Y}$ is required to change in order that the new equilibrium be attained depends (as (11.20) shows) on the sign of $(s_p - s_w)$. If this is negative the profit share is required to fall, while if it is positive the profit share is required to rise: we need a redistribution towards whichever form of income has the higher saving propensity, so that, with aggregate income fixed, saving can match the higher level of investment. But at the initial distribution investment has risen above saving – effective demand (investment plus consumption) has risen above full-employment output – and there is excess demand; and we are assuming that excess demand leads to rising profit margins, and hence a rising profit share. If $s_w > s_p$ the profit share will then be moving in the opposite direction to that required; and only if $s_w < s_p$ will the response of profit margins to the initial disturbance lead the system towards the new equilibrium. If this stability condition is fulfilled, the rise in investment will generate an equal rise in saving – an equal fall in consumption – so that effective demand will be restored to the level which can be feasibly satisfied at full employment. If the condition is not fulfilled, the rise in investment will generate further increases in (consumption) demand, and the disequilibrium will feed on itself.

The need for the neo-Keynesian hypothesis applies in exactly the same way when we consider the consequences of falling investment or changing saving propensities. Thus, *always assuming that profit margins rise flexibly in response to an excess demand for goods, and fall flexibly in response to excess supply, the neo-Keynesian saving hypothesis ensures the stability of the system at full employment, in that starting at a full-employment position the system will remain there, with the flexible profit share and the saving function maintaining effective demand at the appropriate level.*

We have now described the basic essentials of Kaldor's theory. The analysis rests on the following *six main assumptions*:

(i) there is full employment to start with;

(ii) investment *I* is exogenous;

(iii) saving behaviour is described by the neo-Keynesian saving function;

(iv) no constraints on distribution external to the model are effective;

(v) the share of profits may be identified with the profit margin of the 'representative firm';

(vi) at full employment excess demand (excess supply) in the goods market tends to increase (reduce) the representative firm's profit margin, which is flexible both upwards and downwards.

In the remainder of this chapter, and in Chapter 12, we shall be examining the meaning, significance and plausibility of these assumptions. This will provide an opportunity to explore various avenues of neo-Keynesian theory, and to prepare for the growth model of Chapter 13, as well as to clarify the Kaldorian analysis of distribution. We examine the significance of assumption (i) in section 11.5, where we remove it; we discuss the justification for it in section 12.1. We have already, to a large extent, uncovered the significance of the neo-Keynesian saving hypothesis; its validity will be considered in section 12.2. Assumption (vi) is taken up in section 12.3. This leaves (ii) and (iv) – which are discussed in the following section – and (v), which may be treated more briefly here.

It should be obvious that the domestic product of no actual economy is composed simply of the values added of producing units which resemble the 'representative firm'. We have seen that Kalecki recognised that the government sector and parts of the primary and tertiary (services) sectors could not be represented by this device. This suggests that Kaldor's view - that the device may be used to reveal the salient features of pricing behaviour and the determination of distributive shares in advanced economies - may be motivated by a presumption that manufacturing, and other activities where market behaviour is similar, have a dominant influence on the aggregate outcome.

11.4   Investment and external constraints on distribution

The hypothesis that *investment* is independent of the saving function clearly has a Keynesian flavour, and contrasts with almost all neoclassical growth theory. But the model as set out above also entails that investment is independent of profits, which is hardly satisfactory. Kaldor recognised this, and in the later papers setting out his growth model proper he introduces investment functions which always have profits as an independent variable; income distribution is then determined simultaneously with investment as part of the equilibrium (steady-state) solution.

Kaldor (1956), however, merely uses the identity

$$\frac{I}{Y} \equiv \frac{\dot{K}}{K} \times \frac{K}{Y}$$

which shows that in equilibrium steady growth the investment–output ratio is given by the natural growth rate n and the equilibrium capital–output ratio v; and he then simply takes v to be exogenously given by the technology, and so independent of profits. This is the fixed-coefficients, neo-Keynesian-saving world of section 10.5, and the conclusions about the *existence* of a steady-state solution are the same. (It may be seen that by putting $I/Y = nv$ in (11.20), we obtain the same solution for the steady-state profit share as in (10.5).) But we are now concerned with a different kind of *stability*. In section 10.5 we considered an argument whereby, if warranted growth is maintained, P/Y may move towards its steady-state equilibrium from a non-full-employment starting-point. The Kaldorian mechanism in contrast, refers to how, starting at full employment, the system may return to its warranted path following a disturbance from it, with full employment being maintained. That is, the stability mentioned in section 10.5 referred to responses to disequilibrium in factor markets, whereas the Kaldorian mechanism refers to responses to disequilibrium in goods markets.

Now, if an investment function is introduced which has investment varying directly with profits, Kaldorian stability may be impaired since, for instance, a rise in profit margins resulting from excess demand could raise investment by more than it raises saving. Indeed, Hahn and Matthews (1964, p. 34) argue that this is the 'chief threat to stability in the Kaldor model'. We put this question aside until Chapter 13; for the time being we need only note that the absence of an investment function, and particularly the neglect of the dependence of investment on profits, makes the above simple model incomplete, as Kaldor would recognise.[8]

Also, the equilibrium profit share shown in (11.20) must not violate any *external constraint* on distribution. Kaldor (1956) lists three such constraints. First, the profit share P/Y must be such that, for a given capital-output ratio v, the rate of profit P/K is not less than the value $i + r^*$ which, given financial conditions represented by the interest rate i, is needed for producers to undertake investment:

$$\frac{P}{K} \equiv \frac{P}{Y} \times \frac{Y}{K} = \frac{P}{Y} \times \frac{1}{v} \geqslant i + r^* \qquad (11.22)$$

Second, P/Y cannot be less than the prevailing degree of monopoly:

$$\frac{P}{Y} \geqslant \mu' \qquad (11.23)$$

Third, P/Y cannot exceed the level at which the labour force L receives a minimum real wage w':

$$\frac{P}{Y} \leqslant \frac{Y - w'L}{Y} \qquad (11.24)$$

We first consider (11.22) and (11.23). Suppose we are at full employment but that the distribution given by (11.20) does not satisfy (11.22): the rate of profit is too low (in relation to financial conditions) for producers to be willing to invest. Investment therefore falls away, and if we remain at full employment with the Kaldorian mechanism operating, profit margins and the profit share fall, and, with a given capital-output ratio, the profit rate falls further. But eventually the system will come up against restriction (11.23) (assuming it to have been satisfied initially) and we must suppose that at that point profit margins lose their flexibility: producers refuse to accept lower profit margins. The Kaldorian mechanism thus ceases to operate; with rigid profit margins we have left the world of Kaldor and returned to that of Kalecki, with distribution determined by the degree of monopoly. We are then also in a Keynesian world, since with a rigid profit share, the over-all saving propensity is fixed, and it must be aggregate income and output which respond to disequilibrium between saving and investment; quantities, not prices, adjust to demand conditions, and the full-employment assumption must be abandoned. We shall return to this world in section 11.5.

Restriction (11.24) places an upper rather than a lower limit on the profit share. If (11.24) is not satisfied by the solution to (11.20), then if the system is at full employment with the real wage held at w', wages must be too high – and the profit share too low – for saving to attain the given level of investment $\bar{I}$: there is an excess demand for goods which cannot be choked off by the required rise in profit margins without (11.24) being violated. This is the converse of the situation considered above, when, with the profit share at its lower limit, investment fell short of saving at full employment; but there is the asymmetry that whereas in the latter case we could suppose that real output would fall in a Keynesian fashion in response to the deficiency of demand, no upward movement of real output is possible at full employment. Kaldor (for example, 1957, pp. 279–80) considers that in this situation investment will fall back to the level of saving implied by w', and be held there. Distribution will then be governed by w', and investment will be governed by the level of saving implied by w' and the level of output; there is a reversion from neo-Keynesian (and Keynesian) to classical economic behaviour. This fits in with Kaldor's interpretation of w' as a Malthusian subsistence minimum; he considers that the effectiveness of the constraint which it represents can be only a temporary affair for a growing economy.

Kaldor does not specify the mechanism whereby investment is held back to the level of saving consistent with w'. One possibility is that the excess demand which arises if investment is lifted above that level sets up an inflationary process which leads to a tightening of financial conditions. Prices rise in response to the excess demand, and money wages then rise as workers resist the fall in real wages below w' which is entailed in the rise in prices; the demand for nominal active money balances increases as the price level rises; if the money supply is inelastic, interest rates rise in order to release idle balances; and this may cause investment to fall back as required. *Investment is then held in check by the financial consequences of the inflationary response of money wages to the distribution of income implied by any higher level of investment*; this possibility was suggested by Kahn (1959, pp. 151-2). If such a mechanism fails to operate – because of permissive monetary policy, for example – then presumably 'the system explodes in a hyperinflation' (Robinson, 1956, p. 48). Robinson (1956, p. 48; 1962, pp. 58-9) calls the limitation which the minimum real-wage constraint may place on the rate of accumulation the *'inflation barrier'*. Both she and Kahn adopt a broader interpretation of w' than Kaldor: to them it is not necessarily biologically determined in the Malthusian sense, but is more generally the minimum real wage which the labour force will tolerate. The possibility that there may be a 'head-on conflict between the desire of entrepreneurs to invest and the refusal of the system to accept the level of real wages which the investment entails' (Robinson, 1956, p. 48) then acquires a broader and more contemporary significance than is attributed to it by Kaldor. It indicates that even in an advanced economy investment may be restrained by a 'minimum real wage' which is sociologically determined and dependent, in particular, on the power of trade unions. The attainment of Kaldor's equilibrium distribution of income may thus be continuously frustrated, in effect, by the operation of Kalecki's degree of monopoly.

It seems that Kaldor's third constraint, which, at first sight appears so innocuous, 'may very well play an active role in the distribution process' (Rothschild, 1961, p. 184), in which case it cannot satisfactorily be regarded merely as a constraint.[9]

11.5   Distribution as a determinant of output

We now replace the full-employment assumption of the Kaldorian model – expression (11.17) – with the more general condition that output cannot exceed the full-employment level:

$$Y \leqslant \bar{Y} \qquad (11.25)$$

On substitution the equilibrium condition of the model becomes

$$\bar{I} = s_w Y + (s_p - s_w)P \qquad (11.26)$$

Since the value of Y is no longer given, there are now two unknowns; the model as it stands is not closed. We now close it by taking up the Kaleckian strand of neo-Keynesian theory – we postulate that below full employment the profit share is given by the degree of monopoly μ':[10]

$$\frac{P}{Y} = \mu', \text{ when } Y < \bar{Y} \tag{11.27}$$

From (11.26) and (11.27)

$$\bar{I} = [s_w + (s_p - s_w)\mu']\, Y$$

which gives

$$Y = \left(\frac{1}{s_w + (s_p - s_w)\mu'} \right) \bar{I} \tag{11.28}$$

Hence profits, $P = \mu' Y$ are given by

$$P = \left(\frac{\mu'}{s_w + (s_p - s_w)\mu'} \right) \bar{I} \tag{11.29}$$

And finally, the wage bill, $W \equiv Y - P$, is given by

$$W = \left(\frac{1 - \mu'}{s_w + (s_p - s_w)\mu'} \right) \bar{I} \tag{11.30}$$

Thus in our new under-employment model, real output, profits and the wage bill are determined in equilibrium by the saving propensities, investment and the degree of monopoly. But distributive shares are, by hypothesis, dependent solely on μ'.

Now consider the effect of a rise in μ'. By raising the profit share it will raise the over-all saving propensity, and hence produce a fall in aggregate demand and output via the usual Keynesian multiplier mechanism.[11] Equilibrium will be restored when income has fallen sufficiently to offset the rise in the saving propensity, so that total saving is the same as before, equal to $\bar{I}$. The wage bill $[(1 - \mu')Y]$ and saving out of wages $[s_w(1 - \mu')Y]$ must then have fallen; but profits $(\mu' Y)$ must have risen in order to allow an offsetting increase in saving out of profits.[12] Thus an increase in the degree of monopoly will raise the profit share (by definition); it will also raise total profits, but reduce output and the wage bill.

But what if we take the classical case, with $s_w = 0$?[13] Expressions (11.28) – (11.30) become

$$Y = \left(\frac{1}{\mu' s_p} \right) \bar{I} \tag{11.28a}$$

$$P = \left(\frac{1}{s_p} \right) \bar{I} \tag{11.29a}$$

$$W = \left(\frac{1 - \mu'}{\mu' s_p} \right) \bar{I} \tag{11.30a}$$

As before, a rise in μ' will raise the over-all saving propensity (now simply $\mu' s_p$), so that again output must fall via the multiplier. But now saving out of wages is invariably zero, so that for total saving to be restored to its equilibrium value $\bar{I}$, saving out of profits, and hence profits itself, must be the same in the new equilibrium as in the old. That is, the decline in output must exactly offset the rise in the share of profits; and the fall in output is accounted for entirely by a fall in the wage bill and in consumption out of wages.[14] With classical saving, therefore, total profits in equilibrium are independent of the degree of monopoly; they are dependent solely on the investment and consumption decisions of those who receive them. This observation was first made in Kalecki (1933), which anticipated many of the features of Keynes's *General Theory*.[15] Any rise in I or fall in s_p must generate sufficient additional profits for saving and investment to balance. In fact, not only do the workers *spend what they earn*, but also the capitalists *earn what they spend*, since profits must equal the sum of investment and consumption out of profits.

Thus when we remove the full-employment assumption, and regard distributive shares as given exogenously by the degree of monopoly, we arrive very nearly back at the simplest textbook Keynesian model, with output determined by effective demand, which is dependent on investment and thriftiness. The only difference is that with the neo-Keynesian saving function the degree of monopoly enters into the determination of output and wages, and may enter into the determination of profits.

12

Full Employment, Saving and the Flexibility of Profit Margins

12.1 The stability of full employment in neo-Keynesian theory

We saw in section 10.2 that Keynes argued that the only mechanism whereby a closed economy could be expected to attain and maintain full employment naturally, without government intervention, was through the effect of wage and price deflation on the demand for money, and thereby on interest rates. This mechanism has been carried over into growth theory by Kahn (1959, pp. 150-1), who, referring to a steady state without full employment as a 'bastard golden age', argues that:

> the possibility of a bastard golden age turns on the absence of any progressive tendency towards the easing of the state of finance, and more particularly towards a lowering of rates of interest and of yields on ordinary shares. If, for example, money-wage rates tend to fall progressively under the pressure of unemployment or the quantity of money tends to rise faster than money wages or the monetary authority in the face of unemployment deliberately makes credit progressively cheaper, there will be such a progressive tendency.

Then, if other things – including, in particular, profit expectations – remain equal, this easing of financial conditions will tend to raise investment until full employment is restored. Conversely, an excess demand for labour may cause money wages and prices to rise until a consequent increase in interest rates leads to a decline in investment and the elimination of the excess demand.

Keynesian theory thus provides a financial mechanism whereby an economy may be 'tethered' to a full-employment equilibrium growth path; it will then be enjoying a 'legitimate golden age'. But for Kahn the successful operation of this mechanism is one possibility only; and Robinson would certainly give little credence to it.[1] Both Kahn and Robinson are quite prepared to admit the possibility (even the likelihood) of growth without full employment in a capitalist economy without government intervention.

Kaldor, in contrast, concentrates on full-employment growth and distribution. He supports his assumption of full employment, not by means of Kahn's Keynesian mechanism, but partly by reference to economic history,[2] and partly by means of a theorem which purports to show that there cannot be unemployment on a growth path in which the goods market is in equilibrium. This theorem will be considered shortly.

We saw in the previous chapter that *Kaldor's distribution theory* describes a way in which full employment may be maintained in the face of changes in investment and saving behaviour, with flexible distributive shares and different saving propensities out of wages and profits assuring that aggregate demand is held at the appropriate level. Many writers have questioned the plausibility of this mechanism as a natural antidote to demand deficiency, even though most would accept that profit margins and the share of profits are sensitive to demand conditions. Samuelson (1963, p. 345) cynically compared the mechanism with (Jean-Baptiste) Say's Law of pre-Keynesian theory when he wrote that the United States' consistently high unemployment of the late 1950s and early 1960s indicated that 'the mechanism of Jean-Baptiste Kaldor seems to involve an extremely invisible Invisible Hand'. In fact, however, Kaldor (1957, pp. 297–8) had already got himself off the hook of this joke, since he has always been careful to claim that his theory of distribution 'is only acceptable as a "long-run" theory' as he does not expect the assumption of profit-margin flexibility to hold in the short run (see section 12.4). What we need to note here is that Kaldor would not claim that his mechanism will prevent lapses into unemployment in the short term, and that he must therefore consider that its effectiveness (for the long term) is uninhibited by the presence of unemployment (in the short term). It is to be regarded not only as a mechanism whereby full employment is maintained – which is what was to be inferred from the formal presentation of section 11.3 – but also as a mechanism whereby short-term unemployment may 'eventually' be eradicated naturally.

But once we admit that unemployment may occur, and that output rather than distribution may respond to aggregate demand, what is there to prevent output, rather than distribution, from performing the role of equilibrating investment and saving even in the 'long run'? What is there to stop an economy getting stuck in a Kaleckian position, with distribution governed by the degree of monopoly and output governed by effective demand? Kaldor's answer is *growth*, and the kind of investment behaviour which is associated with it. What we may call *Kaldor's full-employment theorem* maintains that any growing economy whose goods market is in equilibrium must tend towards full employment. It is based upon an examination of the stability of various possible positions of goods-market equilibrium, conducted in terms of the supply and 'demand' functions of the representative firm.[3]

The supply function has already been introduced in section 11.3: it was illustrated by the curve SS' in Figure 11.2. Below full employment the supply curve is parallel to the horizontal average prime-cost curve (which is also the average wage-cost curve) and the margin of price over average prime cost is given by the degree of monopoly μ'. As we enter the full-employment range, the supply curve bends upwards – away from Kalecki's supply curve SS – and soon becomes 'well-nigh vertical' (Kaldor, 1961, p. 198), the inference being that within this range changes in demand will bring about changes in price and the profit margin, rather than changes in output.

The 'demand function' of the representative firm is necessarily related to the behaviour of aggregate demand in the economy as a whole. We already know (see expression (11.28)) that, given investment and the saving propensities, the aggregate output and income which gives equality between saving and investment is a function of the profit share:

$$Y = \frac{\bar{I}}{s_w + (s_p - s_w)P/Y} \tag{12.1}$$

In section 11.3 we saw how this relationship determines P/Y when Y is given; and in section 11.5 we saw how it determines Y when P/Y is given. We are now taking the value of neither variable as given, and (12.1) is to be interpreted as showing the combinations of values of Y and P/Y which provide saving equal to the given volume of investment. Now P/Y is the same as the proportional profit margin of the representative firm, $(p - a_w)/p$; and (12.1) may be written equivalently as a relationship between this profit margin and the demand D for the firm's product:

$$D = \frac{\overline{I}}{s_w + (s_p - s_w)(p - a_w)/p} \qquad (12.2)$$

For given aggregate investment, saving propensities and average prime cost this expression describes the relationship between D and p which provides equilibrium between saving and investment at the macro level. From it, we see that

$$\frac{\partial D}{\partial p} = \frac{-a_w \overline{I}(s_p - s_w)}{[ps_p - a_w(s_p - s_w)]^2} \lessgtr 0 \text{ as } s_p \gtrless s_w \qquad (12.3)$$

This is to say that the way in which the demand required for saving–investment equilibrium varies with price depends on the way the saving propensities differ. The higher is price, *ceteris paribus*, the higher will be the firm's profit margin and the economy's profit share. Then with $s_p > s_w$ the higher will be the over-all saving propensity, and the lower will be the output and demand consistent with saving–investment equilibrium; in this case demand varies inversely with price. It may be shown by a similar argument that in the perverse case where $s_p < s_w$ demand varies directly with price. Thus when we come to draw the firm's 'demand curve' in the (quantity, price) plane, it will have a negative slope in the normal case, and a positive slope in the perverse case.

But confusion may be avoided in what follows if we give this 'demand curve' a different name, since it is obviously not a demand curve in the usual sense. It shows the combinations of output and price (for given average prime cost) which provide saving–investment equilibrium. It is thus analogous to Hicks's *IS* curve showing combinations of output and interest rate which allow the same equilibrium condition to be satisfied. It is not unnatural, then, to think of what Kaldor calls the 'demand curve' of his representative firm as an '*IS* curve', and this we proceed to do.

In Figure 12.1(a) the curves IS_1 and IS_2 illustrate the case where $s_p > s_w$, while in Figure 12.1(b) IS_1 and IS_2 are drawn on the perverse assumption that $s_p < s_w$. In both diagrams S' is the inelastic (full-employment range) section of the firm's supply curve. Now for goods-market equilibrium, each firm must be on its supply curve and saving must equal investment, so that if $\overline{I}$, s_p, s_w and a_w are such that the relevant *IS* curve is IS_1, goods-market equilibrium requires price to be p_1 and output to be X_1. We can now obtain a familiar result by asking whether goods-market equilibrium is stable in these two cases.

As in section 11.3, we consider the response to a disturbance of

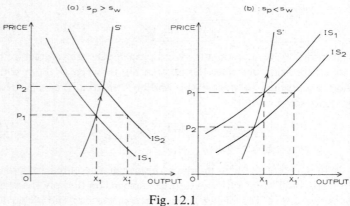

Fig. 12.1

equilibrium caused by a rise in investment. It should be clear that, irrespective of the relationship between the saving propensities, the *IS* curve will shift to the right if investment rises: at any price (or profit margin)[4] output or income must be higher so as to generate the additional saving required to match the new I. Let IS_2 represent the new *IS* curve in both diagrams. Looking first at Figure 12.1(a) we see that at the initial (old equilibrium) price, p_1, the output shown by the supply curve, X_1, implies that investment must now exceed saving: output would have to be X_1' for sufficient saving to be generated at that price. There is therefore excess demand; and by invoking Kaldor's assumption that profit margins are flexible - assumption (vi) of section 11.3 - we can conclude that price will rise along the supply curve until it has reached that level - p_2 in the diagram - at which the profit margin is high enough for saving to have risen to the new level of investment without any substantial increase in output (which is disallowed by the supply assumptions). Thus in this case, equilibrium is stable. Turning to Figure 12.1(b) we see that there is again excess demand at price p_1 following the shift to IS_2 and this will again cause price to rise. But now, as price and profit margin rise, so saving declines, and the gap between saving and investment grows. In this perverse case a fall in price is required for the extra saving to be forthcoming - as is shown by the new equilibrium at p_2 - but the excess demand causes price to move in the opposite direction; thus when $s_p < s_w$ equilibrium is unstable.

These two results are nothing more than a restatement of the stability condition on the saving propensities which was derived in section 11.3.

It is important to note how the disequilibrium behaviour we have been assuming for full employment appears in terms of these diagrams. When the system is out of goods-market equilibrium, we ask whether, at the disequilibrium price, the output given by the supply curve implies that investment exceeds or falls short of saving: in the former case there is excess demand, in the latter excess supply. This question can be answered only by reference to the saving and investment functions which lie behind the *IS* curve. We have been taking investment to be invariant to output (and price), and saving to be an increasing function of output (and price); and this means that there is excess demand or supply according as the *IS* curve lies to the right or to the left of the supply curve at the disequilibrium price. It is just as if the *IS* curve were a demand curve of the usual kind. But, as will be seen shortly, this is not always the case: we cannot rely on a comparison of the positions of our *IS* curve (Kaldor's 'demand curve') and the supply curve always to provide the correct answer.

We now allow for the possibility of unemployment by reintroducing the horizontal stretch of Kaldor's supply curve, drawn in full in Figure 12.2. Assuming henceforward that $s_p > s_w$ the firm's *IS* curve must be downward-sloping; and it may intersect SS' either in the full-employment range, as in Figure 12.1(a) and as shown by IS_f in Figure 12.2, or in a position of unemployment, as shown by IS_u. We already know that in the former case the goods-market equilibrium (with price p_f and output X_f) is stable. To examine stability in the unemployment case we need to amend our assumption about disequilibrium behaviour, since it

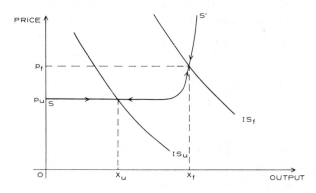

Fig. 12.2

is now output rather than price which is the free variable. When the system is out of equilibrium we ask whether, at the disequilibrium output, the price shown by the supply curve (i.e. the profit margin given by the degree of monopoly) implies that investment exceeds or falls short of saving; in the former case there is excess demand which will cause output to rise in a Keynesian fashion, while in the latter there is excess supply which will cause output to fall. Now at any output below X_u the price given by SS' is below that (shown by IS_u) which would make saving and investment equal. Since we are assuming investment to be invariant to price and saving to be an increasing function of price, saving must be below investment at price p_u, so there must be upward pressure on output. Similarly, at any output above X_u, the price given by average prime cost and the degree of monopoly implies that saving exceeds investment, so that output will tend to fall.

It therefore seems that the system can be in a position of stable goods-market equilibrium with either full employment or unemployment; and that whether it is actually in a Kaldorian position (with output given by the supply constraint and distribution by the position of the *IS* curve) or a Kaleckian position (with output determined by the position of the *IS* curve and distribution by the degree of monopoly) will itself depend on the position of the *IS* curve, and hence on s_p, s_w and $\bar{I}$.

But Kaldor now introduces *endogenous investment*; this changes the picture, and leads to the establishment of his theorem. He assumes that once the representative firm is earning a normal profit – once price (as shown by SS') is covering average total costs (A.T.C.) – as at and beyond output N in Figure 12.3 there is induced investment, A, which is an increasing function of output:

$$A = A(D); A = 0 \text{ for } D \leqslant N; A > 0, A' > 0, \text{ for } D > N$$
$$(12.4)$$

The *IS* function thus becomes

$$D = \frac{\bar{I} + A}{s_w + (s_p - s_w)(p - a_w)/p} \qquad (12.5)$$

We invert this function to make price the dependent variable:

$$p = \frac{a_w D(s_p - s_w)}{s_p D - \bar{I} - A} \qquad (12.6)$$

and then obtain

$$\frac{\partial p}{\partial D} = \frac{a_w(s_p - s_w)[DA'(D) - \bar{I} - A]}{(s_p D - \bar{I} - A)^2}$$

$$> 0 \text{ when } s_p > s_w \text{ if } DA'(D) > \bar{I} + A \qquad (12.7)$$

Kaldor considers that the new *IS* curve has the form shown in Figure 12.3. When output is below N there is no induced investment, and $s_p > s_w$ ensures that the curve is downward-sloping; there is a turning-point at N, where endogenous investment starts, and thereafter the

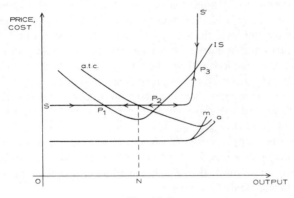

Fig. 12.3

curve is upward-sloping. We see from (12.7) that Kaldor must be assuming that beyond N the function $A(D)$ is such that

$$\frac{dA}{dD} > \frac{\bar{I} + A}{D}$$

That is, the marginal propensity to invest, dA/dD, exceeds the ratio of total investment to output; but the latter, on the *IS* curve, is the same as the over-all average propensity to save, which, for given distributive shares, is the over-all marginal propensity to save. The upward slope of the *IS* curve beyond N is therefore to be interpreted as showing that as output increases, the profit margin must increase as well so as to bring forth sufficient extra saving to counterbalance the excess of the marginal propensity to invest over the marginal propensity to save, so that saving–investment equilibrium is maintained.

Kaldor supposes that with the new *IS* curve there are three goods-market equilibria, as shown by the points P_1, P_2 and P_3 in Figure 12.3. P_1 has the same characteristics as the unemployment equilibrium in Figure 12.2, so we already know it is stable. Turning to the second equilibrium we see that if output is less than that shown at P_2, the price given by SS' is too high for saving–investment equilibrium. Since we are assuming that saving increases with, while investment is invariant to, the profit margin, this means that to the left of P_2 saving exceeds investment, so that output will tend to contract. To the right of P_2 the price shown by SS' is too low for saving–investment equilibrium; this means that investment must exceed saving, so that output will expand. P_2 is therefore an unstable equilibrium. Turning finally to P_3 we see that if price is above the level shown by this point, the output implied by SS' is lower than that required for saving–investment equilibrium. Now if output is lower, we know from the saving function that saving must be lower. But we know from the investment function that investment must also be lower; and since the marginal propensity to invest is being assumed to exceed the marginal propensity to save, the shortfall of investment must be the greater. Thus at any price above P_3 the output shown by the supply curve implies that saving exceeds investment: effective demand is less than output, and price will tend to fall. Similarly, at any price lower than P_3 there will be excess demand, and price will tend to rise. Thus P_3 is stable.

The final step in the argument is the proposition that growth implies positive induced investment; this means that for a growing economy the only relevant section of the *IS* curve is that which is rising, so that the only relevant equilibria are P_2 and P_3. The only relevant stable equilibrium therefore exhibits full employment. The theorem is proved: '*it is impossible to conceive of a moving equilibrium of growth being an under-employment equilibrium*', and '*an under-employment equilibrium is only stable under slump conditions when induced investment is zero*' (Kaldor, 1961, p. 201).

It may now be seen that if we had thought of the *IS* curve as a demand curve in the usual sense, we might have been led to incorrect conclusions about the properties of the three equilibria in Figure 12.3. In particular, it would have appeared that P_3 was unstable: at prices above P_3, for example, the 'demand curve' lies to the right of the supply curve, so that there would have appeared to be excess demand. We cannot tell whether there is excess demand or excess supply at any disequilibrium price or output from the relative positions of the 'demand' and supply curves alone: to know whether investment exceeds or falls short of saving at any (price, output) combination on the supply curve, we also have to refer to the investment and saving functions which lie behind the 'demand curve'. This is particularly clear when P_3 is compared with the equilibrium of Figure 12.1(b) (where saving was perverse and investment was wholly exogenous): the latter is unstable while the former is stable, although the IS and supply curves are related to each other in the same way in the two cases.

Although, if the IS curve is (incorrectly) interpreted as a demand curve of the usual kind, the Walrasian criterion of stability (whereby price rises or falls in disequilibrium according as there is positive or negative excess demand) leads to conclusions about the stability of the three equilibria which conflict with Kaldor, it so happens that the alternative Marshallian criterion does not. In the Marshallian analysis of markets the supply and demand functions are inverted, so that 'supply price' and 'demand price' are the dependent variables, and quantity (supplied or demanded) is the independent variable; it is then assumed that in disequilibrium output rises or falls according as demand price is greater or less than supply price. It is easily seen that by this criterion P_1 and P_3 are stable, while P_2 is unstable. This has led Wan (1971, p. 87) to misinterpret Kaldor's IS curve as a Marshallian demand-price curve. It should be clear from the way the IS curve is constructed that this is just as inappropriate as a Walrasian interpretation.[5]

The validity of Kaldor's theorem rests heavily on the investment function (12.4) which lies behind the U-shaped IS curve. It depends, in particular, on the assumption that the marginal propensity to invest exceeds the marginal propensity to save over a range of output up to full employment, for it is on this account that a small upward disturbance from P_2 leads the system to P_3. It is not difficult to devise alternative assumptions which give different results within the same framework. We could assume that investment is a more sensitive increasing function of the profit margin than is saving. If we took this assumption on its own, we would have an upward-sloping IS curve intersecting the supply curve in an unstable full-employment equilibrium[6] and in a stable unemployment equilibrium. Alternatively we could combine this assumption with Kaldor's hypothesis that investment is an increasing function of output beyond N in Figure 12.3. We would then have an upside-down U-shaped IS curve, again with an unstable full-employment and a stable unemployment equilibrium. But the assumption that investment is related to the level of output is anyway a strange one: we would usually take investment to be related to changes in output – the acceleration principle. And when it comes to his growth model this is of course what Kaldor does: he does not take the investment function used for his full-employment theorem. The static investment function used for the theorem cannot be carried over to the growth model, for in steady-growth equilibrium the marginal propensities to save and invest must be equal; and conversely a dynamic investment function of the accelerator type is disallowed by the static nature of the analysis on which the theorem rests. These considerations indicate that the full-employment theorem, which seems an unusually powerful and profound result, rests on a structure which is probably too weak to support it.

It may now be useful to enumerate the *various arguments we have encountered suggesting that unemployment growth must be, or may be, unstable:*

(i) *Neo-classical*: real wage (determined in labour market) maintains equilibrium between supply and demand for labour by means of *either* variable factor proportions, including variable inter-sectoral factor allocation (Chapters 4–7); *or* variable life of capital equipment (section 7.6); *or* neo-Keynesian saving (section 10.5).

(ii) *Neo-Keynesian*: real wage does not serve to clear the labour market, but the system tends towards full employment because of *either* response of money wages (and hence price level) to labour-market conditions, with implied financial effects (Keynes; Kahn); *or* flexible distributive shares with neo-Keynesian saving (Kaldor: section 11.3); *or* flexible distributive shares with neo-Keynesian saving and induced investment (Kaldor: section 12.1).

The Pigou effect, whereby unemployment causes a deflation of money wages and prices which raises the real value of wealth whose nominal value is fixed (e.g. money), and hence raises consumption, offers a further possibility; but it has not found a prominent place in the growth literature.

12.2   The neo-Keynesian saving function

We have seen how the neo-Keynesian saving function is an essential component of Kaldor's theory of distribution; we now turn to examine the considerations on which it is based. Why should a larger proportion of profits than wages be saved? There are three supporting arguments, each of which has been used by Kaldor.

The first is the fact that *a high proportion of profits is retained at source*; this proportion, not being distributed to households, cannot give rise directly to consumption expenditure.[7] In fact undistributed profits form the most important source of capital funds to the corporate sector in the United Kingdom and elsewhere.[8] These facts are undisputed; but whether the neo-Keynesian hypothesis can be inferred from them is debatable. Additions to the book value of corporate assets which arise from profit retention should, in principle (and in the long run), be reflected in firms' stock-market valuations. The shareholders who have forgone dividends will then enjoy capital gains; and if they regard this rise in the value of their wealth as equivalent to saving out of current income, they will reduce their saving by an amount equal to the capital gain in order to maintain their preferred wealth–income relationship. Company saving will then be offset by dissaving by shareholders to such an extent that total saving out of profits will satisfy shareholders' preferences and be independent of companies' retention policies. This means that to establish that s_p is higher than s_w we would have to fall back on interpersonal differences in saving behaviour, between those who receive dividends (and interest and rent, if profit is defined as including all property incomes) and wage-earners.

This may be restated as follows. Suppose that firms retain a proportion s_1 of profits, that persons proceed to save a proportion s_2 of distributed profits, and that they save a proportion s_3 of wages. Total saving is then given by

$$S = s_p P + s_w W \qquad (12.8)$$

where $s_p = s_1 + s_2(1 - s_1)$ and $s_w = s_3$. At first sight it seems that we can concede that there may be no interpersonal differences in saving behaviour – that s_2 may be equal to s_3 – and still argue that s_p exceeds s_w as long as s_1 is positive. But if share values increase in line with book values as profits are retained, shareholders will perceive $s_1 P$ as an accretion to their wealth and choose a value for s_2 (possibly negative) such that the total increase in their wealth, $s_p P$, satisfies their preferences. Then s_2 will depend upon and vary inversely with s_1. And uniformity of personal preferences in fact implies that s_2 will be such that, for given s_1, s_p will be equal to s_3 and s_w, i.e. s_p will exceed s_w only if shareholders' preferences differ from those of wage-earners.

But while this objection to the retention argument correctly indicates that company saving does not imply saving of an equal amount for the economy as a whole,[9] at least in the short period a rise in a firm's book value does not at all necessarily imply an equal rise in its market value. Indeed, there is a widely recognised trade-off between retention and market valuation.[10] Thus there are a number of empirical studies of movements in security prices in the United States and the United Kingdom which indicate that although 'investors should be indifferent if the present value of the additional future returns resulting from earnings retention equals the amount of dividends forgone. . . higher dividend payout is usually associated with higher price–earnings ratios' (Friend and Puckett, 1964, p. 657). Fisher (1961), for example, found in a cross-section study of U.K. share prices that the proportional effect of dividends on share prices was always greater than the corresponding proportional effect of retentions, and that in some cases the contribution of retentions to the explanation of price was negligible. It therefore seems that in fact the connection between profit retention and market valuation is highly tenuous, so that it is far from clear that firms' retention policies will in practice be wholly or even significantly neutralised by shareholders' dissaving. In terms of (12.8) empirical evidence suggests that, at least in the short term, $s_1 P$ is not perceived by shareholders as an increase in their wealth; this implies that s_2 will be independent of s_1, and that s_p will indeed exceed s_w even if s_2 is no greater than s_3.

But this does not settle the issue. The retention argument may be valid for the short run: but can it be valid for the long run and is it appropriate to growth theory? Bliss (1975, p. 135) accepts that it would be 'wildly unrealistic' to assume that the proportion of profits saved is independent of the proportion retained by firms, and he agrees that 'as a matter of fact company saving is without doubt an important independent cause of aggregate saving'. But he considers that this is irrelevant to long-run analysis (he refuses to accept that 'the peculiarity of business income allows us to attach to it a high saving propensity. . . for an indefinitely long period') and that it can have no place in theories of equilibrium steady growth. This is an important example of the methodological clash betwen the neo-classicals and the neo-Keynesians referred to in Chapter 10. For Bliss, the retention argument has undoubted validity and significance for the short term, but has no place in the inter-temporal equilibrium that is steady growth; for Kaldor, the retention of profits is an essential part of the growth process which no realistic theory can afford to neglect.[11]

The other two arguments in support of the neo-Keynesian saving hypothesis refer to personal saving behaviour. Why might we expect personal income to be saved in a higher proportion if it is in the form of profits than if it is in the form of wages?

Profit is of course generally thought of as a *risky* income – partly, indeed, as a reward for risk-taking. If, then, dividend receipts are more risky and subject to greater fluctuation than labour income, it may be argued that the former will be saved in a higher proportion than the latter; this would follow from the permanent-income hypothesis, for example. In rather different terms it may be argued that if one income stream has the same value on average but greater variability than a second income stream, the receiver of the first stream, if he is a risk-averter, will wish to hold a larger cushion of wealth than the receiver of the second and hence to save a higher proportion of his income as it grows through time. One snag with the application of this argument to the neo-Keynesian saving hypothesis is that if profits are defined as comprising all forms of property income, they will include interest and rent, which are contractual and 'safe', as well as dividends and self-employment income (after deduction from the latter of an imputed labour-income component), which may reasonably be considered residual and 'risky'; and the difference between s_p and s_w may be significantly diluted by the inclusion of the former. Thus Burmeister and Taubman (1969) found that post-war data for the United States indicated that the dichotomy of personal-income types which gave the most significant difference in saving propensities was that between labour income, rent and interest on the one hand, and dividends and self-employment income on the other. They concluded that 'it may be relevant in theoretical models to distinguish between safe versus risky income rather than between labour versus non-labour income'.[12] A second possible objection, which Bliss would presumably raise, is that any hypothesis based on the presence of risk should be considered inappropriate to a theory of steady-state equilibrium.

Finally, there is no question that in most capitalist economies the ownership of wealth is highly concentrated, and that even when pension funds, insurance policies, imputed rents of owner-occupiers, etc., are taken into account the *distribution of personal income from property* is heavily skewed in favour of households with relatively high in-

comes and wealth. If Keynes's (1936, p. 97) argument that 'as a rule . . .
a greater proportion of income' is 'saved as real income increases' is
valid for the cross-section, then it may be inferred that the propensity
to save is higher for personal income from property than for personal
income from labour. But although the cross-section implication of
Keynes's view has not been refuted by subsequent empirical investigations, neither has it been well-established – partly, perhaps, because of
difficulties with the data. Thus Evans (1969, p. 14) considers that 'it
is still an open question whether relatively wealthy individuals save a
greater proportion of their income than do relatively poor individuals'.
It therefore seems that it may be best not to rely on this third argument
to support the neo-Keynesian hypothesis, though Bliss (1975, p. 138) is
in fact fairly sympathetic towards it.

*The validity of the neo-Keynesian saving hypothesis thus appears to
rest more safely on differences between the two forms of income per se
than on any supposed differences between the sets or classes of people
who ultimately receive them.* This is Kaldor's (1966a, pp. 297–8) view,
since he has 'always regarded the high saving propensity out of profits
as something which attaches to the nature of business income, and not
to the wealth (or other peculiarities) of the individuals who own property'. One could adopt a saving function which differentiates not
between different types of income but between different classes of income receiver; but the above considerations make this alternative seem
less compelling. Pasinetti, however, adopted a saving function of this
kind, as we shall see in the next section.

We have already seen why acceptance of the proposition that profits
tend to be saved in a higher proportion than wages does not necessarily
imply acceptance of the neo-Keynesian saving hypothesis as an appropriate component of growth theory. Three further objections to the
neo-Keynesian function may be mentioned.

First, the form of the function entails that for each of the two income types the *average and marginal propensities to save are equal.*
Without this assumption the model would clearly (and probably merely)
become more complicated; and it would be the relationship between
the marginal propensities which would be important for stability.

Second, *why only two income types?* Some writers have been
worried about how the Kaldorian model can survive if there are three,
or four, or more, income types, all with different saving propensities.
Thus Lydall (1971) has objected to the fact that the model becomes
indeterminate when more than two types of income are distinguished.

Suppose there are n income types – $Y_1, Y_2, \ldots, Y_i, \ldots, Y_n$ – and let s_i be the propensity to save out of Y_i. Then the model becomes:

$$Y = \Sigma Y_i = \overline{Y}$$

$$S = \Sigma s_i Y_i$$

$$I = \overline{I}$$

$$I = S$$

from which

$$\sum_{i=1}^{n-1} s_i Y_i + s_n \left[\overline{Y} - \sum_{i=1}^{n-1} Y_i \right] = \overline{I}$$

which is one equation in $n - 1$ unknowns; the model is indeterminate, therefore, unless $n = 2$, which would seem to be a very special case. If, however, we expand the number of expenditure types from 2 (consumption and investment) to n, and assume, for each type of income, given propensities for each kind of expenditure, the model again becomes determinate. This was the subject of a satirical paper by Tobin (1960). In his reply Kaldor (1960a) argued that although there obviously are multifarious kinds of incomes (and expenditures, outputs, inputs, etc.) macro-economics is based on the principle that it is legitimate (and instructive) to aggregate items the differences among which seem inessential to the problem being considered. Thus the Keynesian aggregation of expenditures into consumption and investment serves to highlight a critical distinction between expenditures which are closely dependent on current income and those which are not. And Kaldor's aggregation of incomes into wages and profits is likewise motivated by his view that there is an essential difference between these two kinds of income – not merely because they relate to different factors of production, but because they respond differently to goods-market conditions, and because they are saved in significantly different proportions. Whether one accepts this argument is likely to depend as much on how favourably one is disposed to the Keynesian macro approach to economics as on one's judgement about Kaldor's particular propositions about wages and profits.

Third, there is the question of whether it can be legitimate for long-run analysis and growth theory to assume that the *propensities to save are exogenous (and stable) parameters*. This question was raised at an early stage by Rothschild (1959; 1961), who argued that the propensities will themselves depend on the distribution of income and on historical and sociological influences which can justifiably be ignored only in short-period analysis. This is clearly as much a criticism of the proportional saving function of neo-classical models as of the neo-Keynesian function. But, as we have seen in Chapter 10 many writers of a neo-classical persuasion have been concerned to dissociate themselves (and the neo-classical approach) from any assumption of exogenous propensities, and to argue that neo-Keynesian theory is inconsistent with the more adequate treatment of saving which neo-classical theory can provide.

Finally, it may be of interest to note that a distinction between wages and profits is commonly embodied in *econometrically estimated consumption functions* which form part of short-term macro-economic forecasting models. An example is the consumption function used by the N.I.E.S.R. for its forecasts of the U.K. economy, described by Surrey (1971, ch. 6). The explanatory variables of (real) consumer expenditure in the current quarter are current (real) personal disposable income, the quarter's change in consumer credit and the previous quarter's consumption; but within personal incomes wages and salaries are entered separately from self-employment income, rent, dividends and interest. The estimated coefficient of the 'wages' variable is higher than that of the 'profits' variable; for example, one of Surrey's estimates suggests that the marginal propensity to save out of wages and salaries was about 24 per cent in the short term (i.e. in the quarter in which the change takes place) and less than 10 per cent in the long term, after full adjustment; the corresponding estimates for other personal incomes are about 60 per cent and more than 25 per cent respectively. Another example is found in the Klein–Goldberger model of the U.S. economy (Adelman and Adelman, 1959; Evans, 1969, pp. 44-6). Results such as these may be regarded as providing empirical support for the neo-Keynesian hypothesis separate from any argument over retention;[13] but they do not settle the issue for growth theory.

12.3   The rate of profit and the Pasinetti Paradox

Differentiating between the propensity to save, s_c, of a capitalist class whose members do no work and earn no labour income, and that of a labouring class, s_L, Pasinetti (1962) pointed out that if labourers save –

if $s_L > 0$ – they must acquire wealth and receive profits. He then assumed that these workers' profits, P_L, are saved in the same proportion as the workers' wages, W, so that workers' total saving is described by

$$S_L = s_L(W + P_L)$$

If P_c denotes the profits received by the capitalists, aggregate saving is therefore

$$S = s_L(W + P_L) + s_c P_c; 0 \leqslant s_L < s_c \leqslant 1 \qquad (12.9)$$

This may be compared with what we have been calling the neo-Keynesian function. If we were to ignore the fact that s_L is defined differently from s_w, and s_c differently from s_p, we might infer that the neo-Keynesian function omits P_L. This was the inference drawn by Pasinetti (1962, p. 96), who considered that Kaldor had made a 'logical slip' in ignoring the profits accruing to labourers. But in fact, of course, Kaldor had not: he had assumed that (owing to retention and risk) workers' profits are saved in the same proportion as capitalists' profits, not in the same proportion as wages. For Kaldor (1966a, p. 298), 'the high savings propensity attaches to profits as such, not to capitalists as such'. Pasinetti's model is therefore not to be regarded as a 'correction' of Kaldor's; it represents, rather, a different assumption about saving behaviour. Using (12.9) Pasinetti obtained results which attracted a great deal of interest and controversy in the mid-1960s.[14]

First, when (12.9) replaces the neo-Keynesian saving function in the Kaldorian full-employment model of section 11.3, the equilibrium distribution of income between the classes is given by

$$\frac{P_c}{\overline{Y}} = \frac{\overline{I}/\overline{Y} - s_L}{s_c - s_L} \qquad (12.10)$$

which is the same as the familiar formula (11.20) except that P_c has replaced P, s_L has replaced s_w, and s_c has replaced s_p. The capitalists' share in income, (12.10), lies between zero and unity, given $s_c > s_L$, provided

$$s_L < \overline{I}/\overline{Y} < s_c \qquad (12.11)$$

This condition corresponds to (11.21). But what of the share of total profits in income and the rate of profit on capital? Consider first the latter.

In the Kaldorian model the identity

$$\frac{P}{K} \equiv \frac{P}{Y} \times \frac{Y}{K} \tag{12.12}$$

together with (11.20) gives

$$\frac{P}{K} = \frac{\bar{I}/K - s_w \bar{Y}/K}{s_p - s_w} \tag{12.13}$$

which in the classical case, $s_w = 0$, reduces to

$$\frac{P}{K} = \frac{\bar{I}/K}{s_p} \tag{12.14}$$

Thus with classical saving the steady-state rate of profit may be inferred directly from the natural rate of growth and the propensity to save out of profits, which are both regarded as exogenous parameters; but in the more general case, with $s_w > 0$, the steady-state profit rate is dependent on the output–capital ratio, and hence on the determinants of the choice of technique, among which may be the rate of profit itself.[15]

Now consider the Pasinetti model. In equilibrium the rate of profit must be the same for the capitalists and the workers; and in steady growth capitalists' wealth, K_c, and workers' wealth, K_L, must both be accumulating at the same rate, which must be the natural rate of growth, n. Denoting the uniform rate of profit of the system by r, we therefore have that in steady-state equilibrium:

$$\frac{\dot{K}_c}{K_c} = \frac{s_c P_c}{K_c} = s_c r = n \tag{12.15}$$

$$\frac{\dot{K}_L}{K_L} = \frac{s_L (W + P_L)}{K_L} \equiv \frac{s_L P_L}{K_L} + \left(\frac{s_L (Y - P)}{K} \right) \frac{K}{K_L}$$

$$= s_L r + s_L \left(\frac{Y}{K} - r \right) \frac{K}{K_L} = n \tag{12.16}$$

There are two possible solutions. First, if K_c is positive, (12.15) may be rewritten:

$$r = \frac{n}{s_c} \tag{12.17}$$

Then, using (12.12), we obtain the share of profits:

$$\frac{P}{Y} = \frac{n}{s_c} \times \frac{K}{Y} = \frac{1}{s_c} \times \frac{I}{Y} \qquad (12.18)$$

The steady-state equilibrium rate of profit is thus given simply by the parameters n and s_c, and is independent of the workers' propensity to save and the output–capital ratio. This was the solution derived by Pasinetti; it seemed to him that by 'correcting' Kaldor's 'logical slip' he had shown that the conclusion which had previously been associated with the special classical case in fact obtained much more generally. The only propensity to save which mattered for the rate and share of profit in long-run equilibrium was that of the class which lived on property income and did no work. We could introduce into the model any number of social classes earning labour income and property income in different proportions, but still the only saving propensity which would enter the determination of the profit share and the profit rate in the long run would be that of the widows, playboys, *et al.* who lived off their capital. We could even introduce a neo-classical production function, and the steady-state rate of profit would be quite independent of it.[16] This conclusion became known, not surprisingly, as the *Pasinetti Paradox*.

But (12.15) does not necessarily imply (12.17). The second solution, which is not as trivial as may at first seem, is obtained by satisfying (12.15) with $K_c = 0$: the capitalist class is extinct. Expression (12.16) then yields, since $K_L = K$,

$$\frac{Y}{K} = \frac{n}{s_L} \qquad (12.19)$$

With only one class and only one propensity to save, we might as well drop the subscript L; the obvious neo-classical interpretation is then that we are back in the world of Chapter 4. From a neo-Keynesian point of view this solution clearly makes little sense: so what is the requirement for the Pasinetti solution to be the one which is applicable? In the Pasinetti case $n = s_c r$ and $K > K_L$, so that from (12.16):

$$s_L < (s_c r) \frac{K}{Y} = s_c P/Y \qquad (12.20)$$

The workers' propensity to save must be less than the product of the capitalists' propensity to save and the steady-state profit share. Thus if the system is neo-classical with a Cobb–Douglas production function, the viability of the Pasinetti steady state will depend upon the relationship between the Cobb–Douglas exponent and the saving propensities (Meade, 1963; 1966a). Using (12.18), (12.20) may be expressed alternatively as

$$s_L < I/Y \tag{12.21}$$

which has a clearer neo-Keynesian interpretation: the workers' propensity to save must be insufficient for investment to be financed purely out of workers' incomes. This condition is entailed in (12.11), which is Pasinetti's adaptation of Kaldor's (11.21); and it is this which explains why Pasinetti did not consider the second solution to his model. Now in Kaldor's model, (11.21) serves to ensure that the equilibrium share of profits is positive and less than unity; it ensures, in particular, that the equilibrium share of profits is not zero. That would be a nonsense result, and we saw in section 11.4 that there are reasons for expecting that a decline in the profit share would be halted well before zero is reached, and that the Kaldorian theory would then cease to operate. The problem for Pasinetti is that (12.11) does not have the same logical status, since *there is no reason why his capitalist class should not be saved out of existence by the workers, leaving profits positive and the capitalist system intact.* Thus whereas (11.21) is necessary for the Kaldorian system to make sense, (12.11) 'begs the real question at issue' (Meade and Hahn, 1965, p. 445) in what Bliss (1975, p. 136) calls 'the shameful controversy' over whether Pasinetti's capitalists will, or will not, be eliminated as the system approaches a steady state with constant saving propensities!

12.4   The flexibility of profit margins

This brings us to the last of the six assumptions listed on page 197. We consider three objections to it.

First, *price flexibility is not the same as profit-margin flexibility.* Even if, when output is constrained, goods prices are sensitive to demand, it does not necessarily follow that when, say, demand rises, prices will rise in relation to unit wage costs (or in relation to money wages if we are assuming constant labour productivity), particularly if – as in Kaldor's model – the constraint on output takes the form of full employment of labour. In fact, Rose (1959, p. 332) has argued that full employment 'is just the situation in which money wages tend to rise in proportion to prices', rather than vice versa, when there is excess demand. But one does not have to accept this contrary view (which may also be attributed to Marx)[17] to consider that Kaldor ignores the fact that in his model when there is excess demand for goods, with output restricted, there must also be excess demand for labour which may affect money wages in such a way as to prevent profit margins from rising sufficiently to restore goods-market equilibrium. Meade (1962, p. x) has also criticised Kaldor for apparently taking money wages as given; he considers it implausible that an increase in profitability resulting from an increase in aggregate demand will not, given full employment, induce producers to bid up money wages against one another in order to maintain or increase their respective shares of the scarce factor and hence of total production. If this does happen – and 'how else can one explain the phenomenon of wage-drift?' asks Meade – then profit margins may never attain the level required for the excess demand to be choked off; and government action may be required to stop an inflationary spiral. A similar problem may arise if trade-union strength or employer passiveness is an increasing function of profitability – a view held by Kaldor (1959, pp. 190–4) himself.

Second, *the argument that prices will be flexible in a downward direction is rather less persuasive than that they will be flexible upwards.* Of course, prices will not necessarily rise in response to excess demand at full employment: there may be rationing of some kind, formal or tacit – increasing delivery time, lengthening order books, etc. But at least, in principle, output cannot respond. In the case of excess supply, however, the possibility of output response does arise; and one may consider that this reduces the plausibility of price response (and of the maintenance of full employment – cf. section 12.1).

Third, there is a body of *empirical evidence which suggests that prices of manufactured goods in the United Kingdom and elsewhere are insensitive to short-run (i.e. cyclical) variations in demand.*[18] Since this evidence is drawn from periods of near-full employment, it may seem to run counter to Kaldor's assumption; yet it has, in a sense, provided an unexpected bonus of support for his theory. We now ask how this can be so.[19]

We already know the first part of the answer, from section 12.1: Kaldor holds that his distribution theory is a long-run theory. He considers that in the short run the downward flexibility of profit margins will be limited by producers' resistance and their 'fear of spoiling the market', and that upward flexibility will be limited by workers' resistance to falling real wages (cf. the 'inflation barrier' of section 11.4). He would therefore not be disturbed by evidence that manufacturing prices (or profit margins) are unresponsive to cyclical changes in demand.

Much of this evidence has purported to substantiate the 'normal-cost' pricing hypothesis, according to which prices are formed by the addition of a margin, which is constant in the short term, to the average 'normal' cost of labour and materials – costs being measured by reference to a 'normal' level of output or its trend path. This is closely related to the analysis of Kalecki, but there is an important difference: average 'prime' cost is no longer considered to be invariant to output. The implication is that although prices and planned profit margins over normal cost may not respond to demand in the short run, actual profit margins (and the profit share) will vary over the cycle as actual costs rise and fall in relation to normal costs. Thus if labour costs are closer to being fixed than variable, actual average 'prime' cost[20] will rise in relation to normal average 'prime' cost as output declines in a downswing, and fall as output increases in an upswing. Hence without any variation in prices or planned profit margins, actual profit margins will vary pro-cyclically – which is exactly what Kaldor's theory would predict if its application were extended to the short period.

And this is just what was found by Neild (1963) in his study of cycles in U.K. manufacturing industry between 1950 and 1961. Fluctuations in employment had been relatively small; during periods of low demand firms had tended to employ labour in excess of their current requirements, presumably owing to frictions in the labour market. Average labour costs had therefore fluctuated contra-cyclically; and with prices rigid profit margins had consequently varied procyclically. There had thus been an association between, on the one hand, little deviation from full employment, and on the other, pro-cyclical variation of the profit share – just as one would expect if Kaldor's theory held in the short run. But while the result was the same, the explanation was different:

> As regards the short period, [our results] tend to confirm [Kaldor's theory] that planned profit margins are not flexible but they show that when investment (or some other item of demand) falls, actual profit margins are squeezed and full employment is fairly well maintained, because employers tend to hold on to labour. Thus the net outcome in the short period on our analysis is close to the outcome

in the long period on Mr. Kaldor's, but it depends on a different mechanism - the deviation of actual profit margins from planned profit margins (Neild, 1963, p. 52).

Kaldor, (1964, p. xvi, n. 3) accepted that Neild's findings require the cost curve of his representative firm to be amended, to allow average prime cost to decline as output rises within the full-employment range (which thus becomes a more fuzzy concept) so that *changes in distributive shares may result from changes in output (in the short run) as well as through changes in 'normal' profit margins (in the long run).*[21]

Neither Neild nor Godley and Nordhaus discuss the empirical validity of Kaldor's long-run theory. But both note a secular decline in profit margins, which indicates how the 'normal-cost' hypothesis may be inadequate for the long term, and which is presumably the kind of observation which Kaldor would hope could be explained by his theory, in this case by a decline in investment. We return to this question in Part IV.

Finally, it is interesting to compare Neild's analysis of the cyclical behaviour of prices and distributive shares with that of Kalecki (see section 11.2). First, there is in Kalecki an explicit distinction between prime and overhead labour costs, with wages forming part of the cost base and salaries part of the mark-up; Neild ('for convenience of exposition') refers to all labour costs as 'prime' costs, and includes them all in his cost base. Second, Kalecki assumed constant average prime cost, whereas Neild found falling average 'prime' cost (owing mainly to the overhead nature of part of labour costs). Third, in both analyses demand has no direct impact on prices; but whereas with Kalecki this is due to the constancy of average prime cost, with Neild it is explained by the hypothesis that the cost base refers to 'normal' output. Fourth, Kalecki considered that his profit margin (degree of monopoly), which includes overhead labour costs, would tend to vary contra-cyclically, whereas Neild found that his profit margin (excluding all labour costs) had varied pro-cyclically. But fifth, Kalecki recognised that the share of profits varied pro-cyclically, and explained this by the overhead nature of salaried labour; thus Neild's findings are not so inconsistent with Kalecki's analysis. Indeed, one could argue that the only differences arise from the absence in Neild of an explicit distinction between prime and overhead labour.[22]

13

Investment and Growth – Kaldor's Growth Model

13.1 Introduction

The main components of Kaldor's growth model are as follows: the technical progress function (T.P.F.) of section 9.3; an assumption of constant labour-force growth; and the six main assumptions underlying the distribution model of section 11.3, except that assumption (ii) – that investment is exogenous – is replaced by an investment function. The model has appeared in three versions (Kaldor, 1957; 1961; and Kaldor and Mirrlees, 1962). The investment function is different in each; also, the first version uses period rather than continuous analysis, and in the third version vintage capital is introduced. Although the first and second versions may be regarded as obsolete predecessors of the third, the development of the model and the differences among the three versions are of some interest. It is therefore the first version which we shall examine at length; and the later amendments will be considered more briefly.

Our main interest is in seeing how the components of the model fit together, and in examining the nature of the explanation for steady growth which the model purports to provide. But we shall also pay some attention to the investment function, which is the only component not already discussed.

13.2 Period analysis: steady-state solution

The *investment function* in the first version (Kaldor, 1957) is based on the hypothesis that producers have a desired capital–output ratio which is an increasing function of the expected rate of profit. This in effect constitutes a marriage of the acceleration principle, which assumes a fixed desired capital–output ratio, with Kalecki's principle of increasing risk, which makes investment an increasing function of the profit rate (cf. Kalecki, 1943). Kaldor postulates that higher capital–output ratios entail higher degrees of risk, and that they will therefore require higher expected rates of profit (at a given cost of finance) to be willingly employed. In contrast with Kalecki, he considers that higher rates of growth of capital will not entail higher degrees of risk if they are accompanied by compensatingly higher growth rates of output.

Kaldor's hypothesis is intuitively appealing; but two problems arise in its translation into a precisely formulated investment function which illustrate the difficulties associated with the formulation of investment functions in general. The first concerns the formation of expectations about the profit rate. Here Kaldor adopts the simple expedient of assuming unit-elastic expectations, so that the desired capital–output ratio becomes simply an increasing function of the current profit rate. Denoting the desired capital stock by K^* and taking a linear form

$$\frac{K^*_t}{Y_t} = \alpha' + \beta' \frac{P_t}{K_t} ; \quad \alpha', \beta' > 0 \tag{13.1}$$

The second problem concerns the lag in the execution of investment plans. Again Kaldor adopts an extremely simple assumption – that there is a one-period lag, so that the planned investment of period t is such as will make the actual capital stock in period $t + 1$ equal to the desired capital stock of period t:

$$K_{t+1} = K^*_t \tag{13.2}$$

Thus

$$K_{t+1} = \alpha' Y_t + \beta' \left(\frac{P_t}{K_t}\right) Y_t \tag{13.3}$$

Assuming that this equation for the planned (as opposed to the desired or optimal) capital stock is satisfied by K_t, Kaldor then derives his investment function by first-differencing:

$$I_t \equiv K_{t+1} - K_t = (Y_t - Y_{t-1}) \left(\alpha' + \beta' \frac{P_{t-1}}{K_{t-1}}\right)$$

$$+ \beta' Y_t \left(\frac{P_t}{K_t} - \frac{P_{t-1}}{K_{t-1}}\right) \tag{13.4}$$

Using (13.3) for K_t, we express this in the alternative form:

$$\frac{I_t}{K_t} = \frac{Y_t - Y_{t-1}}{Y_{t-1}} + \beta' \frac{Y_t}{K_t} \left(\frac{P_t}{K_t} - \frac{P_{t-1}}{K_{t-1}} \right) \tag{13.5}$$

Thus if the profit rate is constant, planned investment as a proportion of the capital stock (i.e. the planned growth rate of the capital stock) will be equal to the growth rate of output; but if the profit rate rises (or falls) the planned rate of accumulation will be higher (or lower). Investment in the current period is dependent on the output, profits and capital stock of the current and preceding periods.

This specification of the initial hypothesis about entrepreneurial behaviour has obvious shortcomings. The problem of expectations has been swept aside in cavalier fashion.[1] Also, if investment decisions are regarded as being taken at the beginning of the (gestation) period, (13.5) implies perfect foresight of output and profits during the period. This may be traced back to (13.3); and the inference is that the one-period lag is insufficient, as Kaldor (1962a) later recognised. It was these and other shortcomings which led to the amended investment function of the second version.

Second, we have the neo-Keynesian saving function, now written in terms of discrete rather than continuous time:

$$S_t = s_w Y_t + (s_p - s_w)P_t; \quad 0 \leqslant s_w < s_p \leqslant 1 \tag{13.6}$$

Third, for labour-force growth:

$$L_t = L_o(1 + \lambda)^t; \quad \lambda \geqslant 0 \tag{13.7}$$

Fourth, there is the technical progress function (T.P.F.):

$$\frac{y_{t+1} - y_t}{y_t} = T\left(\frac{k_{t+1} - k_t}{k_t}\right); \quad T' > 0, T'' < 0$$

Kaldor adopts a linear form;[2] in terms of Y, K and λ, it may be written:

$$\frac{Y_{t+1} - Y_t}{Y_t} - \lambda = \alpha'' + \beta'' \left(\frac{K_{t+1} - K_t}{K_t} - \lambda\right);$$

$$\alpha'' > 0, 0 < \beta'' < 1 \tag{13.8}$$

We are now ready to examine the existence, uniqueness and stability of a steady-state solution.

We first reduce the model to a system of two simultaneous difference equations in K and Y. From (13.3) the investment function may be written:

$$I_t \equiv K_{t+1} - K_t = \alpha' Y_t + \beta' Y_t \left(\frac{P_t}{K_t} \right) - K_t \qquad (13.9)$$

Using the equilibrium condition

$$I_t = S_t$$

we eliminate P_t from (13.9) by substitution from the saving function:

$$I_t = \alpha' Y_t + \frac{\beta' Y_t (I_t - s_w Y_t)}{(s_p - s_w) K_t} - K_t \qquad (13.10)$$

We simplify exposition by using the following definitions for the growth rate g of any variable x and the capital–output ratio v:

$$g_t(X) \equiv \frac{x_{t+1} - x_t}{x_t}$$

$$v_t \equiv \frac{K_t}{Y_t}$$

On dividing through by K_t, (13.10) may then be written:

$$g_t(K) = \frac{1}{v_t} \left(\alpha' + \frac{\beta' [g_t(K) - s_w / v_t]}{s_p - s_w} \right) - 1 \qquad (13.11)$$

This is the first of our difference equations. The second is the T.P.F., which may be rewritten:

$$g_t(Y) = \lambda + \alpha'' + \beta'' [g_t(K) - \lambda] \qquad (13.12)$$

Now *steady growth* requires that for all t

$$g_t(K) = g_t(Y) = G > 0$$

where G is a constant. The value of G is then obtained from (13.12):

$$G = \frac{\alpha''}{1 - \beta''} + \lambda > 0 \qquad (13.13)$$

There is thus a unique positive steady-state growth rate for K and Y, given by the technological and demographic parameters. This is the natural growth rate of the system; and when it applies labour productivity and capital per head will be growing at the rate

$$G - \lambda = \frac{\alpha''}{1 - \beta''}$$

which is shown by the intersection of the T.P.F. with the 45° line (Figure 13.1).

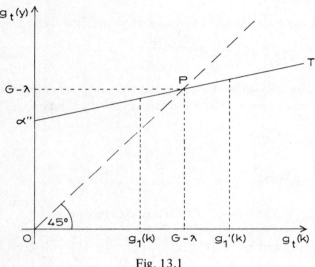

Fig. 13.1

We now need to obtain the steady-state growth paths of the other variables in the model and an expression for the constant capital-output ratio v in terms of the system's parameters. We first obtain expressions for the investment–output ratio, profit share and profit rate; using (13.13)

$$\frac{I}{Y} \equiv \frac{I}{K} \times \frac{K}{Y} = Gv = v\left(\frac{\alpha''}{1 - \beta''} + \lambda\right) \tag{13.14}$$

From the saving function, the saving–investment equilibrium condition, and (13.14):

$$\frac{P}{Y} = \frac{I/Y - s_w}{s_p - s_w} = \frac{v[\alpha''/(1 - \beta'') + \lambda] - s_w}{s_p - s_w} \tag{13.15}$$

Thus

$$\frac{P}{K} \equiv \frac{P}{Y} \times \frac{Y}{K} = \frac{[\alpha''/(1-\beta'') + \lambda] - s_w/v}{s_p - s_w} \qquad (13.16)$$

The ratios between investment, profits, capital and output in the steady state are therefore all determined uniquely in terms of the parameters and the constant capital–output ratio; they are thus all constant, so that P, I and S all grow at the natural rate G of K and Y.

Finally, we obtain a solution for v. From (13.11), with $g_t(K) = G$ and $v_t = v$:

$$G + 1 = \frac{\alpha'}{v} + \frac{\beta'G}{v(s_p - s_w)} - \frac{\beta's_w}{v^2(s_p - s_w)}$$

or

$$(G + 1)(s_p - s_w)v^2 - [\alpha'(s_p - s_w) + \beta'G]v + \beta's_w = 0 \qquad (13.17)$$

The solution of this quadratic in v is

$$v = \frac{\alpha'(s_p - s_w) + \beta'G \pm \sqrt{[\alpha'(s_p - s_w) + \beta'G]^2 - 4(G+1)\beta's_w(s_p - s_w)}}{2(G+1)(s_p - s_w)}$$

Now assuming that

$$[\alpha'(s_p - s_w) + \beta'G]^2 > 4(G + 1)\beta's_w(s_p - s_w) \qquad (13.18)$$

it may be seen that (13.17) has two different real roots; and this is the case taken by Kaldor.[3] It may be shown that both roots are positive.[4] It therefore seems that the model has two steady-state solutions which have the same growth rate but which differ in their other properties. Kaldor obtains uniqueness by excluding the smaller of the two roots, on the ground that it gives an implausibly low capital–output ratio on reasonable parameter values.[5] An alternative argument, used by Allen (1967, p. 309) is that the smaller root is likely to imply – through (13.15) – a negative steady-state profit share. This serves to remind us of assumption (iv) on page 197 (discussed in section 11.4) relating to external constraints on distribution which mean that the steady-state profit share must satisfy

$$0 < \mu' \leqslant \frac{P}{Y} \leqslant \frac{Y - w'L}{Y} < 1$$

where μ' is the prevailing degree of monopoly and w' is the minimum real wage. From (13.15), this may be interpreted as a condition on the relationship between v and the parameters:

$$\frac{s_w}{G} < \frac{s_w + \mu'(s_p - s_w)}{G} \leqslant v \leqslant \frac{(s_p - s_w)(Y - w'L)}{GY} + \frac{s_w}{G}$$

$$< \frac{s_p}{G} \tag{13.19}$$

where G is given by (13.13). Allen considers the weak form of this condition, which is the requirement that v should be such that P/Y lies between zero and unity:

$$\frac{s_w}{G} < v < \frac{s_p}{G} \tag{13.20}$$

(This corresponds to Kaldor's condition (11.21).) Thus for the steady-state profit share to be positive, the steady-state capital–output ratio must exceed s_w/G; and it may be shown not only that this requirement is unlikely to be satisfied by the lower root of (13.17), as Allen claims, but also that it is not implausible that it will be violated by the upper root.[6] We nevertheless follow Kaldor by assuming that the capital–output ratio given by the upper root is such that the constraints on distribution are satisfied; i.e. that (13.19) is satisfied by

$$v = \frac{\alpha'(s_p - s_w) + \beta'G + \sqrt{[\alpha'(s_p - s_w) + \beta'G]^2 - 4(G+1)\beta's_w(s_p - s_w)}}{2(G+1)(s_p - s_w)}$$

$$\tag{13.21}$$

which is thus the steady-state capital–output ratio.

We therefore conclude that *on the assumption that the parameters of the model are such first, that (13.18) is satisfied; second, that the lower root of (13.17) may be excluded as meaningless; and third, that the upper root satisfies (13.19), the model has a unique steady-state solution.* It may be described as follows in terms of the initial labour force L_0, the initial capital–labour ratio, k_0, and the parameters:

$$\left.\begin{array}{l} L_t = L_0(1 + \lambda)^t \\[2mm] K_t = k_0 L_0 (1 + G)^t \\[2mm] Y_t = \dfrac{k_0 L_0}{v}(1 + G)^t \end{array}\right\} \tag{13.22}$$

$$I_t = Gk_oL_o(1 + G)^t$$

$$P_t = k_oL_o\left(\frac{P}{K}\right)(1 + G)^t \qquad \right\} \qquad (13.22)$$

where G is given by (13.13), v is given by (13.21), and P/K is given by (13.16). With *classical saving* the steady state solution becomes much simpler. With $s_w = 0$, (13.11) becomes

$$g_t(K) = \frac{1}{v_t}\left(\alpha' + \frac{\beta' g_t(K)}{s_p}\right) - 1$$

Putting $g_t = G$ and $v_t = v$, as before, we obtain a linear equation in v with solution

$$v = \frac{\alpha' s_p + \beta' G}{s_p(1 + G)}$$

Thus the complication of multiple solutions is avoided. Also, (13.15) and (13.16) now become

$$\frac{P}{Y} = \frac{vG}{s_p} = \frac{1}{s_p} \times \frac{I}{Y}$$

$$\frac{P}{K} = \frac{G}{s_p}$$

which are familiar results. In particular, *the steady-state profit rate is now independent of v, and hence independent of the parameters of the investment function. This is the Kaldorian analogue of the result that the steady-state profit rate is independent of the production function in neo-classical models with classical saving.*

13.3 Period analysis: stability of steady growth

The determination of the steady growth rate G is depicted in figure 13.1 by the intersection of the linear T.P.F. with the 45° line at the point P. Kaldor attempts to show that starting from any position other than P, the system will converge on this point, which will then represent a globally stable steady state. We shall now see that his attempt is not wholly successful.

The question of stability may be considered in three parts. To establish stability (as Kaldor means it) we need to show:

(i) That if in one period the equilibrium growth rate of capital per man k is less than (greater than) the steady-state rate $G - \lambda$, the equilibrium growth rate in the following period will be higher (lower). This is to say that if the system is initially in equilibrium to the left of the point P in Figure 13.1 - say at $g_1(k)$ - in the next period the equilibrium must have moved to the right - and conversely for, say, $g_1'(k)$.

(ii) That these period-to-period movements of equilibrium do not 'overshoot the mark' in such a way that the system oscillates about P without ever reaching it.

(iii) That the equilibrium of each period is stable, so that the system actually follows the period-to-period movements of equilibrium.

The first two requirements are concerned with the convergence of successive equilibria on the steady state; they are matters of equilibrium dynamics. The third requirement is concerned with the attainment in each period, *under the assumption of full employment,* of equilibrium between saving and investment; it is in this sense a matter of disequilibrium dynamics. With (iii) we are in effect returning to the question of the stability of the Kaldorian distribution model, already discussed in section 11.3.

We first consider *requirement (i).* Suppose that in period 1 the growth rate of capital per head is $g_1(k)$ in Figure 13.1; we now need to show that $g_2(k) > g_1(k)$, or equivalently (since labour-force growth is the same in the two periods) that $g_2(K) > g_1(K)$. Now from the investment function, in the form (13.5), we have

$$g_2(K) = g_1(Y) + \frac{\beta'}{v_2}\left(\frac{P_2}{K_2} - \frac{P_1}{K_1}\right) \tag{13.23}$$

Since $g_1(k) < G - \lambda$, the T.P.F. shows that $g_1(y) > g_1(k)$, so that $g_1(Y) > g_1(K)$ and therefore

$$g_2(K) > g_1(K) + \frac{\beta'}{v_2}\left(\frac{P_2}{K_2} - \frac{P_1}{K_1}\right) \tag{13.24}$$

Since β' and v_2 are positive, a sufficient condition for the equilibrium growth rate of capital to be higher in period 2 than in period 1 is there-

fore that the equilibrium profit rate does not fall between the two
periods. But

$$\frac{P}{K} \equiv \frac{P}{Y} \times \frac{Y}{K} \tag{13.25}$$

and since $g_1(Y) > g_1(K)$, Y/K is higher in period 2; it is therefore sufficient that the equilibrium profit share does not fall between the two
periods.

We must therefore focus on the determination of the equilibrium
profit share by the saving and investment functions, which from (13.6)
and (13.9) may be written for the present purpose as:

$$\frac{S_t}{Y_t} = s_w + (s_p - s_w) \frac{P_t}{Y_t} \tag{13.26}$$

$$\frac{I_t}{Y_t} = (\alpha' - v_t) + \left(\frac{\beta'}{v_t}\right) \frac{P_t}{Y_t} \tag{13.27}$$

Thus the over-all saving propensity is a linear function of the profit
share; and the same linear function rules in each period, since both intercept (s_w) and slope ($s_p - s_w$) are constant parameters. In (13.27) the
investment-output ratio is also a linear function of the profit share; but
since both intercept and slope contain v_t, this function will shift from
period to period if the capital-output ratio changes. Now we know that
v is lower in period 2 than in period 1; thus both intercept and slope of
(13.27) will rise between the two periods, while (13.26) remains stable.
There are now two possibilities, shown in parts (a) and (b) of Figure
13.2. Part (a) is drawn on the assumption that

$$s_p - s_w > \beta'/v_2 \tag{13.28}$$

so that the S/Y curve has the greater slope in both periods, while part
(b) is drawn on the assumption that

$$s_p - s_w < \beta'/v_1$$

so that the I/Y curve has the greater slope in both periods.[7] It is only
in part (a) of the diagram that the equilibrium P/Y is higher in period 2
than in period 1; and condition (13.28) is both necessary and sufficient
for this result to obtain. By (13.25) we see that (13.28) is therefore suf-

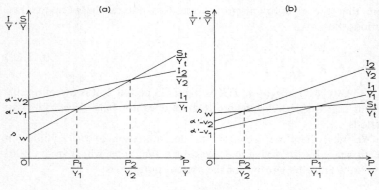

Fig. 13.2

ficient for the equilibrium profit rate to be higher in period 2; and finally, by (13.24), it is sufficient for $g_2(K)$ to be greater than $g_1(K)$.

By a symmetrical argument, it could be shown that if the growth rate of capital per head initally exceeded the steady-state rate, condition (13.28) would ensure a reduction in the equilibrium growth rate in the following period. Generalising, we see that a sufficient condition for requirement (i) to be met is

$$s_p - s_w > \beta'/v_t \tag{13.29}$$

Kaldor assumed this condition to be satisfied.[8]

We can now look at Figure 13.2 and condition (13.29) in a different way by considering *requirement (iii)* for stability. In both parts of the diagram we see that after the investment function has shifted on account of the fall in v between periods 1 and 2, there is, at the equilibrium profit share of period 1, an excess of investment over saving which should, by the familiar argument, drive up profit margins and cause the profit share to rise. But whereas in part (a) the profit share is required to rise, since the equilibrium of period 2 is higher, in part (b) it is required to fall if the new equilibrium is to be attained. In the former case the upward movement of the profit share will tend to restore equilibrium, while in the latter case it will raise investment by more than saving, and so cause the initial discrepancy to widen. The stability of equilibrium also depends therefore on the satisfaction of (13.29). This states that the sensitivity of the investment–output ratio to the profit share must be less than that of the over-all propensity to save; if this condition is not satisfied, the situation is precisely that which we warned in section 11.4 might arise if an investment function with profits as an argument were introduced into the Kaldorian distribution model.[9] We now see that in the first version of Kaldor's growth model, the danger is avoided by the assumption that (13.29) is satisfied. This condition therefore plays a dual role in the stability of steady growth in Kaldor's first version. It is a sufficient – though not necessary – condition for requirement (i) to be fulfilled, and a sufficient and necessary condition for requirement (iii) to be fulfilled. It is thus both a sufficient and a necessary condition for (i) and (iii) to be fulfilled together.

This is as far as Kaldor went to demonstrate stability in his first version. But there remains *requirement (ii)*: we have said nothing which would prevent the period-to-period changes in the equilibrium growth rate of capital from being excessive, in the sense of forming explosive oscillations about the steady-state rate. Expression (13.23) and the form of the T.P.F. imply that for this possibility to be excluded, the sensitivity of the rate of accumulation to changes in the profit rate, or the changes in the profit rate itself, must be limited. Champernowne (1971) has examined what specific parameter restrictions are required, but his results are incomplete. Excluding population growth, he showed that with classical saving a condition sufficient to ensure the absence of anti-damped oscillations would be

$$\beta' < \frac{s_p \alpha'(1 + \beta'')}{2 + \alpha''} \tag{13.30}$$

which is likely to form a more restrictive upper limit on β' than that implied by (13.29). For $s_w > 0$, Champernowne (1971, p. 62) was able to derive an upper limit on β', the satisfaction of which would ensure only local, not global, stability: 'it seems very plausible that the condition also ensures global stability . . . but the author has not yet completed a proof of this conjecture'. We need go no deeper into this question. What is notable is that the fulfilment of requirement (ii), like requirements (i) and (iii), depends on β' being below some level defined by the values of the other parameters of the model.

In sum, *the stability of steady growth in the first version of Kaldor's model seems to rest essentially on an assumption that the preferred capital–output ratio – and hence investment and the rate of accumulation – are not highly responsive to changes in the current profit rate.* It may therefore be argued that the investment function fits uneasily into what is intended to be a model explaining how an economy may be expected to maintain steady growth. One way out of this difficulty would be to amend the assumption about profit-rate expectations, such that the expected rate responds only slowly to changes in the actual rate; we shall see in the next section how Kaldor did amend his assumptions about investment behaviour in the second version.

But we can already see *the essence of the explanation of steady growth being offered by Kaldor: his view is that investment behaviour is such that whenever the system is off its steady-state path, the accompanying changes in the capital–output ratio (implied by the T.P.F.) will induce changes in the rate of capital accumulation in the direction of the steady state.* The contrast with the neo-classical explanation, where investment behaviour plays no independent role, is immediately apparent.

13.4 Continuous analysis

Before turning to the second version, we consider how the *first version* would look *in continuous terms*. This question has been considered by Allen (1967, pp. 306–12), McCallum (1969) and Champernowne (1971).

Following Champernowne, we write the continuous analogue of (13.2) above as

$$K(t) + \dot{K}(t) = K^*(t) \qquad (13.2a)$$

This, together with the continuous equivalent of (13.1), gives the investment function

$$I = \alpha' Y + \beta' Y \left(\frac{P}{K} \right) - K \qquad (13.9a)$$

which corresponds exactly to (13.9). The expressions for labour-force growth, the saving function and the T.P.F. need no explanation:

$$L(t) = L(0)e^{\lambda t}; \quad \lambda \geqslant 0 \qquad (13.7a)$$

$$S = s_w Y + (s_p - s_w)P; \quad 0 \leqslant s_w < s_p \leqslant 1 \qquad (13.6a)$$

$$\frac{\dot{Y}}{Y} = \lambda + \alpha'' + \beta'' \left(\frac{\dot{K}}{K} - \lambda \right); \quad \alpha'' > 0, 0 < \beta'' < 1 \qquad (13.8a)$$

The conclusions about the existence, uniqueness and comparative-dynamics properties of the steady-state solution may be shown to be the equivalent, in continuous terms, of those derived above for the first version proper. But as regards stability Champernowne showed that the satisfaction of the analogue of condition (13.29)

$$s_p - s_w > \beta'/v(t) \tag{13.29a}$$

is sufficient for the steady-state path to be globally stable. No further restriction is required to exclude the possibility of explosive 'cobweb' oscillations, which is thus seen to have been a result of the model being cast in period terms; the possibility does not arise when investment plans are regarded as adjusting continuously to current conditions, rather than at discrete intervals.

Allen's 'Kaldor model' differs from Champernowne's in one respect which turns out to be important. Allen adopts, in place of our (13.2a),

$$K^*(t) = K(t) \tag{13.31}$$

so that the capital stock at any moment satisfies

$$\frac{K}{Y} = \alpha' + \beta' \left(\frac{P}{K}\right) \tag{13.32}$$

Thus, whereas Champernowne, like Kaldor, assumes a time lag in the attainment of the target stock K^*, Allen assumes immediate adjustment. The rest of Allen's version comprises our (13.7a), (13.6a) and (13.8a). The difference in the form of the investment function makes no material difference as far as existence and uniqueness are concerned.[10] Allen does not examine stability, but McCallum has shown that the steady-state path is unstable (in the sense of equilibrium dynamics) irrespective of the parameter values. This indicates the importance for stability in Kaldor's first version of the time lag in the investment function; and it shows that Kaldor's basic hypothesis about the formation of entrepreneurial preferences (which underlies (13.1)) cannot be relied upon to produce stability. This is reminiscent of what we said in section 1.3 about Harrod's model. Here again, important properties of the model are sensitive to the precise specification of the investment function, and to features of the specification which one would probably not regard as of fundamental economic significance.[11]

The *second version* – Kaldor (1961) – can now be treated briefly. Expressions (13.7a), (13.6a) and (13.8a) are carried over from the first version in continuous terms. The basic hypothesis about investment is also retained, but the specification of the function is amended in ways which reflect the problems arising from the specification of the first version.

The new *investment function* has two components. The first is based on the assumption that, apart from changes in the expected rate of profit, producers will wish the capital stock to grow at the rate required for its capacity output to keep pace with actual output. (This compares with the corresponding assumption of the first version that with a constant expected profit rate firms will wish the capital stock to grow in line with output, so as to maintain a constant capital–output ratio.) From the T.P.F., (13.8a), we know that for capacity output to grow at the rate $\dot{Y}/Y$, capital must grow at the rate

$$\frac{\dot{K}}{K} = \lambda + \frac{\dot{Y}/Y - \lambda - \alpha''}{\beta''}$$

Hence, on the assumption that producers are aware of the technological possibilities described by the T.P.F., and on the further assumption of a lag of length θ between their observation of output growth and the execution of their investment plans, the first term of the investment function is given by:[12]

$$I_1(t + \theta) = \lambda K(t + \theta) + \left(\frac{\dot{Y}/Y(t) - \lambda - \alpha''}{\beta''}\right) K(t + \theta); \quad \theta > 0$$

The second component of investment is assumed to vary directly with the rate at which the expected profit rate is currently increasing. A new assumption about expectations is now introduced: that expectations about profit margins (and hence the profit share) are inelastic (being based on an average of observed values in which the present and the recent past have a low weight), while expectations about output are relatively elastic. This assumption is based on the idea that profit margins are subject to a long-term norm, while output is following a long-term upward trend; changes in margins, if they occur, are expected to be short-lived. The implication is that the current change in the expected profit rate will be given (roughly) by the current change in the observed capital–output ratio; if the capital–output ratio is currently rising, the expected profit rate will be falling, and conversely. Again assuming a lag of length θ, and adopting a proportional form, we may therefore write the second term of the investment function as

$$I_2(t + \theta) = \gamma \frac{d}{dt}\left[\frac{Y(t)}{K(t)}\right]; \quad \gamma > 0$$

The addition of the two components gives the new investment function:

$$I(t + \theta) = \lambda K(t + \theta) + \left(\frac{\dot{Y}/Y(t) - \lambda - \alpha''}{\beta''} \right) K(t + \theta) + \gamma \frac{d}{dt} \left[\frac{Y(t)}{K(t)} \right]$$

$$(13.33)$$

Regarding the questions of existence and uniqueness, we see from the T.P.F. that, as in the first version, there is a unique steady-growth rate G, as shown by (13.13); and G may be seen to be compatible with the new investment function by substituting

$$\frac{d}{dt} \left[\frac{Y(t)}{K(t)} \right] = 0$$

into (13.33). As before, the steady-state values of I/Y, P/Y and P/K may be expressed in terms of the constant capital–output ratio v and the parameters of the model. But there is a difference: owing to the change in the investment function, it is now not possible to solve for v. (In order to close the model Kaldor expands it by introducing additional relationships which we do not need to describe.)

Turning to the question of stability, the second version plainly differs from the first in the important respect that, owing to the new assumption about expectations, investment is no longer dependent on current profits. This is significant for both the disequilibrium and equilibrium dynamics of the model. First, whereas in the first version the investment–output ratio was dependent on the current profit share (see (13.27)) because of the dependence of the preferred capital–output ratio on the current (= expected) profit rate, the ratio is now independent of the current profit share owing to the inelasticity of expectations about the profit share. Thus the new investment function does not threaten to destabilise the Kaldorian distribution mechanism; and there is no longer need for a restriction like (13.29) to ensure the stability of saving–investment equilibrium. Second, the growth rate of the capital stock implied by the new investment function is independent of the current profit rate. In fact (13.33) and (13.8a) show that

$$\frac{I(t + \theta)}{K(t + \theta)} = \frac{I(t)}{K(t)} + \gamma \frac{d}{dt} \left[\frac{Y(t)}{K(t)} \right]; \quad \gamma > 0 \qquad (13.34)$$

Thus if at time t the growth rate of the capital stock is below the steady-state rate G, so that the output–capital ratio is rising, the equilibrium rate of accumulation at time $t + \theta$ will be higher. The system will move in the direction of the steady state. Whereas in the first version the direction of the change in the equilibrium growth rate of capital depended partly on the effect on the equilibrium profit share of the change in the capital–output ratio, it is now determined unambiguously by the direction of change in the capital–output ratio and is always directed towards the steady-state path. There remains, however, the possibility of unstable oscillations of equilibrium about the steady state. To remove this danger, and hence to establish in full the stability of steady growth, it seems that some upper limit would need to be placed on the value of γ.

The differences between the first and second versions are due primarily to the different assumptions about producers' expectations. In the first version it was assumed that expectations with regard to the profit rate are unit-elastic, while the second version assumes expectations about profit margins to be inelastic and expectations about output to be elastic so that the expected profit rate changes according as the actual output–capital ratio changes. There are obviously other assumptions about expectations which could be adopted, within the framework of the basic hypothesis about investment behaviour that is common to both versions.

We could assume, for example, that the expected profit rate is related to current and past actual rates by a geometric or exponential distributed lag;[13] and in fact Champernowne (1971) has examined such an *'adaptive expectations' version* of the Kaldor model. Taking the investment function of the first version in continuous terms, (13.9a), he replaces P/K with the expected profit rate, which he then assumes to be related to current and past rates by a continuously distributed lag with an exponential weighting function. He shows that if the speed at which expectations respond is sufficiently slow, local stability is ensured irrespective of the value of β'; and that otherwise the upper limit on β' which shows the sufficient condition for stability is higher, the slower is the speed of response, always exceeding the upper limit in the first version, (13.29a), as long as response is not immediate. This result is as would be expected. *The more sluggish is the adjustment of profit-rate expectations to current experience, the higher can be the elasticity of investment with respect to the expected profit rate; for it is the responsiveness of investment to the current profit rate which is important for stability.*[14]

13.5 Vintage capital and the pay-off period

The *third version* – Kaldor and Mirrlees (1962) – differs from the variants considered above in two radical respects.

First, there is explicit recognition of the heterogeneity of capital goods owing to the embodiment of technical progress. Kaldor (1957, p. 268) had emphasised earlier that with technical progress 'the capital goods produced in any one period are physically non-identical with the capital goods produced in previous periods'; and this had been the most important consideration underlying his scepticism about capital aggregation in the earlier versions of his model. The idea that 'improved knowledge is, largely if not entirely, infused into the economy through the introduction of new equipment' (Kaldor, 1961, p. 207) had also formed one of the bases of the T.P.F., as we saw in section 9.3. It was therefore natural for Kaldor to introduce vintage capital explicitly into his model.

Second, there is a fundamental change in assumptions about investment behaviour. The basic hypothesis underlying the new *investment function*, replacing that adopted for the first and second versions, is that firms aim to maximise their growth rates, subject to the constraint that profitability is sufficient for 'risks of bankruptcy or take-over bids' (Kaldor, 1961, p. 168) to be avoided. This hypothesis is closely related to the 'managerial' critique of the orthodox neo-classical theory of the profit-maximising firm, and in particular to Marris (1964).

The profitability constraint implies that firms will invest only if the relevant projects are expected to earn a rate of profit at least equal to a certain minimum, ρ, which is given by the profitability of new investment in the economy generally. Thus if t' is the expected life of equipment, aggregate investment at time t, $I(t)$, must satisfy the constraint

$$I(t) \leqslant \int_t^{t+t'} L_t \left[q_t - w^*(\tau) \right] e^{-(\rho+\delta)(\tau-t)} d\tau \qquad (13.35)$$

where L_t is employment on vintage-t machines when new, q_t is output per head on these machines, $w^*(\tau)$ is the expected real wage at time τ, and δ is the rate of depreciation. But in addition to this requirement of satisfactory profitability, it is assumed that projects must, for adoption, satisfy the *'pay-off period' criterion*. That is, owing to the uncertainty at time t of expectations regarding the course of technical progress beyond the near future – beyond, say, $t + h$, where $h < t'$ – a project, to be adopted at time t, must at least repay its cost within the time span to $t + h$, for which expectations are relatively confident. Thus investment at time t cannot exceed the (undiscounted) sum of profits over the pay-off period:

$$I(t) \leqslant \int_t^{t+h} L_t \left[q_t - w^*(\tau) \right] d\tau \qquad (13.36)$$

Now on the assumption that any project which satisfies the pay-off period criterion satisfies the minimum-profitability constraint, investment at time t will be carried on up to the point where equality holds in (13.36). Thus our investment function is given (on dividing though by L_t) by

$$i_t = \int_t^{t+h} \left[q_t - w^*(\tau) \right] d\tau = hq_t - \int_t^{t+h} w^*(\tau) d\tau \quad (13.37)$$

This represents a radical change from the investment function of the second version. But in common with the change between the first and second versions it is due largely to an amendment of assumptions about producers' expectations. *Now the stress is on the uncertainty of expectations about the real wage beyond the pay-off period.* This new view is linked to the form of technical progress assumed in the third version; in fact Kaldor supports his new function with the claim that the pay-off period criterion is commonly used by firms in the 'putty–clay' world of reality, because of the uncertainty bred by the danger of obsolescence.

The model is completed, briefly, by: a T.P.F. (which is now a relationship between the growth rate of investment per man working on new equipment and the growth rate of their productivity); the neo-Keynesian saving function (Kaldor and Mirrlees in fact take the classical case); a constant labour-force growth rate; an assumption that machines are retired when their quasi-rents fall to zero;[15] and an assumption that firms expect the real wage to rise in the foreseeable future at the rate observed over the recent past.

Kaldor and Mirrlees proceed to show that there is a unique steady-state solution, with i, q and the real wage w all growing at a constant rate determined by the T.P.F., and with t', the lifetime of machines, constant. They provide no formal proof of stability; but they do infer from the investment function and the assumption about wage expectations that if i and q are growing at different rates, the growth rate of i will be moving in the appropriate direction – towards the steady-state rate – unless the growth rate of w diverges significantly from the growth rate of q.

13.6 Conclusion

In all three versions of the model it is the response of investment to the non-steady-state expansion of output which is meant to make steady growth the stable condition; it is this which is the distinctive core – though not the whole – of the Kaldorian explanation of steady growth. The investment decisions of producers play an independent and central role, which is in marked contrast with the neo-classical theory of Part II. But the development of Kaldor's model through its three versions shows the difficulties involved in formalising plausible assumptions about investment behaviour in such a way as to obtain an unambiguously stable result – difficulties which are partly related to the fact that such a result requires that the responsiveness of investment to current profitability is strictly limited.

Part IV

STEADY GROWTH
AND
ECONOMIC HISTORY

14

Stylised Facts, Steady Growth and Structural Change

14.1 Kaldor's stylised facts and steady growth

Whatever the objective of other growth theorists Kaldor has consistently stated the purpose of his models to be the explanation of what he regards as salient features of macro-economic history. In 1956 he argued that no theory of distribution could be satisfactory unless it could account for 'the relative stability of [distributive] shares in the advanced capitalist economies over the last 100 years or so'. He introduced the first version of his growth model with the claim that 'A satisfactory model concerning the nature of the growth process in a capitalist economy must . . . account for the remarkable historical constancies' (Kaldor, 1957, pp. 260-1) not only of distributive shares but also of the capital–output ratio and the rate of profit. (Since the share of profits is identical to the product of the rate of profit and the capital–output ratio if the definitions are consistent, the constancy of any two of these variables of course implies the constancy of the third.) In 1961 he amplified his summary of history by listing the following six *stylised facts*:

    (i) growth of output and labour productivity 'at a steady trend rate' – in particular, no evidence of falling growth rates;

    (ii) a continuing growth in capital per worker;

    (iii) a 'steady' rate of profit on capital;

    (iv) 'steady capital–output ratios over long periods . . . if differences in the degree of utilisation of capacity are allowed for' – i.e. 'income and capital tend to grow at the same rate';

(v) (a) long-term steadiness of the share of profits (and of wages) and of the investment–output ratio, and (b) a high positive correlation, in the shorter term, between the share of profits and the investment-output ratio;

(vi)' differences in growth rates among different economies at any one time.

Since our main concern is the historical growth process rather than international growth comparisons, we can neglect (vi)'. We replace it with:

(vi) little deviation, over the long term, from full employment of labour.

Although not listed explicitly by Kaldor, this additional 'stylised fact' may be attributed to him since he argues that his assumption of full employment is justified not only on theoretical considerations (see section 12.1 above) but also by the history of the advanced economies since the late nineteenth century. He infers from history that the depression of the 1930s was the exception which proves the rule, and that 'it does not ... seem unrealistic to assume that capitalist economies operate under full-employment conditions in all such periods (and these appear to be the more frequent, in terms of chronological time) when capital is accumulating and the national income is growing' (Kaldor, 1957, p. 264).

We thus have six 'stylised facts' which (excluding v(b), which refers to fluctuations about the trend rather than the trend itself) together suggest that the long-run history of advanced capitalist economies is very much like the steady-state growth paths described by the theories discussed in earlier chapters.

Kaldor's purpose in enunciating them is partly to draw attention to what he sees as the inconsistency with economic history of the pessimistic predictions of pre-Kaldorian macro-dynamic theory. We saw in section 10.4 how Ricardo inferred from the law of diminishing returns that as capital accumulated in relation to land, the rate of profit and rate of accumulation would decline until growth would eventually cease. The stationary state seemed inevitable; and moreover it seemed likely that wages would not for any length of time rise above subsistence levels. This grim prospect earned for political economy the description 'the dismal science',[1] by which it was known for much of the nineteenth century. As the economy approached the stationary state, the distribution of income would of course be changing: 'in different stages of society, the proportions of the whole produce of the earth which will be allotted to each of these classes, under the names of rent, profit and wages will be essentially different' (Ricardo, 1817, p. 5). The contrast with steady growth and Kaldor's stylised facts is very clear. Then there was Marx, for whom capitalism was a system with inherent internal contradictions which would inevitably lead to its collapse; in particular, profit-seeking accumulation and expansion by competing firms would tend to exhaust the 'reserve army' of unemployed and thereby result in crises in which profits would be wiped out and accumulation halted. The long-term prospect generally inferred from pre-modern neoclassical theory was little less dismal than that held forth by Ricardo. With the accumulation of capital in relation to labour (as well as to land – classical theory had for the most part, in effect, treated capital and labour as complements) the marginal product of capital, and hence the rate of interest, would decline, and consequently so would saving and the rate of accumulation. Even Keynes, when contemplating the long run, envisaged a progressive decline in the rate of profit. With the growth of the capital stock the marginal efficiency of capital schedule would shift inwards, and the rate of interest required to induce the investment needed for full employment might decline to zero unless there was a corresponding long-term decline in the propensity to save (Keynes, 1936, pp. 374-7). For Keynes (1936, p. 376), however, the 'euthanasia of the rentier' – 'the euthanasia of the cumulative oppressive power of the capitalist to exploit the scarcity value of capital' was not so dismal a prospect: in fact it seemed to him to be 'the most sensible way of gradually getting rid of many of the objectionable features of capitalism' (Keynes, 1936, p. 221). Finally, there were the obstacles to steady growth emphasised by Harrod.

But, Kaldor is saying, we know that while capital has certainly grown in relation to labour (and land), the rate of profit and rate of interest have not declined, and nor has the rate of growth. The 'stationary state' and the 'euthanasia of the rentier' have not materialised, and there is no sign of their doing so. The history of advanced economies over the long run contradicts the predictions of Ricardo, Marx, the neoclassicals, and even Keynes and Harrod. The stylised facts call for a theory of – an explanation for – steady growth; and this is what Kaldor's model purports to provide.

But Kaldor's view of the empirical inadequacy of neo-classical (and even classical) theory is valid only on account of their neglect of technical progress. We know from Part II that when technical progress is introduced, neo-classical theory does not necessarily predict that the accumulation of capital in relation to labour will entail a declining rate of profit or an approach to a stationary state. In fact, with appropriate assumptions about technical progress (and population growth and saving), neo-classical theory is quite consistent with steady growth (with growing capital per head) and quite capable of providing an explanation, of sorts, for Kaldor's stylised facts. Kaldor is, of course, critical of the neo-classical treatment of technical progress (cf. section 9.3) and of other features of the neo-classical 'explanation' of steady growth. But these are separate issues. The fact is that although the long-run predictions of pre-modern neo-classical theorists may not have been verified by the passage of history, neo-classical theory does not necessarily entail those predictions, and modern neo-classical theory has been concerned almost exclusively with the characterisation and explanation of steady growth, just as Kaldorian theory has been. It is therefore not surprising, though ironic, that neo-classical writers have adopted Kaldor's stylised facts as empirical support for their own models. Solow's view of neo-classical growth theory as an explanation for the stylised facts was cited in section 2.3. Samuelson (1973, pp. 746–7) lists six 'trends' which, he claims, summarise 'the basic facts of economic history in the advanced nations', and these are essentially the same as Kaldor's (i) – (v)(a) as listed above. Contrary to Kaldor's hope, his stylised facts do not succeed in distinguishing between neo-classical and Kaldorian growth theory, or in demonstrating the superiority of the latter in relation to the former.[2] Nor do they demonstrate the superiority of the former in relation to the latter. Nevertheless, Brems (1977) turns Kaldor's argument on its head by claiming the validity of what are basically the stylised facts –though without any reference to Kaldor – and by arguing that this shows that neo-classical growth theory is not only realistic, but superior to neo-Keynesian theory! Unfortunately for both Kaldor and Brems, the device of the stylised fact is of little help in distinguishing between theories which make the same predictions.

A second weakness of the device lies in the danger that stylised facts may turn out to be more stylised than factual. Chapter 15 will examine the extent to which the particular stylised facts proposed by Kaldor are confirmed by historical (mainly national accounts) data, and will indicate some of the problems entailed in such an examination. We shall refer mainly to data for the U.K. economy. Meanwhile, in the following section, we suggest that there are reasons for considering the U.K. economy to be particularly well-suited to the test.

14.2 Structural change and a missing stylised fact

The theories described in previous chapters are aggregative models referring to whole economies. Kaldor (1957, p. 259), for example, states that the purpose of his growth theory is to explain the determination of 'the rate at which the general level of production of an economy is growing'. If the models seem most applicable to non-agricultural or industrial activity, this is not because they are meant to refer to any particular sector or sectors. Rather, it is because they are meant to describe advanced or 'mature' industrialised economies in which the agricultural sector – Colin Clark's (1940, p. 182) 'primary' sector – is relatively small, and in which the industrial or 'secondary' sector is presumed to have a dominant influence on the course of over-all growth. It is to such economies that the theories and the stylised facts refer; and it is to such economies that we should look for data to check against Kaldor's summary of history.

Apart from indicating which economies of the modern period are relevant to a study of the validity of the stylised facts, this also indicates, for any such relevant economy, how far back in time the enquiry should extend; the starting-point of the data period should be more recent than the period during which industrialisation took place. Obviously there cannot in practice be a clear-cut division between a period of industrialisation and a period of 'maturity'; all we can hope to identify is a span of years in which the characteristic features of industrialisation shaded into relative unimportance and from which the choice of starting-point will be more or less arbitrary. We may illustrate by considering the choice of a starting-point for data for the U.K. economy, with reference to two features of industrialisation.

The first is the urbanisation of the population. Deane and Cole (1967, p. 7) estimate that in 1801 about 25 per cent of the population of Great Britain lived in concentrations of 5000 or more, and that this proportion had already doubled over the previous century under the impact of the early stages of the Industrial Revolution. They report that the process of urbanisation continued unabated into the nine-

teenth century, but that it reached its peak around 1850, clearly declined in importance after 1870, and became insignficant after 1880:
'in the last two decades of the century. . . a change in the pattern of
internal migration was evident in the population records. It seems as
though the urbanisation which was particularly associated with the
process of industrialisation had been completed' (Deane and Cole,
1967, p. 11). The implication is that for the U.K. economy we would
be justified in using data extending as far back as 1880 or 1870 to test
the stylised facts.

The second feature of industrialisation is what may be regarded as
one of its defining characteristics: the reallocation of productive resources (in particular, the labour force) away from the primary sector
into the secondary sector. This is obviously a more fundamental feature
than urbanisation, which is largely a consequence of it. Deane and Cole
(1967, table 30) report that in 1801 the proportions of the British
labour force employed in the primary, secondary and tertiary (i.e. services) sectors were practically the same: 36, 30 and 34 per cent respectively.[3] Their estimates suggest that the subsequent ninety years
can be divided into three periods of equal length characterised by
different kinds of reallocation among the three sectors. Between 1801
and 1831 there was a large increase in the secondary sector's share of
total employment – from 30 to 41 per cent – wholly at the expense
of agriculture. Between 1831 and 1861 there was a much smaller rise
in the share of the secondary sector, from 41 to 44 per cent, accompanied by a similar increase in the share of the tertiary sector (mainly
in trade and transport) from 34 to 37 per cent. Finally, between 1861
and 1891 there was a larger increase in the share of the tertiary sector,
from 37 to 45 per cent (again accounted for mainly by an increase in
trade and transport), wholly at the expense of the primary sector. The
share of the secondary sector was virtually stable. Over the ninety-year
period as a whole, then, the primary sector's share of employment fell
continuously and dramatically, from 36 to 11 per cent; but it was only
up to 1861, and mainly up to only 1831, that industry gained (relatively) from the release of labour from agriculture. This evidence seems
to point towards a rather earlier date as a starting-point for our investigation than was suggested by the data on urbanisation: perhaps 1860 or
even earlier, rather than 1880 or 1870.

But as we said, we are not seeking a precise date or a clear-cut division; and it seems that we may reasonably conclude, taking both sets of

evidence together, that the characteristic features of the industrialisation process became relatively unimportant in the United Kingdom in the third quarter of the nineteenth century. In any case the choice of starting-point is subject to the constraint of the availability of reliable data. As will be seen in the following chapter, some of the series of national-income accounts data available for the United Kingdom begin in 1889, others in 1870, and others in 1855; none begins earlier. From the above it seems that each of these dates may be considered admissible as a starting-point for our investigation, so that for the U.K. economy there would appear to be a century or so of evidence which may legitimately be used to test the validity of the stylised facts.

For most other economies which would now be considered advanced, the starting-point for the investigation would, by the above criteria, have to be more recent than the third quarter of the last century. In 1870, when in the United Kingdom the primary sector employed only 15 per cent of the labour force, the corresponding proportion was 85 per cent in Japan, and above 40 per cent in the United States, France, Italy, Norway and Sweden (Kuznets, 1966, table 3.2). In 1910, by which time the proportion had fallen below 10 per cent in the United Kingdom, it was still above 50 per cent in Japan and Russia, and above 30 per cent in the United States, France, Italy, Norway, Sweden and Canada (Kuznets, 1966). All these countries have experienced much larger transfers of resources out of the primary sector during this century than has the United Kingdom. Even in the post-war period there has in some advanced economies been quite dramatic structural change by Clark's classification, the most striking case being Japan, where the proportion of the labour force engaged in agriculture fell from about a half to a third between 1950 and 1960. If one accepts that the large-scale shift of resources from the primary to the secondary sector is essentially a feature of the industrialisation process, then it would appear that for most economies other than the United Kingdom there will be much less time-series evidence that can legitimately be used to check against the stylised facts, which are, after all, meant to be 'broad facts about the growth of advanced industrial economies' (Solow, 1970, p. 2). *The history of the U.K. economy is particularly well suited to a test of the stylised facts because that economy was the first to become industrialised.*

If one adopts a broader conception of 'advanced industrial economies' – so that one includes, for instance, the United States in this category from, say, 1910, though in the following forty years there was a decline of 20 per cent in agriculture's share of the labour force (from 32 to 12 per cent) – then a limitation of the description and explanation of economic history which growth theory provides is immediately apparent. To the extent that structural change by Clark's classification is an important feature of the historical development of *advanced* economies, aggregative models which abstract from such shifts must be considered deficient, not only because they cannot explain them, but also because the structural change which they exclude may in reality form an important part of the explanation of the features of aggregate growth which they purport to provide. Thus, even if the stylised facts are found to hold true for the U.S. economy since 1910, theories which profess to explain them in abstraction from the fundamental structural changes which were occurring at the same time may omit a large part of the true story.

This point of course has broader significance. Changes in the distribution of the labour force (or productive resources generally) among Clark's three sectors did not come to a halt in the United Kingdom at the end of the nineteenth century. Since 1891 the proportion of the labour force employed in agriculture has continued to decline, though obviously more slowly than in the nineteenth century – by about 1 per centage point, rather than 3, a decade. It now stands below 3 per cent. The main beneficiary has been the tertiary sector. There has, moreover, obviously been radical structural change within each of the three sectors. Structural change, whether by Clark's classification or by any other, has continued in the U.K. economy since its industrialisation. Structural change is invariably a concomitant of growth, even in the most mature of advanced economies. This indicates that even if one accepts the validity of the stylised facts, the kind of steady growth which they represent is rather different from the strict theoretical conception of an economy in which 'all elements. . . are growing at the same [constant] rate – so that, although there is an absolute expansion, every element remains in the same proportion to every other' (Hicks, 1965, p. 133). Kaldor does not, of course, claim that the absence of structural change is a feature of the history of advanced economies, and this omission may be regarded as one significant respect in which his stylised facts (quite justifiably) do not conform to the steady state of theory, strictly defined. They conform to the steady state of his model because of its aggregative structure, implicit in which is the view that they can be explained without reference to structural change.

In sum, *even if the stylised facts are found to be valid, 'Inasmuch as economic growth in practice is observed to be intimately associated with changes in the structure of production, this. . . reduces the real-life applicability of the steady growth concept'* (Hahn and Matthews, 1964, p. 39), *more generally defined* outside 'one-sector' models.

It is interesting to note, in this context, that when Kaldor (1966) sought to explain the United Kingdom's poor post-war growth performance in relation to other 'advanced' economies, he derived little help from his growth model; he did not, for example, seek to explain why his technical progress function appeared to be lower in the United Kingdom than elsewhere. He abandoned his aggregative model, returned to Clark's sectoral classification, and argued that international growth differences could be explained by differences in the rate of growth of employment in the secondary sector, on account of the particular importance to productivity growth in manufacturing of dynamic economies of scale, i.e. the particular applicability to manufacturing industry of *Verdoorn's Law* that the growth rate of productivity is positively associated with the growth rate of output. With differences in the rate of growth of employment in the secondary sector held to be dependent on differences in the availability of labour from agriculture, his thesis, briefly stated, was then that 'the trouble with the British economy is that it has reached a high stage of "maturity" earlier than others' (Kaldor, 1966, p. 3). Primary-sector labour was no longer available to the secondary sector on the same scale as in the faster-growing economies. Whether or not this thesis is accepted,[4] it at least serves to add emphasis to the point that different economies which are usually classified as 'advanced' are in fact in different stages of development, and that even in advanced economies structural change (and Clark's sectoral classification) may be of some significance even for the analysis of growth in aggregate terms.

15

Stylised Facts and Historical Statistics

15.1 Introduction

This chapter is concerned with examining the validity of Kaldor's stylised facts, mainly using the historical national-accounts data for the United Kingdom provided by Feinstein (1972). In doing so, we shall need to consider some of the problems and ambiguities which arise in the identification of appropriate statistical variables to correspond to the variables of the theories. (Although Kaldor quotes empirical evidence in support of his stylised facts, the precise statistical interpretation of the variables to which they refer is sometimes unclear.) We shall also consider some of the problems with the data themselves. There are particular problems with the statistical measurements of capital. These are discussed in section 15.2, which attempts to elucidate the meaning and shortcomings of the available capital-stock data. Section 15.3 proceeds to examine the historical movements of output, capital and employment, and their correspondence with stylised facts (i), (ii), (iv) and (vi), as listed in section 14.1. This leaves (iii) and (v), which refer to the rate of profit and distributive shares: these are investigated in section 15.4. The final section offers some conclusions.

15.2 Capital statistics: problems and methods

The meaning and shortcomings of the capital-stock data for the United Kingdom provided by Feinstein (1972) and the *National Income and Expenditure* Blue Book (Central Statistical Office, 1977) may be described partly in terms of coverage and partly in terms of the method of measurement.[1]

First, we investigate *coverage*. If we were to adopt a broad view of capital, defined as 'produced means of production', we might include all the following:

(i) *Human capital*: the qualities of the labour force 'accumulated' through investment in health, education and training.

(ii) *Circulating or working capital*: stocks of materials, work in progress, and finished goods in the hands of producers; and stocks of finished non-durable goods in the hands of consumers.

(iii) *Consumers' fixed capital*: dwellings and other consumer durables.

(iv) *Social fixed capital*: roads, government offices, schools, etc.

(v) *Fixed capital* being used in the production of goods and services for sale.

(vi) *Land*, or at least those 'natural' resources which are partly 'produced' (e.g. livestock, standing timber, accessible mineral wealth).

The measured capital stock has a narrower coverage: (i), (ii) and (vi) are excluded altogether, and so is (iii), apart from dwellings. What remains may be described as the 'tangible, reproducible, fixed capital stock' - 'tangible' indicating the exclusion of human capital, 'reproducible' the exclusion of natural resources, and 'fixed' the exclusion of stocks - though none of these adjectives indicates the exclusion of cars and other consumer durables. This coverage is the same as that of fixed capital formation; in fact, as will be seen below, the capital stock is measured largely on the basis of data for fixed investment. The exclusions may therefore be regarded partly as a reflection of the separation of investment in stocks from fixed investment in the expenditure analysis of national income,[2] and partly as a reflection of omissions from conventionally defined investment expenditure; household expenditure on durable goods, private and public expenditure on health, education, etc. are all counted as consumers' or government current expenditure rather than investment.

The coverage of the measured capital stock is therefore rather narrower than one might prefer. It is true that in growth models the capital stock is often described as comprising only 'machines'. But in the real world capital comprises much more than machines; and it may be argued that it consists of much more than the tangible reproducible fixed capital that is measured in the statistics. An implication is that since measured output for the most part includes the contribution of unmeasured capital (an exception being the value of the services of consumer durables other than dwellings), measured capital-output and capital–labour ratios will tend to understate the actual capital-intensity of production. Moreover, unless the relationship between unmeasured and measured capital is relatively stable, movement over time in these ratios will fail to provide an accurate description of the way in which actual capital is changing in relation to output and employment. If, for example, human capital has grown faster than measured capital in the post-war period, the growth of capital may on this account be understated in the statistics. Clearly the difficulties of interpretation thrown up by limited coverage may be quite serious.[3]

Another question of coverage is whether we should want to use a measure of national or domestic capital: the former (for the United Kingdom) comprises assets owned by U.K. nationals, whether located in the United Kingdom or abroad, while the latter comprises assets located in the United Kingdom, whether owned by U.K. nationals or foreigners. If we were interested in the distribution of wealth among U.K. citizens, the first would be the natural concept to use; but for the analysis of domestic economic activity and its growth, it is the second concept which is appropriate. And it is the *domestic tangible reproducible fixed capital stock* which is measured in the national accounts, so that in this respect our requirements are met. Henceforward, we shall usually be referring to the capital stock in this sense, and the string of adjectives can be left unsaid.

We now turn from coverage to *measurement*. In the measurement of national income (in terms of income, expenditure, or output) most components are given observable values by current transactions in goods and factor markets; in consequence the need for imputation is relatively rare. In the case of the capital stock, however, very few components will be changing hands, and thereby being given market values, at or around any point in time at which we want to measure it. Satisfactory information is available only for new assets (the components of investment); for existing assets the second-hand market is too thin to provide reliable information.

Thus transactions in the markets for goods and services, which provide the observable values which facilitate the measurement of income, are of little help in the measurement of capital. The only other way in which the capital stock might be measured in terms of directly observable market values would be by reference to financial markets, i.e. to the *stock-market valuations* of companies. But this method would have a number of drawbacks, at least for our purposes.[4] Without observable market values, we have to fall back on imputation. In the measurement of income imputed values are the exception; but in the measurement of capital they must be the rule. This, Hicks (1961, p. 19) has argued, 'marks the great practical distinction between the problem of measuring capital and the problem of measuring income'. So how can imputed values be derived?

One possibility would be to use the balance-sheet or *book values* calculated by businesses for tax purposes (for the calculation of depreciation allowances) and in accordance with company legislation. Such valuations are readily available; but they have several drawbacks, the chief one being that they are generally in terms of historic cost. Since different assets will have been acquired at different times – at different levels and configurations of factor and product prices – the sum of the original prices of assets, written down for depreciation calculated on the basis of these prices – which is what historic-cost valuation means – can have little economic meaning. A further problem is that the rates of depreciation used are probably unreliable; as will be seen below, Barna (1957) found a tendency for depreciation to be overstated, owing to a cautious underestimation of asset lives. Notwithstanding these problems, Feinstein's estimates are partly based, as we shall see, on a resort to book valuation.

A second method of imputation is the *capitalisation of property incomes*. Each type of property income is multiplied by the reciprocal of an estimate of the corresponding rate of yield – this multiplier is known as the 'number of years' purchase' – to provide the estimated value of the wealth from which the income is derived. The main problem is to obtain appropriate yield estimates; in practice they are usually based either on accounting (often Inland Revenue) convention, or on the yields of financial securities. Estimates of national capital were obtained by this method in the nineteenth century by Giffen, and in the interwar period by Stamp (1920) and Campion (1939). Stamp's estimates provided the starting-point for Phelps Brown *et al.'s* (1952; 1953) series for the domestic capital stock; and Deane and Cole (1967, pp. 269–77) also use estimates obtained by this method. The capitalisation method plays no part in the Feinstein or Blue Book estimates, however, and it may now be regarded as obsolete.

The third and fourth methods to be considered both purport to measure the capital stock in terms of its replacement cost. In competitive equilibrium with perfect foresight the value of any capital asset – the discounted future income stream expected from it – would be equal to its replacement cost: profit-maximising firms would increase the number of units of each asset employed until its value no longer exceeded the cost of acquisition of an identical asset, while with perfect foresight asset values would never fall short of acquisition costs. In the hypothetical conditions of long-run competitive equilibrium, therefore, the value of the capital stock at any point in time could be measured by the aggregation of replacement costs. In the real world, however, replacement costs, even if they could be measured accurately, would not provide a reliable reflection of capital values. Most modern capital measurement is in terms of replacement cost; and it is in these terms that the capital stock is measured in the Blue Book and in Feinstein. But estimates of replacement costs, obtained by the methods now to be described, can be regarded only as distant approximations to the value of capital as conceived in economic theory. It is best to regard them as estimates of replacement costs, and of nothing more.

Before proceeding to the methods, we need some definitions. First, *replacement cost new* (or gross) refers to the cost of replacing existing assets with assets which are new but otherwise identical, while *replacement cost written down* (or net) refers to the cost of replacing existing assets with identical assets. The former measure is gross of depreciation, and corresponds to the concept of gross value; the latter is net of depreciation, and corresponds to net value, which is what we would usually mean by the value of capital in theory. Second, a time series can be in terms either of current prices – *current replacement cost* (new or written down) – or in terms of the prices of some base year – *constant replacement cost* (new or written down). These terms define the four different kinds of time-series data which are available.

The third method – the *perpetual inventory (P.I.) method* – is the central method of modern capital measurement. It is based on the idea that the replacement cost of an asset can be measured by its actual original cost, corrected for price changes, and, in the case of replacement cost net, corrected for depreciation. The implication is that the capital stock can be measured by the cumulation of past investment expenditures corrected by appropriate price indices, using appropriate assumptions about asset lives and depreciation rates. The method was pioneered in the United States by Goldsmith (1951); it was first applied in the United Kingdom by Redfern (1955). Redfern's estimates were refined and developed by Dean (1964), and his work forms the basis of Feinstein's estimates for the post-war period, and of the estimates currently published in the Blue Book.

We first make more explicit what the method entails, and then consider some of the problems involved.

First, suppose we wish to measure the current replacement cost new of the capital stock at end of year T. Let $I_t(T)$ and $D_t(T)$ denote respectively gross fixed investment in year t and replacement cost new of assets scrapped in year t, both in the prices of year T. Then the replacement cost new of the capital stock at end of year T would be given by

$$G_T(T) = \sum_{t=0}^{T} [I_t(T) - D_t(T)] \qquad (15.1)$$

But we neither have data for I back to the beginning of time, nor for D in any year; we therefore need assumptions about asset lives. Suppose every asset lasts L years:

$$D_t(T) = I_{t-L}(T) \qquad (15.2)$$

By substitution:

$$G_T(T) = \sum_{t=0}^{T} I_t(T) - \sum_{t=L}^{T} I_{t-L}(T) = \sum_{t=T-L+1}^{T} I_t(T) \qquad (15.3)$$

The only investment data needed, therefore, are for the years from $T - L + 1$ to the present; all assets installed earlier are irrelevant since they have, by hypothesis, been discarded.

For replacement cost written down, estimates of depreciation are needed. Assume that assets depreciate according to the straight-line rule: each asset loses, during every year of its life, the same proportion $1/L$ of its replacement cost new. Depreciation in year t in year-T prices is therefore

$$d_t(T) = \frac{G_t(T)}{L} = \frac{1}{L} \sum_{t'=t-L+1}^{t} I_t'(T) \qquad (15.4)$$

Net investment in year t in year-T prices is then

$$I_t(T) - d_t(T) = I_t(T) - \frac{1}{L} \sum_{t'=t-L+1}^{t} I_t'(T) \qquad (15.5)$$

so that the current replacement cost written down of the capital stock at the end of year T is given by

$$N_T(T) = \sum_{t=0}^{T} [I_t(T) - d_t(T)] = \sum_{t=0}^{T} [I_t(T) - \frac{1}{L} \sum_{t'=t-L+1}^{t} I_t'(T)] \qquad (15.6)$$

which may be compared with the corresponding expression (15.1) for the gross stock. Just as (15.1) could be reduced to the more manageable form (15.3), (15.6) may be re-expressed as

$$N_T(T) = \sum_{t=T-L+1}^{T} \left\{ \frac{t - (T - L + 1)}{L} \right\} I_t(T) \qquad (15.7)$$

Expressions (15.3) and (15.7) show how the current replacement cost of the capital stock may be calculated for any year T, given our assumptions about asset lives and depreciation. To obtain a series at constant replacement cost – say year-T replacement cost – we would need to measure I_t in the prices of year T for every year $T + i$ for which the capital stock was measured. But there is an invaluable short cut. From (15.1) and (15.2):

$$G_{T+1}(T) = G_T(T) + I_{T+1}(T) - I_{T+1-L}(T) \qquad (15.8)$$

and

$$G_{T-1}(T) = G_T(T) - I_T(T) + I_{T-L}(T) \qquad (15.9)$$

Thus once the year-T replacement cost new of the capital stock in year T has been calculated, a constant replacement-cost series can easily be built up using successive years' investment data in the prices of year T. Similarly, for constant replacement cost written down, (15.6) shows

$$N_{T+1}(T) = N_T(T) + I_{T+1}(T) - \frac{1}{L} G_{T+1}(T) \qquad (15.10)$$

and

$$N_{T-1}(T) = N_T(T) - I_T(T) + \frac{1}{L} G_T(T) \qquad (15.11)$$

Short-cut formulae like these are not available for the construction of series in current replacement cost; to calculate $G_{T+1}(T + 1)$, for instance, $G_T(T)$ would have to be revalued before $I_{T+1}(T + 1)$ could be added to it. But once a constant replacement-cost series has been obtained, the current-price series can be derived from it simply by application of the appropriate price index; and this is the procedure which is followed in practice.

It may be seen that the P.I. method requires four sets of information or assumptions, i.e. those regarding asset lives, investment in current prices, price indices for deflation, and depreciation. The problems involved may be considered under these headings.

volved may be considered under these headings.

As regards asset lives, the practice is to distinguish various classes of asset for which different mortality assumptions are appropriate, and to assume the same constant average life for all assets in the class. The only difference from the method as described above is therefore that the assumed L is not the same for all assets. The average lives assumed by Redfern (1955) were in most cases those implicit in the depreciation rates allowed by the Inland Revenue. Considerable doubt was laid on the accuracy of these lives by Barna (1957), who estimated the replacement cost new of the capital stock in U.K. manufacturing by an alternative method. This is the fourth and final method of capital measurement which we need to mention; it is based on *insurance valuation*. It makes use of the fact that fixed capital assets are regularly valued for fire-insurance purposes in terms of replacement cost. Barna obtained from a sample of manufacturing firms estimates of replacement cost new of their fixed assets, and on the basis of this sample obtained a figure for manufacturing industry as a whole. His estimates exceeded the comparable P.I. calculation of Redfern by about 50 per cent; and he put about half of this discrepancy down to an underestimation of asset lives in income-tax depreciation rates. The Central Statistical Office later amended their asset-life assumptions, partly to take account of Barna's findings (Dean, 1964; Griffin, 1976). This illustrates the lack of precise information about asset mortality, the sensitivity of capital measurement to mortality assumptions, and the value to the P.I. method of supplementary information like that obtained by Barna. Although the insurance-valuation method used by Barna has several drawbacks,[5] it may usefully provide occasional 'bench-mark' guidance.

The second requirement of the P.I. method is investment data extending as far back as is needed by the mortality assumptions. Since some assets (e.g. dwellings) are assumed to last 100 years, estimates of the capital stock in 1855 (which is where Feinstein's series began) would require, on the P.I. method, investment data for as early as 1756; yet official Blue Book investment-expenditure figures are available for no earlier than 1948! The problem – which is less acute for shorter-lived plant and machinery – has been tackled in two ways. First, investment estimates for earlier years have been constructed by various means, usually from output rather than expenditure data, and by extrapolation with reference to other economic time series (see Feinstein, 1965; Dean, 1964). The Feinstein–Dean investment estimates lie behind the post-war capital-stock series published in the Blue Book and in Feinstein (1972). But adequate investment figures are unavailable for years prior to the mid-nineteenth century. Therefore – and this is the second way the problem has been tackled – Feinstein's pre-1939 capital-stock figures are not based on the P.I. method, at least as described by the above formulae. For the interwar period his estimates are derived from balance-sheet information converted from historic to replacement cost by means of 'heroic assumptions' (Feinstein, 1972, p. 198). For years prior to 1920 the net stock estimate for 1920 was decumulated by means of expression (15.11), while the gross estimate for 1920 was decumulated by means of expression (15.9) with scrapping assumed to be equal not to investment L years earlier but to a constant proportion of the current gross stock for each type of asset.

But before any of the P.I. calculations can be performed – before the investment expenditures of different years can be aggregated – the current-price investment data have to be converted to a common price basis by means of price indices. This is so whether the series being constructed is in terms of constant or current replacement cost. As already described, the procedure followed by the Central Statistical Office is first to obtain (using the formulae) series at constant replacement cost, which requires a price index to convert all investment data to the prices of the base year, and then from this to derive current replacement-cost series by means of the same index. Before describing the price index actually used at these two stages, we briefly consider four possibilities which, in principle at least, are open to the statisticians. Investment expenditure could be deflated by:

(i) An index of money wage rates, to give a series purporting to measure the replacement cost of the capital stock in terms of labour time. Joan Robinson (1956, p. 121) has argued that 'This is in some ways the most significant way of measuring capital. . . . capital goods in existence today can be regarded as an embodiment of past labour time to be used up in the future.'

(ii) An index of prices of investment goods unadjusted for quality change. This will not give a measure of the capital stock in terms of its cost of replacement by identical assets, but will give a capital-stock series from which quality improvement has been eliminated. This kind of measure has been advocated by, for example, Denison (1967, p. 144) on the ground that, in 'accounting for' growth, improvements in the quality of capital goods should be classified as productivity growth rather than as a growth in input.

(iii) An index of prices of investment goods which takes quality change into account. This will, in principle, give a measure of the capital stock in terms of the cost of its replacement by identical assets.

(iv) An index of the prices of consumer goods. The constant-price investment series will then measure the volume of consumption goods forgone each year to permit the accumulation of capital; and the capital-stock series would measure the consumption which would have to be forgone in order to replace it. This kind of measure has been advocated by, for example, Scott (1976).

It should now be clear that behind the choice of price index lie conceptual questions of some importance.

In general the four measures will give different results. With growth and technical progress, wages will be rising faster than prices, so that constant replacement cost measured by (i) will be growing most slowly. Also, with capital goods improving in quality, the capital stock measured by (ii) will be rising more slowly than that measured by (iii). The difference between the series obtained by (iv) and by (iii) will depend on how consumption-good prices are changing in relation to capital-good prices, and hence on the relation between the rates of technical progress in the two sectors; if capital goods are becoming cheaper in relation to consumption goods, measure (iv) will be growing faster than measure (iii).

Each of the four kinds of measure has its own appeal, and which is preferred will depend on the intended use. Measures (ii) and (iii) seem preferable from our point of view since they treat the capital stock as consisting of actual capital goods rather than reducing it to equivalent labour or equivalent consumption goods; it is capital *qua* capital goods which most growth theorists have usually had in mind.[6] And it is measure (ii) which is in fact used, (iii) being rejected because of the difficulty of quantifying quality change; it is indices of type (ii) which are used by the Central Statistical Office to deflate investment expenditure and the capital stock for the Blue Book. This reflects not so much a deliberate preference, but rather the non-existence in general of 'identical assets' at different points in time when technology is changing.

Finally, we consider depreciation. We would generally think of depreciation as the decline in the value (discounted future income stream) of a capital asset which occurs with the passage of time on account of falling physical efficiency, obsolescence, and pure ageing – these three processes being conceptually distinct. It is generally recognised that physical decay is a relatively unimportant part of depreciation; and because of the difficulty of taking account of obsolescence, estimated depreciation is usually thought of as referring primarily to pure ageing – to the pure effect of the passage of time on values of assets with finite lives. The problem is therefore treated as one of choosing the best assumption about the way the services rendered by assets are distributed through their lives. The solution adopted in practice is the straight-line rule inherited from accounting convention: depreciation is thus estimated in the way shown in the above description of the P.I. method, except that different lives are assumed for different kinds of asset. Clearly these estimates can only be rough.[7]

We may now *summarise*. The difficulties involved in empirical capital measurement arise mainly from two essential properties of capital: the absence of suitable observable market valuations of most capital assets; and index-number problems stemming from the limited comparability of assets existing in different years. The first feature has given rise to the convention of measurement in terms of replacement cost; but this, except in particular hypothetical conditions, is conceptually different from value. Further, replacement cost is estimated by the P.I. method, using investment data in terms of actual past cost and price indices unadjusted for quality change, so that in practice even 'replacement cost' does not mean what it says. But not only does true replacement cost differ from value and measured replacement cost differ from true replacement cost, but even in terms of what measured replacement cost represents – 'the actual past cost of the creation of the stock of assets' (Feinstein, 1972, p. 196), or 'doctored historical cost' (Hicks, 1974b, p. 164) – significant errors are liable to occur on account of incorrect assumptions about mortality and depreciation, and inaccurate investment and price data. It is not surprising that the Central Stastical Office assesses the margin of error in its estimates of some components of the capital stock to be wider than for any other figures published in the Blue Book (Maurice, 1968, p. 387).

It is clear, therefore, that for these reasons and because of the problems of coverage discussed earlier, the published capital-stock estimates can be used only with great caution.

15.3 Output, capital and employment

The following variables now need to be specified in terms of the available statistical series:

(i) capital stock;
(ii) output (or income);
(iii) employment of labour;
(iv) capital per worker (capital–labour ratio) (from (i) and (iii);
(v) output per worker (labour productivity) (from (ii) and (iii);
(vi) capital–output ratio (from (i) and (ii); and
(vii) degree of full employment of labour.

First, the *capital stock*. For the examination of the pattern of growth of the capital stock and the capital–labour ratio it is clearly constant rather than current replacement cost which is relevant. Replacement cost written down corresponds to the usual conception of capital in theory; but it will simplify matters to some extent if we take all variables gross of depreciation.[8] We therefore take *constant replacement cost new as our measure of capital stock K* (variable (i)), as the numerator of the capital–labour ratio (variable (iv)), and as the numerator of a version of the capital–output ratio (variable (vi)), a second version of which will be introduced below. As was seen in the previous section, the evidence is that declining physical efficiency is a relatively insignificant component of the depreciation of most capital assets.[9] This means that the replacement cost written down of most assets declines much faster than their ability to contribute to current production: 'after some years of use [an] asset may be as productive as ever, and physically almost as new, despite having become less valuable to its user as the stock of unexpired services it represents has diminished' (Dean, 1964, p. 328). The implication is that 'Accrued capital consumption . . . not an appropriate deduction from the gross capital stock if the aim is to measure capital as a factor in current production' (Dean, 1964, p. 328). Although this view[10] may reflect an interest in measuring the productive capacity of the capital stock rather than the capital stock *per se*, it is of interest to note that since the meaning of measured depreciation implies that 'the relationship between replacement cost new and output may be more stable than between written-down replacement cost and output' (Barna, 1961, p. 80), by examining the former we shall be tending to overstate, rather than understate, the stability of the capital–output ratio.

For *output*, as for capital, we require a domestic rather than a national measure. We choose *gross domestic product (G.D.P.) at constant factor cost* as our measure of output or income *Y* (variable (ii)), as the numerator of output per worker *y* (variable (v)), and as the denominator of the first version of the *capital–output ratio* (variable (vi)) which may now be written as

$$v \equiv \frac{K}{Y} \equiv \frac{\text{constant replacement cost new of the capital stock}}{\text{G.D.P. at constant factor cost}}$$

(15.12)

Both numerator and denominator of v are in constant prices. If we multiply both by their respective deflators – p_k representing the price of capital goods, and p_y representing the price of output goods in general (the G.D.P. deflator) – we obtain a capital–output ratio in current prices, V:

$$V \equiv \frac{p_k}{p_y} \times \frac{K}{Y} \equiv \frac{\text{current replacement cost new of the capital stock}}{\text{G.D.P. at current factor cost}}$$

(15.13)

This is our second version of the capital–output ratio. Movements in v will differ from those in V according as the price level of capital goods, p_k, develops differently from the general level of output prices, p_y; if, for example, there is a relative increase in the prices of capital goods, V will rise in relation to v.

For *employment*, L, the only suitable measure available is the *total number in employment*, which comprises employees in civil employment, members of H.M. Forces, and the self-employed. This becomes the denominator for the capital–labour ratio k (variable (iv)) and labour productivity y (variable (v)), now specified as:

$$k \equiv \frac{K}{L} \equiv \frac{\text{constant replacement cost new of the capital stock}}{\text{total in employment}}$$

(15.14)

$$y \equiv \frac{\text{G.D.P. at constant factor cost}}{\text{total in employment}}$$

(15.15)

Perhaps the most notable drawback of this measure is that it is a simple unweighted aggregate of 'man-years' which are far from homogeneous. Apart from qualitative differences among the 'men', the 'year' does not represent a uniform length of time at work – part-time and suspended workers are counted as equivalent to full-time workers,[11] and no account is taken of changes in standard working hours or overtime. These deficiencies would be remedied by a measure in terms of man-hours per annum; but such a series is not available.[12] We therefore have to note that changes in our measure of labour productivity may reflect unmeasured changes in labour input per man-year – changes in hours worked, quality and composition – as well as changes in other factor inputs and technical progress.[13]

For the *degree of full employment of labour* (variable (vii)) the choice is again clear cut: we take *the number estimated as unemployed as a percentage of the civilian working population.* For years after 1939 the number unemployed is measured as the number registered as wholly unemployed and available for work. There are a number of reasons why the unemployment percentage thus defined is an imperfect measure either of the general degree of utilisation of the labour force, or of the level of Keynesian 'involuntary' unemployment, or of the pressure of demand in the labour market; but having said this it is probably as reliable an indicator of any of these as any other simple measure. For years before 1939 the unemployment estimates conform in principle to the modern definition; but they have been obtained from different sources (from trade-union records before 1920) and are less reliable, so that for these years 'it would not be worthwhile to attempt to specify the definition too minutely' (Feinstein, 1972, p. 216).

The data relating to the growth of output, capital and employment between 1855 and 1976 are summarised in Table 15.1.[14] The 'Feinstein period', 1855–1965, after the exclusion of the years around the two world wars, has been split into five sub-periods of roughly equal duration. The interwar and post-war sub-periods distinguish themselves naturally; and the fifty-nine years before the First World War have been divided into three sub-periods by isolating the period of the 'Great Depression', 1871–95. For each sub-period, cols (1)–(5) show the average annual growth rates of Y, K, L, y and k, as defined above; col. (6) shows the initial value of the constant-price capital–output ratio, v, and col. (7) shows the subsequent percentage change; cols (8) and (9) give the same information for the current-price ratio, V; finally, cols (10) and (11) reconcile the changes in v with those in V by describing the implied changes in capital-good prices in relation to output prices in general. Row (6) refers to the whole Feinstein period, including the war years, while row (7) brings Feinstein's data up to date, using the Blue Book.

One of the most striking features of the three earliest sub-periods is the rise in the rate of capital accumulation: the growth rate of the capital stock in sub-period (3) was almost twice that of sub-period (1), and

Table 15.1

Growth of output, capital and labour in the United Kingdom, 1855-1976*

| Period | Average annual growth rates (%) | | | | | v | | V | | $p_k/p_y \equiv v/V$ | |
| | Y | K | L | y | k | Initial value | % change during period | Initial value | % change during period | Initial value | % change during period |
	(1)	(2)	(3)	(4)	(5)	(6)	(7)	(8)	(9)	(10)	(11)
(1) 1855–70	2.2	1.0	0.8	1.4	0.2	5.1	−14	5.5	−22	1.08	− 9
(2) 1871–95	1.7	1.4	0.7	1.0	0.7	4.2	−10	4.2	−14	1.00	− 5
(3) 1896–1913	1.7	1.9	1.0	0.7	0.9	3.7	+ 3	3.6	+11	0.97	+ 8
(4) 1920–38	1.9	1.6	0.3	1.6	1.3	4.2	− 5	4.7	−15	1.12	−11
(5) 1948–65	3.0	2.7	0.7	2.3	2.0	3.7	− 5	4.6	−13	1.24	− 8
(6) 1855–1965	1.8	1.5	0.7	1.1	0.8	5.1	−31†	5.5	−27†	1.08	+ 6†
(7) 1966–76	2.1	3.8	−0.2	2.3	4.0	3.9	+18†	3.9	+39†	1.01	+19†

*For definitions, see text.

†End-period values:

	v	V	p_k/p_y
1965 Feinstein (1972)	3.5	4.0	1.13
C.S.O. (1977)	3.8	3.9	1.03
1976 C.S.O. (1977)	4.6	5.5	1.19

Source: Feinstein (1972, tables 1, 20, 46); Central Statistical Office (1977, tables 1.1, 2.1, 11.12; 1977 ...)

the comparison is even more dramatic in terms of capital per head (col. (5)). But while accumulation was gathering pace, the growth of output and labour productivity was stagnant or declining: the growth rate of output per head between 1896 and 1913 was half that of the sub-period 1855-70, while the growth rate of capital per head was four times higher. In fact, 1896-1913 is the only Feinstein sub-period in which output grew more slowly than capital, so that - as col. (7) shows - v rose, albeit by only 3 per cent in seventeen years.

In terms of Kaldorian theory these features of pre-1914 growth suggest that the technical progress function (T.P.F.) shifted downwards; this is the only way the retardation of productivity growth can be reconciled with accelerating capital per head. More precisely, the data may be interpreted as showing that initially the economy was out of steady-state equilibrium, to the left of the point P in Figure 9.1. With Y thus growing faster than K - at least in sub-periods (1) and (2) - producers were encouraged to raise the rate of capital-deepening; but the T.P.F. was meanwhile shifting downwards at such a rate that the beneficial effects on productivity growth of accelerating capital per head were more than cancelled out. The data for sub-period (3) may then be taken as an indication that producers overshot the mark: that the system was by then to the right of the steady-growth point on the new, lower T.P.F. With the capital-output ratio rising, Kaldor's theory would suggest that the rate of deepening would drop back; and Feinstein's data do indeed show a clear deceleration in k after about 1904 - in fact almost all the increase during sub-period (3) had occurred by 1907. It therefore seems that the salient features of growth between the mid-nineteenth century and the First World War can be interpreted in terms of a Kaldorian story. It is a *simpliste* story, ignoring such influences as the trade cycle; but perhaps it is an illustration of what growth theory can tell. At least there seems to be nothing in the data - such as an advancing rate of accumulation at the same time as a rising capital-output ratio - which is inconsistent with the theory.

In terms of the neo-classical aggregate production function, accelerating k with decelerating y implies either a declining profit share (falling marginal product of capital and/or falling capital-output ratio) or technological regress. Section 15.4 will show that there is some evidence of a decline in the share of profits during sub-period (2), though not in sub-periods (1) and (3). In any event it seems that neo-classical theory also implies that there was some decline in the 'technical dynamism' of the economy towards the end of the nineteenth century. In fact

Matthews (1964, table 1) has calculated that in the United Kingdom between 1899 and 1913 Solow's 'residual' (cf. section 7.7) was negative, suggesting negative technical progress.

Both the Kaldorian and the neo-classical analyses therefore suggest that there was a deceleration of technical progress, or even technical regress for part of the period, during the last decades of the nineteenth century and the first decade of the twentieth century. Phelps Brown *et al.* (1952; 1953) have offered an explanation. They suggest that by about 1895 the opportunities stemming from the advent of the railway and advances in steel production had been largely exhausted, and that new advances, although being developed, were not to become widely applicable until after the First World War. This may explain the apparent decline in the rate of technical progress; but it does not account for the negative residual observed by Matthews. Phelps Brown and Weber (1953, p. 271) recognised this, in effect, and went on to suggest that the exhaustion of natural resources, particularly in coal mining (i.e. diminishing returns from land), and 'a decreased efficiency, or annual effort, of managers and men' might provide the explanation.

During the interwar period the advances referred to by Phelps Brown – electricity, the motor-car, chemical engineering, etc. – did become widely applied. The growth rate of y in sub-period (4) was higher than in any of the earlier sub-periods; and the same is true of k. But the growth of Y and K was not so exceptionally fast: one of the most striking features of the interwar period is the low growth rate of L. In fact the whole of the growth in employment in this sub-period occurred in the final three years: L fell dramatically in the early 1920s, and did not recover its 1920 level until 1936. The reverse side of this coin is, of course, the exceptionally high unemployment depicted in figure 15.1, though there was also in fact some decline in population growth. Y again grew faster than K, so that v fell, by about 5 per cent.

In sub-period (5) the growth rates of Y, K, y and k were all higher than in any earlier sub-period; and v is estimated again to have fallen slightly. The more recent data in row (7) show a further strong rise in the rate of capital accumulation, in spite of the post-1973 recession; but the recession is clearly reflected in the decline in L in col. (3), the rise in U in Figure 15.1,[15] the slower growth of Y in col. (1), and the large increase in v shown in col. (7) and the chart. Between 1966 and 1976 the difference between the growth rates of K and Y was larger than in any other sub-period, and v grew at an annual rate of 1.7 per cent. There was, moreover, a significant increase in the relative price

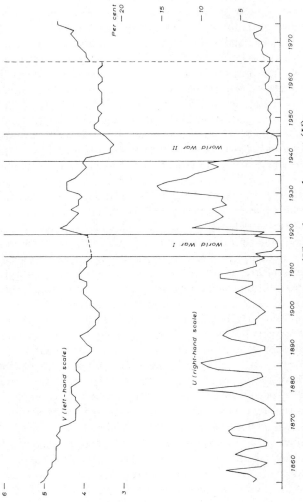

Fig. 15.1   The physical capital-output ratio (*V*) and unemployment (*U*),
United Kingdom, 1855–1976*

*For definitions, see text.
Sources: Feinstein (1972, tables, 20, 57); C.S.O. (1977, tables 2.1, 11.12; 1977a, p. 85).

of capital goods (col. (11)), so that the current-price capital–output
ratio V grew, remarkably, more than twice as fast (col. (9)): by 1976 it
was back at its 1855 value of 5.5. But even with the years since 1973 included, rows (5) and (7) show quite clearly that the growth of the U.K.
economy in the post-war period has exceeded its growth in any other
period of comparable duration, over at least the last 120 years.

We can now make some judgement on the validity, for the United
Kingdom, of the relevant stylised facts. There is no question as to the
validity of (ii): there has obviously been 'a continued increase in the
amount of capital per worker', apart from over periods short enough
not to have shown through in our summary of the data in Table 15.1.
But a more interesting question is whether the growth rate of capital
per head has been steady – a question we need to ask in relation to stylised facts (i) and (iv). The table in fact shows a continuous acceleration
of k through the period: the growth rate may be seen to have increased
tenfold between sub-periods (1) and (5), and twentyfold between sub-
periods (1) and (7). For K also, the evidence of acceleration is fairly
clear, despite the dip in the interwar years. The evidence for output and
labour productivity is rather less clear. The table shows quite a marked
acceleration since the turn of the century; but whether there has been
a long-run acceleration in any meaningful sense seems open to interpretation. Matthews (1964, p. 4) argues, rather, in favour of 'identifying
three broad phases in the economic history of the past hundred years:
an initial phase of fairly rapid growth, terminating in the 1870s or in
1900. . . a doldrums period, running from then until the early 1930s;
and a concluding period of faster growth, beginning in the 1930s, inter-
rupted by World War II, and carrying on up to the present time'.

In any event the *data for the United Kingdom provide little support
for the hypothesis that there is some 'steady trend' or 'normal' growth
rate of capital or output or both* running through economic history –
which is what Kaldor's stylised facts suggest – unless the interpretation
of the hypothesis is so liberal as to bear little meaning.

There is, however, another sense in which the course of growth in
modern economies may be claimed to have been relatively steady. Although the evidence (at least for the United Kingdom) does not support
the idea that the growth rates of industrialised economies are trendless,
it is probable that the variability of growth from year to year about
whatever trend there may be in any period is considerably less for industrialised economies than it was for the same economies in pre-
modern times. This is what Kuznets (1966, p. 70) means when he

claims that one of the main features 'of modern aggregative growth. . . is the relative steadiness of its rate over time'. The explanations for this are: the decline in the importance of agriculture in favour of activities more susceptible to human control; technical progress in agriculture itself; improvements in transportation, which have widened sources of supply; advances in medicine, which have made possible a 'steadier' rate of population growth; and, in the post-war period, Keynesian demand management. That the variance of growth through time has been reduced by these developments is hardly open to doubt, though it is difficult to obtain adequate quantitative support for the proposition. And the relative steadiness of growth in this sense may be a factor which could help to explain the apparent acceleration of growth in the United Kingdom during the 'modern epoch': the relative 'steadiness' of growth in Kuznets's sense may have a part to play in explaining the 'unsteadiness' of growth in the sense in which we are more interested.[16]

Turning to the capital–output ratio and stylised fact (iv), we have already seen that v, the ratio in constant prices, is estimated to have fallen in each of the five Feinstein sub-periods other than (3); and Table 15.1 also shows that over the period 1855–1965 as a whole, v is estimated to have fallen by about a third. This seems to indicate that the physical capital–output ratio has a secular downward trend: that the average productivity of capital, as well as labour, tends to rise with economic growth. But on the other hand most of the estimated decline occurred before 1895, when the data – particularly for the capital stock – are weakest; and furthermore since the end of the Feinstein period, as we have seen, there has been a large rise in the ratio. Thus whereas between 1855 and 1965 v is estimated to have fallen by a third, between 1871 and 1976 there appears to have been a rise of a tenth. It may therefore be argued that *it is difficult to discern any definite long-run trend in the capital–output ratio in the United Kingdom*, and that stylised fact (iv) stands up reasonably well.

One problem in identifying the secular trend of the capital–output ratio is the 'noise' in the statistics which is due to the strong dependence of v on the degree of utilisation of capacity. That v is strongly contra-cyclical may be seen from Figure 15.1, which shows a clear positive correlation between v and unemployment: the high level of v in the interwar period, and the strong rise since the mid-1960s are of particular interest in this regard. Maywald (1956) attempted to eliminate this source of variation by taking as the denominator of V, the current-price ratio, the 'full-employment' national income for each year, estimated on the basis of unemployment figures. With data for the numerator derived from fire-insurance capital valuations, he constructed a series for V between 1870 and 1952 which, by his judgement, showed secular stability.[17]

Also, *the experience of other industrialised countries appears to support the conclusions drawn from U.K. data.*

It seems, first, that the concept of a 'steady trend' rate of growth is no more applicable elsewhere than it is in the United Kingdom. For example, Paige (1961, table 1) found the post-war acceleration of growth to have been quite a general phenomenon; in each of eleven industrialised countries studied the average growth rate of labour productivity in the post-war period was higher than the long-term average calculated from data running back into the nineteenth century. And Paige (1961, p. 37) concluded from her investigation that there seemed to be no 'normal' or predictable pattern in countries' growth rates (apart from the fact that Japan's always seemed the highest): 'It is naive to regard a process as complex as the expansion of economic output as following some necessarily predetermined pattern; the main lesson of the historical figures is simply that no such pattern does in fact appear in them'

As regards the capital–output ratio, Klein and Kosobud (1961) found a statistically significant downward trend in v in the United States between 1900 and 1953; and data for the United States quoted by Kravis (1959) and Domar (1961) show quite large falls in capital–output ratios, variously defined, between the 1930s and the 1950s. Between 1950 and 1962 Denison's (1967) estimates show the capital–output ratio stable in the Netherlands, rising in the United States, Denmark, Norway and the United Kingdom, and falling in Belgium, France, West Germany and Italy. Kuznets (1966, p. 77), summarising evidence from various countries over periods extending back into the ninteenth century, writes that 'by and large, the trends in the ratios of reproducible capital to product have been upward, though tempered by recent declines, often to particularly low levels in the post-World War II years'. The international evidence thus appears to confirm that although there may be quite pronounced swings in the capital–output ratio in different periods, there is no well-defined or generally applicable long-term trend, upwards or downwards; in this sense stylised fact (iv) may be accepted as valid.

15.4 Distributive shares and the rate of profit

For an examination of the validity of stylised facts (iii) and (v), the following variables (others stated on p. 271) remain to be specified:

(viii) the shares of profits and wages in income;
(ix) the rate of profit on capital; and
(x) the ratio of investment to output.

Kaldor's stylised facts refer to a decomposition of aggregate income into wages and profits; and in most growth models (including Kaldor's) these are the only types of income distinguished, since capital and labour are the only factors of production. But in reality land exists as a factor which is, in principle, distinct, and whose reward, rent, ought in principle to be distinguished. It therefore seems that we should seek a three-part division of our measure of aggregate income, G.D.P., into wages, profits and rent – the rewards to labour, capital and land respectively. In the national-income accounts, however, G.D.P. is described as comprising five main kinds of income:

$$G.D.P. \equiv E + F + PC + PP + R - A \qquad (15.16)$$

where E is income from employment, F is income from self-employment, PC is gross trading profits of companies, PP is gross traging surpluses of public corporations, etc., R is rent, and A is stock appreciation.[18] It is natural to include PC and PP in our 'profits' variable; it then seems that the only problem in obtaining our three-part division is the treatment of F. But unfortunately 'rent' does not mean what it says.

The statistical variable 'rent' refers to the income derived from the ownership of land and buildings, except that where property is owner-occupied the coverage excludes trading property other than farms. It therefore differs from the conception of rent as the income of the factor of production land in two respects. First, R includes the earnings of buildings, which are part of the capital stock – indeed, 'the figures relate principally to buildings' (Maurice, 1968, p. 473). Second, R excludes the earnings of land which is owner-occupied by trading concerns other than farms; these are included (with the earnings of buildings) in F, or PC, or PP, as appropriate. The first feature is a reflection of the common institutional arrangement whereby land and buildings are rented together in the same transaction; the second reflects the impracticability of distinguishing the part of profit (or self-employment income) which represents a return to land from that which represents a return to capital. In sum, for the United Kingdom – and other economies with similar institutional arrangements – there is no direct way of obtaining a measure of the rent of land; and 'rent' as measured for the national-income accounts has little significance as a category of income distinct from profits: 'Rent is better-regarded as a form of trading profits – the surplus on operating account derived from the business of letting real estate – than as the earnings of a specific and distinguishable factor of production' (Maurice, 1968).

We therefore have to revert to the two-category classification – 'wages' and 'profits' – with which we started: R must be included with PC and PP in the latter, which must now be understood as the income of property generally, including land.

There remains the question of how self-employment income, F, should be treated. F refers to the incomes of unincorporated businesses: sole traders and partnerships, including professional people. It is to be regarded as a combination of a return on the labour contributed by the self-employed, and a return on their capital and land (except that for farmers, as has been seen, the rent of land and buildings is included in R). As far as the national-income statisticians are concerned, 'there is no way of distinguishing between these two elements' (Maurice, 1968, p. 103). Various methods have nevertheless been used to split F, though only roughly, into its labour income (F_w) and property income (F_p) components. Using Kravis's (1959, pp. 924–5) terminology we may list the main possibilities as follows:

(i) *Labour basis*: impute to each self-employed person a 'wage' – based on either a national or an appropriate sectoral average – and count the remainder of the income of each enterprise as 'profit'.

(ii) *Asset basis* (converse of (i)): impute to each enterprise a 'profit' – based on either a national or an appropriate sectoral average profit rate – and count the residual as 'wages'.

(iii) *Economy-wide basis*: split F into F_w and F_p for each year by applying the current ratio between labour income and property income in the remainder of the economy.

(iv) *Proportional basis*: assume that F_w (or F_p) is some constant proportion of F, perhaps on the basis of information for a particular year, or some hypothesis about the composition of F.

Kravis made calculations for the United States using each of these methods. Feinstein (1968, pp. 124–6) applied the labour basis, with sectoral wages, to U.K. data. Kuznets (1966, pp. 177–80) also prefers the labour basis, but considers unnecessary the refinement of taking account of inter-sectoral wage differences. Denison (1967, pp. 37–9), however, prefers the economy-wide and proportional bases; and these have the advantage of being directly calculable from the national-income accounts alone – no additional information is needed. Partly for this reason we shall use the economy-wide basis.

We can now offer a provisional specification of *distributive shares*. With all variables at current factor cost, we define 'wages' as

$$W_1 \equiv E + F_w \qquad (15.17)$$

where

$$\frac{F_w}{F} \equiv \frac{E}{G.D.P. - F} \qquad (15.18)$$

Then define 'profits' as

$$P_1 \equiv G.D.P. - W_1 \equiv F_p + PC + PP + R - A \qquad (15.19)$$

where

$$F_p \equiv F - F_w \qquad (15.20)$$

As is appropriate, P_1 excludes stock appreciation. Our provisional specification of the shares of 'wages' and 'profits' follows directly:

$$\left[\frac{W}{Y}\right]_1 \equiv \frac{W_1}{G.D.P.} \equiv \frac{E + F_w}{G.D.P.} \equiv \frac{E}{G.D.P. - F} \qquad (15.21)$$

$$\left[\frac{P}{Y}\right]_1 \equiv \frac{P_1}{G.D.P.} \equiv \frac{F_p + PC + PP + R - A}{G.D.P.} \equiv$$

$$\equiv \frac{PC + PP + R - A}{G.D.P. - F} \qquad (15.22)$$

It will be noted that use of the economy-wide basis means that the specified factor shares depend only on the distribution of income outside the self-employment sector; in effect self-employment income is neutralised.

Three other alternative specifications may be considered. First, some may prefer to specify the share of 'wages' as the share of income from employment:

$$\left[\frac{W}{Y}\right]_2 \equiv \frac{E}{G.D.P.} \qquad (15.23)$$

Thus Deane and Cole (1967, p. 241) argue that 'In the end it seems best to focus on incomes from employment as being the least ambiguous of the factor shares.' But there is the drawback that the complement of $(W/Y)_2$ – the implicit corresponding 'profit' share – includes the whole of self-employment income.

Second, even E may be considered too broad a specification of 'wages'. E is made up of four main components: wages; salaries (including directors' fees); the pay of H.M. Forces; and employers' contributions to national insurance, pensions, etc. There are reasons why one might prefer to exclude salaries from a specification of 'wages', or to examine the share of wages, as defined by the statisticians – call it W^* – alone. Thus one might argue that a high proportion of salaries must represent a return to human capital, and that W^* – the incomes of manual labour – represent a purer form of labour income: or one's theory of distribution may involve a distinction between different kinds of labour income resembling the distinction between the statistical variables wages and salaries (cf. Kalecki's distinction between prime and overhead labour costs, discussed in section 11.2). The latter argument would have more force if the distinction between prime and overhead labour had been retained by Kaldor and other growth theorists; but it has not. The first argument correctly questions the legitimacy of treating the whole of income from employment as a return to labour; but it is doubtful whether the exclusion of salaries can help to solve the problem. For in fact, the distinction between wages and salaries turns out to be rather meaningless: administrative, technical and clerical workers are classified as salary-earners, while operatives, shop assistants and the police are treated as wage-earners. It seems that the statistical distinction cannot satisfy the requirements of either of the arguments to which we have referred; for example, many skilled operatives must embody more human capital than many clerical workers. Thus the Central Statistical Office considers that 'Only a limited importance can be attached to the separation of wages from salaries in the national accounts' (Maurice, 1968, p. 121); and in fact the distinction has not appeared in the Blue Book since 1970. We shall nevertheless examine the movements in the share of wages

$$\left[\frac{W}{Y}\right]_3 \equiv \frac{W^*}{G.D.P.} \tag{15.24}$$

over the period covered by Feinstein's data, partly because it has figured prominently in the literature.

Third, one may wish to focus on the share of corporate profits, PC, preferably after deduction of company-sector stock appreciation, A_{PC}. Feinstein does not provide a breakdown of stock appreciation A among PC, PP and F, but the Blue Book does. It is therefore only for years since 1948 that we are able to deduct direct estimates of A_{PC} from PC; for earlier years for which Feinstein provides estimates of A, we have arbitrarily assumed that A_{PC} forms 70 per cent of A; but before 1914 even estimates of A are unavailable, so that no deduction can be made. We shall therefore examine movements in the share of PC, both before deduction of stock appreciation

$$\left[\frac{P}{Y}\right]_4 \equiv \frac{PC}{G.D.P.} \tag{15.25}$$

and, for years since the First World War, after the deduction

$$\left[\frac{P}{Y}\right]_5 \equiv \frac{PC - A_{PC}}{G.D.P.} \tag{15.26}$$

but with A_{PC} only roughly estimated for years up to 1947.

Our original provisional specification of distributive shares – $(W/Y)_1$ and $(P/Y)_1$ – comes nearer than any of these alternatives to identifying categories of 'wages' and 'profits' which together exhaust the total product. It also seems consistent with Kaldor's specification; for example, 'I use the terms "profits" and "wages" in an inclusive sense, to embrace all forms of income from property and work, respectively' (Kaldor, 1957a, p. 251). But while it does seem the most satisfactory from our point of view, it is clearly not ideal; in particular the split of F is fairly arbitrary, and it does not distinguish the returns to human capital from labour income.

Given that we are omitting to deduct depreciation, only one meaningful measure of the *rate of profit on capital* can be derived from the data we are using:

$$r \equiv \frac{P_1}{p_k K} \equiv \frac{F_p + PC + PP + R - A}{\text{Current replacement cost new of the capital stock}}$$

(15.27)

At most this provides a measure of the average rate of profit, before depreciation and taxation; it is far removed from the marginal rate of profit or the inducement to invest. But even on its own terms r has several limitations; thus returns to land and circulating capital are included in the numerator, while the values of these assets are excluded from the denominator. But without, for example, a sectoral analysis of the capital stock (other than for recent years in the Blue book), this seems the best that can be done.

Expressions (15.12), (15.13), (15.22), and (15.27) show that $(P/Y)_1$ may be decomposed as follows:

$$\left[\frac{P}{Y}\right]_1 \equiv rV \equiv rv\,\frac{p_k}{p_y}$$

(15.28)

Hence movements in $(P/Y)_1$ can be analysed in terms of movements in our measure of the rate of profit on the one hand, and movements in either our current-price capital–output ratio, or our constant-price capital–output ratio, and the relative price of capital goods, on the other.

Finally, we need to identify an appropriate statistical measure of the *investment–output ratio*. In the growth models there are two kinds of expenditure, consumption and investment. But the expenditure analysis of the G.D.P. of an open economy with a government is not so simple: in the Blue Book six types of expenditure are distinguished:[19]

$$G.D.P. \equiv C + I_f + H + G + X - M$$

(15.29)

where C is consumers' expenditure, I_f is gross domestic fixed capital formation, H is stock-building, G is government current expenditure, X is exports of goods and services, and M is imports of goods and services. We would usually think of 'investment' as expenditure which adds to the stock of capital. On this basis we might specify 'investment' as the sum of $I_f + H$ (which relates to domestic investment) and $X - M$ (the trade balance, which relates to foreign investment); this would leave $C + G$ as our specification of 'consumption', though we might have reservations about the inclusion in $C + G$ of expenditures which add to the 'unmeasured' capital stock (cf. section 15.2). But this specification seems inappropriate to our purpose, and we take a different approach.

One specification we shall adopt is simply

$$\left[\frac{I}{Y}\right]_1 \equiv \frac{I_f}{G.D.P.} \tag{15.30}$$

where the variables are in constant prices. This omits foreign investment and stock-building, and measures domestic fixed investment gross of depreciation. Its rationale is that in attempting to identify a statistical variable analogous to the variable 'I' in Kaldor's distribution model, it seems appropriate to measure investment gross (since it is gross, not net, expenditure which is important for aggregate demand); to restrict attention to domestic investment; and also to exclude stock-building, since although it is – like fixed investment – a capital rather than a current expenditure, it is unlike fixed investment in being (like consumer spending) sensitive to current income and output flows. This last point has wider implications. If we were to take the simple Keynesian closed-economy multiplier model, and apply it in simple fashion to an open economy with a government, we would tend to treat G and X, like I_f, as autonomous, and M, like C, as endogenous. We could then show how output is determined, given the marginal propensities to save and import (and given tax rates), by the level of total 'autonomous' expenditure, including G and X. This is of course done in introductory textbooks. There would seem to be a case for adopting a similar approach in extending the Kaldorian distribution model to an open economy with a government. Thus assuming, in a 'Keynesian' spirit, that C, H and M are endogenous, while I_f, G and X are autonomous, our second specification of the 'investment'-output ratio is

$$\left[\frac{I}{Y}\right]_2 \equiv \frac{I_f + G + X}{G.D.P.} \tag{15.31}$$

Its rationale is essentially that Kaldor's theory implies that with output given at full employment a change in any kind of autonomous demand will affect the share of profits in the same way: there is no reason why a change in I_f should have an effect any different from a change in G or in X. $(I/Y)_2$ is, however, based on a classification of expenditure types into 'autonomous' and 'endogenous' components which is obviously *simpliste* and which Kaldor might not accept.

We can now examine the validity of stylised facts (iii) and (v), which refer to the alleged long-run steadiness of the rate of profit and distributive shares, and the alleged positive correlation, in the shorter term, between the share of profits and the investment–output ratio.

Kaldor was not the first to claim that distributive shares have been stable over the long run. Phelps Brown (1968, p. 2) writes that the apparent stability of labour's share 'first made a powerful impression on the minds of British economists in 1927, when Bowley and Stamp published their study of the British national income in 1924, and compared it with Bowley's earlier analysis of national income in 1911'. Indeed, the 'stylised fact' that the share of wages has been constant is sometimes referred to as 'Bowley's Law'. Kalecki (1939) adopted this 'Law', which appeared to be supported by data for the United States, as one of the features to be explained by his theory of distribution. Keynes (1939, p. 48) claimed that 'the stability of the proportion of the national dividend accruing to labour, irrespective apparently of the level of output as a whole and of the phase of the trade cycle. . .is one of the most surprising, yet best-established, facts in the whole range of economic statistics, both for Great Britain and for the United States'. If Kaldor was not the first to adopt Bowley's Law, he is also not the last. Kennedy (1964, p. 542) argued that 'one of the advantages of a theory of induced bias in innovation is that it can explain this. . . tendency, for advanced economies at any rate, towards constancy in distributive shares'. And Drandakis and Phelps (1966, p. 823) accepted that 'distributive shares have been remarkably constant in most western economies . . . the modern economist has almost ceased to wonder at Bowley's Law'. Even when Solow (1958) was in a sceptical mood he was more concerned to question the idea that distributive shares fluctuate less from year to year in the aggregate than in individual industries. than to question the 'Law' that there is no trend.

The movements of labour's share in income, by each of the three definitions set out above, for the United Kingdom over the period 1855–1976, are shown in Figure 15.2. The variable which captured the attention of Bowley, Kalecki and Keynes corresponds (though not exactly) to $(W/Y)_3$, the share of wages. To Kalecki and Keynes, writing in the late 1930s, this share seemed to have been remarkably stable, in both the long and short runs. From our vantage point in the 1970s it appears to have declined, though not dramatically, through every period of peacetime since about 1890. During the two world wars the share fell –

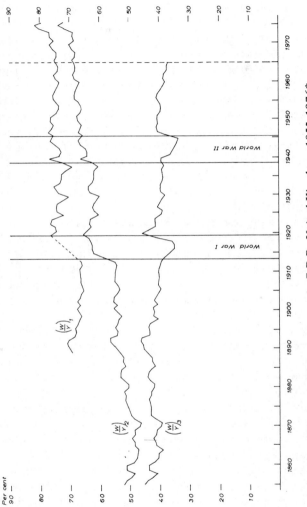

Fig. 15.2   The share of labour income in G.D.P., United Kingdom, 1855–1976*

*For definitions, see text.

Sources: Feinstein (1972, tables 18, 21); C.S.O. (1977, table 1.1).

wages do not, it will be recalled, include H.M. Forces' pay – thereafter to recover sharply at least to pre-war levels before the decline proceeded. Through the Feinstein period as a whole $(W/Y)_3$ fell moderately, from around 43 per cent in the late 1850s to around 37 per cent in the early 1960s.

The second line in the chart shows the movements of $(W/Y)_2$, the share of income from employment. Up to 1890 it may be seen to have moved roughly in parallel with $(W/Y)_3$. But between 1890 and the First World War, whereas the share of wages was falling, the share of employment income was stable; and the widening of the gap between $(W/Y)_3$ and $(W/Y)_2$ which began around 1890 has continued since. This decline in the share of wages in income from employment is not surprising, in view of the large fall in the number of wage-earners in relation to the number of salary-earners. Feinstein (1968, table 3) reports that the ratio of wage-earners to salary-earners declined from about 9 in 1911 to about 2 in 1961, the effect on the share of wages in employment income being offset to some extent by a doubling of the ratio between the average wage and the average salary over the same period. It is clear from the chart that the growth of employment incomes other than wages has been more than sufficient to offset the secular decline in $(W/Y)_3$. After the period of stability between 1890 and 1913, $(W/Y)_2$ increased from 55 to 65 per cent during the First World War, and although there was some decline in the interwar period, the share was still above 60 per cent at the start of the Second World War. There was a further significant rise through the Second World War, and this has not been eaten up at all in the post-war period; in fact the upward trend has continued. Over all, $(W/Y)_2$ may be seen to have increased from around 50 per cent in the third quarter of the last century to around 70 per cent in the 1970s.

The third line depicts $(W/Y)_1$, which we suggested is probably the most satisfactory of the three measures of labour's share. The inclusion of labour's estimated share of self-employment income gives a series with a rather less pronounced upward trend than $(W/Y)_2$: the gap between the two lines narrows significantly through the period. And the presence of an upward trend in the post-war period is less clear, certainly up to the late 1960s. Nevertheless, as with $(W/Y)_2$, there has been a definite upward movement through the period as a whole. The difference is that the rise in $(W/Y)_1$ seems to have taken place almost wholly during the First World War and since the mid-1960s; between 1920 and 1965 hardly any trend is discernible.

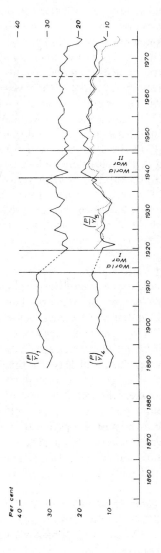

Fig. 15.3   The share of property income in G.D.P., U.K., 1889–1976*

*For definitions, see text.

Sources: Feinstein (1972, table 18); C.S.O. (1977, tables 1.1, 5.1); and earlier *National Income and Expenditure* Blue Books.

Movements in the share of profits, again by three definitions, are shown in Figure 15.3. The top line shows $(P/Y)_1$; this is merely the complement of $(W/Y)_1$ and requires no further comment. The $(P/Y)_4$ line shows the share of corporate profits before allowance for stock appreciation, while the broken line depicts $(P/Y)_5$, the same share after deduction of stock appreciation. These two lines diverge in periods of rapidly changing prices; otherwise they move roughly in step. $(P/Y)_4$ confirms the impression given by $(P/Y)_1$ that there was some rise in the share of property income in the twenty-five years preceding the First World War. The fall in $(P/Y)_4$ during the First World War is rather less than that in $(P/Y)_1$, indicating that most of the decline in the share of property income between 1913 and 1920 is to be accounted for by rent and the property share of self-employment income. Both $(P/Y)_4$ and $(P/Y)_5$ declined in the 1920s, but had at least recovered their 1920 levels by 1938. Between 1938 and 1960 the share of corporate profits seems to have shown no trend; but since the mid-1960s there has been a marked decline, particularly if profits are measured net of stock appreciation. In fact in 1974–6 $(P/Y)_5$ was lower than in any other part of the period.

When interpreting the $(P/Y)_4$ and $(P/Y)_5$ series one should bear in mind the considerable increase in the size of the corporate sector, at the expense of the self-employment sector, since the late nineteenth century. It then seems difficult, unless one attaches importance to $(W/Y)_3$, to avoid the conclusion that *on the above evidence labour's share in aggregate income in the United Kingdom has increased over the long run.* And Feinstein (1968) has shown, at least for the period 1910–63, that the same conclusion follows when self-employment income is allocated on the labour basis; when the rental income of dwellings is excluded from property income and from the total; and when allowance is made for depreciation. For the post-war period the conclusion is supported by, for example, the results of Neild (1963) and Godley and Nordhaus (1972), which show a downward trend in profit margins for manufactured goods, and by King's (1975) study of the share of profits in manufacturing.[20]

Nor is the apparent upward trend in labour's share unique to the United Kingdom. Kravis (1959) found a pronounced upward trend in the United States between 1900 and 1957 whichever method was used to allocate self-employment income. And he found that the trend was still present when estimates of returns to consumer durables and government property were included in the profit share, and when the government sector was excluded altogether. Kravis (1959, p. 930) concluded that 'Taking all factors into account. . . the decline in the property share in national income over the first half of the twentieth century has been substantial, and. . . it cannot be explained away either by our methods of estimation or by the vagaries of the social accounting system.' For the period 1950–62 Denison (1967) found a declining profit share in each of his nine countries, although in Denmark and West Germany the fall appeared to have been negligible. In a study of seventeen industrialised countries over the period 1938–63 Heidensohn (1969) found an increasing share of employment income to have been a practically universal phenomenon. And the evidence presented by Kuznets (1966, table 4.2) indicates that there has been a general decline in the share of profits in industrialised economies since the beginning of the century.

All this casts considerable doubt on the validity of Bowley's Law, and on the validity of Kaldor's stylised fact (v) in so far as it claims that distributive shares have been stable over the long run.

But stylised fact (v) also refers to a positive correlation between the share of profits and the investment–output ratio, and we may now ask whether this proposition is supported by the data for the United Kingdom. In Figure 15.4 $(P/Y)_1$ is drawn alongside $(I/Y)_1$, the share of fixed investment, and $(I/Y)_2$, which we identified as the share of total autonomous expenditure. For the period before the First World War both $(I/Y)_1$ and $(I/Y)_2$ follow an upward trend until the early 1900s; $(I/Y)_2$ then flattens out, while $(I/Y)_1$ falls substantially. $(P/Y)_1$ follows an upward trend until about 1906, and then levels out. This does not seem markedly inconsistent with Kaldor's theory. During the First World War, however, there appears to have been no change in either investment ratio sufficient to account for the dramatic fall in $(P/Y)_1$. In the interwar period $(P/Y)_1$ and $(I/Y)_1$ appear to have shared an upward trend, and all three series dip in the early 1930s and recover thereafter, though the fall is much larger in $(I/Y)_2$ than in $(I/Y)_1$. But perhaps the most striking feature of the chart is that in the period since the Second World War there has been a substantial rise in the investment ratio, by either definition, without any corresponding rise in the share of profits. It therefore seems that *at least in the United Kingdom in the post-war period the share of profits has not changed in the way which would have been required, on the neo-Keynesian saving hypothesis, to generate the additional saving required to match the increasing investment or autonomous expenditure.* And this refers to a period of fuller employment than either the interwar period or the pre-1914 period,

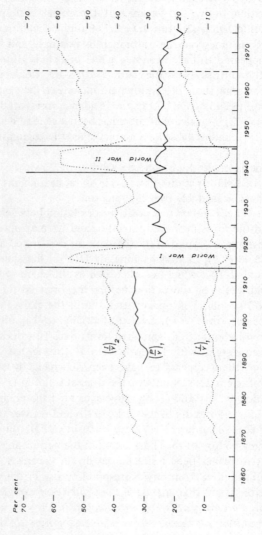

Fig. 15.4   The share of profits and the ratio of investment to output, U.K., 1870–1976*
*For definitions, see text.
Sources: Feinstein (1972, tables 5, 18); C.S.O. (1977, tables 1.1, 2.1).

and to a period long enough, surely, for profit margins to have over-come any short-term rigidities of the kind referred to by Kaldor (cf. sections 12.1 and 12.4). That the Kaldorian distribution model seems unable to account for the secular path of distributive shares in the United Kingdom in the post-war period may be considered to form a significant criticism of the empirical applicability of the theory.

Reder (1959) Gallaway (1964) and Phelps Brown (1968, pp. 30–7) have examined data for the United States and other countries for con-sistency with the Kaldorian correlation between the investment ratio and the profit share. The results, as for the United Kingdom, are mixed.

How else have movements in distributive shares been explained? With neo-classical theory it is possible to do little more than say *ex post* what combinations of values of the elasticity of substitution and the degree of factor-saving bias of technical progress are consistent with the observed changes in shares: 'what can be done is to measure changes in observable inputs and then, in light of theoretical concepts, interpret the outcome' (Johnson, 1973, p. 191). Solow (1958), for example, pointed out that the rise in labour's share in the United States in the first half of the twentieth century was consistent with an elasticity of substitution of 2/3, given the magnitude of the growth of capital per head in this period. But he claimed no empirical support for this value of the elasticity, nor did he justify the assumption of Hicks-neutrality on which his calculation was implicitly based. Thus Kravis (1959) pointed out that the observed combination of decline in the profit share and growth of capital per head was consistent with either Hicks-neutrality, or labour-saving bias, or capital-saving bias, together with an elasticity of substitution less than unity in the first two cases, and less than, equal to, or greater than unity in the third.

Other writers have attempted to explain distributive shifts in what may be regarded as Kaleckian terms - for example, Phelps Brown and Hart's (1952) study of changes in distributive shares in the United Kingdom between 1870 and 1950. They argue that the period 1870–1913, for example, may be divided into two sub-periods, during the first of which - 1870–95, the Great Depression - there was a general downward pressure on goods prices, and during the second of which demand conditions were such that producers had greater freedom to raise or maintain prices and profit margins. In the first sub-period, when producers were weak in goods markets, there were, according to the historians, two occasions when trade unions were strong in labour mar-kets. Each of these occasions was found by Phelps Brown and Hart to have had associated with it an upward shift in labour's share, the explanation being the impotence of producers to respond to upward pressure on wages by raising prices. And on the one occasion of recognised trade-union weakness, labour's share did not fall, presumably because of the depressed condition of goods markets. In the second sub-period, when producers were strong in goods markets, the reverse was found to be true: when unions were strong, labour's share failed to rise and profit margins were maintained, while union weakness led to a redistribution in favour of profits. Similarly, Glyn and Sutcliffe (1972) sought to explain the post-war decline in the share of profits in the United Kingdom in terms of a falling 'degree of monopoly', in effect stemming from an intensification of international competition among producers on the one hand and increased trade-union militancy on the other.

Other factors which have been invoked have included institutional changes (e.g. government rent control) and inter-sectoral shifts – in particular the relative growth of the labour-intensive government sector, whose 'return to capital' as imputed for the measurement of 'rent' in the national-income accounts may well be significantly understated. The results obtained by Feinstein and Kravis, however, suggest that these factors may not be as important or as distortionary as might have been thought. Another possible influence left out of account in growth theory is government fiscal policy. Thus Nordhaus (1974) attributes the post-war decline in the share of profits in the U.S. non-financial corporate sector to a fall in the cost of finance, stemming partly from a decline in the burden of corporate taxation and partly from a willingness on the part of savers to accept lower returns on equities. Sargent (1968) suggested that the ratio of fixed investment to output in the United Kingdom had risen between the early 1950s and the mid-1960s on account of government investment incentives, but that goods-market equilibrium had been maintained by an autonomous increase in the propensity to save. Meanwhile, the demand for labour to man the new equipment had persistently exceeded supply. The decline in the share of profits was therefore attributable to a chronic tendency to excess demand in the labour market, unmatched by any corresponding excess demand in the goods market. Sargent thus supplied a neat explanation for the concurrent rise in the investment ratio and fall in the profit share. (Sargent's analysis suggests that the post-war acceleration of growth in the United Kingdom may have been a purely temporary 'capital-deepening' phenomenon: that there may have been no increase in the natural growth rate.)

Table 15.2

*The share of property income, the rate of profit, and the capital–output ratio,
United Kingdom, 1896–1976**

	$\left[\dfrac{P}{Y}\right]_1$ Initial Value (1)	$\left[\dfrac{P}{Y}\right]_1$ % change during period (2)	$r \equiv \left[\dfrac{P}{Y}\right]_1 \times \dfrac{1}{V}$ Initial Value (3)	% change during period (4)	% change during period V (5)	v (6)	p_k/p_y (7)
(1) 1896–1913	0.317	+ 7	0.089	− 4	+11	+ 3	+ 8
(2) 1913–20	0.339	−30	0.085	−41	+18	+11	+ 7
(3) 1920–38	0.236	+31	0.050	+53	−15	− 5	−11
(4) 1938–48	0.308	−22	0.077	−32	+15	− 8	+24
(5) 1948–65	0.240	+ 8	0.052	+25	−13	− 5	− 8
(6) 1896–1965	0.317	−19	0.089	−27	+11	− 5	+18
(7) 1966–76	0.250	−18	0.064	−59	+39	+18	+19

*For definitions, see text.

Sources: Feinstein (1972, tables 1, 18, 20, 46); Central Statistical Office (1977, tables 1.1, 11.12).

One way of analysing - though not of explaining - movements in distributive shares is illustrated in Table 15.2. This also takes us on to stylised fact (iii), concerning the rate of profit. The period 1896–1965 has been split into five sub-periods - among which are the two world wars - and the Feinstein data are brought up to date in row (7). For each sub-period (and for the Feinstein period as a whole, in row (6)) the percentage change in $(P/Y)_1$ is shown in col. (2). Cols (4) and (5) show how the data imply that these changes may be broken down into changes in the average rate of profit on the one hand, and changes in the value capital–output ratio on the other (see expression (15.28)). In cols (6) and (7) the changes in V have then been broken down further into the changes in v and the relative price of capital goods. What stands out from the table is that in every sub-period except the first, and in the Feinstein period as a whole, the change in the rate of profit on capital is more than sufficient to account for the change in the share of profits in income: the rate of profit has generally moved in the same direction as the share, but more pronouncedly. What we have said about the 'empirical law' that the share of profits has been stable also applies, therefore, only more so, to Kaldor's third stylised fact, at least for the United Kingdom.[21]

15.5 Conclusions

When Solow (1970, p. 7) confronted Kaldor's stylised facts with the data, his conclusion was that 'the steady state is not a bad place for the theory of growth to start, but it may be a dangerous place for it to end'. The evidence reported in this chapter, however, suggests that by this Kaldorian criterion the steady state is not a particularly good place for the theory to start either. In so far as the data to which we have referred provide satisfactory measures of the theoretical variables - a qualification which, we have been concerned to indicate, is an important one - and in so far as we have succeeded in identifying the aggregative characteristics of long-run growth in 'industrialised' economies generally - and our examination of the data even for the United Kingdom cannot be claimed to be much more than cursory - these characteristics do not seem to coincide with the features of the theoretical concept of the steady state.

It is true that as far as the direction of movement of capital–output ratios is concerned, 'The unstylised facts will hardly justify anything more than an agnostic conclusion' (Solow, 1970, p. 6); there appears to have been no systematic tendency, over the long term, for capital to grow faster than output or vice versa. But there are indications that if there has been a common experience of trends in growth rates among industrialised countries, it has been an experience of acceleration, rather than of steadiness. And with regard to the distribution of income, there is quite strong evidence of a common experience of labour benefiting at the expense of capital, rather than of stable distributive shares. On the above evidence even the *aggregative* features of long-run growth in industrialised economies do not look very much like a steady state. If modern growth theory as represented in this book is regarded as a collection of attempts to explain how real economies come to be, in the long run, in a state of steady growth, it seems that the theory has been seeking to explain the wrong thing.

This is of course not necessarily to condemn the theory. Kaldor's stylised facts do not provide the sole justification for steady-state theory (cf. Chapter 2); and the models do provide a framework within which the implications for a growing economy of changes in behaviour and technology can be analysed. It may be argued, for example, as Mirrlees (1973, p. xii) has done (in his list of eight 'uses' for growth theory) that 'Probably there is no other way of discussing how increased saving (brought about by new habits of thriftiness, or changes in taxation) can affect the distribution of wealth and income' other than in the framework of a growth model. And as has been illustrated in this and earlier chapters, the models can aid the interpretation of history even if history has been out of steady state: 'It would be as philistine and silly to write off modern growth theory as it would be to take it as a completed theory of the world' (Hahn, 1971, p. xv).

What is to be inferred from this chapter is that the validity of one rather common interpretation of the significance and usefulness of steady-state analysis can seriously be questioned.

What are the implications for the future of growth theory? The inconsistencies with economic history of Kaldor's stylised facts, which have become clearer in the twenty years since they were formulated, do not mean that a new set of 'stylised facts', more empirically valid but less convenient for theoreticians, should be drawn up to describe the equilibrium solution of a new set of models. For one lesson to be learned is that simple 'stylised facts' or 'empirical laws' of economics – 'Bowley's Law of constant relative wage share; Long's Law of constant population participation in the labour force; Pareto's Law of unchangeable inequality of incomes; Denison's Law of constant private saving ratio; Colin Clark's Law of a 25% ceiling on government expenditure and taxation; Modigliani's Law of constant wealth–income ratio; Marx's Law of the falling rate of real wage and/or the falling rate of profit; Everybody's Law of a constant capital–output ratio' – are treacherous: 'they do describe the facts, up until they cease to describe the facts. If these be laws, Mother Nature is a criminal by nature' (Samuelson, 1963, p. 336).

But the questionable validity of Kaldor's stylised facts does imply that there are empirical grounds for shifting attention away from the steady state. Otherwise, if steady growth continues to be thought of as the stable condition of modern economies, the attention of the theories may remain focused on the conditions in which an economy will be in a steady state, and, in particular, the natural growth rate may remain, for the most part, an exogenous parameter. Yet it is the determination of this parameter, and in particular of the rate of technological change, which should, from many points of view, be at the centre of the stage.

Meanwhile, with regard to the work so far, it seems that 'The theory of growth is not a theory of economic history. . . If a historical theory ever comes to be formulated, the growth literature may be of some use; the bulk of the work will remain to be done' (Hahn, 1971, p. vii).

Notes and References

CHAPTER 1

[1] To say that Keynes was not interested in the long run is, of course, an overstatement. He was interested, for example, in the long-term implications of capital accumulation for the rate of return on capital (Keynes, 1936, pp. 220-1). (See also below, Chapter 14.) This was, however, peripheral to the main theme of his work.

[2] This and all other variables are defined in real terms, i.e. in terms of goods, or in terms of money deflated by a suitable price index.

[3] In common parlance 'rate of growth' almost invariably means 'percentage rate of growth', which is the proportional growth rate expressed as a percentage.

[4] More formally, mathematicians will recognise (1.6) as a first-order linear differential equation, with solution

$$Y(t) = Y(0)e^{(s/v)t} \qquad (1.6a)$$

where $Y(0)$ is initial output, which is taken to be given and assumed to be positive. (If $Y(0)$ were zero, the solution would imply constant $Y(t)$; if $Y(0)$ were negative, it would imply declining $Y(t)$.) The solution of the model is completed from (1.3) and (1.5):

$$S(t) = S(0)e^{(s/v)t}; I(t) = I(o)e^{(s/v)t}$$

where $S(0) = I(0) = sY(0)$. It may be observed from (1.6) and (1.6a) that in continuous time the (proportional) growth rate is an *exponential* growth rate.

[5] Harrod (1939, p.16) preferred 'warranted' to 'equilibrium' here not for this reason but because he considered the warranted path to be

highly unstable, a question to be considered in the next section.

[6] Note the way we add λ to τ. Full-employment output is the product of the labour force L and output per head y; and the growth rate of a variable which is the product of other variables is equal to the sum of the growth rates of these other variables. (In continuous time this is exactly true. In discrete time it is generally a good approximation.) Formally, if $L(t) = L(0)e^{\lambda t}$ and $y(t) = y(0)e^{\tau t}$, then full employment output, $\bar{Y}$, is given by

$$\bar{Y}(t) = L(t)y(t) = L(0)y(0)\,e^{(\lambda + \tau)t}$$

Thus for $Y = \bar{Y}$, $Y(t) = Y(0)e^{(\lambda + \tau)t}$, where $Y(0) = L(0)y(0)$.

[7] Note that the growth rate of a variable which is the ratio between two other variables is equal to the difference between the growth rates of these other variables.

[8] Chapter 7 expands on the meaning and role of the neutrality of technical progress.

[9] He also recognised that it was a simplification to regard the whole of investment expenditure as being dependent on and generated through the acceleration principle, and that autonomous investment might dampen the instability of warranted growth (Harrod, 1939, pp. 26–8).

[10] For example, Harrod (1948, p. 85) argues that if a surplus of capital develops, then 'orders will be reduced' and vice versa. More recently, Harrod (1973, p. 34) argues that a redundancy of capital 'will tend to cause an abatement in the rate of increase of new orders'. These propositions are not quite the same, though the difference probably does not indicate any significant change in Harrod's thinking over the twenty-five years between them. The point is that either is subject to different precise interpretations.

[11] From note 10, it may be seen that this specification seems close to Harrod (1948), whereas (1.10) seems close to Harrod (1973). Harrod gives no indication that the *apparent* change in his assumption about behaviour (which, as we said, may not be real) is an attempt to defend his Instability Principle from Rose's results.

[12] Sen's analysis is in terms of discrete time.

[13] I.e. $\hat{G}_t = (1-\alpha)\,[G_{t-1} + \alpha G_{t-2} + \alpha^2 G_{t-3} + \ldots + \alpha^n G_{t-n-1} +]$; $0 < \alpha < 1$, where $\hat{G}_t$ is the expected growth rate of output between periods t–1 and t. The Koyck transformation of this expression gives

$$\hat{G}_t - \alpha\hat{G}_{t-1} = (1-\alpha)G_{t-1}$$

or

$$\hat{G}_t = \alpha \hat{G}_{t-1} + (1 - \alpha) G_{t-1}$$

so that the expression implies that the expected rate of growth in the current period is a weighted average of the expected and actual growth rates of the previous period. This is the form used by Sen.

[14] Harrod did not accept this well-known 'knife-edge' analogy, which he considered exaggerated his view of the degree of instability (see Harrod, 1970, pp. 740-1 and Harrod, 1973, pp. 32-3).

[15] Formally, (1.20) may be written as

$$(s - v) \, Y_t + v \, Y_{t-1} = 0$$

which is a first-order difference equation, with solution

$$Y_t = Y_o(1 + \frac{s}{v - s})^t$$

where Y_o is initial output, assumed to be positive.

These complications, which do not arise when the model is constructed in continuous terms, can be avoided by assuming that planned saving is related to income in the previous, rather than the current, period:

$$S_t = sY_{t-1}$$

Then steady warranted growth at the rate s/v is the unambiguous solution, as long as s, v and initial output are all positive. But Harrod was keen to avoid lags. This is one reason why we preferred to construct his model in continuous terms in 1.2.

CHAPTER 2

[1] For instance, in 1970-1 the American Economic Association, the Royal Economic Society and the Economics Section of the British Association each received presidential addresses devoted to critiques of current progress in economics; and in two of the three (those of Phelps Brown, 1972; and Worswick, 1972) specific reference was made to growth theory. The main theme of all three (the third being Leontief, 1971) was the allegation of a serious imbalance between sophisticated advances in economic theory and the slow progress of empirical knowledge; and each emphasised the need for a more effective dialogue between these two branches of the subject.

[2] See Hicks's (1965, ch. IV) description of how Adam Smith and Ricardo did so.

[3] But recall that Keynesian under-employment 'equilibrium' is a balance of forces in which all preferences are not satisfied; in particular, there is involuntary unemployment.

CHAPTER 3

[1] 'Monetarists' might be an exception; but few monetarists have been involved with growth theory.

[2] Meade (1962), for example, assumes that factor prices in money terms are determined competitively. To get over the Keynesian problem that real (as opposed to money) wages might not adjust perfectly to conditions in the labour market, he introduces a monetary authority whose operations (through the interest rate) ensure that demand in the market for consumer goods is always equal to supply at a constant price. The monetary authority thus ensures that real wages change if and only if money wages change. Since the money wage is assumed to adjust perfectly to labour-market conditions, continuous equilibrium and full employment are also ensured.

[3] Keynes was here, of course, including what is now generally referred to as neo-classical theory. 'Keynes impatiently threw all economics from Adam Smith to Pigou into one box and called them "classical". For him they were all alike for they did not take account of his problem – the influence of effective demand on the level of employment' (Robinson, 1970). It was only heretics on this question (like Malthus) who were excluded.

CHAPTER 4

[1] It may be shown that (4.4) and (4.5) together imply that $F_{KL} > 0$, i.e., that the marginal product of each factor increases when the input of the other factor is raised, *ceteris paribus*.

[2] In the Harrod–Domar model, of course, it is not possible to compare two steady-state equilibria which differ only in their saving propensities because v is a parameter, not a variable, and there is only one value of s which is consistent with it (and λ). Consideration of the implications of differences in s must involve disequilibrium; Harrod's analysis of the consequences of a change in s was discussed in section 1.3.

[3] The values of t_1, t_2 and t_3 depend upon the difference between λ

and λ'' and the shape of the productivity function. The latter determines, for a given difference in natural growth rates, the initial differences in K and Y; and the former then determines how quickly this difference will be eliminated. The reader may care to derive the values of t_1 and t_2 in terms of λ, λ'' and the value of k on the two paths, using (4.18) and (4.19). He will then show that $t_2 > t_1$, as should be obvious: the K paths cannot meet until after the $S = I$ paths have met at t_1.

[4] We can, of course, have different steady states with the same k and hence the same factor shares. This will be the case when both λ and s differ but λ/s, the steady-state output–capital ratio is the same. In Figure 4.2 the comparison would be shown by paths of differing slope which have the same starting-point.

[5] This concept was introduced by Hicks (1963).

[6] The reader may verify this by re-expressing (4.21) as

$$\sigma \equiv \frac{w}{rk} \bigg/ \frac{d(w/r)}{dk}$$

and differentiating.

[7] It is derived and discussed in, for example, Allen (1967, pp. 52–5) and Brown (1966, Ch. 4).

[8] Formally, using (4.22):

$$\frac{d}{dk}\left(\frac{P}{Y}\right) = \frac{d}{dk}\left(\frac{kf'}{f}\right) = -\frac{kf''(\sigma - 1)}{f} = 0$$

for all k, if and only if $\sigma = 1$ for all k.

[9] We have already seen that the share of profits at any k is the same as the elasticity of the labour-productivity function $f(k)$ at that k (see p. 41 and (4.23)). In terms of the production function the share of profits (for example) is

$$\frac{P}{Y} = \frac{K}{Y} \times r = \frac{K}{Y} \times \frac{\partial Y}{\partial K} = \frac{\partial \log Y}{\partial \log K}$$

which is the elasticity of Y with respect to K.

[10] More formally:

$$c = f(k) - \lambda k$$

$$\frac{dc}{dk} = f'(k) - \lambda = 0, \text{ when } f'(k) = \lambda$$

$$\frac{d^2c}{dk^2} = f''(k) < 0$$

CHAPTER 5

[1] Note that, however large is σ, the rise in s can never offset the fall in Y/K as k rises. We have already seen from (5.7) that $\dot{K}/K = sY/K$ is a monotonically decreasing function of k if f is well-behaved and $s_p > s_w$, irrespective of the value of σ.

[2] This possibility is discussed by, for example, Solow (1956, pp. 185-7).

[3] Johnson (1967, pp. 150-2) considers a function with a similar rationale. He assumes there is a desired capital–output ratio, v^*, and that at any K and Y, saving differs from what would be required for steady growth (λK) by an amount proportional to the difference between v^* and K/Y. He also shows how the value of human capital may be measured in the one-sector model, and how it may be taken account of in a saving function of a similar kind.

[4] Apart from population growth the growth of the labour force also depends on changes in participation rates and hours worked, which may also be increasing functions of the real wage or income per head.

[5] And it provides a fairly obvious way of eliminating the possibility, which arose in section 5.2 when s was assumed to be zero at low incomes, that if k is initially low enough it may decline without interruption towards zero, for it is not implausible to suppose that the decline will be halted when the wage falls to a level, corresponding to a positive k, at which λ is reduced to equality with $\dot{K}/K$. This may occur when $\dot{K}/K$ is zero; there will then be a low-level equilibrium trap which is a stationary state.

[6] This holds for discrete changes if the two components are defined consistently. Suppose that yesterday N = \$120 and p = \$5, so that M = 24 units of the good, and that today N = \$160 and p = \$4, so that M = 40 units of the good. M has thus risen by *16*. The real value of the increase in N at yesterday's price is $40/5 = 8$. The change in the price level, as a proportion of yesterday's price, is $-1/5$ or -0.2. There has been a 20 per cent fall in price, so 20 per cent of today's M, i.e. 8, is attributable to it. The two components thus defined (which happen to be equal) sum to the increase in M.

[7] It will be noted that in the real world there is no monetary asset which is outside money *and* a medium of exchange *and* interest-bearing. Currency has the first and second characteristics but not the third; bank deposits do not have the first, and do not always have the third; government bonds have the first and third, but not the second.

[8] Strictly speaking these should all be defined in terms of expectations; we shall ignore this discrepancy.

[9] Consider its steady-state solution. Let steady growth require constancy of m, so that $\dot{p}/p$ is again the difference between $\dot{N}/N$ and λ; with i given, the r required for portfolio balance is then obtained from (5.40). In the second quadrant of Figure 5.3 draw a curve showing $r = f'(k)$ and indentify the portfolio balance r; this determines the steady-state k and Y/K. The steady-state m may then be read off the upward-sloping curve in the third quadrant, which is the same as before; the $m(Y/K)$ curve is now of course irrelevant. Note that $\dot{N}/N$ and i again help to determine the 'real' characteristics of the steady state.

[10] The preference for (5.38) may be justified by reference to uncertain expectations and risk-averse behaviour. The reader may already be familiar with Tobin (1958); for a briefer treatment, see Tobin (1955, section 1.3).

[11] This is one of the main concerns of Tobin (1955).

[12] When gross saving is proportional to gross income, the ratio of gross output to capital is $(\lambda + \delta)/s$; when gross saving is proportional to net income it is $\delta + (\lambda + \delta)/s$.

[13] Similarly, since the value of each machine must depend on its age, the valuation of the capital stock must depend on its age distribution.

CHAPTER 6

[1] A useful exposition is provided by Allen (1967, ch. 12).

[2] Note that this is quite different from the meaning of p in section 5.5.

[3] With classical saving, (6.24) shows that $\dot{K}/K$ is simply a continuous function of k_1, taking all positive values if f_1 is well-behaved. The well-behavedness of f_1 alone is then sufficient for existence.

[4] We could have obtained this result more directly from the previous note, for the well-behavedness of f_1 (which ensures existence when $s_w = 0$) also ensures that $\dot{K}/K$ is a monotonically decreasing function of k_1, so that there is a unique steady-state k_1; and this determines unique steady-state values of z and k. This shows more clearly the similarity of the one-good and two-good models in the case of classical saving, as far as the existence and uniqueness of steady growth are concerned.

[5] That is, the ratio of output to capital, with both aggregates measured in terms of the same good by means of the relative values of the two

goods as indicated by p. In terms of the consumption good the numerator in the ratio is Y and the denominator pK; in terms of the capital good the numerator is Y/p and the denominator is K.

[6] This is most easily shown by means of Figure 6.1. The term $(q_2/p)^2 \div k_2$ is the output–capital ratio in Sector 2 when output is measured in terms of the capital good. We know that in the diagram p is shown by OW_2/OW_1. Thus at $k_2{}^*$, output per head in Sector 2 in terms of the capital good, q_2/p, is obtained by extending $k_2{}^* X_2$ in the proportion OW_1/OW_2, to meet the projection of the line RX_1 at a point X_2' (which is not drawn). The slope of the ray OX_2' then shows $(q_2{}^*/p) \div k_2{}^*$, and this is clearly less than the slope of OX_1, which shows $q_1{}^*/k_1{}^*$. The reason is that $k_2{}^* > k_1{}^*$.

[7] Results for this case (but with $s_p = 1$) were obtained by Uzawa (1961).

[8] This case was examined by Uzawa (1963).

[9] Results for this case were obtained by Inada (1963).

[10] See Drandakis (1963). The connection between the monotonicity of $k(z)$ and the 'overall' elasticity of substitution is easy to see, since if z rises, an over-all elasticity of substitution greater than or equal to unity means that the share of wages cannot rise, which in turn means that k cannot fall.

CHAPTER 7

[1] It may (in principle) and does (in fact) also imply changes in the quality of output and the appearance of new goods. (The latter may be regarded as the extreme case of the former.) For present purposes this may be considered 'merely' as a problem complicating the measurement of output, and may be neglected. It obviously does not arise under the assumption of one good, which we are about to adopt.

[2] Note that the fixed-coefficients production function (3.2) is a particular case of the factor-augmenting function (7.2). ($\overline{K}$ and $\overline{L}$ have now, of course, been given a different meaning.)

[3] This is the natural neo-classical adaptation of Harrod's original definition, given in section 1.3, except that we are now holding the capital–output ratio (rather than the interest rate or marginal product of capital) constant, and referring to the implication of technical progress for the factor price. This may be regarded as more appropriate for the economy as a whole; from the point of view of the firm, the alternative is more suitable (see Chapter 8).

[4] With more than two factors technical progress would need to be augmenting all factors other than capital.

[5] With increasing returns to scale steady growth is possible if the production function is of the corresponding Cobb–Douglas form:

$$Y = [K^\alpha (e^{\tau t} L)^{1-\alpha}]^h$$

The steady-state growth rate of output and capital is then

$$\frac{\dot{Y}}{Y} = \left\{ \frac{(1-\alpha)h}{1-\alpha h} \right\} (\lambda + \tau) > \lambda + \tau$$

Cf. section 5.4.

[6] On the assumption of purely labour-augmenting (Harrod-neutral) progress, we could of course measure $\bar{k}$ and $\bar{y}$ on the axes, and draw $g(\bar{k})$, which would be stable over time (see (7.8) and (7.9)).

[7] It may also be shown by the same kind of argument that Harrod-neutrality implies Hicks labour-saving bias when $\sigma < 1$ and Hicks capital-saving bias when $\sigma > 1$; and that Hicks-neutrality implies Harrod capital-saving bias when $\sigma < 1$ and Harrod labour-saving bias when $\sigma > 1$. (We return to the relationship between the two sets of definitions of neutrality and bias in Chapter 8.)

[8] See, for example, Hahn and Matthews (1964, p. 48).

[9] The Hicks notion has the advantages of being associated with what may be considered a more natural measure of the rate of progress, and of being easily redefinable when there are more than two factors, in which case the marginal product of capital may vary at a constant capital–output ratio merely because of changing proportions among the other factors. On the other hand, rising capital per head is unquestionably a feature of real-world growth, so that the Hicks bench-mark is inoperative; and Harrod-neutrality is the requirement for steady growth. For more detail, see Meade (1962, ch. 6).

[10] Advances in knowledge are infused into the productive system through the education and training of labour as well as through the design of capital goods. However, the idea of embodiment is rather less compelling when applied to labour, partly because the design of new 'machines' is more readily improved and is more an object of improvement than is the 'design' of new 'men', and partly because, after 'installation', 'men' are more adaptable, and more receptive to new knowledge, than are 'machines'. The idea is nevertheless applicable.

[11] It reflects a judgement about priorities for a text of this scope, given the mathematical complexity of much of the work done in this area.

[12] The unit of capital may be thought of as the amount of equipment which, when new, has a price equal to that of output, which is homogeneous.

[13] Solow-neutrality (introduced in Solow, 1963) is the obverse of Harrod-neutrality. It implies that at constant output per head the real wage (and hence distributive shares) are unchanged.

[14] The only exceptions known to the present writer form a mixed bag: Stalinist Russia (Kuznets, 1966, p. 84n.); Edwardian Britain (Matthews, 1964, p. 13); post-war Israel (Kennedy and Thirlwall, 1972, p. 18); and post-war Australia (Harcourt, 1972, p. 48n.).

[15] See Kuznets (1966, pp. 75–80) and Part IV of this book.

[16] If the starting-point was a steady state, of course, this effect should ultimately exactly offset the rise in the saving ratio, and the change in the growth rate should ultimately be zero.

[17] In the long run, of course, after the re-establishment of steady growth, the growth rate will again be the natural growth rate, independent of the propensity to save.

[18] After a French economist; for references, see Jorgenson and Griliches (1967).

[19] Jorgenson and Griliches (1967) appeared to have reduced it to 3.3 per cent for the United States over the period 1945–65! But Denison (1969) showed the validity of their result to be dubious, largely because of the way they had adjusted their measure of capital input to allow for its increased utilisation through the period.

CHAPTER 8

[1] This is apart from Kaldor's theory (considered in Chapter 9 and Part III).

[2] These definitions of Hicks-neutrality and bias are analogous to those of section 7.5, the only difference being that whereas for the economy as a whole a given K/L was taken as the bench-mark, and the implication for w/r was taken as the criterion, at the level of the firm it is more appropriate to take given (market-determined) relative factor prices as the bench-mark, and to examine the implications of technical progress for the firm's choice of technique.

[3] In fact Hicks (1963, p. 120) himself referred to induced bias as a form of substitution, and later recalled in his Nobel lecture that 'whether . . . "induced inventions" were to be regarded as shifts in the Production Function, or as substitutions within an unchanged Production Function, was left rather obscure' (Hicks, 1973, p. 2).

[4] A corresponding Salterian explanation of Harrod-neutrality would

require σ (as described by his isoquants, or Ahmad's I.P.C.s) to be unity.

[5] Although most econometric estimates of σ from time-series data are below unity, they are usually dependent on an assumption about the factor-saving characteristics of technical progress. Generally, identification problems mean that it is impossible to disentangle from data the theoretically separate influences of σ and bias. See, for example, Nadiri (1970), and Kennedy and Thirlwall (1972).

[6] In competitive equilibrium, of course, c will equal the price of the good, which is unity. But for the analysis of the firm's decisions with regard to the reduction of costs, it is clearly inappropriate to assume that this equality is always satisfied.

[7] He also shows that when a distinction is drawn between a capital good and a consumption good, technical progress will in the long run be Harrod-neutral in the sense that with a constant interest rate the value capital–output ratio (rather than v) will be constant. If technical progress is confined to the consumption-good sector, the long-run equilibrium may be shown to be at the intersection of the I.P.F. and the 45° line (see Figure 8.5); with technical progress in both sectors, it is located between that intersection and P.

[8] In fact $\sigma = 1$ (with constant returns and factor-augmenting technical progress) gives a special case of equal augmentation, for the production function must be of the Cobb–Douglas form

$$Y = [a(t)K]^\alpha [b(t)L]^{1-\alpha}$$

which may be written alternatively as

$$Y = c(t)K^\alpha L^{1-\alpha} = [c(t)K]^\alpha [c(t)L]^{1-\alpha}$$

where $c = a^\alpha b^{1-\alpha}$, so that both factors can be regarded as being augmented at the same rate. (Recall from section 7.5 that (i) equally augmenting progress is equivalent to Hicks-neutrality; (ii) factor-augmenting progress with $\sigma = 1$ is both Hicks- and Harrod-neutral; (iii) unless technical progress is factor-augmenting it is neither Hicks- nor Harrod-neutral.)

[9] Some familiar results may be obtained from (8.21) and (8.22). Thus they show under what circumstances constant factor shares are possible when the capital–labour ratio is growing. In (8.21), which applies even when technical progress is not factor-augmenting, π is constant with K/L growing only if:

(i) $\sigma = 1$ and $B = 0$ (Hicks- and Harrod-neutral; factor-augmenting);

or

   (ii) $\sigma < 1$ and $B > 0$ (Hicks labour-saving); *or*
   (iii) $\sigma > 1$ and $B < 0$ (Hicks capital-saving).

In (8.22), which applies only to factor-augmenting progress, π is constant with K/L growing only if:

   (i) $\sigma = 1$ (which now implies Hicks- and Harrod-neutrality); *or*
   (ii) $\hat{b} > \hat{a}$ (Hicks labour-saving if $\sigma < 1$, capital-saving if $\sigma > 1$).

[10] Solow (1970, p. 34) seems doubtful: 'it is possible to give theoretical reasons why technological progress might be forced to assume the particular form required for the existence of a steady state. They are excessively fancy reasons, not altogether believable.' ('But,' he adds, 'that is more of a lead than we have on the side of increasing returns.' See section 5.4.) Nordhaus (1973) reopens the question of whether it is plausible to assume that the frontier of rates of factor augmentation is independent of the initial position, and shows that, more generally, when the relationship between $\hat{b}$ and $\hat{a}$ is dependent on a and b, the Drandakis–Phelps result does not hold.

CHAPTER 9

[1] It will be recalled from section 8.2 that Salter preferred to regard technical progress as 'purely technically determined' and free from economic influences, so that he excluded from his definition the development of basic scientific knowledge. On diffusion, Kennedy and Thirlwall (1972, p. 12) argue that in theory 'technical progress should not be confused with the diffusion of existing technical knowledge, which does nothing to change production possibilities'; but one may easily take a contrary view, that the 'confusion' is unavoidable because diffusion does indeed change production possibilities for the economy as a whole.

[2] This was suggested to me by D. M. G. Newbery.

[3] Since in our model technical progress is wholly disembodied, it would make rather more sense to use cumulative past gross *output* as the proxy for experience. We nevertheless stay with Arrow. In fact, however, the choice has little significance for equilibrium growth, because with a proportional saving function cumulative gross investment is equal to cumulative output *times* the constant saving propensity.

[4] If the elasticity were not less than unity, the labour force, in efficiency units, would be growing faster than the capital stock, and steady growth would be possible only if there were offsetting decreasing returns to scale, with the sum of the exponents of K and bL in (9.1) less than unity.

[5] The fact that the steady-growth rates are proportional to λ seems to imply that if the labour force is stationary, the only feasible steady state is a stationary state. It should be remembered, however, that (9.6)–(9.8) were all based on the assumption that $\lambda > 0$. If $\lambda = 0$ (9.5) shows that steady growth requires m to be unity. Indeed, if $m = 1$ so that b grows at the same rate as K, steady growth (with constant returns) requires $\lambda = 0$; but the steady-growth rate G can then take any value – the natural growth rate is indeterminate, and not necessarily zero. This contrasts with the case, $0 < m < 1$, considered in the text, where λ can take any (positive) value, G then being determined uniquely in terms of λ and m. Similarly with increasing returns: if the degree of homogeneity, β, in (5.13) is $1/\alpha$, steady growth requires $\lambda = 0$; and the natural growth rate is then indeterminate.

[6] Robinson (1975, p. 39) endorses this view: 'There is no such phenomenon in real life as accumulation taking place in a given state of technical knowledge. The idea was introduced into economic theory only to give a meaning to the marginal product of capital.'

[7] Essentially the same point has been made by others; for example, 'firms venturing into technologies with significantly higher capital-labour ratios than actually have been experienced will tend initially to make mistakes, and will experience a considerable amount of learning costs before achieving significant gains in output per worker' (Nelson, 1973, pp. 467–8).

[8] Kaldor (1962) welcomed Arrow's learning model as 'a refreshing departure from the arid neo-classical orthodoxy which has hitherto characterised the growth theories of our great partners in the Atlantic Alliance'.

[9] *Dynamic* economies of scale imply a relationship between the *growth* of output and the *growth* of productivity. The alleged empirical prevalence of this kind of relationship has become known as *Verdoorn's Law*. Kaldor (1966) sought to explain international growth differences on the basis of the idea that this 'Law' applies to manufacturing rather than to primary or tertiary activity (see Chapter 14). Kaldor (1972) uses the same idea as part of an explanation of how growth can be a self-generating process.

[10] Although Eltis's (1973, p. 130) relationship is partly based on the proposition that 'it will be more profitable to invent and develop superior methods of production where the rate of investment is high', technical progress is still only a by-product of investment which is undertaken for other reasons.

[11] This could be inferred from the first half of Hicks's statement quoted in section 8.2 (p. 125): 'A change in the relative prices of the factors of production is itself a spur to invention.'

[12] See also Robinson (1962, pp. 51–2). She attributes these propositions to Marx; indeed, Robinson (1963, p. 410) considers that they form 'the most interesting and important Marxian idea incorporated in' her growth theory.

CHAPTER 10

[1] The title of Harcourt's (1969; 1972) surveys is a play on 'Some Cambridge Controversies in Monetary Theory', the title of a paper by H. G. Johnson concerned with controversies within Cambridge, England, published in *Review of Economic Studies*, vol. XIX, 1951–2, p. 90.

[2] 'Clearly I need to change my name. Let it be understood that *Value and Capital* (1939) was the work of J. R. Hicks, a "neoclassical" economist now deceased; while *Capital and Time* (1973) – and *A Theory of Economic History* (1969) – are the work of John Hicks, a non-neoclassic who is quite disrespectful towards his "uncle" ' (Hicks, 1975, p. 365). (*Capital and Growth* (1965) appears to mark the transition.) He accepted the 1972 Nobel Prize for his work on general equilibrium and welfare economics 'with mixed feelings' (Hicks, 1977, p.v) and his Nobel lecture (1973) was on economic growth, with prominent acknowledgements to Harrod, Robinson and Kaldor.

[3] After the French economist, Jean-Baptiste Say (1767–1832).

[4] *Memoranda on Certain Proposals Relating to Unemployment* (London: H.M.S.O., 1929) Cmd 3331.

[5] That he succeeded in so doing is not disputed by the leading neoclassical growth theorists. But this is, of course, a controversial issue even today; and pre-Keynesian theory and policy prescriptions live on in much of present-day monetarism. Witness also the recent debate over whether expansionary fiscal policy will tend to 'crowd out' private expenditure through its financial side-effects (for example, Carlson and

Spencer, 1975). The 'crowding-out' argument is first cousin to the argument of the 1929 White Paper; both represent a similar pessimism about the efficacy of fiscal policy for raising employment. (The 'market optimism' of the argument about real wages which balanced the old 'intervention pessimism' has played a less prominent role in recent debates.)

[6] Hicks in fact uses this theorem in the context of inflation rather than wage reductions. He deduces the theorem from the convention which Keynes adopted of measuring variables in wage units, rather than from Keynes's explicit analysis of the consequences of wage changes (in chapter 19 of the *General Theory*).

[7] See the discussion of dynamics in section 2.2.

[8] For a statement by Keynes himself of the importance of uncertainty to his analysis – in particular, to his treatment of money and investment – Keynes (1937).

[9] For a contrary view, see, for example, Leijonhufvud (1968, esp. p. 33).

[10] Kalecki's distinction between 'demand-determined' and 'cost-determined' prices is congruent with Hicks's (1974a, p. 23) more recent distinction between 'flexprice' and 'fixprice' markets.

[11] See also the further reading to Chapter 5.

[12] See, for example, Robinson (1971, pp. 45–6) and Kaldor (1956, p. 368n.). Also, in the *General Theory*, Keynes (1936, p. 262) argued in his discussion of the effects of falling real wages that 'The transfer from wage-earners to other factors is likely to diminish the propensity to consume.'

[13] After Kalecki's death, Robinson (1977a, pp. 8–9) brought to light his personal experience of what must have been one of the most remarkable coincidences in the history of economic thought: 'He told me that he had taken a year's leave from the institute where he was working in Warsaw to write the *General Theory*. In Stockholm someone gave him Keynes's book. He began to read it – it was the book that he intended to write. He thought that perhaps further on there would be something different. No, all the way it was his book. He said: "I confess, I was ill. Three days I lay in bed. Then I thought – Keynes is more known than I am. These ideas will get across much quicker with him and then we can get on to the interesting question, which is their application. Then I got up." '

[14] Meade was in fact following Kaldor (1957): in the first version of Kaldor's (1957, pp. 268–9) growth model (see Chapter 13) capital is considered to be measured by the 'total weight of steel embodied in the

capital equipment'. Kaldor considers that the capital stock must be measured by some arbitrary convention, and that this is as good as any. It does not, of course, play the same role as in Meade.

[15] In a section with the heading 'A Curiosium' and the warning that it was 'concerned with a somewhat intricate piece of analysis which is not of great importance'! (Robinson, 1956, p. 109).

CHAPTER 11

[1] The 'representative firm' was a device introduced by Marshall (1920, e.g. pp. 264-5).

[2] A similar problem has arisen in investigations of the influence of trade-union strength on wage inflation. The percentage of the labour force unionised and the incidence of strikes have both been used in this context to measure union militancy; but both have fairly obvious drawbacks (see Laidler and Parkin, 1975, pp. 761-3). Thus industrial unrest may be related to employer resistance as much as to labour 'pushfulness'.

[3] The allegation that 'there is no theory provided of the determination of the profit margin' (Johnson, 1973, p. 198) certainly seems extreme.

[4] On the assumption of profit maximisation Lerner's degree of monopoly measures the excess of price over marginal revenue in proportion to price, and it may be shown that this is the reciprocal of the price-elasticity of demand for the product. This was how Lerner originally conceived his measure of monopoly power.

[5] This may be regarded as an implicit rejection of the Kaldorian theory.

[6] He thus anticipated the observations of Neild and others (see section 12.4).

[7] As will be seen shortly, this amendment is related to the application of the neo-Keynesian saving function to the income categories thus defined; for example, 'the wage-category comprises not only manual labour but salaries as well, and profits the income of property-owners generally, and not only of entrepreneurs; the important difference between them being in the marginal propensities to consume (or save), wage-earners' marginal savings being small in relation to those of capitalists' (Kaldor, 1956, p. 370).

[8] The absence of an investment function, or the associated absence

of a relationship between the capital–output ratio and profitability, in this model has been a popular target for attack. Sen (1963) objects to the implicit assumption that investment is unaffected by movements in the price level which may accompany changes in profit margins. Johnson (1973, pp. 202–4) makes great play of the omission, arguing that 'The crucial weakness in the Kaldor theory is that the capital–output ratio is assumed not to be influenced by the rate of profit . . . the Kaldor theory begs all the interesting questions of capital theory, through its assumption of a constant capital–output ratio.' Johnson's criticisms appear to ignore Kaldor's full growth model.

[9] Although Kaldor associates restriction (11.24) with a subsistence real wage, he in fact takes a more broadly interpreted minimum into account as one of the factors limiting the specifically short-run flexibility of distributive shares (see section 12.4).

[10] There are, of course, other ways of closing the model below full employment. Schneider (1958), for instance, introduces a relationship which states that at a given wage rate the wage bill created by producers is a simple function of expected profits. Riach (1969), on the other hand, assumes that labour receives its marginal product, a position which he considers to be closer to Keynes. Hahn (1972) – the published version of a Ph.D. thesis begun under Kaldor's supervision in the late 1940s – introduces a relationship showing supply as an increasing function of the profit margin. But we remain within the neo-Keynesian framework.

[11] Note that we are assuming investment to be independent of profits.

[12] Formally, from (11.28) – (11.30):

$$\frac{\partial Y}{\partial \mu'} = \frac{-\overline{I}\,(s_p - s_w)}{[s_w + (s_p - s_w)\mu']^2} < 0$$

$$\frac{\partial P}{\partial \mu'} = \frac{s_w\,\overline{I}}{[s_w + (s_p - s_w)\mu']^2} > 0$$

$$\frac{\partial W}{\partial \mu'} = \frac{-s_p\,\overline{I}}{[s_w + (s_p - s_w)\mu']^2} < 0$$

[13] Here we follow Robinson (1970a).

[14] Formally, from (11.28a), (11.29a) and (11.30a):

$$\frac{\partial Y}{\partial \mu'} = \frac{-s_p \overline{I}}{(s_p \, \mu')^2} < 0$$

$$\frac{\partial P}{\partial \mu'} = 0$$

$$\frac{\partial W}{\partial \mu'} = \frac{\partial Y}{\partial \mu'}$$

[15] The degree of monopoly was introduced into the analysis in Kalecki (1942).

CHAPTER 12

[1] Robinson (1962, p. 27) ridicules the idea that, in the process described by Kahn, falling prices will leave profit expectations in money terms unchanged.

[2] In effect he adopts full employment as an additional 'stylised fact' to be explained by growth theory (see Chapter 14).

[3] The theorem appears in both Kaldor (1961, pp. 197–201) and Kaldor (1959, pp. 171–6); it had been at least hinted at in Kaldor (1957, pp. 262–3).

[4] We are assuming that a_w is constant.

[5] Wan's Marshallian interpretation makes Kaldor's distribution model stable when the saving function is perverse (see Figure 12.1(b)). Also, Marshallian disequilibrium behaviour depends upon the short-run flexibility of profit margins; when, for instance, demand price exceeds supply price following an upward shift of demand, it is the rise of actual price above supply price and the emergence of super-normal profit which are supposed to provide producers with the incentive to expand output towards the new equilibrium. Both these implications of Wan's interpretation are in conflict with Kaldor.

[6] We encountered this possibility in section 11.4.

[7] For example, taking the years 1960–76, on average 44 per cent of the income of U.K. industrial and commercial companies (comprising gross trading profits net of stock appreciation, rent and non-trading income arising in the United Kingdom, plus income from abroad), after deduction of taxes, was undistributed. (In most of the years the proportion was between 40 and 50 per cent.) (Central Statistical Office, 1977a, table 134).

[8] Between 1963 and 1976 undistributed income formed on average 60 per cent of the increase in capital funds of U.K. industrial and commercial companies (Central Statistical Office, 1977a, table 142).

[9] And the view that the propensity to consume out of current income will tend to be raised by capital gains is well-founded in the Keynesian theory of the consumption function (Keynes, 1936, pp. 92–3).

[10] More correctly, between retention ratio and ratio of market valuation to book valuation.

[11] We need not consider in any depth the reasons either for the extent to which firms rely on internal funds, or for investors' apparent preference for dividends over retentions. The former is clearly related to imperfections in capital markets; but to Kaldor its main significance is that firms need to save in an uncertain world in order to grow, and that they need to grow in order to maintain or advance their relative positions in the competitive struggle, because of economies of scale. (See, for example, Kaldor (1966a); this view is closely related to that of Marx.) Williamson (1966) has pointed out that the second observation is consistent with the proposition that while shareholders are rational wealth maximisers, the manager-controlled firms push their retention ratios beyond the point where present value is maximised (the firms may, for instance, be growth maximisers, rather than profit maximisers). The two observations may therefore be related. The theory of the firm constructed by Marris (1964), a Cambridge economist, is based on the assumption that firms aim to maximise their growth rates within the constraint represented by a trade-off between retention (as a means to growth) on the one hand and market valuation (as a defence from takeover) on the other.

[12] Kaldor does not regard this as a problem because of his confidence in, and reliance on, the retention argument. In fact he considers his saving hypothesis to be based on an assumption that the propensity to save out of 'profits' is greater than the propensity to save out of 'wages (and other contractual incomes)' (Kaldor, 1961, p. 194) or 'wages, salaries [and] rentier income' (Kaldor, 1959, p. 170).

[13] But recall the findings of Burmeister and Taubman. (Surrey explains his results in terms of the concentration of income and wealth; Evans explains Klein's results in terms of the riskiness of property income.)

[14] See Meade (1963), Pasinetti (1964), Meade and Hahn (1965), Pasinetti (1966) and Meade (1966a) for the debate as it ran in the

Economic Journal, and Samuelson and Modigliani (1966) and accompanying papers in the October 1966 issue of the *Review of Economic Studies*. Meade (1966a) is a helpful synthesis.

[15] See section 5.2 for a neo-classical, and Chapter 13 for a Kaldorian, interpretation.

[16] Cf. our treatment of classical saving in section 5.2.

[17] Marx held that if the accumulation of capital ran ahead of the labour supply, so that the 'reserve army' of unemployed became exhausted, a crisis would ensue in which competition for labour would cause wages to rise and profits to fall until accumulation would come to a halt. Kaldor (1957a) examines this proposition in the light of Keynes, and contrasts it with his own (purportedly Keynesian) analysis.

[18] For example, the analysis by Godley and Nordhaus (1972) of quarterly price movements in U.K. manufacturing between 1955 and 1969.

[19] We are not concerned to assess the validity or significance of the evidence, which is not uncontroversial. See the surveys by Nordhaus (1972), and Laidler and Parkin (1975). (Laidler and Parkin (1975, p. 768) dismiss the conclusions of Godley and Nordhaus.)

[20] We continue to use the word 'prime' for labour and material costs, though we admit that they may be overheads.

[21] Joan Robinson (1969, Preface, p. viii) also accepts Neild's findings. She writes, for example: 'With short-period fluctuations in demand, prices vary very little as long as money costs are constant. Output rises and falls with demand and (as the overhead per unit of output falls and rises) the share of net profit rises and falls still more. . . . Movements of demand affect profits strongly, but prices hardly at all.'

[22] It is doubtful whether the statistical distinction between wages and salaries which Kalecki employed is nowadays of any economic significance (see section 15.4).

CHAPTER 13

[1] He brings in another assumption about expectations: that the growth rate of output expected for period $t + 1$ at the beginning of the period equals the actual growth rate of output between periods $t - 1$ and t. He considers that this makes sense of the first term in the right-hand side of (13.5). In fact, however, the appearance of this term follows from his assumption of a one-period lag, without any assumption about expectations.

[2] We saw the significance of the linear form in section 9.3.

[3] The reader might like to check that (13.18) is satisfied by empirically reasonable parameter values. For example, if $s_p = 0.7$, $s_w = 0.1$ and, with the 'period' being the year, $G = 0.03$ and $\alpha' = 3.5$, (13.18) is satisfied for any value of β'.

[4] With G, α', β' and $(s_p - s_w)$ all positive, and s_w non-negative, any negative v would violate (13.17) since its left-hand side would be positive.

[5] If we denote the quadratic in v by the function $\psi(v)$, it is easy to see that $\psi(o) = \beta' s_w > 0$ and that $\psi(v) \to +\infty$ as $v \to +\infty$. Also, it may be shown that the parameter values assumed in note 3 imply that $\psi(1) < 0$ if β' is less than 21. This means that the lower root is less than unity (and that the upper root is greater than unity) unless β' exceeds 21; and a capital–output ratio less than unity is implausible on annual data. A value of β' higher than 21 implies that investment is highly sensitive to the profit rate – probably too sensitive for stability as well as uniqueness, as will be seen in section 13.3.

[6] We saw in the last note that reasonable parameter values suggest that the lower root will be less than unity; it will therefore be less than our 'reasonable' estimate of s_w/G, which is 3.33. It then follows that a necessary and sufficient condition for the upper root to exceed s_w/G is that the quadratic $\psi(v)$ is such that $\psi(s_w/G) < 0$. It may be shown from (13.17) that this will be the case if and only if $\alpha' > s_w(G + 1)/G$. With $s_w = 0.1$ and $G = 0.03$, this means that we require $\alpha' > 3.43$. This is satisfied by our assumed α' of 3.5, but only just: if we were to assume $\alpha' = 3$, which is not particularly implausible for this parameter (which is in the nature of an accelerator coefficient), even the upper root of (13.17) would give a negative profit share.

[7] We have also assumed, for part (a), that $\alpha' - v_1 > s_w$, and for part (b) that $\alpha' - v_2 < s_w$. These respective conditions ensure that the I/Y and S/Y curves intersect at a positive P/Y in both periods.

[8] Alternatively, we see from (13.26) and (13.27) that the equilibrium profit share in period t is

$$\frac{P_t}{Y_t} = \frac{\alpha' - s_w - v_t}{s_p - s_w - \beta'/v_t}$$

If (13.29) is not satisfied, the denominator is negative, and for P/Y to be positive the numerator must be negative as well. Then if v is falling (to the left of the point P in Figure 13.1), the numerator is decreasing numerically while the denominator is rising numerically, so that the equilibrium profit share is falling, whereas for the satisfaction of requirement (i) of stability to be met, it should be rising; and so on. Readers seeking a more formal proof should consult Kubota (1968), which suggested that Kaldor had not derived the correct sufficiency condition, and Kaldor's (1970) reply.

[9] Without an investment function of this kind, i.e., with $\beta' = 0$, (13.29) reduces to $s_p > s_w$, and it is only perverse saving which can threaten instability (cf. sections 11.3 and 12.1).

[10] The steady-state growth rate, being determined by the parameters of the T.P.F. alone, is unaffected. The different investment function does, however, affect the solution for the steady-state capital–output ratio and hence also the investment–output ratio, profit share and profit rate. In fact the quadratic in v in Allen's version, to be compared with our (13.17), is

$$(s_p - s_w)v^2 - [\alpha'(s_p - s_w) + \beta'G]v + \beta's_w = 0$$

For the reason described in section 13.2 Allen considers that there is only one meaningful solution for v, so that there is a unique steady-state solution.

[11] McCallum (1969, p. 57) did not consider the difference between Allen's version and Kaldor's model to be significant: he took Allen's version rather than Kaldor's own merely 'owing to the analytical "messiness" of the latter'.

[12] This expression incorporates a correction made in Kaldor (1970).

[13] Explained by, for example, Allen (1967, ch. 5).

[14] McCallum (1969) introduced adaptive profit-rate expectations into Allen's 'Kaldor model' and obtained results for stability similar, but not identical, to those of Champernowne. In particular, as we already know, Allen's steady-growth path is unambiguously unstable if the response of expectations is immediate.

[15] Nuti (1969) has pointed out that this assumption may be regarded as inconsistent with the imperfectly competitive environment in which the model is meant to be working.

CHAPTER 14

[1] Coined by the English writer Thomas Carlyle (1795–1881).

[2] Even Kaldor's (1961, p. 179) claim that (v)(b) 'cannot be accounted for at all on the basis of the marginal productivity theory – if we

assume, as I believe we must, that the fluctuations in the level of investment are the causal factor, and the fluctuations in the share of profits consequential, rather than the other way round' may be considered invalid, in that a positive correlation between the saving (or investment) ratio and the profit share is consistent with neo-classical theory if the elasticity of substitution exceeds unity.

[3] Mining is included with manufacturing in the secondary sector, rather than with agriculture in the primary. (This is in line with Clark's definitions.)

[4] See Wolfe (1968), Kaldor (1968; 1975), Cripps and Tarling (1973), Rowthorn (1975; 1975a) for discussions of some of the issues it raised. Kaldor has now abandoned the thesis of 'premature maturity' as an explanation for the United Kingdom's poor growth performance, though he still holds to Verdoorn's Law and the strategic importance of the growth rate of the secondary sector. He now emphasises the importance of demand – 'economic growth is demand-induced, and not resource-constrained' (Kaldor, 1975, p. 895) – and, in particular, the role of exports and international competitiveness.

CHAPTER 15

[1] For fuller accounts of the methodology of official U.K. capital statistics, see Griffin (1975; 1976). Although this section refers specifically to U.K. data, it is of more general relevance since the data for most other countries are constructed by essentially the same method and have a broadly similar coverage. Ward (1976) is a comprehensive survey of capital measurement in O.E.C.D. countries. Patterson and Schott (1978) is a useful collection of papers describing recent work on theoretical and practical aspects of capital measurement.

[2] Note that stock-building includes expenditure on items in our category (vi) – livestock, crops, forestry, etc. Also, limited estimates of the value of stocks are available. Feinstein (1972, table 110) provides estimates of the book value of stocks in thirteen selected years over the period 1856-1965, based partly on the rule of thumb that the value of stocks is about 40 per cent of G.D.P. A similar rule was used by Phelps Brown *et al.*. (1952; 1953) to estimate series for the fixed and circulating capital of the U.K. economy over the periods 1860-1912 and 1924-38.

[3] Scott (1976) puts forward strong arguments in favour of a broader conception of capital for the analysis of growth than is conventionally

adopted in national-accounts statistics. For the United States Kendrick (1976) has provided more broadly defined estimates of capital.

[4] First, it would not help in the valuation of assets owned by un-quoted companies, unincorporated businesses, households, or the state. Second, stock-exchange values relate to the capital owned by companies, including assets employed in production abroad. Third, stock-exchange values reflect companies' ownership of financial, as well as physical assets. Finally, stock-market prices are subject to speculative influences which could not be allowed for in any straightforward way.

[5] Apart from sampling problems, assets tend to be under-insured, and some assets regarded as indestructible are not insured at all. Also, the method is too costly to be applied annually. The great advantage of the P.I. method is the ease with which a series can be built up on the basis of one year's valuation and continued from year to year.

[6] This is certainly true of Kaldor (1957), who expresses a clear preference for measuring capital in terms of its physical character-istics. Cf. Hicks's (1974b) distinction between Fundist and Materialist approaches to capital measurement. Kaldor, like the neo-classicals, is a materialist, at least in his growth models.

[7] Unlike capital-stock estimates, depreciation estimates are relatively insensitive to mortality assumptions. Expression (15.3) shows that $G_T(T)$ will vary directly with L, and (15.4) shows that depreciation will, on this account, tend to be understated if L is underestimated. But (15.4) also shows that estimated depreciation varies inversely with L; and this provides an offset.

[8] Partly because a breakdown of depreciation by type of property in-come is not provided by Feinstein (cf. section 15.4).

[9] That is, that most capital goods suffer something close to 'sudden death' (cf. section 5.6).

[10] Expressed in similar terms by Redfern (1955, p. 143), Barna (1957, p. 7), Maurice (1968, p. 384) and Griffin (1976, pp. 132-3).

[11] An exception is that for 1921-38 Feinstein's (1972, p. 216) series excludes the number involved in 'temporary' stoppages because of their abnormally high incidence.

[12] Denison (1967, appendix D) estimates that in the United King-dom between 1950 and 1962 average hours per man-year fell 3.8 per cent, thus offsetting almost half of the 8.1 per cent rise in the number in employment. Matthews (1964, pp. 3-6), however, estimates that over 1948-62 the growth of labour input in man-hours was no different from that in man-years. His estimates also indicate that the growth of

man-hours was rather lower over 1856–99, about the same over 1899–1913, and rather higher over 1924–37, than the growth in man-years.

[13] Denison (1967) estimates that in the United Kingdom between 1950 and 1962 'total labour input' (taking into account hours worked, age and sex composition, and education) increased 10 per cent whereas the number in employment rose 8.1 per cent.

[14] As elsewhere, the data refer to the United Kingdom, inclusive of Southern Ireland before 1920.

[15] The working population $(L + U)$ grew by 0.2 per cent per annum between 1966 and 1976.

[16] It has sometimes been suggested that the poor growth performance of the United Kingdom in the post-war period, in relation to other countries, has been partly due to the relative instability of the economy deriving from deficiencies in macro-economic management. Wilson (1966), however, in a study of seven industrial countries, found no significant positive correlation between the growth rate and its stability.

[17] His evidence showed a rising, rather than falling, V during our sub-period (2); and the series for v constructed by Phelps Brown and Weber (1953) showed stability over those years of the Great Depression. These inconsistencies are an indication of the uncertainty of nineteenth century capital-stock data.

[18] R is gross of depreciation; F, PC and PP are gross of both depreciation and stock appreciation.

[19] G.D.P. is now at market prices rather than at factor cost.

[20] King shows, however, that there was no decline in the *post-tax* share of profits in manufacturing until the late 1960s.

[21] For an account of the decline in rates of profit, before and after tax, in the U.K. corporate sector between 1960 and 1974, see Flemming *et al.* (1976).

Bibliography

Abramovitz, M. (1956), 'Resource and Output Trends in the United States Since 1870', *American Economic Review*, Papers and Proceedings, vol. 46, 1956, pp. 5–23, as reprinted in Rosenberg (1971).

Adelman, I. and Adelman, F. L. (1959). 'The Dynamic Properties of the Klein–Goldberger Model', *Econometrica*, vol. 27, 1959, pp. 596–625, as reprinted in American Economic Association, *Readings in Business Cycles* (London: Allen & Unwin, 1966).

Ahmad, S. (1966). 'On the Theory of Induced Invention', *Economic Journal*, vol. 76, 1966, pp. 344–57.

Ahmad, S. (1967), 'Reply to Professor Fellner', *Economic Journal*, vol. 77, 1967, pp. 664–65.

Ahmad, S. (1967a), 'A Rejoinder to Professor Kennedy', *Economic Journal*, vol. 77, 1967, pp. 960–3.

Allen, R. G. D. (1967), *Macro-Economic Theory: A Mathematical Treatment* (London: Macmillan, 1967).

Arrow, K. J. (1962), 'The Economic Implications of Learning by Doing', *Review of Economic Studies*, vol. 29, 1961–2, pp. 155–73, as reprinted in Hahn (1971).

Atkinson, A. B. (1975), *The Economics of Inequality* (Oxford University Press, 1975).

Atkinson, A. B. and Stiglitz, J. E. (1969), 'A New View of Technological Change', *Economic Journal*, vol. 79, 1969, pp. 573–8.

Barna, T. (1957), 'The Replacement Cost of Fixed Assets in British Manufacturing Industry in 1955', *Journal of the Royal Statistical Society*, Series A, vol. 120, 1957, pp. 1–36.

Barna, T. (1961), 'On Measuring Capital', in *The Theory of Capital*, ed. F. A. Lutz and D. C. Hague (London: Macmillan, 1961).

Black, J. (1962), 'The Technical Progress Function and the Production Function', *Economica*, vol. 29, 1962, pp. 166–70.

Blaug, M. (1974), *The Cambridge Revolution: Success or Failure?* (London: Institute of Economic Affairs, 1974).

Bliss, C. J. (1968), 'On Putty-Clay', *Review of Economic Studies*, vol. 35, 1968, pp. 105–32.

Bliss, C. J. (1975), *Capital Theory and the Distribution of Income* (Amsterdam: North-Holland, 1975).

Brems, H. (1977), 'Reality and Neoclassical Theory', *Journal of Economic Literature*, vol. 15, 1977, pp. 72–82.

Brown, M. (1966), *On the Theory and Measurement of Technological Change* (Cambridge University Press, 1966).

Burmeister, E. and Dobell, A. R. (1970), *Mathematical Theories of Economic Growth* (London: Macmillan, 1970).

Burmeister, E. and Taubman, P. (1969), 'Labour and Non-Labour Income Saving Propensities', *Canadian Journal of Economics*, vol. 2, 1969, pp. 78–89.

Campion, H. (1939), *Public and Private Property in Great Britain* (Oxford University Press, 1939).

Carlson, K. M. and Spencer, R. W. (1975), 'Crowding Out and Its Critics' *Federal Reserve Bank of St Louis Review*, Dec 1975, pp. 2–17.

Cass, D. and Yaari, M. E. (1967), 'Individual Saving, Aggregate Capital Accumulation and Efficient Growth', *Essays on the Theory of Optimal Economic Growth*, ed. K. Shell (Cambridge, Mass.; M.I.T. Press, 1967).

Central Statistical Office (1977), *National Income and Expenditure, 1966–76* (London: H.M.S.O., 1977).

Central Statistical Office (1977a), *Economic Trends: Annual Supplement* (London: H.M.S.O., 1977).

Champernowne, D. G. (1971), 'The Stability of Kaldor's 1957 Model', *Review of Economic Studies*, vol. 38, 1971, pp. 112–35.

Chiang, A. C. (1967), *Fundamental Methods of Mathematical Economics* (New York: McGraw-Hill).

Clark, C. (1940), *The Conditions of Economic Progress* (London: Macmillan, 1940).

Clark, J. B. (1891), 'Distribution as Determined by a Law of Rent', *Quarterly Journal of Economics*, vol. 5, 1891, pp. 289–318.

Cobb, C. W. and Douglas, P. H. (1928), 'A Theory of Production', *American Economic Review*, Supplement, vol. 18, 1928, pp. 139–65.

Coddington, A. (1976), 'Keynesian Economics: The Search for First Principles', *Journal of Economic Literature*, vol. 14, 1976, pp. 1258–73.

Conlisk, J. (1969), 'A Neoclassical Growth Model with Endogenously Positioned Technical Change Frontier', *Economic Journal*, vol. 79, 1969, pp. 348–62.

Cripps, T. F. and Tarling, R. J. (1973), *Growth in Advanced Capitalist Economies, 1950–1970* (Cambridge University Press, 1973).

Dean, G. (1964), 'The Stock of Fixed Capital in the United Kingdom in 1961', *Journal of the Royal Statistical Society*, Series A, vol. 127, 1964, pp. 327–51.

Deane, P. and Cole, W. A. (1967), *British Economic Growth 1688–1959: Trends and Structure*, 2nd ed. (Cambridge University Press, 1967).

Denison, E. F. (1962), *The Sources of Economic Growth in the United States and the Alternatives Before Us* (New York: Committee for Economic Development, 1962).

Denison, E. F. (1962a), 'United States Economic Growth', *Journal of Business*, vol. 35, 1962, pp. 109–21, as reprinted in Rosenberg (1971).

Denison, E. F. (1967), *Why Growth Rates Differ: Postwar Experience in Nine Western Countries* (Washington, D. C.: Brookings Institution, 1967).

Denison, E. F. (1968), 'Economic Growth', in *Britain's Economic Prospects*, ed. R. E. Caves *et al.* (London: Allen & Unwin, 1968).

Denison, E. F. (1969), 'Some Major Issues in Productivity Analysis: An Examination of Estimates by Jorgenson and Griliches', *Survey of Current Business*, vol. 49, 1969, May (Part II), pp. 1–27.

Denison, E. F. (1974), *Accounting for United States Economic Growth. 1929–1969* (Washington, D.C.: Brookings Institution, 1974).

Diamond, P. A. (1965), 'National Debt in a Neo-Classical Growth Model', *American Economic Review*, vol. 55, 1965, pp. 1126–50.

Diamond, P. A. (1965a), 'Disembodied Technical Change in a Two-Sector Model', *Review of Economic Studies*, vol. 32, 1965, pp. 161–8.

Dixit, A. K. (1976), *The Theory of Equilibrium Growth* (Oxford University Press, 1976).

Dixit, A. K. (1977), 'The Accumulation of Capital Theory', *Oxford Economic Papers*, vol. 29, 1977, pp. 1–29.

Domar, E. D. (1946), 'Capital Expansion, Rate of Growth, and Employment', *Econometrica*, vol. 14, 1946, pp. 137–47.

Domar, E. D. (1947), 'Expansion and Employment', *American Economic Review*, vol. 37, 1947, pp. 34–55.

Domar, E. D. (1961), 'The Capital–Output Ratio in the United States: Its Variation and Stability', in *The Theory of Capital*, ed. F. A. Lutz and D. C. Hague (London: Macmillan, 1961).

Drandakis, E. M. (1963), 'Factor Substitution in the Two-Sector Growth Model', *Review of Economic Studies*, vol. 30, 1963, pp. 217–28.

Drandakis, E. M. and Phelps, E. S. (1966), 'A Model of Induced Invention, Growth and Distribution', *Economic Journal*, vol. 76, 1966, pp. 823–40.

Eltis, W. A. (1973), *Growth and Distribution* (London: Macmillan, 1973).

Evans, M. K. (1969), *Macroeconomic Activity, Theory, Forecasting, and Control: An Econometric Approach* (New York: Harper & Row, 1969).

Fabricant, S. (1974), 'Perspective on Productivity Research', *Review of Income and Wealth*, vol. 20, 1974, pp. 235–49.

Feinstein, C. H. (1965), *Domestic Capital Formation in the United Kingdom, 1920–38* (Cambridge University Press, 1965).

Feinstein, C. H. (1968), 'Changes in the Distribution of the National Income in the United Kingdom', in *The Distribution of National Income*, ed. J. Marchal and B. Ducros (London: Macmillan, 1968).

Feinstein, C. H. (1972), *National Income, Expenditure, and Output of the United Kingdom, 1855-1965* (Cambridge University Press, 1972).

Feiwel, G. R. (1975), *The Intellectual Capital of Michal Kalecki* (Tennessee University Press, 1975).

Fellner, W. (1961), 'Two Propositions in the Theory of Induced Innovations', *Economic Journal*, vol. 71, 1961, pp. 305–8, reprinted in Rosenberg (1971).

Fellner, W. (1966), 'Profit Maximization, Utility Maximization, and the Rate and Direction of Innovation', *American Economic Review*, Papers and Proceedings, vol. 56, 1966, pp. 24–32.

Fellner, W. (1967), 'Comment on the Induced Bias', *Economic Journal*, vol. 77, 1967, pp. 662–4.

Fisher, G. R. (1961), 'Some Factors Influencing Share Prices', *Economic Journal*, vol. 71, 1961, pp. 121–41.

Flemming, J. S., Price, L. D. D. and Ingram, D. H. A. (1976), 'Trends in Company Profitability', *Bank of England Quarterly Bulletin*, vol. 16, 1976, pp. 36–52.

Foley, D. K. and Sidrauski, M. (1971), *Monetary and Fiscal Policy in a Growing Economy* (New York: Macmillan, 1971).

Friedman, M. (1953), 'The Methodology of Positive Economics', in *Essays in Positive Economics* (Chicago University Press, 1953).

Friend, I. and Puckett, M. (1964), 'Dividends and Stock Prices', *American Economic Review*, vol. 54, 1964, pp. 655–82.

Gallaway, L. E. (1964), 'The Theory of Relative Shares', *Quarterly Journal of Economics*, vol. 78, 1964, pp. 547–91.

Glyn, A. and Sutcliffe, B. (1972), *British Capitalism, Workers and the Profits Squeeze* (Harmondsworth: Penguin, 1972).

Godley, W. A. H. and Nordhaus, W. D. (1972), 'Pricing in the Trade Cycle', *Economic Journal*, vol. 82, 1972, pp. 853–82.

Goldsmith, R. W. (1951), 'A Perpetual Inventory of National Wealth', in *Studies in Income and Wealth*, vol. 14 (New York: N.B.E.R., 1951).

Griffin, T. J. (1975), 'Revised Estimates of the Consumption and Stock of Fixed Capital', *Economic Trends*, no. 264, October 1975, pp. 126–9 (London: H.M.S.O., 1975).

Griffin, T. J. (1976), 'The Stock of Fixed Assets in the United Kingdom: How to Make Best Use of the Statistics', *Economic Trends*, no. 276, October 1976, pp. 130–43 (London: H.M.S.O., 1976).

Gurley, J. G. and Shaw, E. S. (1960), *Money in a Theory of Finance* (Washington, D.C.: Brookings Institution, 1960).

Hahn, F. H. (1965), 'On Two-Sector Growth Models', *Review of Economic Studies*, vol. 32, 1965, pp. 339–46, as reprinted in Sen (1970).

Hahn, F. H. (1966), 'Equilibrium Dynamics with Heterogeneous Capital Goods', *Quarterly Journal of Economics*, vol. 80, 1966, pp. 633–46.
Hahn, F. H. (ed.) (1971), *Readings in the Theory of Growth* (London: Macmillan, 1971).
Hahn, F. H. (1972), *The Share of Wages in the National Income* (London: Weidenfeld & Nicolson, 1972).
Hahn, F. H. (1975), 'Revival of Political Economy: The Wrong Issues and the Wrong Argument', *Economic Record*, vol. 51, 1975, pp. 360–4.
Hahn, F. H. and Matthews, R. C. O. (1964), 'The Theory of Economic Growth: A Survey', *Economic Journal*, vol. 74, 1964, pp. 779–902, as reprinted in American Economic Association/Royal Economic Society, *Surveys of Economic Theory*, vol. II: *Growth and Development* (London: Macmillan, 1968).
Hahn, F. H. and Matthews, R. C. O. (1968), 'Stability of Harrod's Model: A Reply', *Economic Journal*, vol. 78, 1968, p. 940.
Harcourt, G. C. (1969), 'Some Cambridge Controversies in the Theory of Capital', *Journal of Economic Literature*, vol. 7, 1969, pp. 369–405.
Harcourt, G. C. (1972), *Some Cambridge Controversies in the Theory of Capital* (Cambridge University Press, 1972).
Harcourt, G. C. (1976), 'The Cambridge Controversies: Old Ways and New Horizons – Or Dead End?' *Oxford Economic Papers*, vol. 28, 1976, pp. 25–65.
Harcourt, G. C. and Laing, N. F. (eds) (1971), *Capital and Growth: Selected Readings* (Harmondsworth: Penguin, 1971).
Harrod, R. F. (1939), 'An Essay in Dynamic Theory', *Economic Journal*, vol. 49, 1939, pp. 14–33.
Harrod, R. F. (1948), *Towards a Dynamic Economics* (London: Macmillan, 1948).
Harrod, R. F. (1959), 'Domar and Dynamic Economics', *Economic Journal*, vol. 69, 1959, pp. 451–64.
Harrod, R. F. (1963), 'Themes in Dynamic Theory', *Economic Journal*, vol. 73, 1963, pp. 401–21.
Harrod, R. F. (1970), 'Harrod after Twenty-One Years: A Comment', *Economic Journal*, vol. 80, 1970, pp. 737–41.
Harrod, R. F. (1973), *Economic Dynamics* (London: Macmillan, 1973).
Heidensohn, K. (1969), 'Labour's Share in National Income – A Constant?', *Manchester School of Economic and Social Studies*, vol. 37, 1969, pp. 295–321.
Hicks, J. R. (1949), 'Mr. Harrod's Dynamic Theory', *Economica*, vol. 16, 1949, pp. 106–21.
Hicks, J. R. (1950), *A Contribution to the Theory of the Trade Cycle* (Oxford University Press, 1950).
Hicks, J. R. (1961), 'The Measurement of Capital in Relation to the Measurement of Other Economic Aggregates', in *The Theory of Capital*, ed. F. A. Lutz and D. C. Hague (London: Macmillan, 1961).

Hicks, J. R. (1963), *The Theory of Wages*, 2nd ed. (London: Macmillan, 1963); first published 1932.
Hicks, J. R. (1965). *Capital and Growth* (Oxford University Press, 1965).
Hicks, J. R. (1973), 'The Mainspring of Economic Growth', *Swedish Journal of Economics*, vol. 75, 1973, pp. 336–48, as reprinted in Hicks (1977).
Hicks, J. R. (1973a), *Capital and Time: A Neo-Austrian Theory* (Oxford University Press, 1973).
Hicks, J. R. (1974), 'Industrialism', *International Affairs*, vol. 50, 1974, pp. 211–28, as reprinted in Hicks (1977).
Hicks, J. R. (1974a), *The Crisis in Keynesian Economics* (Oxford: Blackwell, 1974).
Hicks, J. R. (1974b), 'Capital Controversies: Ancient and Modern', *American Economic Review*, vol. 64, 1974, as reprinted in Hicks (1977).
Hicks, J. R. (1975), 'Revival of Political Economy: The Old and the New', *Economic Record*, vol. 51, 1975, pp. 365–7.
Hicks, J. R. (1977), *Economic Perspectives: Further Essays on Money and Growth* (Oxford University Press, 1977).
Inada, K. (1963), 'On a Two-Sector Model of Economic Growth: Comments and a Generalisation', *Review of Economic Studies*, vol. 30, 1963, pp. 119–27.
Johansen, L. (1959), 'Substitution vs. Fixed Production Coefficients in the Theory of Economic Growth: A Synthesis', *Econometrica*, vol. 27, 1959, pp. 157–75.
Johnson, H. G. (1967), 'Money in a Neo-Classical One-Sector Growth Model' in *Essays in Monetary Economics* (London: Allen & Unwin, 1967).
Johnson, H. G. (1973), *The Theory of Income Distribution* (London: Gray-Mills, 1973).
Jorgenson, D. W. and Griliches, Z. (1967), 'The Explanation of Productivity Change', *Review of Economic Studies*, vol. 34, 1967, pp. 249–83.
Jorgenson, D. W., Griliches, Z. and Denison, E. F. (1972), 'The Measurement of Productivity: An Exchange of Views', *Survey of Current Business*, vol. 52, (1972), May (Part II); also in *Brookings Reprint No. 244* (Washington, D.C.: Brookings Institution, 1972).
Kahn, R. F. (1931), 'The Relation of Home Investment to Unemployment', *Economic Journal*, vol. 41, 1931, pp. 173–98.
Kahn, R. F. (1959), 'Exercises in the Analysis of Growth'. *Oxford Economic Papers*, vol. 11, 1959, pp. 143–56, as reprinted in Sen (1970).
Kaldor, N. (1956), 'Alternative Theories of Distribution', *Review of Economic Studies*, vol. 23, 1955–6, pp. 83–100, as reprinted in *The Labour Market: Selected Readings*, ed. B. J. McCormick and E. O. Smith (Harmondsworth: Penguin, 1968).

Kaldor, N. (1957), 'A Model of Economic Growth', *Economic Journal*, vol. 67, 1957, pp. 591–624, as reprinted in Kaldor (1960).

Kaldor, N. (1957a), 'Capitalist Evolution in the Light of Keynesian Economics', *Sankhya*, vol. 18, 1957, pp. 173–82, as reprinted in Kaldor (1960).

Kaldor, N. (1959), 'Economic Growth and the Problem of Inflation', *Economica*, vol. 26, 1959, pp. 212–26, 287–98, as reprinted in Kaldor (1964).

Kaldor, N. (1960), *Essays on Economic Stability and Growth* (London: Duckworth, 1960).

Kaldor, N. (1960a), 'A Rejoinder to Mr. Atsumi and Professor Tobin', *Review of Economic Studies*, vol. 27, 1959–60, pp. 121–3.

Kaldor, N. (1961), 'Capital Accumulation and Economic Growth', in *The Theory of Capital*, ed. F. A. Lutz and D. C. Hague (London: Macmillan, 1961).

Kaldor, N. (1962), 'Comment' (in Symposium on Production Functions and Economic Growth), *Review of Economic Studies*, vol. 29, 1961–2, pp. 246–50.

Kaldor, N. (1962a), 'A Comment', *Economic Journal*, vol. 72, 1962, pp. 739–40.

Kaldor, N. (1964), *Essays on Economic Policy*, vol. 1 (London: Duckworth, 1964).

Kaldor, N. (1966), *Causes of the Slow Rate of Economic Growth of the United Kingdom*, Inaugural Lecture (Cambridge University Press, 1966).

Kaldor, N. (1966a), 'Marginal Productivity and the Macro-Economic Theories of Distribution', *Review of Economic Studies*, vol. 33, 1966, pp. 309–19, as reprinted in Harcourt and Laing (1971).

Kaldor, N. (1968), 'Productivity and Growth in Manufacturing Industry: A Reply', *Economica*, vol. 35, 1968, pp. 385–91.

Kaldor, N. (1970), 'Some Fallacies in the Interpretation of Kaldor', *Review of Economic Studies*, vol. 37, 1970, pp. 1–7.

Kaldor, N. (1972), 'The Irrelevance of Equilibrium Economics', *Economic Journal*, vol. 82, 1972, pp. 1237–55.

Kaldor, N. (1975), 'Economic Growth and the Verdoorn Law: A Comment on Mr. Rowthorn's Article', *Economic Journal*, vol. 85, 1975, pp. 891–6.

Kaldor, N. and Mirrlees, J. A. (1962), 'A New Model of Economic Growth', *Review of Economic Studies*, vol. 29, 1961–2, pp. 174–92, as reprinted in Hahn (1971).

Kalecki, M. (1933), 'A Macrodynamic Theory of Business Cycles', published in Polish, 1933; *Econometrica*, vol. 3, 1935, pp. 327–44; as reprinted in Kalecki (1971).

Kalecki, M. (1939), 'The Distribution of the National Income', in *Essays in the Theory of Economic Fluctuations* (London: Allen & Unwin, 1939).

Kalecki, M. (1942) 'The Determinants of Profits', *Economic Journal*, vol. 52, 1942, pp. 258–67, as reprinted in Kalecki (1971).

Kalecki, M. (1943), 'Determinants of Investment' in *Studies in Economic Dynamics* (London: Allen & Unwin, 1943), as reprinted in Kalecki (1971).

Kalecki, M. (1954), 'Costs and Prices', in *Theory of Economic Dynamics* (London: Allen & Unwin, 1954), as reprinted in Kalecki (1971).

Kalecki, M. (1954a), 'Distribution of National Income', in *Theory of Economic Dynamics* (London: Allen & Unwin, 1954), as reprinted in Kalecki (1971).

Kalecki, M. (1971), *Selected Essays on the Dynamics of the Capitalist Economy, 1933-1970* (Cambridge University Press, 1971).

Kalecki, M. (1971a), 'Class Struggle and Distribution of National Income', in Kalecki (1971).

Kamien, M. I. and Schwartz, N. L. (1975), 'Market Structure and Innovation: A Survey', *Journal of Economic Literature*, vol. 13, 1975, pp. 1–37.

Kendrick, J. W. (1976), *The Formation and Stocks of Total Capital* (New York: N.B.E.R., 1976).

Kennedy, C. (1964), 'Induced Bias in Innovation and the Theory of Distribution', *Economic Journal*, vol. 74, 1964, pp. 541–7.

Kennedy, C. (1966), 'Samuelson on Induced Innovation', *Review of Economics and Statistics*, vol. 48, 1966, pp. 442–4.

Kennedy, C. (1967), 'On the Theory of Induced Invention – A Reply', *Economic Journal*, vol. 77, 1967, pp. 958–60.

Kennedy, C. and Thirlwall, A. P. (1972), 'Technical Progress – A Survey', *Economic Journal*, vol. 82, 1972, pp. 11–72.

Keynes, J. M. (1936), *The General Theory of Employment, Interest and Money* (London: Macmillan, 1936).

Keynes, J. M. (1937), 'The General Theory of Employment', *Quarterly Journal of Economics*, vol. 51, 1937, pp. 209–23.

Keynes, J. M. (1939), 'Relative Movements in Real Wages and Output', *Economic Journal*, vol. 49, 1939, pp. 34–51.

King, M. A. (1975), 'The United Kingdom Profits Crisis: Myth or Reality?', *Economic Journal*, vol. 85, 1975, pp. 33–54.

Klein, L. R. and Kosobud, R. F. (1961), 'Some Econometrics of Growth: Great Ratios of Economics', *Quarterly Journal of Economics*, vol. 75, 1961, pp. 173–98.

Kravis, I. B. (1959), 'Relative Income Shares in Fact and Theory', *American Economic Review*, vol. 49, 1959, pp. 917–49.

Kubota, K. (1968), 'A Re-Examination of the Existence and Stability Propositions in Kaldor's Growth Models', *Review of Economic Studies*, vol. 35, 1968, pp. 353–60.

Kuznets, S. (1966), *Modern Economic Growth: Rate, Structure and Spread* (Yale University Press, 1966).

Kuznets, S. (1973), 'Modern Economic Growth: Findings and Reflections', *American Economic Review*, vol. 63, 1973, pp. 247–58.

Laidler, D. E. W. and Parkin, J. M. (1975), 'Inflation – A Survey', *Economic Journal*, vol. 85, 1975, pp. 741–809.

Leijonhufvud, A. (1968), *On Keynesian Economics and the Economics of Keynes* (New York: Oxford University Press, 1968).

Leontief, W. (1971), 'Theoretical Assumptions and Nonobserved Facts', *American Economic Review*, Papers and Proceedings, vol. 61, 1971, pp. 1–7.

Lerner, A. P. (1934), 'The Concept of Monopoly and the Measurement of Monopoly Power', *Review of Economic Studies*, vol. 1, 1933–4, pp. 157–75.

Levhari, D. and Patinkin, D. (1968), 'The Role of Money in a Simple Growth Model', *American Economic Review*, vol. 58, 1968, pp. 713–53.

Lydall, H. (1971), 'A Theory of Distribution and Growth with Economies of Scale', *Economic Journal*, vol. 81, 1971, pp. 91–112.

McCallum, B. T. (1969), 'The Instability of Kaldorian Models', *Oxford Economic Papers*, vol. 21, 1969, pp. 56–65.

Mansfield, E. (1968), *The Economics of Technological Change* (New York: Norton, 1968).

Marris, R. (1964), *The Economic Theory of 'Managerial' Capitalism* (London: Macmillan, 1964).

Marshall, A. (1920), *Principles of Economics*, 8th ed. (London: Macmillan, 1920).

Matthews, R. C. O. (1959), *The Trade Cycle* (Cambridge University Press, 1959).

Matthews, R. C. O. (1964), 'Some Aspects of Post-War Growth in the British Economy in Relation to Historical Experience', *Transactions of the Manchester Statistical Society*, 1964–5, pp. 1–25.

Maurice, R. (ed.) (1968), *National Accounts Statistics: Sources and Methods* (London: H.M.S.O., 1968).

Maywald, K. (1956), 'Fire Insurance and the Capital Coefficient in Great Britain, 1856–1952', *Economic History Review*, new series, 1956, vol. 9, pp. 89–105.

Meade, J. E. (1962), *A Neo-Classical Theory of Economic Growth*, 2nd ed. (London: Allen & Unwin, 1962).

Meade, J. E. (1963), 'The Rate of Profit in a Growing Economy', *Economic Journal*, vol. 73, 1963, pp. 665–74.

Meade, J. E. (1966), 'Life-Cycle Savings, Inheritance and Economic Growth', *Review of Economic Studies*, vol. 33, 1966, pp. 61–78.

Meade, J. E. (1966a), 'The Outcome of the Pasinetti Process: A Note', *Economic Journal*, vol. 76, 1966, pp. 161–5, reprinted in Harcourt and Laing (1971).

Meade, J. E. (1968), *The Growing Economy* (London: Allen & Unwin, 1968).

Meade, J. E. and Hahn, F. H. (1965), 'The Rate of Profit in a Growing Economy', *Economic Journal*, vol. 75, 1965, pp. 445–8.

Mirrlees, J. A. (1973), 'Introduction', in Mirrlees and Stern (1973).

Mirrlees, J. A. and Stern, N. H. (eds.) (1973), *Models of Economic Growth* (London: Macmillan, 1973).

Moggridge, D. (ed.) (1973), *The Collected Writings of John Maynard Keynes*, vol. 14: *The General Theory and After* – Part II: *Defence and Development* (London: Macmillan, 1973).

Nadiri, M. I. (1970), 'Some Approaches to the Theory and Measurement of Total Factor Productivity: A Survey', *Journal of Economic Literature*, vol. 8, 1970, pp. 1137–77.

Neild, R. R. (1963), *Pricing and Employment in the Trade Cycle* (Cambridge University Press, 1963).

Nelson, R. R. (1956), 'A Theory of the Low-Level Equilibrium Trap in Underdeveloped Economies', *American Economic Review*, vol. 46, 1956, 894–908.

Nelson, R. R. (1973), 'Recent Exercises in Growth Accounting: New Understanding or Dead End?', *American Economic Review*, vol. 63, 1973, pp. 462–7.

Nelson, R. R. and Winter, S. G. (1974), 'Neoclassical vs. Evolutionary Theories of Economic Growth: Critique and Prospectus', *Economic Journal*, vol. 84, 1974, pp. 886–905.

Nelson, R. R. and Winter, S. G. (1975), 'Growth Theory from an Evolutionary Perspective: The Differential Productivity Puzzle', *American Economic Review*, Papers and Proceedings, vol. 65, 1975, pp. 338–44.

Nordhaus, W. D. (1969), *Invention, Growth and Welfare: A Theoretical Treatment of Technical Change* (Cambridge, Mass.: M.I.T. Press, 1969).

Nordhaus, W. D. (1972), 'Recent Developments in Price Dynamics', in *The Econometrics of Price Determination*, O. Eckstein, ed. (Washington, D.C.: S.S.R.C., 1972).

Nordhaus, W. D. (1973), 'Some Skeptical Thoughts on the Theory of Induced Innovation', *Quarterly Journal of Economics*, vol. 87, 1973, pp. 208–19.

Nordhaus, W. D. (1974), 'The Falling Share of Profits', *Brookings Papers on Economic Activity*, 1974(I), pp. 169–208.

Nuti, D. M. (1969), 'The Degree of Monopoly in the Kaldor-Mirrlees Growth Model', *Review of Economic Studies*, vol. 36, 1969, pp. 257–60.

Paige, D. (1961), 'Economic Growth: The Last Hundred Years', *National Institute Economic Review*, no. 16, July 1961, pp. 24–49.

Pasinetti, L. L. (1962), 'Rate of Profit and Income Distribution in relation to the Rate of Economic Growth', *Review of Economic Studies*, vol. 29, 1961–2, pp. 267–79, as reprinted in Sen (1970).

Pasinetti, L. L. (1964), 'A Comment on Professor Meade's "Rate of Profit in a Growing Economy"', *Economic Journal*, vol. 74, 1964, pp. 488–9.

Pasinetti, L. L. (1966), 'The Rate of Profit in a Growing Economy: A Reply', *Economic Journal*, vol. 76, 1966, pp. 158–60.

Pasinetti, L. L. (1974), *Growth and Income Distribution: Essays in Economic Theory* (Cambridge University Press, 1974).

Patterson, K. D. and Schott, K. (eds) (1978), *The Measurement of Capital: Theory and Practice* (London: Macmillan, 1978).

Phelps, E. S. (1961), 'The Golden Rule of Accumulation: A Fable for Growthmen', *American Economic Review*, vol. 51, 1961, pp. 638–43.

Phelps, E. S. (1963), 'Substitution, Fixed Proportions, Growth and Distribution', *International Economic Review*, vol. 4, 1963, pp. 265–88.

Phelps Brown, E. H. (1968), *Pay and Profits* (Manchester University Press, 1968).

Phelps Brown, E. H. (1972), 'The Underdevelopment of Economics', *Economic Journal*, vol. 82, 1972, pp. 1–10.

Phelps Brown, E. H. and Hart, P. E. (1952), 'The Share of Wages in National Income', *Economic Journal*, vol. 62, 1952, pp. 253–77.

Phelps Brown, E. H. and Handfield-Jones, S. J. (1952), 'The Climacteric of the 1890s: A Study in the Expanding Economy', *Oxford Economic Papers*, vol. 4, 1952, pp. 266–307.

Phelps Brown, E. H. and Weber, B. (1953), 'Accumulation, Productivity, and Distribution in the British Economy, 1870–1938', *Economic Journal*, vol. 63, 1953, pp. 263–88.

Pigou, A. C. (1933), *The Theory of Unemployment* (London: Macmillan, 1933).

Pratten, C. F. (1971), *Economies of Scale in Manufacturing Industry* (Cambridge University Press, 1971).

Reder, M. W. (1959), 'Alternative Theories of Labour's Share', in *The Allocation of Economic Resources* ed. M. Abramovitz *et al.* (Stanford University Press, 1959).

Redfern, P. (1955), 'Net Investment in Fixed Assets in the United Kingdom, 1938-53', *Journal of the Royal Statistical Society*, Series A, vol. 118, 1955, pp. 141–82.

Riach, P. A. (1969), 'A Framework for Macro-Distribution Analysis', *Kyklos*, vol. 22, 1959, pp. 542–65.

Ricardo, D. (1817), *On the Principles of Political Economy and Taxation*, in *The Works and Correspondence of David Ricardo, Vol. 1*, ed. P. Sraffa (Cambridge University Press, 1951).

Robinson, J. V. (1938), 'The Classification of Inventions', *Review of Economic Studies*, vol. 5, 1937-8, pp. 138–42.

Robinson, J. V. (1954), 'The Production Function and the Theory of Capital', *Review of Economic Studies*, vol. 21, 1953-4, pp. 81–106.

Robinson, J. V. (1956), *The Accumulation of Capital* (London: Macmillan, 1956).

Robinson, J. V. (1961), 'Equilibrium Growth Models', *American Economic Review*, vol. 51, 1961, 360-9, as reprinted in Robinson (1965a).

Robinson, J. V. (1962), *Essays in the Theory of Economic Growth* (London: Macmillan, 1962).

Robinson, J. V. (1963), 'Findlay's Robinsonian Model of Accumulation: A Comment', *Economica*, vol. 30, 1963, pp. 408–12.

Robinson, J. V. (1964), *Economic Philosophy* (Harmondsworth: Penguin, 1964).

Robinson, J. V. (1965), 'Pre-Keynesian Theory After Keynes', *Australian Economic Papers*, vol. 3 1965, pp. 25–35, as reprinted in Robinson (1965a).

Robinson, J. V. (1965a), *Collected Economic Papers*, vol. 3 (Oxford: Blackwell, 1965).

Robinson, J. V. (1967), 'Marginal Productivity', *Indian Economic Review* new series, vol. 2, pp. 75–84, as reprinted in Robinson (1973a).

Robinson, J. V. (1969), *The Economics of Imperfect Competition*, 2nd ed. (London: Macmillan, 1969); first published 1933.

Robinson, J. V. (1970), 'Economics Today', in Robinson (1973a).

Robinson, J. V. (1970a), 'Harrod after Twenty-One Years', *Economic Journal*, vol. 80, 1970, pp. 731–7.

Robinson, J. V. (1971), *Economic Heresies* (London: Macmillan, 1971).

Robinson, J. V. (1971a), 'Solow Once More', *Kyklos*, vol. 24, 1971, pp. 189–92, as reprinted in Robinson (1973a).

Robinson, J. V. (1971b), 'The Relevance of Economic Theory', in Robinson (1973a).

Robinson, J. V. (1972), 'The Second Crisis of Economic Theory', *American Economic Review*, Papers and Proceedings, vol. 62, 1972, as reprinted in Robinson (1973a).

Robinson, J. V. (1973), Preface to J. Kregel, *The Reconstruction of Political Economy: An Introduction to Post-Keynesian Analysis* (London: Macmillan, 1973).

Robinson, J. V. (1973a), *Collected Economic Papers*, vol. 4 (Oxford: Blackwell, 1973).

Robinson, J. V. (1975), 'The Unimportance of Reswitching', *Quarterly Journal of Economics*, vol. 89, 1975, pp. 32–9.

Robinson, J. V. (1977), 'What are the Questions?', *Journal of Economic Literature*, vol. 15, 1977, pp. 1318–39.

Robinson, J. V. (1977a), 'Michal Kalecki on the Economics of Capitalism', *Oxford Bulletin of Economics and Statistics*, vol. 39, 1977, pp. 7–17.

Robinson, J. V. and Eatwell, J. (1973), *An Introduction to Modern Economics* (New York: McGraw-Hill, 1973).

Rose, H. (1959), 'The Possibility of Warranted Growth', *Economic Journal*, vol. 69, 1959, pp. 313–32.

Rosenberg, N. (ed.) (1971), *The Economics of Technological Change: Selected Readings* (Harmondsworth: Penguin, 1971).

Rothschild, K. W. (1959), 'The Limitations of Economic Growth Models', *Kyklos*, vol. 22, 1959, pp. 567–86.

Rothschild, K. W. (1961), 'Some Recent Contributions to a Macro-Economic Theory of Income Distribution', *Scottish Journal of Political Economy*, vol. 8, 1961, pp. 173–99.

Rowthorn, R. E. (1975), 'What Remains of Kaldor's Law?', *Economic Journal*, vol. 85, 1975, pp. 10–19.

Rowthorn, R. E. (1975a), 'A Reply to Lord Kaldor's Comment', *Economic Journal*, vol. 85, 1975, pp. 897–901.

Salter, W. E. G. (1966), *Productivity and Technical Change*, 2nd ed. (Cambridge University Press, 1966); first published 1960.

Samuelson, P. A. (1939), 'Interactions between the Multiplier Analysis and the Principle of Acceleration', *Review of Economics and Statistics*, vol. 21, 1939, pp. 75–8.

Samuelson, P. A. (1947), *Foundations of Economic Analysis* (Harvard University Press, 1947).

Samuelson, P. A. (1963), 'A Brief Survey of Post-Keynesian Developments' in *Keynes' General Theory: Reports of Three Decades*, ed. R. Lekachman (New York: St Martin's Press, 1964).

Samuelson, P. A. (1965), 'A Theory of Induced Innovation along Kennedy–Weizsacker Lines', *Review of Economics and Statistics*, vol. 47, 1965, pp. 343–56.

Samuelson, P. A. (1966), 'Rejoinder: Agreements, Disagreements, Doubts and the Case of Induced Harrod-Neutral Technical Change', *Review of Economics and Statistics*, vol. 48, 1966, pp. 444–8.

Samuelson, P. A. (1973), *Economics*, 9th ed. (New York: McGraw-Hill, 1973).

Samuelson, P. A. and Modigliani, F. (1966), 'The Pasinetti Paradox in Neo-Classical and More General Models', *Review of Economic Studies*, vol. 33, 1966, pp. 269–301.

Sargent, J. R. (1968), 'Recent Growth Experience in the Economy of the United Kingdom', *Economic Journal*, vol. 78, 1968, pp. 19–42.

Schneider, E. (1958), 'Income and Income-Distribution in Macro-Economic Theory', *International Economic Papers*, no. 8, 1958, pp. 111–21.

Scott, M. FG. (1976), 'Investment and Growth', *Oxford Economic Papers*, vol. 28, 1976, pp. 317–63.

Sen, A. K. (1963), 'Neo-Classical and Neo-Keynesian Theories of Distribution', *Economic Record*, vol. 39, 1963, pp. 53–64.

Sen, A. K. (1965), 'The Money Rate of Interest in the Pure Theory of Growth', in *The Theory of Interest Rates* ed. F. H. Hahn and F. P. R. Brechling (London: Macmillan, 1965), as reprinted in Sen (1970).

Sen, A. K. (ed.) (1970), *Growth Economics: Selected Readings* (Harmondsworth: Penguin, 1970).

Shell, K. and Stiglitz, J. E. (1967), 'The Allocation of Investment in a Dynamic Economy', *Quarterly Journal of Economics*, vol. 81, 1967, pp. 592–609.

Solow, R. M. (1956), 'A Contribution to the Theory of Economic Growth', *Quarterly Journal of Economics*, vol. 70, 1956, pp. 65–94, as reprinted in Sen (1970).

Solow, R. M. (1957), 'Technical Change and the Aggregate Production

Function', *Review of Economics and Statistics*, vol. 39, 1957, pp. 312–20.

Solow, R. M. (1958), 'A Skeptical Note on the Constancy of Relative Shares', *American Economic Review*, vol. 48, 1958, pp. 618–31.

Solow, R. M. (1959), 'Investment and Technical Progress', in *Mathematical Methods in the Social Sciences*, ed. K. J. Arrow, S. Karlin and P. Suppes (Stanford University Press, 1959).

Solow, R. M. (1961), 'Note on Uzawa's Two-Sector Model of Economic Growth', *Review of Economic Studies*, vol. 29, 1961–2, pp. 48–50.

Solow, R. M. (1963), *Capital Theory and the Rate of Return* (Amsterdam: North-Holland, 1963).

Solow, R. M. (1970), *Growth Theory: An Exposition* (Oxford University Press, 1970).

Solow, R. M. (1975), 'Brief Comments', *Quarterly Journal of Economics*, vol. 89, 1975, pp. 48–52.

Solow, R. M., Tobin, J., von Weizsacker, C. C. and Yaari, M. (1966), 'Neo-Classical Growth with Fixed Factor Proportions', *Review of Economic Studies*, vol. 33, 1966, pp. 79–115.

Sraffa, P. (1926), 'The Laws of Returns under Competitive Conditions', *Economic Journal*, vol. 36, 1926, pp. 535–50, as reprinted in American Economic Association, *Readings in Price Theory* (London: Allen & Unwin, 1953).

Sraffa, P. (1960), *Production of Commodites by Means of Commodities: Prelude to a Critique of Economic Theory* (Cambridge University Press, 1960).

Stamp, J. C. (1920), *British Incomes and Property* (London: P. S. King, 1920).

Stiglitz, J. E. (1974), 'The Cambridge–Cambridge Controversy in the Theory of Capital; A View from New Haven: A Review Article', *Journal of Political Economy*, vol. 82, 1974, pp. 893–903.

Surrey, M. J. C. (1971), *The Analysis and Forecasting of the British Economy* (Cambridge University Press, 1971).

Swann, T. W. (1956), 'Economic Growth and Capital Accumulation', *Economic Record*, vol. 32, 1956, pp. 334–61.

Swan, T. W. (1963), 'Growth Models: of Golden Ages and Production Functions', in *Economic Development with Special Reference to East Asia*, ed. K. E. Berrill (London: Macmillan, 1963).

Takayama, A. (1963), 'On a Two-Sector Model of Economic Growth: A Comparative Static Analysis', *Review of Economic Studies*, vol. 30, 1963, pp. 95–104.

Tobin, J. (1955), 'A Dynamic Aggregative Model', *Journal of Political Economy*, vol. 63, 1955, pp. 103–15, as reprinted in Sen (1970).

Tobin, J. (1958), 'Liquidity Preference as Behaviour Towards Risk', *Review of Economic Studies*, vol. 25, 1957–8, pp. 65–86.

Tobin, J. (1960), 'Towards a General Kaldorian Theory of Distribution', *Review of Economic Studies*, vol. 27, 1959–60, pp. 119–20.

Tobin, J. (1965), 'Money and Economic Growth', *Econometrica*, vol. 33, 1965, pp. 671–84.

Tobin, J. (1967), 'Life-Cycle Saving and Balanced Growth', in *Ten Economic Studies in the Tradition of Irving Fisher*, ed. W. Fellner (New York: Wiley, 1967).

Uzawa, H. (1961), 'On a Two-Sector Model of Economic Growth', *Review of Economic Studies*, vol. 29, 1961–2, pp. 40–7.

Uzawa, H. (1961a), 'Neutral Inventions and the Stability of Growth Equilibrium', *Review of Economic Studies*, vol. 28, 1960–1, pp. 117–24.

Uzawa, H. (1963), 'On a Two-Sector Model of Economic Growth II', *Review of Economic Studies*, vol. 30, 1963, pp. 105–18.

Wan, H. Y. (1971), *Economic Growth* (New York: Harcourt Brace Jovanovich, 1971).

Ward, M. (1976), *The Measurement of Capital: The Methodology of Capital Stock Estimates in O.E.C.D. countries* (Paris: O.E.C.D., 1976).

Williamson, J. H. (1966), 'Profit, Growth, and Sales Maximisation', *Economica*, vol. 33, 1966, pp. 1–16.

Wilson, T. (1966), 'Instability and the Rate of Growth', *Lloyds Bank Review*, no. 81, July 1966, pp. 16–32.

Wolfe, J. N. (1968), 'Productivity and Growth in Manufacturing Industry: Some Reflections on Professor Kaldor's Inaugural Lecture', *Economica*, vol. 35, 1968, pp. 117–26.

Worswick, G. D. N. (1972), 'Is Progress in Economic Science Possible?', *Economic Journal*, vol. 82, 1972, pp. 73–86.

Index